D1564205

Yearnings of the Soul

Yearnings of the Soul

*Psychological Thought in
Modern Kabbalah*

JONATHAN GARB

The University of Chicago Press   Chicago and London

JONATHAN GARB is the Gershom Scholem Professor of Kabbalah in the department of Jewish thought at the Hebrew University of Jerusalem. He is the author of several books, most recently *Kabbalist in the Heart of the Storm* and *Shamanic Trance in Modern Kabbalah*, the latter also published by the University of Chicago Press.

The University of Chicago Press, Chicago 60637
The University of Chicago Press, Ltd., London
© 2015 by The University of Chicago
All rights reserved. Published 2015.
Printed in the United States of America

24 23 22 21 20 19 18 17 16 15   1 2 3 4 5

ISBN-13: 978-0-226-29580-0 (cloth)
ISBN-13: 978-0-226-29594-7 (e-book)
DOI: 10.7208/chicago/9780226295947.001.0001

Library of Congress Cataloging-in-Publication Data
Garb, Jonathan, author.
   Yearnings of the soul : psychological thought in modern
Kabbalah / Jonathan Garb.
      pages cm
   Includes bibliographical references and index.
   ISBN 978-0-226-29580-0 (cloth : alk. paper)—ISBN 978-0-226-29594-7
(e-book)   1. Cabala—Psychological aspects. 2. Psychology. 3. Judaism
and psychology.   I. Title.
   BM526.G38 2015
   296.1'6—dc23

                                                      2015017044

♾ This paper meets the requirements of ANSI/NISO Z39.48-1992
(Permanence of Paper).

In memory of James Hillman, who

spoke with passion for the soul

Contents

Preface

As I shall write on its last page, the book was written in joy, as a song of the soul. I wish to thank true friends who have shared of their own creative joy:

My thoughts on the general direction of the book were presented at lectures in 2012 in the Judaic Studies Programs at the Department of Religions at Rice University and Yale University, and many thanks for the learned comments and warm welcome. Parts of the Habad-related portions of the book were presented at the 2012 conferences "Habad and the Academe" at the University of Pennsylvania and "Epic Exposition: The Ayin Bet Discourses and the Mystical Thought of Rabbi Shalom DovBer Schneersohn of Lubavitch (RaShaB)" at the Center for Jewish History, and warm thanks are due to the participants.

My "wanderyear of the soul" in the United States (quoting the late lamented John S. Dunne, as encountering his work and corresponding with him truly transformed the last part of this year) was made possible mostly through the wonderfully challenging, yet supportive atmosphere of the Tikvah Center for Law and Jewish Civilization at New York University, and special thanks are due to its visionary leaders, Moshe Halbertal and Joseph Weiler. My time in New York was greatly enriched by deep conversations with Elliot Wolfson. At the same time, the sabbatical that enabled this year of immersion in the "story of the soul" was enabled by Hebrew University's continued insistence on the vital need for periods of reflection, a laudable policy that will hopefully survive the deadening pressures exerted on academia these days. My ability to join the resources of the excellent

American library system with the textual riches of Jerusalem was not the result of any magical feat. Rather, it resulted from the dedicated efforts of an excellent team of young scholars: Avishai Bar-Asher, Ido Harari, Patrick Koch, Yakov Meir, Avital Sharon, and Elchanan Shilo, as well as by the excellent databases created in the Haredi world. My ability to avail myself of these felicitous circumstances was greatly helped by Israel Science Foundation Grant 57/09, as well as by a publication grant from the Hebrew University Humanities Research Committee. I am delighted to thank the University of Chicago Press for placing the book in an ideal home and especially T. David Brent for his broad vision and warm support, Ellen Garnett Kladky for her courteous and thoughtful assistance while escorting the book to production, and Michael Koplow for his sensitive and meticulous editing. Finally, I wish to warmly thank the readers appointed by the press for their learned, helpful, and supportive comments.

During the period of writing, and especially while in the United States, I enjoyed a rich variety of intellectual, spiritual, and political exchanges with many friends and colleagues, especially Daniel Abrams, Michael Vannoy Adams, Shazad Bashir, Courtney Bender, Yoram Bilu, Gad Buchbinder, Jonathan Alexander Daniel, April Deconick, Yaron Ezrahi, David Greetham, Ruth HaCohen, Maoz Kahana, Patrick E. Kelly, Jeffrey Kripal, Tanya M. Lhurmann, Menachem Lorberbaum, David Loy, Shaul Magid, Itzhak Melamed, Christia Mercer, David L. Miller, Dan Nussbaum, William Parsons, William Pinar, Barbara Pitkin, Dan Russell, Bracha Sack, Orit San-Gupta, David Shulman, Jason Siff, Moshe Schatz, Moshe Sluhovsky, Joseph Spinner, Steven P. Weitzman, and Philip Wexler. As always, my reflection on the relationship of textual study and theoretical analysis is greatly indebted to my dialogue with Moshe Idel.

This journey could not have happened without the adventurous spirit of my own "soul family." As the Kabbalist R. Isaac Haver wrote, one names sons according to divine inspiration concerning the root of their soul. Ronna and I gave Evyatar David one name each, yet it was she who named Ariel; this can be seen as a sign of the beneficial transitions in the engenderment of the soul in our times.

This book is dedicated to the ongoing "uplifting," as the classical Hebrew expression has it, of the fierce and wide-ranging soul of James Hillman, who is one of the righteous of whom it is said that they are even more present in their afterlife than in embodied life.

ONE

The Return of the Soul: Psychology and Modern Kabbalah

The Return of the Soul

In the end, it mattered not that you could not close your mind. It was your heart that saved you. **ALBUS DUMBLEDORE TO HARRY POTTER**

In the last two volumes/movies of *Harry Potter*—the most widespread myth of our times—two clusters of objects compete for the attention of Harry and his friends, and thus of the readers and viewers. On the one hand, we have the Deathly Hallows, with all the connotations of sacredness and power, as well as their close association with the archetypal figure of Death. On the other hand we have the Horcruxes, in which the satanic Lord Voldemort protected the fragments of his soul, culminating with the accidental displacement of yet another fragment in the soul of Harry, whose Christ-like self-sacrifice destroyed it. This enabled Harry to fulfill the plan of Professor Dumbledore by defeating Voldemort, even when the latter was armed with one of the Hallows (and allied with soul-destroying Dementors). Harry's victory was prepared by a complex strategy, which included Dumbledore's care for the soul of Harry's youthful antagonist Draco Malfoy.[1]

This foray into popular culture not only expresses my sharing of Jeffrey Kripal's conviction that this is a central arena for the study of modern mysticism (requiring university professors to study the likes of Professor Xavier, leader

1

of the X-men, and Professor Dumbledore) but also my sense that after centuries of neglect, the soul is once more claiming its due central place in cultural life. Here I join the recent call of Joseph Grange, who has alerted us to the startling gap between the resonance that the idea of the soul still possesses and its marginality in academic discourse. I also share his concern that contemporary cultural and technological developments are leading towards a civilization in which it would be difficult to recapture the world of images and ideas that created the rich history of discourse on the soul throughout the centuries. This is all the more troubling if one accepts Grange's compelling argument that it is soul that enables a sense of the alternative to what he describes as the heartlessness of the corporate-dominated world, including the soul-silencing technocratic management of academia itself.[2]

One may indeed ask, as did Julia Kristeva, in what now looks like an innocent, pre-app decade, "in the wake of psychiatric medicines, aerobics, and media zapping, does the soul still exist?" Kristeva's own answer, though acknowledging "new maladies" not covered in the traditional taxonomy of psychoanalysis, still remains deeply rooted in the Freudian tradition (though via the mediation of Jacques Lacan), the critique of which is one of the main goals of this chapter. Even when acknowledging "Talmudic and cabalistic traditions" in general terms, her move straight from the Bible to Freud bypasses millennia of Jewish psychology, especially the prolific modern centuries covered here.[3]

However, as we shall see in chapter 6, I am encouraged by the return in contemporary mysticism and spirituality of the soul, whose presence has at last begun to command intensive academic attention. In saying this, I must stress that we are not talking here of a religious belief system, but rather of forms of psychological thought and cultural reflection, as well as a form of poetics (as I hope to elaborate elsewhere). As Erich Fromm put it in his pioneering *Psychoanalysis and Religion*: "It is not true that we have to give up the concern for the soul if we do not accept the tenets of religion." However, I must confess to some sympathy with Christopher Dawson's saying "religion is the soul of culture."[4]

This being said, it is not a religious, but a cultural stance, that is championed when Martha Nussbaum, in her inspiring defense of the humanities, repeatedly appeals to the soul: "We seem to be forgetting about the soul, about what it is for thought to open out of the soul and connect person to world in a rich, subtle, and complicated manner; about what it is to approach another person as a soul . . . to talk as someone who has a soul." Nussbaum goes on to say, in a locution that

I would wholeheartedly espouse: "the word 'soul' has religious connotations for many people, and I neither insist on these nor reject them. Each person may hear them or ignore them."[5]

A striking example of the return of the repressed soul is Victoria Nelson's *The Secret Life of Puppets*. This beautiful book shows how the soul denied in modern discourse morphed into various artistic, literary, theatrical, and later cinematic forms, especially in the image of artificial humans (the Kabbalistic variant, which is the *golem*, as Nelson indeed notes, following the studies of Gershom Scholem and Moshe Idel). From the many rich cultural lodes that she has uncovered, I shall note here only her description of romantic travel adventures as "vehicles for a new kind of soul quest," moving from the physical world to "an internalized soul region outside time and space," as in her analysis of fictional journeys to the poles as "journey to the center of the soul."[6]

Reworking Nelson's historical narrative, one may say that the soul was gradually displaced over the modern centuries, as the body-soul dualism of Descartes and the extreme dualism of Malebranche gave way to entirely materialistic psychologies and philosophies. Hegel's "beautiful soul," maintaining its "purity of heart" through self-defeating withdrawal from the world, can perhaps be said to have marked the last significant presence of the soul in authoritative philosophical conceptualization. I believe that one can locate evidence of awareness of this shift in materials from the turn of the nineteenth century, as in churchman-academic Isaac Milner's complaint: "the great and high have forgotten that they have souls." At the end of Hegel's nineteenth century, the return of the soul to authoritative discourse (as opposed to literature, where it still held sway, as described by Nelson and as evident throughout the poetry of that century) was marked by the inception of the ultimate modern mythology—psychoanalysis, with all of its scientific veneer. Naturally, this schematic, perforce linear, narrative leaves out transitional phases, such as attempts to create an empiricist "science of the soul" in the eighteenth century.[7]

This book emerged from the realization that Kabbalah, as an important player in contemporary culture, has consistently preserved the centrality of the soul throughout modernity (second only to God and the Torah as a theme of discourse), while at the same time profoundly changing its psychological theories under its impact. The affinity between these two psychological discourses was expressed in a classic of twentieth-century Jewish literature—Chaim Potok's *The Chosen*. The main theme of the novel (as well as its sequel *The Promise*) is the clash between the Hasidic care of the souls as represented by Reb Saunders and the modern science of the soul (first Freudian and then experimental), which inescapably draws his son and heir, Danny. When the patriarch capitulates (on the symbolic date of Passover), it is out of deference to the cry of Danny's soul. It is highly likely that the model for Daniel Saunders is the twentieth-century psychologist Fischel Schneerson, a grandson of a Hasidic rebbe, whose main novel *Hayyim Gravitzer* describes not only the travails of the soul of Gravitzer but also numerous Hasidic teachings on psychology.[8]

While Potok's narrative is heavily modernistic, depicting the move from the Hasidic court to the laboratory as liberation from bondage (as well as strongly Freudian in centering on the Oedipal drama), its valuable insight is that modern Jewish mysticism and the heavily Jewish field of psychology are both concerned with the "yearnings of the soul," as Scholem (who emerged from the same central European Jewish culture as Freud) defined mysticism itself.[9]

In the broadest sense, this work merges with the field of psychology of religion, while aspiring to carve out a place of pride for the psychology of mysticism. At the same time, I shall not even attempt to encompass the vast range of scholarship on psychology and religion, especially as the rather influential cognitivist, empiricist, evolutionary, neurological, and poststructuralist approaches leave little room for theories of the soul. Yet within the ever-expanding subfield of psychology of mysticism this is less so, as evidenced in the central treatment of mysticism in the first major twentieth-century work on psychology of religion—*The Varieties of Religious Experience* (based on the 1901–2 Gifford lecture by William James). Pragmatist that he was, James still used an expression such as "the sick soul" in bringing together melancholic religious writers and psychological aspects of religious pessimism.[10]

Indeed, it was the issue of mysticism that contributed significantly to the great divide between Sigmund Freud and Carl Jung, whose debt to James is rather unrecognized. This was the "central tension" (to use Peter Homans' felicitous phrase) that set the stage for all subsequent splits while transforming psychoanalysis from a joint exploration of the depths of the psyche to a set of competing schools and institutions. The Freudian controversies also included Freud's later and lesser-known schism with Otto Rank, whose analysis of the roots of *Seelenglaube* (soul-belief) deserves far more attention than it has received (despite its later propagation by important psychological thinkers such as Ernest Becker and Rollo May). Rank forcefully criticized Freud for his denial of the centrality of the soul for psychology while camouflaging its presence by means of the ideology of scientism. In presenting his alternative psychology, Rank boldly claimed that "religion was and is as much psychology as our modern scientific psychology is, unavoidably, soul-study" and that "in the animistic era, psychology was soul-creation; in the religious era it was soul-representation; in the scientific era, it has become knowledge of the individual soul," a formulation that will be highly suggestive for my own investigation.[11]

Lately, the history of the movement, as described in John Kerr's groundbreaking *A Most Dangerous Method*, has also moved into the cinema, the shared language of twentieth-century culture, which was born and grown in tandem with psychoanalysis. Kerr shows that it was Jung (and his mentor Eugen Bleuler) at Zurich who provided the institutional and public ground in which Freud's Vienna-based work could take root. Jung's position on psychology of religion, on mysticism, and on the soul thus plays a central role in our history of the psychology of mysticism.[12]

Another ramification of this finding is that one should view even more skeptically the claims as to Freud's alleged sources in Jewish texts and as to the Jewishness of psychoanalysis, culminating the claim (mentioned by Stephen Frosh) that it is properly part of Jewish studies! Going back to popular culture, it is interesting to note that the notion of Freud as a "closet Kabbalist" has spread from academia to literature (as in *Darkness Rising* by Frank Tallis). At the same time, one should not entirely remove the soul from Freud's orbit. Bruno Bettelheim, in his *Freud and Man's Soul*, has persuasively argued that the mistranslation of Freud's German texts in the English standard edition, motivated to a large extent by the attempt to cast a scientific veneer over his writing, has excised the prominent presence of the soul in his writings. Bettelheim sees this as a prominent example of the omission of an entire rich world of cultural allusions, often with religious or mythic antecedents. Furthermore, the gap between Freud and Jung's respective views of mysticism has been somewhat narrowed in an innovative discussion by William Parsons.[13]

Jung's 1937 Terry lectures at Yale University, published as *Psychology and Religion*, are a relatively early self-formulation of the field that I myself also belong to—the phenomenology of religion—boldly claiming, as part of his self-distancing from materialism, that "the only form of existence that we know of immediately is psychic." In a key formulation that will be relevant to my later discussion of dreams, Jung said: "The very common prejudice against dreams is but one of the symptoms of a far more serious undervaluation of the human soul in general." Despite this, Jung's extensive and multiyear opus cannot be seen as a true return of the soul, due to his constant efforts to cloister his discourse in the rhetoric of scientism: Thus Jung wrote in a central work, *Psychological Types* (first published in 1921): "By Soul I understand a clearly demarcated functional complex that can best be described as 'personality.'" Yet soon after this passage, Jung inserts the Latin term for psyche, *anima*, as the inner, feminine, soul-life, largely complementing the outward-directed "persona" (this duality being in turn a major theme in Jung's autobiographical reflection).[14]

Following James Hillman, one may posit that this is a thinly veiled theoreticization of the interior feminine figures Jung encountered and recorded in his visions, together with Elijah, a known favorite of Kabbalistic visions (as is the *Shekhina* or divine feminine). In doing so, he (like Otto Rank) acknowledged a long-standing relationship between the soul and the feminine (including the narrative of the denial of the soul of women by the council of Macon), profoundly affecting the more recent gender-oriented study of religion. Indeed, it is not surprising that much of the work on Kabbalah's psychology (mostly following Lacanian variants in French feminist theory) focuses on gender. Nonetheless, I shall address treatments of the engenderment of the soul only when it is called for in the modern Kabbalistic texts under survey. This move away from a gender-centric approach to the soul resonates with the approach of the school in which the return of the soul was fulfilled—archetypal psychology.[15]

For it was precisely at the time when the Jungian "heresy" solidified and at times ossified into a set of "second wave" schools, the new heresy of archetypal psychology emerged. In his 1972 Terry lectures, published as *Re-Visioning Psychology*, James Hillman most eloquently called for restoring the central place of the soul in the life of psychology, especially through John Keats' poetic idea of the world as the "vale of Soul-making." While Hillman himself attacked the Western importation of "Oriental transcendent methods" (which was just then moving towards its present popularity), mysticism has played a central role in the creative work of his "fellowship," perhaps the most vital psychological circle since Freud. Already in this lecture, Hillman claimed mystics such as Plotinus and Marsilio Ficino as partaking in his "ancestral tree of thought" (itself a somewhat Kabbalistic image!).[16]

I cannot do justice here to the ongoing and prolific output of this school that has also been somewhat institutionalized through the Pacifica Graduate Institute, and has developed its own schisms, as in the case of Wolfgang Giegerich, whose massive and innovative contribution to the history of the soul deserves a separate study (though see my brief

discussion in chapter 6). However, two major discussions of soul in religious texts, resonate with my own project: David L. Miller's archetypal
reading of Christianity (though not necessarily mystical Christianity)
belongs to the mytho-poetic reading that is currently gaining ground in
Kabbalah scholarship. Generally speaking, this approach subordinates
soul to myth, while in my reading that of Hillman himself takes the opposite track. However, Miller's reading of Christian texts, though using
the term "soul" relatively rarely, brings a religious tradition that shall be
much addressed here within the orbit of archetypal psychology. Likewise, Robert Sardello's synthesis of Hillman and early twentieth-century
mystic Rudolf Steiner is not merely a representation of a current "spiritual culture based in the reality of the soul," but also an illuminating
reflection on classical religious studies themes such as shamanism, apoc-
alypticism, and magic. I was particularly inspired by his depiction of the
very act of research on this topic as part of the work of soul-making.[17]

In those terms, the figures, places, books, and events discussed immediately below and throughout the book can be read on one level as a
historical survey (partaking in academic ritual, which has its own psychological life), and on another as an archetypal narrative of the "ancestors" or "lineage" of this work. Thus, if a picture of Hillman at the site of
Eranos, which played such a crucial role in the development and reception of Jungian thought, is the frontispiece of the Festschrift dedicated
to the former, one can regard it as an image for reflection on a certain
constellation (itself a mystical-magical term), just as the opening section
of that textual gift is devoted to "reverie, ancestry, photography, inter-
view," including "a celebration of images."[18]

It was at Eranos that Hillman interfaced with Henry Corbin, the great
French scholar of Islamic mysticism and philosophy, who helped him to
create a link with the secondary theme of this book—the heart. Although
this is less evidenced in Hillman's own treatment of him, "throughout
the entire range of Corbin's work, the emphasis is everywhere upon the
secret hidden realities of soul," as Tom Cheetam, Corbin's most important interpreter in the Anglophone world, put it. It is of portent for my
own study that Eranos was also where the ever-looming father of modern Kabbalah scholarship, Scholem, presented the more phenomenological and comparative of his writings. Besides his influence on Hillman's
school, Corbin also markedly informed the interpretation of the role of
the imagination in Kabbalah by Elliot Wolfson, the leading theoretician
of the post-Scholem era.[19]

In his 1979 Eranos paper in memory of Corbin, "The Thought of the
Heart," Hillman relates Corbin's "imaginal heart" to Freud's psychology

as a "paradigmatic occasion for the appearance of the thought of the heart within that Western modern consciousness which is bereft of a philosophy for adequately mediating its own heart." In other words, Corbin should be read as a "classic of psychoanalysis." Hillman prefaces his reading of Corbin with three imaginings of the heart in contemporary culture: The first of these, the "heart of the lion," the heart as courage and as virtue, is described as a response to the world-soul or *anima mundi*. The second, mechanistic heart is that of William Harvey, who graduated from the faculty of medicine at Padua one hundred years before the members of the Kabbalistic circle of R. Moshe Hayyim Luzzatto, which shall much concern us in this book. Hillman indeed places Harvey within the same historical and modern framework—of the move towards industrialization—that I have placed the circle of Luzzatto in. Following Thomas Fuchs, one must also note the connections between Harvey's revolutionary concept of the heart and Descartes' body-soul dualism.[20]

The third heart discussed in the lecture, clearly at the heart of the present (to use a Foucauldian phrase), is that of personal feeling, a philosophy that goes back to Augustine, yet "better belongs" to the formative modern figure of Rousseau. It is striking that Hillman contrasts this heart with that of "the Hebrews," as well as "the Persian thought presented by Corbin." It is also significant that Hillman describes this as the "confessional mode," so that it is also the heart captured and critiqued in the writings of Michel Foucault. This contextualizing critique of "confessional psychology" is extremely important for any reflection on psychology of religion, or indeed psychology as religion, for Hillman correctly identifies it as the source of the "secondary religious aura" pervading psychotherapy. The desire to move beyond this heart is one of the reasons for my decision to focus on theories of the soul and the heart, rather than those of emotion as such, or specific emotions (usually referred to as *middot* in Kabbalistic writing). It is also one reason for my reluctance to engage the frequently anachronistic discourse of psychobiography.[21]

It was more than a mere editorial decision to join this essay to Hillman's 1982 lecture and article "*Anima Mundi*: The Return of the Soul to the World." Hillman's call for the return of soul to psychology, "the renaissance of its depth" is founded on Marsilio Ficino's idea that the heart is the organ of perception responsive to the *anima mundi*. However, I believe that this is not merely a Renaissance, Florentine mode, as Hillman puts it. As Idel has shown (perhaps with some exaggeration), Renaissance thought (profoundly Judeo-Christian) was one of the streams that fed into the modern renaissance of psychic immanentism—Eastern European Hasidism.[22] In foregrounding two lectures by Hillman, both delivered in what I see as the approximate decade of his creative breakthrough, I have not done justice to earlier works such as *Suicide and the Soul*, *Insearch*, which is devoted to psychology of religion, or the more recent and popular *The Soul's Code*, which includes brief discussions of Kabbalah.[23] However, these works, each a world of its own, will reverberate in later chapters.

Hillman's exposition is of great portent for me, as throughout I shall claim that one cannot approach the soul without constantly touching on the heart, yet another classical psychological image or trope suppressed in modernity, and particularly in modern philosophy. In fact, despite several insightful comments, the heart as a coherent theme has not been the subject of any existing article-length study in Kabbalah studies. This relative disregard should be contrasted with the more extensive discussions of the heart as psychic center in various domains of religious studies, to be discussed in chapter 6 (as well as the popular writings I shall address in chapter 5).[24]

In a previous book, I claimed that the hypnotic method that Freud failed at and soon abandoned is far more useful for the study of many kinds of mysticism than the later technique of psychoanalysis. However, when moving from the realm of experience and technique to that of thought and theory (also in the classical and Christian senses of *theoria*, especially as contemplation and even prayer of the heart), I am compelled to follow the movement that has most influenced religious studies (as well as Kabbalah and its research) precisely at the moment when it has finally lost its hegemony. Yet one must again maintain a constant connection to the psychology of religion that is barely developed in Israeli academe (one major exception, referred to here and elsewhere, being the work of Yoram Bilu). Thus, researches on Kabbalah have not yet articulated theories of personality and emotion, even after several decades of advances in these areas.[25]

Of course, even when dwelling on the level of thought, collective representations can never be entirely divorced from individual experience and practice, as I myself have repeatedly claimed in the past. Nonetheless, I follow Hillman in his insistence on the need for "dehumanizing" for soul-making, and thus liberating the soul from the narrow frame of personal experience and autobiographical confession. As Hillman has put it, the thought of the heart, and the work of thought and image-making, should be restored to their due place, especially at a time when experience is foregrounded even when the texts do not especially call for it. In doing so, and denaturalizing "experience," one would be deconstructing an entire Western edifice of this complex cultural construction, as magisterially surveyed by Martin Jay.[26]

One cannot depart the history of psychology of mysticism without mentioning the works of Michael Eigen, that also encapsulate earlier theorists, such as Donald Winnicot, Marion Milner, and W. B. Bion. Eigen, who regards psychoanalysis and mystical states as part of one inseparable reality, is surely the most prominent psychological thinker to be significantly influenced by Kabbalistic and other Jewish texts, as well as by meetings with figures such as R. Menahem Mendel Schneerson, the last rebbe of Habad Hasidism. Eigen's deeply personal writing, interspersed with prayers and consciously designed to evoke experiencing, is explicitly an expression of his "Jewish soul" and "cry from the heart." Charmingly, in following the psychoanalytic ritual of writing up a case study, Eigen writes of a patient that "Jesse's soul would tickle me," as well as using vivid and manifold imagery such as ripping the soul, tearing its garments, "soul space," growing by "eating each other's souls" (as well as eating the "tiger soul" or "predator soul" of God), "the naked soul," and "soul price."[27]

In his most recent book, the autobiographical and confessional *Kabbalah and Psychoanalysis*, Eigen goes a step further and devotes an entire work to this comparison. To the extent that Eigen builds on concrete examples and textual allusions, he focuses on R. Nahman of Bratzlav, a figure who is certainly central for the Western reception of Hasidism since Martin Buber's publication of his tales (1906—just when Freud began formulating his critique of religion and shortly after James' lectures). However, we shall see in chapter 3 that R. Nahman's thought is but a marginal portion of a much wider context involving many dozens of schools in the Hasidic world alone. This choice and similar moves in Eigen's book illustrate the inherent gap between historically oriented and textually based scholarship and a praiseworthy effort to reflect on the implications of certain Jewish mystical teachings (within an eclectic selection from spiritual-mystical tradition in general) for clinical practice.

In my reading, the main innovation here relative to Eigen's earlier writing is his sensitive discussion of the work of the Tzaddik or righteous person with souls (see chapters 3 and 5 on this topic). His Winnicotian description of a Tzaddik such as R. Nahman as containing what each soul lost by being born is a true contribution towards understanding the psychology of Hasidism. Although this deserves a separate study, Eigen helps us to locate the soul repair or retrieval performed by the Tzaddik in a psychic field of loss, lack, and fall (the fall of the soul, through the figure of the antihero as faller, *nofel*, is a central theme in Gravitzer's novel).[28]

Modern Kabbalah and the Psychology of Mysticism

Whoever lacks the capacity to put on blinders, so to speak, and to come up to the idea that the fate of his soul depends on whether or not he makes the correct conjecture at this passage of his manuscript may as well stay away from academics. MAX WEBER

Like psychoanalysis and indeed like modern thought in general, modern Kabbalah was produced by circles or fellowships centered on teacher-figures and usually formalized through contracts (*shitrei hitqashrut*) and written regulations.[29] The earliest of these emerged not long after the Florentine Renaissance in the Galilean town of Safed. It was the sixteenth-century Safedian circles of R. Moshe Cordovero and R. Yitzhaq Luria that created the psychology of modern Kabbalah. In the new social structure of the fraternity, Kabbalistic life departed from the premodern and more intellectualist psychology dominated by neo-Platonic and Aristotelian philosophy. As we shall see in chapter 2, the rich Safedian discourse on the soul, together with its Italian and Middle Eastern reception, is crucial for understanding subsequent developments in Kabbalah's psychology. In the course of the long eighteenth century, these varied reworkings gradually gave way to new forms of authoritative psychological discourse that emerged in the fellowships of R. Shalom Shar'abi, R. Luzzatto, R. Elijah Kremer of Vilna (also known as the Vilna Ga'on or the Gra), and the Besht, founder of Hasidism (as described mostly in chapters 3 and 4). At this point, Kabbalah's psychology truly came into its own, almost entirely jettisoning residual attempts to match philosophical schemes. As a result, although I shall generally follow my customary method of thematic organization, these chapters (as well as chapter 2) will loosely follow a historical narrative. To the not insignificant extent that the book contains a historical argument, it is that one must understand modern Kabbalah on its own terms, and in this sequence. However, it must be stressed that this book is but part of a much wider ongoing project of discovering the uniqueness and importance of modern Kabbalah.[30]

A closely related claim is that despite the great achievements in recent decades in writing on psychology and Kabbalah, the way forward is to release our dependence on psychoanalysis, and instead bring to the forefront the indigenous psychological theories developed in the

Kabbalistic world that shared the modern period with psychology. In other words, we should not overly attempt to interpret texts written in sixteenth-century Galilee, seventeenth- and eighteenth-century Italy, or nineteenth-century Lithuania through the prism of the products of Central European culture in the late nineteenth and early twentieth centuries. To do so would be to accord a universal, ahistorical status to an interpretative method that is embedded in a very specific socioeconomic, cultural, and historical moment.[31]

Although Suzanne Kirschner risks overlooking the more immediate historical origins of psychoanalysis, one can indeed follow her in observing the similar chronology of the these two modern psychologies. Although her focus is on the Romantic period (somewhat later than the crest of the wave of modern Kabbalah) and its move from the soul to the self, she also includes the interiorizing moves of earlier Protestant mystics such as Jacob Boehme that were still framed in terms of the soul, while touching on more distant origins.[32]

Again following Kirschner, we are also speaking of two movements emerging from religious thought, one of which went to great lengths to repress its origins. The present post-Foucauldian climate, in which psychoanalysis is regarded as but one of numerous forms of power/knowledge created within later Western modernity is an apt time for denying such theories' privileged hermeneutical status. In this context, one should mention Joel Whitebook's important argument that Foucault's work, also a major influence on my own writing, is a "counterproject" to Freudianism.[33]

Therefore, I shall not add much to the brief synopsis of the history of scholarly, as well as popular, writing on psychology and Kabbalah in my last book, as I am again taking the road less traveled. However, there is room for two main exceptions that reflect a growing interest in the intersection of Kabbalah and psychoanalysis. One is Elliot Wolfson's recent *A Dream Interpreted within a Dream*, which offers a rich treatment of a major theme of Kabbalah's psychology. In doing so, Wolfson extensively addresses Foucault, Corbin, and Jungian thought (including that of Hillman). Both in his comparative scope and his bold transcendence of both philology and phenomenology in rooting his own philosophical reflections in the Kabbalistic texts, Wolfson's approach inspired my own efforts. Furthermore, together with his previous *Open Secret: Postmessianic Messianism and the Mystical Revision of Menaḥem Mendel Schneerson*, it reflects his increasing engagement with modern Kabbalah.[34]

At the same time, one should note two important differences (rather than disputes). Firstly, while Wolfson's reflections are in dialogue with the best of contemporary philosophy and theology, my own inclination is towards explicitly psychological discourse, as well as the best of contemporary mysticism and spirituality (including critical consideration of New Age materials). Secondly, Freud, a constant inspiration for Wolfson, famously described the dream as *via regia zur Kenntnis des Unbewußten* (the royal road to knowledge of the unconscious activities of the mind). Here (to some extent departing from my own previous work on hypnosis), I deliberately address more conscious forms of the psyche's own self-reflection—that being my favored characterization of psychological thought as such.[35]

A second recent work, of a very different nature, is Sanford Drob's *Kabbalistic Visions: C. G. Jung and Jewish Mysticism*. It shows a slightly (in my view) stronger influence of Kabbalah on Jung than previously suspected. However, generally speaking, the comparison between the two worlds is based on a selection of secondary sources and translations (some popular), rather than on any sustained reading of Kabbalistic texts sensitive to the variety of cultural contexts in which they were penned. Thus, I find it highly problematic for a writer with this kind of linguistic background to critique the textual interpretations given by a scholar like Wolfson (who is immersed in the original sources) when they disturb his argumentation. I am not at all persuaded that the various Jungian themes discussed here cannot be attributed, in the greater part, to Jung's extensive exposure, mostly in the original languages, to the Gnostic, alchemical, and modern Western esoteric literature that was far more significant for the formation of his views than his limited knowledge of Kabbalah, mediated largely through Christian reworking. I believe that to deduce otherwise from the very sources that Drob has assembled simply reflects an approach that bypasses the cultural, linguistic, and textual base of Jung's ideas.[36]

Despite these reservations, psychoanalysis indeed played an increasing role in the Kabbalistic discourse created after the early twentieth century, when the Kabbalists encountered the Freudians. From this point on, it would actually be contextually appropriate to follow the increasing influence of Western psychology on Kabbalah (as I shall do in chapter 5). Indeed, even when pursuing "indigenous knowledge," one should by no means view the Kabbalistic world as operating in isolation from general culture and history, as some Jewish studies scholars are prone to do. As I have argued in recent years in several studies, Kabbalah closely and increasingly interacted with various forms of modernity even prior to its encounter with psychoanalysis and similar trends. In other words, reading modern Kabbalah on its own terms is not merely a matter of periodization or demarcation within a vast textual domain. Rather, a central proposal here is that the very shift to a more psychological discourse was one of the markers of the interaction between the Kabbalists and the modern world at large. In other words, Kabbalah partakes of modernization qua psychologization. At this point it would be wise to quote a central researcher of modernity and religion, Peter Berger:

> The relatively frequent references to previous writings of my own should in no way be construed as a conviction on my part that these writings are terribly important . . . But every process of thinking must be a conversation with oneself and particularly with one's previous thought, and one cannot at each step start all over again from the beginning. Not to have to do this should perhaps be one of the fringe benefits of having written more than one book.[37]

This being said, this is a good point to encapsulate the reasons for my customary stress on the autonomy of the modern, joining a far broader move in current scholarship in European intellectual and cultural history. Besides the psychological and social psychological changes already mentioned, one should add some of the wider historical sea changes around the sixteenth century—the demographic revolution, especially in the Jewish world, the advent of print culture, profound religious transition such as the Reformation and the accompanying Catholic revival, geopolitical changes such as the establishment of the Ottoman Empire and the reorganization of Europe following the Peace of Westphalia and the European discovery of the Americas—for all of their implications for the very idea of religion, as discussed recently by Guy G. Stroumsa.[38] Above all, modern religion is characterized by historical self-awareness of innovation, as presaged by the *devotio moderna* movement and the theological approach known as *via moderna*.[39]

However, autonomy is not complete independence. Obviously, there are threads of continuity between modern Kabbalah and earlier periods, and I shall allude to these briefly when appropriate (as at the beginning of chapter 2, and see the methodological discussion in chapter 3). Furthermore, I do not wish to give the impression that premodern Kabbalah gave way to modernity in one fell swoop at some sixteenth-century point, even though I shall speak of the Safedian revolution (in chapter 2). Rather, in Foucauldian fashion, one may conceptualize a series of revolutions, in the sixteenth-seventeenth, eighteenth-early nineteenth, and currently in the late twentieth-early twenty-first centuries, each building on the other. Following the prolific and eloquent Sinologist François Jullien (applying his insights to French history), one can speak of silent transformations in between and even alongside this sequence of revolutions.[40]

It is this very focus on modern Europe and the Ottoman Empire (which ruled over several Kabbalistic centers for much of the modern period) that moves my approach away from the more universalistic views of the Eranos circle (including of course Mircea Eliade).[41] Attempting to move beyond the universalist-contextualist debate, the ongoing "paradigm clash" in the study of mysticism, I make a claim for contextualized comparison. In other words, when dealing with theories and images, as opposed to the more socially embedded world of practices and experiences, one can draw on the entire range of religious and mystical writing (as I shall do in chapter 6). However, one must then make every effort to relate the resultant insights to specific social and cultural contexts. Thus, it makes sense to focus one's comparative endeavor on cultures that were proximal to the world of modern Kabbalah, culturally and geographically.

Such contextualizing requires placing phenomenological observations within the broader frame of the cultural, intellectual, and social history of modern Judaism. It is especially important to trace the numerous connections between the psychology of modern Kabbalah and reflections on the soul and heart found not only within other foci of modern Kabbalistic discourse (such as ideas of the text, as in chapter 7) but also in other forms of modern Jewish writing, especially Mussar (so-called ethics). I believe that this is an important bulwark against the tendency among some academics, consciously or unconsciously joining with neo-Kabbalistic marketing experts, to downplay the more religious and traditional aspects of modern Kabbalah.[42]

It is this insistence of controlled and focused comparison that sharply distinguishes my project from the recent extensive study by Ron Margolin, *Inner Religion: The Phenomenology of Inner Religious Life and Its Manifestation in Jewish Sources (From the Bible to Hasidic Texts)*. There is some overlap here with my own investigation, as Margolin takes care to address cognition and thought as well as emotion, in addressing interiorization within a wider frame of selfhood and subjectivity. Furthermore, Margolin critically engages the literature on psychology of religion. However, as its title indicates, his study explicitly avoids historical and geographical contextualization, ranging as far as Far Eastern religion.[43]

Psychology and the Emerging History of Modern Kabbalah

The Struggle with history . . . is a way of soul-making. The occupation with history . . . reflects *anima*. JAMES HILLMAN

As I have claimed in the past, there is a glaring discrepancy between the fact that the greater part of Kabbalistic literature was penned in the modern period and the focus on the premodern periods in academic training. This is certainly true in the case of psychology, as almost the entirety of research on the soul in Kabbalah is devoted to the medieval period.[44] Since my last book on modern Kabbalah, and perhaps at least partly in response to it, the study of modern Kabbalah has indeed been burgeoning, creating a much-needed setting for the investigation of specific themes. David Ruderman's wide cultural history of Jewish early modernity and Maoz Kahana's groundbreaking work on Central Europe in the eighteenth century have greatly improved our understanding of the cultural and intellectual context in which modern Kabbalists operated. The updated publication of David Sorotzkin's work on Orthodoxy and modern disciplination has joined the publication of Roni Weinstein's above-noted *Kabbalah and Jewish Modernity*. Yaacob Dweck's work on R. Yehuda Modena used Modena's seventeenth-century critique of Kabbalah as a case study for examining the interrelationship of Kabbalah and modernity. Pawel Maciejko's work on the Frankist movement, joined by Ada Rapoport-Albert's work on Sabbateanism, take up Scholem's main inquiry (at least in the modern period) and deal with a world whose psychological thought deserves further investigation, yet not in the present study, for reasons that will be discussed in chapter 7.[45]

As we shall see in that chapter, I continue to focus my exploration of modern Kabbalah on the more nomian and mainstream streams of Jewish modernity, all the while seeking to illuminate schools and texts, especially between the late sixteenth and early twentieth centuries, which have enjoyed less scholarly attention. Among these, I would include the Middle Eastern reception of Safedian Kabbalah (which has now received an important historical study by Jonatan Meir), the above-mentioned Luzzatto circle, and works that have barely been mentioned in English, such as the seventeenth-century *Nishmat Adam* by R. Aharon of Kremnitz (devoted entirely to the topic of the soul), the nineteenth-century works of R. Isaac Haver of Lithuania, and the voluminous works of R. Ya'aqov Abuhatzeira of Morocco in the same century. In addition, I propose to move through psychology towards a new reading of better-known schools, such as the Lithuanian Mussar movement and the Hasidic schools unfolding from the circle of the Seer of Lublin. In this analysis, to be offered in chapter 3, I hope to be able to show that specific developments in European modernity impacted on these strongly psychological views of the soul.

Generally speaking, I follow Daniel Abrams in seeking to correct the ever-increasing academic tendency, in both research and teaching, to repeatedly focus on a limited corpus, especially when we are speaking of the modern period. Although the recent developments surveyed above have somewhat improved this sad state of affairs, one cannot but note the gap between the sheer volume of material available now through vast Haredi databases such as Otzar HaHokhma, not to mention the manuscript material that Abrams focuses on (gradually being published in Haredi editions), and the generally repetitive selection in the universities. This slow migration of cultural capital (and of the emotional energy associated with it, paraphrasing Randall Collins) away from the university reflects the crisis of both the Zionist and the liberal American Jewish enterprises, both of which include a strong drive towards canonization.[46]

In any case, we are still very far from a general theory of Kabbalistic modernity. I feel that one vital step towards this goal is a much fuller and consciously comparative treatment of one of the key characteristics of European modernization—the psychological realm. I believe that the recent debates surrounding the modern selfhood that emerged over the course of the eighteenth century (the notion of interiority and uniqueness as articulated in the philosophical tradition versus cultural configurations of gender, race, and class) will be cast in a different light once one places this discussion in a more panoramic context. Namely, if we allow Raymond Martin and John Baressi (as well as their duly acknowledged predecessors) to remind us that the modern self could emerge only once it was reimagined, in this period, as mind rather than as soul, especially in the case of John Locke and his respondents, or alternatively, that the modern self has often replaced the soul. As we shall soon see, this period of what is increasingly termed "the long eighteenth century" will be cardinal in our narrative of the modernization of Kabbalah.[47]

However, in order to avoid universalizing the Western psychological mind-set, even when more broadly construed, it must be remembered at all times that this is but one of "multiple modernities," to use the late lamented S. N. Eisenstadt's felicitous phrase. While including Ottoman Kabbalah obviously requires addressing modern Sufism to some extent (in chapter 2), other mystical traditions on the soul can be addressed mainly in order to illustrate both the uniqueness of the European case and the profoundly European nature of much of modern Kabbalah.

In view of these cautions, the comparative discussion in chapter 6 will mostly juxtaposition Kabbalah's psychology with Christian contexts such as the seventeenth-eighteenth century "religion of the heart" (also comparing the recent Kabbalistic writing on the soul covered in chapter 5 to similar discourse in mystical Christianity and Western Sufism, no less than "unchurched" mysticism). In doing so, one cannot but extend Wolfson's formidable study of attitudes to non-Jews in Kabbalah and address the role of nationalization on the evolution of what I have elsewhere termed "national psychology" within Kabbalah, to be addressed in detail in chapter 4. One of the key shifts from premodern Kabbalistic thought to the psychology of modern Kabbalah was the victory of the doctrine of the divinity of the soul, which was almost always interpreted as the Jewish soul.[48]

At the same time, that chapter will show that even in the depths of national psychology, as in the writings of Rabbi Avraham Yitzhaq Kook, one may find insights conducive for psychological thought and imagination. Furthermore, my comparative chapter will disclose the paradoxical similarity between Jewish national mystical psychology and parallels in modern Europe. All of these moves require relinquishing the insistence on "panoramic" continuity between modern Kabbalah and premodern modes of thought. Specifically, the decline of Greek-influenced philosophy in increasingly nationalized Jewish culture from the sixteenth century precludes reading later developments as "neo-Platonic." The retreat of Jerusalem (literally in the case of sixteenth-century Jerusalemite Kabbalah) from dialogue with Athens also creates a certain distance from psychoanalysis, including archetypal psychology, as an heir not only of Greco-Latin terminology, but also of Greek mythology. In other words, I part ways with Hillman, with his conscious return to the Renaissance and through Florence to Greece, in attempting to present a thoroughly modern imagination of the soul as an inspiration for its return.[49]

Our tale of the soul in modern mysticism will weave together numerous images and motifs arising from both Jewish and Christian sources discussed throughout the book, following rich accounts of the wandering and return, renewal, recovery, rebirth, growing, proliferation, migration, transformation, and personalization of the soul. All these are gerunds, for just as process theology claims that "God is a verb," a process-oriented study of mystical psychology reveals that the soul is seen as a verb more often than as a noun (although, as we shall see, this view is also not absent among the numerous manifestations of the modern mystical imagination).

Neighboring Areas

Everybody seems to be publishing a psychology these days.
WILLIAM JAMES

The sheer quantity of unstudied Kabbalistic material and the need for comparative contextualization necessitate leaving numerous themes outside the scope of the present work (especially as some of these have been admirably covered by others). As Brad Gregory put it very well:

Any attempt to "cover everything" would succeed only in producing a completely unmanageable mountain of data. Indeed, in proportion to its increase, which has been enormous . . . the sheer volume of historical scholarship—what Daniel Lord Smail has recently called "the inflationary spiral of research overproduction'"—paradoxically militates against comprehension of the past in relationship to the present. A different approach is needed if we are to avoid being overwhelmed by specialized scholarship, the proliferation of which tends to reinforce ingrained assumptions about historical periodization.[50]

First and foremost, although I shall often touch on the body/soul relationship, I remain focused on the soul itself. Thus, although one does not need to be a Freudian to realize the intimate connection between Amor and Psyche, this book is not part of the Foucauldian project of the history of sexuality nor the wider project of the history of the body (including the physical heart). From my earlier comments on the "heart of Foucault" it should be clear that I regard even the modern soul as far more than "the prison of the body" (as "the effect and instrument of a political anatomy"). Rather, like Kristeva, I regard the "iron cage" (Weber) of modernity primarily as a "prison of the soul."[51]

While reincarnation of souls (*gilgul neshamot*) plays a key role in Kabbalistic discussions of the soul, I regard it as a separate topic, interlaced with other questions of eschatology and soteriology (such as the interrelationship of the resurrection at the end of days and the "world of the souls" in the afterlife) as well as time and sacral history. This concern peaked in Safed and continued to receive much attention in the Middle Eastern reception of Luria (as in R. Yehuda Petaya's twentieth-century practice of soul retrieval), but is far less present in the writings of the circle of Luzzatto, Lithuanian Kabbalah (including Kook), and most streams of Hasidism.[52]

As Kerr has shown, psychoanalysis as a modern movement originated in the mental hospital at Burghölzli in Zurich, and of course it is difficult to address the soul without what Hillman has termed "pathologizing." However, my concern is with the illumination and transformation of the soul rather than with madness, which has received some scholarly attention in the pioneering psychological-anthropological work of Bilu and later in Jewish studies that joins a recent interest in trauma in Israeli Kabbalah scholarship, probably reflecting the posttraumatic and traumatic character of Israeli society. Although I share Barbara Ehrenreich's eloquent social critique of the current avoidance of the suffering of the soul in positive psychology, I am following here the mainstream and authoritative, rather than the marginal (as we shall see further in chapter 7).[53]

Finally, we must bear in mind that the psychological thought of modern Kabbalah must be differentiated from related but separate areas of investigation, such as the psychology of God, as discussed in an important study by Abrams. The modern victory of the doctrine of the divine soul much deepened the already intimate relationship between theosophy and Kabbalah's psychology, as well put by Wolfson: "If we are to accept the language of the secrets of the divine being presented in the guise of the secrets of the soul, then we must equally posit that the secrets of the soul are presented in the guise of the secrets of the divine." However, my concern is with the secrets of the soul rather than the secrets of the divine. Thus, while dissolving Rudolph Otto's geocultural distribution of the "Eastern" soul-mysticism and the "Western" god-mysticism, I support his essential phenomenological intuition, while opting to address the former. Others, especially Idel, have already dealt with the modern psychological reinterpretation of the supernal realm, in doing so reinforcing my argument as to the uniqueness of modern Kabbalistic discourse on such areas.[54]

On the broad cultural level, my attempt to regard Kabbalah as a form of indigenous knowledge that may contribute to psychology rather than just being interpreted through it joins the extensive dialogue between Buddhism and psychology as well as rapidly developing directions such as spiritual psychotherapy and pastoral psychology. Here I join Philip Wexler, who has pioneered the extraction of models of social psychology—rooted in classical social theory—from Hasidic texts. As Wexler has more recently and generally put it: "in the new mystical scholarship, one can find . . . models of social interaction, of mystical interaction, that may again become analytically resonant, especially with the declining intuitive validity of modern sociological theory." As we shall see in chapter 2, the Safedian conceptualization of social interaction in the fellowship as reflecting the internal interaction within a plural psyche (closely linked to what Wexler's hero William James termed "a pluralistic universe") clearly bears out Wexler's own intuition.[55]

More generally, it is my hope that this study, like previous works of mine, will contribute somewhat towards a fuller integration of religious studies and the social sciences, an interrelationship presently confined mostly to current phenomena. I believe that this synthesis is crucial for the joint struggle of the humanities and the "softer" social sciences in face of the managerial trends mentioned at the beginning of the chapter, epitomized by the physical and conceptual relocation of psychology at my university away from both the humanities and social sciences to the natural sciences. Again quoting Wexler (following Weber, who I shall return to at the very end of the book): "in the contemporary social world of incessant rationalization and commodification . . . 'imparting training,' the hallmark of the 'specialist type of man' remains the prevailing type of pedagogy."[56]

TWO

The Safedian Revolution

Before Safed: A Brief Overview

True to the temporal boundaries explained in chapter 1, I shall treat developments prior to the sixteenth century very sparsely. Stemming from the premodern predilection of existing scholarship, there are relatively extensive discussions of psychology in general and the soul in particular, in philosophical literature (reaching back to Philo), that I shall not even attempt to summarize here. I shall not at all enter the voluminous material on psychological thought in Jewish spiritual literature, whether overlapping with or extending beyond the early Kabbalah, including Mussar as well as Ashkenazi and Egyptian pietism, although clearly there is more work to be done here. However, it may be wise to repeat my previous comments as to the greater influence of philosophy on premodern, as opposed to modern, Kabbalah. This change went along with the decrease in reading (and translation) of Arabic-language texts in the Jewish world (as discussed below).

Scholem already pointed out this fact, in a discussion of "the new Kabbalah," some seven decades ago, although, as was his wont, he tied it to the trauma of the expulsion from Spain, which can indeed be said to mark the beginnings of Kabbalistic modernity. In contradistinction, after the sixteenth century, Mussar, with its psychology, was largely integrated within mystical discourse. (We shall see in chapter 3 that even the later Lithuanian Mussar movement is no true exception to this rule. In discussing this movement, I shall also point out the unrecognized influence of the twelfth-century philosopher R. Abraham ibn Ezra.)[1]

I shall certainly not attempt to address the more rudimentary rabbinic discussions of the soul. At the same time, one cannot but note the need for a more thorough examination of the relationship of Gnostic and other late antique ideas and images of the soul and early Kabbalistic writing, especially if one does not entirely accept Idel's revisionary theory of the relationship of Gnosis and Kabbalah. A recently published collection, including the text *The Exegesis on the Soul* (from the Nag Hammadi Library), discloses a rich poetics of the journey of the soul. Likewise, April DeConick's excellent treatment of the "recovery of the soul" in Hermetic circles (including Jewish advocates) discloses an equally rich discourse on the divinization of the soul. The current proliferation of writing on Jungian psychology and Gnosis would greatly benefit from a close reading of the relevant texts in their overall context and in light of recent scholarship. However, the decisive demarcation seems to be the transition to modernity rather than the lesser shift from late antiquity to the Middle Ages, the latter again being largely a scholarly construct.[2]

Beginning then with early Kabbalah, the logical starting point is a lengthy discussion by Idel that mostly ends in the thirteenth century. Based on Idel's discussion, one can trace two basic models of the divinity of the soul. That developed in the school of Nahmanides treats the soul as primordial, given with the divine breathing into Adam (Genesis 2:7). The other model, found in the earlier Provencal school of R. Isaac the Blind, is that of the soul as acquired through a process of ascension, moving up to the divine world as a result of human deeds in the material world. These models are both found in the Zoharic literature of the late thirteenth and early fourteenth century.[3] Here we find, developing the second model, a more nuanced system of gradual acquisition of the three levels of *nefesh*, or body-soul, *ruah*, or spirit (which often accompanies soul in Western mystical literature), and *neshama*, or true soul. As we shall see in chapter 7, there is also a "soul of soul," more of eschatological relevance. At least according to one Zoharic passage, the true soul is attained only by the righteous. Margolin has recently noted an important passage that reads several Biblical verses on the human heart as referring to "the Holy One, Blessed be He," pointing towards what I call the divinization of the heart. This finding reinforces the sense of a wide range of views on the divinity of the psyche in this nonetheless important corpus.

As social psychology should usually accompany psychology, this premodern debate that shall reverberate throughout this chapter and the entire book can be described as a theory of entitlement and immediacy versus one of effort and hierarchy (somewhat comparable to the never-ending works vs. grace debate in Christianity). While the first model regards the soul as a static substance, the second seems to treat it more as a process or activity, as in soul-making, and thus has a certain elective affinity with modernity. As we shall see, these basic models continued to play out throughout modernity, yet in very different intellectual and social contexts, and thus in far greater degrees of complexity.[4]

Idel's distinction is thus highly useful for organizing premodern discussions, yet discussions of the *tzelem* or "divine image," especially in the school of Nahmanides, need to be also revisited in view of explicating the psychological theory that they contain. Likewise, one must consider the theory of the four worlds (Emanation, Creation, Formation, and Making, *atzilut, beri'a, yetzira, 'asiya*) that, as we shall see, was later interwoven with the various soul levels. Such examinations need to take into account the marked diversification of Kabbalistic thought in the first great wave of proliferation in the thirteenth and early fourteenth centuries.[5] Before turning to the shift to modern Kabbalistic psychology in a second and even greater wave in sixteenth-century Safed, I must caution that I shall go into some detail of a more technical nature, as these texts lay a necessary foundation for understanding the subsequent diversification and unfolding of modern Kabbalistic psychology. At the same time, the more expert readers need to bear in mind that the vast scope of material available to us from the era of printing (and in the era of databases) precludes an extensive analysis of any single corpus or figure.

The Psychological Revolution of Safed

Friend of the Soul. . . . My soul is sick with your love.
EL'AZAR AZIKRI, "YEDID NEFESH"

By far, the greater amount of research on Kabbalistic psychology has focused on the Kabbalistic circles of sixteenth-century Safed, and justly so. As I have claimed elsewhere, the Kabbalah underwent a "psychological turn" in the sixteenth century, a period that by many accounts saw a decisive intensification in discourse of individuality. The numerous textual witnesses for this shift include Italian Renaissance Kabbalah (influenced in turn by neo-Platonism as briefly mentioned in chapter 1) and the trance-oriented Kabbalists of Jerusalem, numerous psychological passages in the less obviously mystical writings of R. Yehuda Loew ben Bezalel (1520–1609, famous as Maharal) of Prague, and the Greco-Turkish Kabbalah of R. Meir ibn Gabbai, where one can find a very important discussion of "soul" as the Kabbalistic term of choice for the deity. Nonetheless, it is only Safed that can be said to have been the one site of a veritable psychological revolution, manifested in autobiography, hagiography, possession-related phenomena, a renewed focus on *teshuva* (so-called repentance), psychological techniques related to master-disciple relationships, and various psychodiagnostic methods, not to mention the gender-related issues discussed in chapter 1.

It was this revolution, in newly conquered Ottoman Palestine (the Land of Israel to Safedian Jews), that truly inaugurated the modern era in Kabbalah while effecting sharp discontinuity with earlier periods. Thus, my choice of the quintessentially modern term "revolution" is entirely deliberate. As I have stated elsewhere, different mystical traditions moved on divergent timelines, thus undermining facile periodizations. However, the material assembled in this chapter, tip of the proverbial iceberg though it is, shall demonstrate that the modern timeline for Kabbalah should also be joined to a specific geographical site, that of Safed.[6]

There is a recent awakening of the thesis (most developed by Paul Fenton), that the Safedian revolution has much to do with contacts with Sufi circles in the Galilee. Avraham Elqayam has offered an interesting psychological speculation on the guilt experienced by a major Safedian Kabbalist and Halakhist, R. Joseph Karo, after entering a Sufi center (an autobiographical testimony first discussed by Zwi Werblowsky). According to his interpretation, the term *tiul* found in this account refers to a spiritual, ecstatic experience (rather than merely a walk through the garden of the center), while the adjacent description of "seeing sexual organs" (*'erva*) refers to exposure to an ecstatic Sufi ceremony in which the participants tore off their clothes. As a result, the angel communicating with Karo, serving as his superego (following Werblowsky's psychobiographic interpretation of Karo's mystical life), rebuked him for the homoerotic arousal that this occasioned. Thus, Elqayam posits that Karo experienced both attraction and repulsion towards "Sufi spirituality." Elqayam relates these claims to Safedian critiques of ecstatic dances in which the participants tear off their clothes (according to Elqayam "undoubtedly" remaining partially or fully naked). If one is to accept this speculation, this would markedly change our understanding of the individual psychology of Karo, not merely an important Kabbalist but actually (through his Code of Law and other Halakhic works) one of the makers of modern Judaism. Yet interesting as this analysis is, it is very much to build on a few lines in the partial printed version of Karo's diary, even should one accept all of Elqayam's interpretations and connections (Elqayam quoted these lines throughout via Werblowsky, and it would have been helpful had he presented his readers with the full entry in its context).[7]

Likewise, Haviva Pedaya has ascribed the rise of ecstatic musical composition and performance in sixteenth-century Kabbalistic circles, alongside other developments (such as the replacement of reclusive meditation with group activity) to encounters with the Islamic world in the Ottoman domain. She partly explains this shift (especially as exemplified in the influential yet controversial poetry of R. Israel Najjarah) to a joint Jewish-Islamic space of popular religion. However, Pedaya herself notes the reservations of the leading Safedian Kabbalist, R. Yitzhaq Luria, with regard to such a receptive approach. One can compare Pedaya's hypothesis to Idel's more cautious claim as to the influence of Ottoman popular religion, especially storytelling, on early Hasidism. One direction that has not yet come up in scholarly discussion is the possible relationship between Safedian messianism (for all of the questions as to its nature and extent) and the general awakening of messianism in the ascendant Islamic empires of the sixteenth century, including the Ottoman Empire that ruled over the Galilee and its surroundings.[8]

However, there are substantial methodological obstacles to be cleared for this thesis to be established. Firstly, unlike Fenton, Elqayam and Pedaya move freely over centuries of Sufi writing and between continents, without grounding their comparison in the specific context of Galilee and the surroundings in the sixteenth century. Secondly, the level of knowledge of literary Arabic in the Jewish world had much declined in this period, as attested in a testimony from sixteenth-century Safed, discussed by Fenton himself and addressed in my article on sixteenth-century psychology and its Middle Eastern context. Therefore, it is harder to imagine Kabbalists actually reading Sufi texts. This, however, is not to preclude contacts on a more popular or oral level, such as the known encounters between a central Safedian Kabbalist, R. Hayyim Vital, with Muslim sorcerers. However, unlike Europe in both the Renaissance and the modern period, we cannot find evidence for any reciprocal influence of Kabbalistic psychological thought on non-Jewish writers in the Ottoman Empire.[9]

I shall further address the question of Kabbalistic and Sufi social psychology below. For now let me say that it is obviously impossible to do justice to the social psychology implicit in all of the above-mentioned themes, due to our focus on the soul and the heart. Here one can but note that this topic needs to be reexamined thoroughly following the work of Eyal Davidson, who has explored the actual social structure of the wider learning community of Safed, which was the necessary infrastructure for the revolutionary process. Recently, Safedian social psychology has been touched on in two works in Hebrew (although neither of these utilize social psychological theory). Weinstein has analyzed Lurianic Kabbalah from the perspective of comparative social history. Although psychology, and certainly the soul, are not specific focal points of this innovative effort (which stresses the history of the body), it has contributed to a reading of Lurianic theosophy in terms of the art of memory, that Weinstein follows into the early modern period.[10]

Although the theme of *teshuva* had been discussed in previous scholarship, Weinstein greatly advances this inquiry by describing a joint Judeo-Christian early modern "culture of sin," leading to similar social constructions of emotion and imagination. In this context, one should add that Shaul Magid has devoted an English-language discussion to the impact of the *converso* phenomenon at the end of the period of Spanish Jewry, and thus of Catholicism, on Safedian Kabbalah. It is possible that the true beginning of modern Kabbalah was in *converso* circles (such as that of the *Book of the Responding Entity*) responding to the persecutory effect of the rise of one of the first modern states by imagining the magical interventions of Kabbalists in the course of national history (as described by Idel, also in earlier studies). As a result, these texts disclose strong Catholic influence, as in incarnational language, alongside with a political denouncement of Christianity. One can speculate as to the connection of these visionary circles to the heterodox *alumbradismo* (illuminism) movement that was also persecuted by the Spanish Inquisition in the same period. However, this question can be answered only after the relevant manuscripts are fully published.[11]

Haviva Pedaya has addressed various psychological issues in her study of "rituals of movement," including those related to exile. Generally speaking, although she mentions the "post-Jungians" (in tandem with self-psychology), she maintains a binary scheme opposing ego and self, thus not truly integrating their model of a "plural psyche." Nonetheless, she has contributed valuable insights on ritual as "metamorphosis" or transformation of the heart, as well as intergenerational psychology (which I shall touch on in chapter 3). Pedaya attempts to somewhat revive the Scholemian hypothesis as to the effect of the expulsion of Spain on Safedian Kabbalah, yet in a more culturally nuanced manner. In and of itself, this theory removes the Safedian revolution from the wider setting of the sixteenth century, linking it instead to the late fifteenth-century event of the expulsion from Spain. From a psychological point of view, Pedaya's development of this connection is highly interesting, as it foregrounds the currently popular notion of trauma.[12]

However, while—for all of its uniqueness—one cannot isolate the Safedian center from the rest of the sixteenth-century Jewish Mediterranean world; one must bear in mind some sense of "interactive history" (to use Idel's phrase). Furthermore, I do not believe that it is possible, even on a merely textual level, to contain the Safedian revolution within the sixteenth century. As Yosef Avivi has recently demonstrated at great length, the very Safedian corpus that has reached us is indelibly marked by the effect of later copying and editing, not to mention interpretation, after the heyday of Safed and in other locations, in the late sixteenth and early seventeenth centuries.

This is true not only of the Lurianic corpus, where it is very difficult to separate "original" and "later" versions of any given work, but even of the texts of the rival major school, that of R. Moshe Cordovero (1522–70), which were mostly printed in later periods and more significantly were mediated by extensive summarizing, quotation, and simplification by seventeenth-century exegetes. These included R. Avraham Azulai (1570–1643) of Morocco and Palestine as well as R. Menahem 'Azaria da Fano (1548–1620) of Italy, of whom I shall have more to say below. In doing so, these writers fulfilled the original mission of Cordovero and his Safedian disciples, who strove, in a more modern manner, for popular reach, as opposed to the Lurianic esotericism. Generally speaking, seventeenth-century Kabbalah still needs to be released from the thrall of the excessive focus on the Sabbatean movement in order to be studied in context and in toto.[13]

Previous scholarship, as well as the more recent contributions mentioned just now, have placed the fellowship or circle at the center of the spiritual life of Safed. As described in chapter 1, this is essentially a social-psychological structure. A Lurianic autobiographical text explicitly frames this form of mystical organization in terms of the soul. R. Hayyim Vital, the main disciple of R. Yitzhaq Luria, quotes his teacher on the process of sifting (or "clarifying," using the term *birur*) members that is pivotal in the formation of any circle:

My teacher . . . told me that not all of our colleagues will be permanently established and a few of them still need to be clarified and changed and others will be put in their place . . . I will now write about the colleagues who study with us, though I do not know which ones will have others exchanged in their places. Since these colleagues are not complete, that is, there are those among them who have a small amount of that aspect of the garment of the superior Soul.[14]

The text then details this imperfection in saying that several fellows (including the highly original R. Joseph Tabul) were "cast aside" due to psychological flaws such as anger. Obviously, the impact of internal power struggle on such an account is well conceivable, yet it is not our concern here. One should rather view this text in light of Luria's admonition, placed strategically at the beginning of Vital's rendition of the Lurianic mystical manual *Sha'ar ha-Kavvanot*, on the love of fellows in study, extending to each member imagining himself as "one limb" in a collective body. Tellingly, this tradition adds a special stress on those merited with "knowledge and attainment to know and recognize his friend in the aspect of his soul."[15] As we shall see, this privileging of psychic imagery over somatic imagery is typical of Lurianic thought.

As I have written in a study on Safed (cited above), charismatic leaders and their autobiographically or hagiographically detailed inner life were the keystones of the Safedian fellowships. I shall focus here on two much-studied and prolific figures, due to their profound impact on subsequent Kabbalistic modernity as well as their focal position in the modern Kabbalistic imaginaire: Cordovero and Luria. It should be noted here that certain disciples, including Vital himself, learned from both Cordovero and his successor, further justifying a dual focus on these teachers. Perforce I must set aside important earlier figures such as R. Lapidot Ashkenazi and R. Yehuda Hallewa, as well as any further discussion of R. Joseph Karo.[16]

R. Moshe Cordovero

Once the reader delves through our words into the depths . . . His soul shall bless him.
R. MOSHE CORDOVERO

Cordovero's most important and lasting contribution to psychological theory was his elaboration of the Nahmanidean theory of the divinity of the soul. As Cordovero put it at the beginning of the last and decisive of the thirty-two "gates" of his much-printed magnum opus *Pardes Rimonim*: "Man is a part of divinity above" (*heleq eloah mi-ma'al*, quoting Job 31:2). Here, he both explicitly summarizes the preceding "gate of the soul" and then immediately applies this principle to the connection of the soul to the supernal, in a "chain of being" theory (the "part" being part of a chain). This more complex theoretical position is stated more simply in the popular treatise advocating widespread Kabbalah study, *Or Ne'erav*, where Cordovero encourages his reader to aspire to Kabbalah study, as the portion of God is his portion and his soul is "part of God above."

I do not think that the source for Cordovero's precise formulation is necessarily found in the esoteric texts of Nahmanides (1194–1270). A more likely premodern candidate, especially for the *Or Ne'erav* text (and also amplified in the text from R. Elijah de Vidas' "Sha'ar ha-Ahava (Gate of Love)" mentioned below), is the much-cited (especially by Cordovero) thirteenth-century Kabbalist R. Yosef Gikatila (1248–1325), who developed the biblical formulation "For the portion of the Lord is his people" (Deuteronomy 32:9) into a theory of the Jews being the portion of God.[17]

Furthermore, close as Cordovero's formulation may seem to a Nahmanidean theory (and thus it was interpreted influentially in the following century, as we shall see), the third chapter of the "Gate of the Soul" clearly states that the acquisition of the four levels of the soul (including the "soul of the soul"), overlapped with the four-worlds theory, is dependent on human action. Indeed, as a modern Kabbalist, Cordovero greatly stressed the importance of human activity. It is only after this earthly process that one becomes "a son" of the divine house, implying relocation to the divine world. Including yet another model popular in Safed, this time that of becoming a chariot to the divine, he goes on to say, even more explicitly that:

[. . .] there is a vital natural *nefesh* that is a chariot for the divine *nefesh* . . . and though one may be alive, it is possible that the [divine] *nefesh* will not be emanated in him, but he shall live from the vital *nefesh*, and when he merits, the divine *nefesh* will be influenced on him (*yoshp'a 'alav*) and if he merits further, then the *ruah* and the *neshama* shall be influenced on him.[18]

It should be clear even from this brief selection that Cordovero's encyclopedic writing indebted him to a great variety of models and traditions, thus rendering problematic the later identification of his position with a simple theory of the divinity of the soul.

Later in this gate, he writes of the *tzelem*, which is beyond the tripartite division, and is attained by some of the *hasidim*, or pietists. It is plausible that he (following an above-noted Zoharic view) reserved the full divinity of the soul mainly for the righteous or *hasidim*, the soul and the righteous being two overlapping and central heroes of his writing, that partakes in what I have described as the Safedian "cult of the saints." This was clearly the opinion of the seventeenth-century R. Avraham Azulai, who ascribed the divinity of the soul mostly to the righteous (thus continuing the trope of the "souls of the righteous," found in rabbinic literature as well as earlier Kabbalistic texts, which will recur throughout the book).[19]

Having looked into these better-known texts, I wish to now follow my inclination to pursue exegetical texts. Though far more voluminous, Cordovero's texts in this genre have been somewhat less studied (with the major exception of Bracha Sack's careful readings), due to the residual tradition of avoidance of the nomian and seeking out of the non-canonical in Kabbalah studies. I turn first to Cordovero's innovatively extensive commentary on the prayer book (*Tefillah le-Moshe*) described at the very end of *Pardes Rimonim* as its successor volume, or in contemporary terms "companion workbook." In his long commentary on the "wonderful secrets" of the prayers of the New Year, described at the outset as continuing the end of his magnum opus, he indeed applies a model that we have just seen, in describing a meditative practice of adherence of thought to the divine as connecting the soul as "part" to the divine whole (using the organic metaphor of connecting the branch to the root). However, this text is also pervaded by a strong exilic consciousness that I shall later contrast with Luria's views. For instance, in describing the state of the exile, Cordovero writes that "there is no power in the reality of the souls" to perform the necessary unification of the divine name in prayer.[20]

In his multivolume commentary on the *Zohar*, *Or Yaqar* (also described as the basis of his above-mentioned prayer manual), Cordovero branches out yet further, developing a model of the purification and renewal of the soul through the rite of *nefilat appayim* (lit. "falling on the face"), a practice of "soul descent" that I have dwelt on at length elsewhere. There and elsewhere in his commentary, he also dwells on the *diyuqan* or "image" of the soul. I believe that the latter passages point towards a model in which the soul has what we might term "virtual reality." In another text in this commentary, he writes of the "sparks" of the soul, shining according to one's deeds. Both of these terms will recur much in later Kabbalistic writing; however, what is significant for our purposes is that though the divinity of the soul is given, the extent to which it is present in the body depends on human action.[21]

When considering the place of psychology in Cordovero's hermeneutics, one must also recall his crucial role in popularizing the pluralistic theory of the dependence of exegetical and scholastic insight on the root of one's soul (a theme first discussed by Scholem in more general terms). Thus, in *Or Yaqar* he exemplified this approach by stating that each soul has its aspect in the Torah that cannot be revealed by another, that enables it to reveal secrets known only to God.[22]

I would like to conclude my discussion of Cordovero's psychology by briefly mentioning its development and dissemination in the greatly popular Mussar treatise *Reshit Hokhma* by his student R. Elijah de Vidas. As Patrick Koch has written extensively on this large and rich work, I shall only note a few crucially important texts: In his "Gate of Love" ("love" having being defined at its beginning as action stemming from the desire of the soul and heart), de Vidas commences with an almost entirely Cordoverian discussion of love of the soul for God as "part" of a chain linked with the divine, as branch of the root, as hewn from a quarry, and as chariot to the king. However, he then moves to a description of love as soul-making, based on the idea of the ascent along rungs of the ladder leading from *nefesh* to *neshama*. He concludes with the proclamation of the superiority of the love of one who has acquired the latter, thus translating the language of the soul into emotional terms.

Although this very gate and its impact have been oft-discussed in discussions of *eros*, its implications for psychological theory, which I have barely touched on here, have been overlooked, surprisingly so as these texts seem to clearly subordinate *eros* to *psyche*. In light of this text, we can well understand the idea (found in the same gate) that the heart can be made a dwelling-place for the divine through the process of the rectification of the *middot*, or emotional traits, that were the main subject of earlier Mussar literature. In my view this can be seen as a general theory of the relationship of Mussar-style psychological work and mystical experience that resonates well with the Sufi theories that were undoubtedly prevalent in sixteenth-century Galilee. In a somewhat overlooked essay, Sara Sviri has differentiated between the Kabbalistic approach, focused on theurgical effects of ritual, and the Sufi (and medieval Judeo-Sufi) stress on the heart and its inner life, and the accompanying cultivation of ethical interpersonal behavior. I have reason to believe that Sviri would be open to the hypothesis that the rise of Safedian psychology and social psychology can be partly ascribed to its location in close proximity to the Sufi world.[23]

More generally speaking, the mostly Cordoverian Kabbalistic Mussar literature was a significant factor in the extension of the Safedian psychological revolution into subsequent centuries. One popular treatise from this school, *Sefer Haredim*, was written by Cordovero's student, R. El'azar Azikri, who wrote the "Yedid Nefesh" poem on the yearnings of the soul quoted at the beginning of an earlier section. As noted above, of course, Cordovero's own highly psychological and much-studied treatise *Tomer Devorah*, played a major role in this process. Interestingly, this book itself contains a psychological theory of mentoring and influence. Elsewhere, I have noted the importance of this literature for understanding one facet of modern Kabbalistic psychology. Here I shall only say that the work of Koch and other emerging scholars offers hope that Kabbalah scholarship will emerge from its (at times increasing) self-enclosure to examine the close relationship of the mystical corpus to at least one other major genre in modern Jewish writing.[24]

Among Safedian works of mystical Mussar one should of course note *Sha'arei Qedusha*, written by none other than Vital, this after his period of tutelage with Luria, when he reverted somewhat to Cordoverian views. Vital's main contribution to the theory of the soul is his model of the various "quarries" (*mahtzavim*): This term reflects the predilection of Luria's school for Mishnaic terminology (reflecting the Safedian use of the Mishna in psychological techniques, as discussed in chapter 7). In a consciously esoteric, and thus difficult, discussion of the "essence of Man" and the need for a very strong soul-body dualism, Vital describes the cosmic structure as anthropomorphic ("all the worlds are human forms"), but in the psychic sense of being composed of the five aspects of the soul. However, he then goes on to differentiate this general structure into the light of the ten Sefirot, or divine potencies, in human form and its exact parallel in the "quarry of souls."

At the beginning of this discussion, Vital explains that he needs to go into these "wonderful secrets" due to the need to explain prophecy, the stated goal of his entire treatise. He concludes this discussion with a slightly cryptic comment on the possibility of prophecy being opened due to the greatest closeness between the light of the quarry of souls and that of the Sefirot. One must note that this discourse was preceded by an exoteric discussion of the structure of the psyche that quotes the "words of the philosophers." In other words, it is just here that we can discern the above-mentioned shift from the premodern Kabbalistic-philosophical synthesis and the modern synthesis of Kabbalah and Mussar. This observation is reinforced by the use of the term "quarry," as we have seen above in the far more Cordoverian Mussar work *Reshit Hokhma*.[25]

R. Yitzhaq Luria

As shown in Gam-Hacohen's dissertation, Lurianic Kabbalah has a persistent place of pride in academic research and teaching in Israel and also abroad, thus requiring an introduction positioning the current discussion within the history of scholarship. Scholem largely treated this vast corpus in terms of myth, guided by orientations described above (mostly restricting his discussion of Lurianic psychology to reincarnation). Yehuda Liebes, while maintaining this paradigm, took matters further towards the psychological in foregrounding the self-perception of Luria and his main student Vital. The latter was indeed greatly concerned with the origins and destiny of his soul, yet this reduction of theory to a personal exchange, for all of its hermeneutical force, is an example of what Hillman has described as "personalizing." A true breakthrough took place around the time of Liebes' writing, when Mordechai Pachter disclosed the centrality of the psychological realm within the biological imagery central to the Lurianic edifice. In textual terms, while Scholem (and his main student Tishby) focused mostly on the structure of contraction (*tzimtzum*), cosmic disaster (*shevira*), and rectification (*tiqqun*), and Liebes moved aside from theory to hagiography, Pachter took on the central part of the Lurianic magnum opus *'Etz Hayyim*, especially focusing on the psychological ramifications of the concepts of "smallness" and "greatness" of the *mohin*, or intelligences.[26]

As its title shows, Lawrence Fine's *Physician of the Soul, Healer of the Cosmos* has given the soul its due place in his overview of Lurianic Kabbalah. However, the two terms making up the title remain rather separate in the book's structure and argumentation. Fine addresses the soul in terms of practice, focusing on Luria's diagnostic and therapeutic techniques (as well as on reincarnation). When addressing the theoretical part of Lurianic Kabbalah, in what I regard as the less innovative part of his book, Fine treats it as "myth," along the path of Scholem and Liebes, focusing on the *tiqqun* portion of the triune structure, without significantly incorporating the findings of Pachter as to the centrality of the psychological in other Lurianic structures. In a discussion largely focused on gender (see chapter 1) Wolfson has made an important contribution towards understanding the ontological significance of the highest level of the soul, *Yehida*, as undifferentiated unity. This conjoining of psychology and ontology can be seen as a correction to the separation in Fine's analysis.[27]

More recently, Avivi has attempted to simplify his earlier model of no less than nine diachronic stages of "order of teaching" (i.e., unfolding rather than actual shifts) and reduced the vast textual complexity that he himself has exposed to two aspects (*behinot*). In this scheme, the soul, associated more with the aspect of influx (as opposed to light) is largely subsumed in the concept of "intelligences" (*mohin*) that plays out differentially in the two schemes. Although this central concept has important ramifications for contemporary psychological theory, it requires a separate study. What is most important in Avivi's vast project is that it represents a strong effort to reestablish the contested textual centrality of the transmission by R. Hayyim Vital, especially in his main compilation of Lurianic teachings, 'Etz Hayyim, which I shall focus on in subsequent discussion.[28]

Moving from research to the texts themselves, one should commence with two texts that place the vast Lurianic system in relation to that of Cordovero. True to my method of respecting hagiographical texts as reflections of the imaginaire of a period, I turn to a statement found in the greatly popular Shivhei ha-Ari (In Praise of the Ari [Luria]), where Luria is quoted as saying that although he appears to dispute the theories of Cordovero, nonetheless, this is what his soul received. In another hagiographical account, Vital's Sefer ha-Hezyonot (Book of Visions), he recounts that Cordovero informed him in a dream that in the "world of souls" it is the teachings of Luria that are followed rather than his own. In other words, Luria utilizes Cordovero's own theory of psychological pluralism in order to establish a route of direct revelation from his soul that he himself described as the superior source of mystical insight, free of the problems that accompany angelic revelation. Paradoxically, it is this revelation that then enables Luria (and also Vital, as claimant for the position of true successor) to move away from Cordovero's above-discussed eclectic pluralism and establish a narrow line of transmission of revelatory truth.[29]

Thus, in an influential treatise by Vital (often printed at the beginning of 'Etz Hayyim), while surveying Luria's dismissal of most forms of earlier Kabbalistic writing, the theme of the need for revelation from souls of the righteous is stressed, Luria's special achievement in this area being repeatedly emphasized. Finally, in a text echoing an increasingly influential view of Cordovero's teachings as belonging to the "world of chaos" (which Luria's tiqqun comes to emend), a seventeenth-century Lurianic Kabbalist, R. Naftali Bakhrakh, cites a legend according to which R. Joseph Karo, the recipient of famous angelic and other supernal revelations, fell asleep whenever he heard Luria expounding on Kabbalah, as his soul belongs to the world of chaos and is thus unsuitable for this teaching. In other words, the new teaching, based on the construction of the compelling image of superior souls in contact with other reliable souls, breaks with and supplants earlier sources of revelation, and certainly mere intellectual attainment.[30]

It is thus highly fitting, at this point, to compare this almost triumphalist sense of confidence, to the more hesitant approach of the former major Safedian school: In the context of a discussion of the light of the soul, Cordovero mentioned the presently inaccessible yet vastly superior form of mystical intention, or *kavvanah*, as drawing the "median soul" (*neshama ha-tikhona*) of the worlds through the "line of measurement" (*qav ha-midda*) as the main source for the power of the Sefirot, or divine powers. This typically multisourced text merges a theory of the world-soul, with an axis-mundi-style Zoharic idea that itself goes back to the Greek *arête*.[31] In Avivi's reading, Cordovero presages the superiority of the Lurianic system. The latter is described as emanating new souls through the very practice described by Cordovero as inaccessible. Although this is obviously a retroactive reading, it is valuable in illustrating the gap between the approach of Luria and that of his illustrious predecessor, whose exilic consciousness could be said to illustrate Scholem's hypothesis as to the effect of the expulsion.[32]

Arriving now at Luria's own theory, one can show that the soul is central to the complex and multilayered Lurianic structure, whose very textual nature precludes even a three-part (and certainly a binary "two-aspect") scheme. Quite early in *'Etz Hayyim*, Vital records a teaching according to which the *Ein Sof*, or infinite, the starting point of the entire map of emanation in this transmission, is the "soul of the soul." The infinite then

emanated one *Adam* that includes all of the worlds, whose aspect of essence [*'atzmut*], that is the aspect of the five levels of the soul [adding *haya and yehida* to *nefesh, ruah,* and *neshama*], is called *adam qadmon* [primordial man] and the aspect of the body in it, is the world of emanation [*atzilut*], and the garments are the worlds of creation, formation and action [*beri'a, yetzira,* and *'assiya*].[33]

This complex text combines a largely Cordoverian distinction between essence and body or container, the above-mentioned four-worlds theory, the expansion of the three or four ("soul of soul") part Zoharic model to a five-fold psychic structure, as well as Luria's famous theory of the macroanthropos. However, what is important for our purposes is that both the infinite and the macroanthropos are described in thoroughly psychic terms. In other words, Lurianic Kabbalah reconfigures the more morphic structures of premodern Kabbalah, assigning them to a container for the soul that is itself the true connection to the infinite, understood now as the soul of souls. In other words, *adam qadmon* is the primordial form of revelation due to its connection, as world-soul, to infinity as soul, reminiscent of Heraclitus' famous saying on the limitless depths of the soul.[34]

This connection is elaborated in an under-researched yet highly influential text that is central for the very structure of 'Etz Hayyim: Luria describes an intermediate aspect between the creator and the created, identified with the notion of Israel being the sons of God. He then goes on to say that "the meaning is that there is a very small spark that is the aspect of divinity, drawn from the last level of the creator, and this spark enclothes itself through the power of one created spark that is a very very subtle soul," that is the highest *yehida* level of the soul. Again, it is the soul that affords the possibility of the subtle connection between the divine and the created worlds. These formulations should be seen as a far subtler reworking of the Cordoverian view of the divinity of the soul, as stated quite explicitly in the practice-centered *Sha'ar Ruah ha-Qodesh*.[35]

Vital returns to the structure of the soul at the very end of 'Etz Hayyim. After a fascinating discussion of the practical and theoretical intellect in relation to imagination and dreams, he concludes with a brief treatise on the "principle of the essence of the soul" (returning to the concept of essence from our first theoretical text). The body is made up of the four physical elements, and from these also extend the four souls—synthetic, vegetative, animal, and discursive—familiar from the psychological terminology of philosophy. However, all of these are merely the "powers of the body," and thus are not the true soul. Above this we have the "servants," or the *nefesh*, *ruah*, and *neshama* of the three lower worlds (creation, formation, and action), and only then do we reach, again, the aspect of the sonship of God, also divided into three aspects. Here we curiously have no mention of the two highest aspects of the quintuple division.

However, Vital then summarizes the summary, in a "short way," in which we have the body, its power, and then *nefesh*, *ruah*, *neshama*, and *haya*, corresponding to the four worlds. Characteristically, the earlier division is here subverted, as in lieu of three aspects corresponding to the three lower worlds and then three belonging entirely to the fourth, we now have four aspects of the soul corresponding to four worlds. It is fascinating that he concludes the entire book by opposing these four to the four demonic husks, which correspond to Rome (which the Italian-born Vital dreamt of), "Salamanca of Spain," site of the expulsion, Egypt, where Luria lived prior to his move to Safed, and Damascus, where Vital lived after Safed. The most central work of the Lurianic corpus ends with what one should term imaginal geography.[36]

At the same time, the focus on the demonic realm can be said to reinforce Tishby's stress on the problem of evil in Lurianic Kabbalah. The same could be said for a historiosophical working of this mythic geography in the practice-oriented *Pri 'Etz Hayyim*, which relates the rabbinic theme of the "four exiles" to the "four husks" of the demonic realm:

[. . .] just like the main holiness (*'iqar ha-qedusha*) is the four rivers of Eden, which are the four letters of the Tetragammaton, so they are paralleled by four other rivers that emerge from the husk, and these include everything. And when the souls were exiled, the main part of the sparks of the souls went there to these four rivers emerging from the husk, and thus all of Israel had to be exiled in one of these four, because according to their aspect (*behina*) each and every person according to the root of his soul can sift and extract from there.[37]

This text also confirms Scholem's intuition that the theurgical project of sifting the divine spark, closely related to soul sparks, from their fallen location in the husks is a manifestation of exilic consciousness, even if one does not reify it by stressing the event of the expulsion. Thus, earlier scholarly interpretations also have their due place within the infinitely intricate Lurianic universe, surely one of the greatest creations of mystical thought. In this pluralistic perspective, my reading, stressing the centrality of the soul, is but another offering, important mostly as part of a wider history.

This being said, I turn to yet another cardinal text from *'Etz Hayyim*, in which Luria states that the souls of the righteous are the internal aspect (*penimiyut)* of the worlds. Here we have a focus on an elite, whose nature I have already discussed elsewhere. As we have seen, there are very similar formulations in the works of Cordovero, mitigating against scholarly accounts that overly differentiate between the two masters. Through this focusing of the general theory, the soul can be readily integrated in theurgical practice.[38]

One must compare this text to the strong statement in another practice manual, *Sha'ar ha-Kavvanot*, according to which the fallen kingdom can be uplifted only by *tzaddiqim* with pure and holy souls who have the power to ascend to the correct psycho-cosmic location (*imma* or the aspect of the mother). Vital's exilic conclusion, perhaps reflecting the missed messianic moment of Luria's death, is that the exile is protracted, causing most of the troubles and evil in the world, due to the absence of one who could hasten the redemption through such an ascent. However, there is a "small rectification" through whole-hearted martyrological, self-sacrificial intention. The theoretical root for this practice-centered discussion is found in the fascinating discourse in *'Etz Hayyim* on the salvation of the world from near-destruction by the famous ten martyrs of the Roman period. It is fascinating that a contemporary American Kabbalist renders this level as accessible to all and also relates it to the mass martyrdom of the Holocaust.[39]

I shall conclude my discussion of Luria with one more practice-focused, less theoretically sophisticated text, found in a seventeenth-century canonical editing of Lurianic teachings of the mystical intention of prayer: 'Olat Tamid. Following a dualistic distinction between matter, derived from the husks, and soul, which is "part of divinity from above," the main theme is introduced by saying that sin creates "blemish, stain, and rust" in the soul, which is also an illness. In this state it cannot see and attain the "true perfection" that is the secrets of the Torah, which is the way to restore the soul as part to the whole. When the soul is impure in this manner, "it cannot see, and the pure things [the supernal worlds] do not shine in her just as they do not shine in the copper mirror when it is full of stains and rust." This text clearly relates the attainment of Kabbalistic insight to the purity and perfection of the soul. However, what is significant here is the image of the mirror, extremely common in Sufi writing (as well as in the writing of R. David ben Yehuda he-Hasid, a possible fourteenth-century source of Luria's who was clearly influenced by Sufism).

What is even more significant is the immediate turn from within the mirror imagery to a medical model:

[. . .] when she is rusty and stained then all bitter is sweet, like the ill person rejects the good things and likes those that worsen the disease, and the physician in order to restore him to health gives him bitter herbs . . . thus the ill soul in order to remove the illness must accept the bitterness of the medicine of repentance in mortifications.

Here, the complex Lurianic system of mortifications as rectifications of the soul is summarized as the healing of the soul. It is only this health that enables attaining the secret wisdom concealed from the time of R. Simeon bar Yohai, the mythical author of the *Zohar*, until the last, messianic generation "which is this time, when through our teacher the holy divine R. Yitzhaq Luria z"l [of blessed memory] who by means of the spirit of prophecy that was in him began to enlighten our eyes in the light of this divine wisdom." Luria is described here in visionary, prophetic, and messianic terms. The text then immediately relates this role once more to the rectification of the soul, stating that he

would not reveal any secret of the secrets of this holy wisdom to one in whose holy spirit that he had a blemish in his soul until he gave him a rectification to emend what he distorted. And just as the expert physician prescribes the drug this is needed to heal each illness, so he, peace be on him, would recognize the sin and tell him the place where he blemished and give him the rectification (*tiqqun*) needed for that sin in order to launder his soul so that he can receive the supernal light.[40]

In other words, prophecy was not only the source of Luria's teachings, but also the inspiration for the methods of rectifying the souls who are to receive it. One can regard this text as a blend of two discourses: One is that of prophetic authority, presaging Sabbatean, Luzzattoian, Hasidic, and Kookian claims to this authority. In the Lurianic context, we can better understand the move described above from the less confident, pluralistic, and eclectic discourse of Cordovero (despite his own experiences of inspiration, recorded in his *Sefer Gerushin*), to the more absolute claims of Luria. Surprisingly, this discourse merges with another discourse of certainty that also developed through erasing earlier forms of knowledge—that of medicine. It is in such texts that I find vindication for my assertion that modern Kabbalah truly begins in Safed. Paradoxically, it is this very sense of a self-enclosed and absolute discourse that generated an entire universe of editing, transmission, and interpretation, inter alia aiming at resolving the many lacunae and ambiguities created by the vast system delivered in Luria's extremely short sojourn in Safed.

Seventeenth-Century Syntheses

As noted above, Safedian Kabbalah continued to unfold in different locales in the seventeenth century, with the very proliferation of Lurianic Kabbalah being described in this period (by R. Moshe of Prague) as reflecting the pre-Messianic shining of souls from the world of rectification.[41] One of these was Italy, where one should especially note the complex, voluminous, influential yet rather under-researched corpus of R. Menahem 'Azaria da Fano that is currently enjoying a vogue, including extensive reprinting. As already discussed in scholarship, R. Menahem 'Azaria, who began operating in the late sixteenth century, maintained a complex relationship to the canons of Cordovero and Luria, and his writing can be best described as a synthesis of these two worlds.[42] However, here I wish to emphasize his independent contribution that in my view may reflect the influence of Christian thought, typical of Italian Jewish writing.

R. Menahem 'Azaria composed a précis (entitled *Pelah ha-Rimon*) of the first twenty-four gates of Cordovero's *Pardes Rimonim*, and adds in his introduction that of the last eight gates he only summarized that of the soul. It is likely, as noted by Avivi, that he refers to *Ma'amar ha-Nefesh*, the treatise of the soul, which not only summarizes but greatly embellishes Cordovero's discussion. R. Menahem 'Azaria clearly subordinates the Safedian theories to the Nahmanidean model, as the divine soul, described by him as the "first icon," and as including *nara"n ha"y* [i.e., the five levels of the Lurianic system] from the world of emanation—is described as being blown from "the essence of the blower." Under this highest soul, we have the second icon, the divine *nefesh, ruah*, and *neshama* from the lower worlds of creation, formation, and action. Finally, we have the third icon—two shadows (*tzelalim*), closely related to the *tzelem*, which guard and rule the last aspect of the soul, the vital soul, or lowly fourth icon, which enables sin (and punishment), with some assistance from the *tzelem*.[43]

Here, the Nahmanidean interpretation of Genesis controls both Cordovero's theory of the divinity of the soul and Luria's five-fold division, as mapped onto the four-world theory as well as the *tzelem* theory. However, this is not merely an elaborate synthesis, expressing the level of complexity of Kabbalah at this historical juncture. Rather, the author goes on to develop an elaborate epistemological theory: "from it [the divine soul] come to Man all true and divine intellections . . . we ascribe all the sayings of Man to the higher soul . . . which controls the second, third, and fourth icons, and is enclothed in them, at times with shining of countenance, at times with hiding of countenance." He describes this theory as a "great key for the enlightened to contemplate the words of the sages."[44] Despite its remarkable complexity, one can still observe the dominance of those aspects of the soul that emanate from the essential aspects of divinity. Although the term "icon of the king" is found in the rabbinic theory of the *tzelem*, one cannot but suspect Christian influences behind its extensive use here.

The gradual takeover of the model of the divine soul that will be even more apparent in our discussion of later periods in chapter 3 can also be seen in writings from the center in Prague flourishing in this century, while maintaining a complex relationship with Italy throughout the early modern period. Sack has already discussed at length the influential elaboration of Cordovero's system in the popular *Shef'a Tal* by R. Shabbetai Sheftel Horowitz. Generally speaking, one can say that this writer somewhat narrowed down the options found in the writings of his predecessor in order to stress the divinity of the soul, with which he opens his large work. Another striking example is that of the rich psychological discourse in a hugely influential and largely Cordoverian work, *Shnei Luhot ha-Brit,* by R. Shabbetai's father, R. Isaiah Horowitz, of seventeenth-century Prague, blending Kabbalah, Mussar, and other genres. Finally, one should note the important recent findings of Avivi as to the early diffusion of Lurianic Kabbalah in Central Europe, independent of R. Menahem 'Azaria's mediation and related to Horowitz's transmission of Safedian material in the wake of his travel to the Middle East. These findings, crucial for the history of early modern Kabbalah in Europe, have yet to be fully digested in academic writing.[45]

However, the most important discussion of the soul in this century is found in a work dedicated to it, *Nishmat Adam* by R. Aharon Shmu'el of Kremnitz (Ukraine), reflecting the beginning of the move of the main center of Jewish learning to Eastern Europe. Although rhetorically R. Aharon Shmu'el joins the tide in stressing the Nahmanidean model of the divine soul, if one carefully follows his argumentation it is apparent that he restricts it to the righteous, or *hasidim.* Concomitantly, he stresses the need for ordinary mortals to adhere to such exalted figures. As I shall partly show in chapter 3, this work substantially influenced the Hasidic world, whose different schools stressed, to different degrees, the divinity of the soul and the inherent superiority of the righteous and their veneration.[46]

In concluding this brief discussion of what was ultimately a median period, one must note that the divinity of the soul was still frontally contested, albeit rarely so, as in the seventeenth century in the important treatise on the soul, *Nishmat Hayyim,* by R. Menashe ben Israel (Dias Soeiro), of Amsterdam and London, one of the earlier examples of Jews who wielded considerable political influence in early modernity. Although he prominently and approvingly cites the Nahmanidean view on the divinity of the soul, he disputed R. Shabbetai Sheftel Horowitz's interpretation of Cordovero as holding that the soul is literally part of the divine essence. It is interesting that he also attributes this view to unnamed gentile philosophers.[47]

The Eighteenth-Century Breakthrough of R. Shalom Shar'abi

As briefly claimed in chapter 1, the next great wave of Kabbalistic writing took place in the eighteenth century, when it also guided the formation of a true social movement, Hasidism, as well as the strong reaction to this development. In this movement, as well as in the schools of R. Moshe Hayyim Luzzatto (1707–46) and, influenced strongly by Luzzatto, R. Elijah Kremer of Vilna (1720–97), one may find a conscious

move towards independence from the Lurianic paradigm.[48] Therefore, I shall wait with all these for chapters 3 and 4, and focus here on
R. Shalom Shar'abi (1720–77), originally of Yemen, a Kabbalist who saw
himself as a reincarnation of Luria, itself a reflection of a strong self-
consciousness of continuity. His school developed in a strikingly continuous manner in the same country as Safed (though in Jerusalem), as
well as other Middle Eastern locations, to this day.[49]

As Frederic William Maitland put it in his inaugural lecture on the
history of English law as Downing Professor at Cambridge in 1911:
"There are vast provinces that lie unclaimed, not outlying provinces
but the very heart of the country."[50] Certainly, the Shar'abian school
is one of these provinces. Despite Meir's important historical work and
an earlier discussion by Pinchas Giller (heavily based on the writings of R.
Ya'aqov Moshe Hillel, the main propagator and ideologue of this Kabbalah today, thus demonstrating the growing influence of Kabbalists on
scholars), its texts are still terra incognita, having never been taught as
such in universities (to the best of my knowledge). Indeed, the current
sad state of textual training makes it unlikely that texts studied by at
least hundreds of Kabbalists (as evidenced by demand in bookshops in
Israel and New York, as well as internal circulation deliberately aimed at
avoiding academic attention) will be studied in academia in the foresee-
able future. In this context one should note the extremely detailed and
learned discussion of the system of Shar'abi in the recent *Yira'ukha 'im-
Shamesh* and *Ke-Tze'et ha-Shemesh* (and the more concise *Tevu'ot Shemesh*) by R. Shmu'el Arenfeld, a student of R. Yitzhaq Me'ir Morgenstern
(who shall be discussed below and in chapter 5).[51]

In a purist manner, Shar'abian Kabbalah zealously and exclusively
restricts itself to the writings of Luria, almost entirely according to the
version of Vital. I believe that this marked difference from European
schools, as well as the disinclination to translate Lurianic terms into psychological or other conceptual terminologies, reflects the uniqueness of
Ottoman, versus European, Kabbalah. It chose to abstain from the conceptualization that has greatly hampered academics in appreciating the
complexity and subtlety of this vast corpus. Similarly, its rhetoric of continuing and interpreting Luria has occluded its profound, at times revolutionary, innovations, which are duly recognized and celebrated by its
contemporary heirs. In other words, the European eighteenth-century
movements should be described as extrinsic reorganizations of Lurianic
Kabbalah, and the Ottoman movement as an intrinsic reorganization.

In his magnum opus, *Nahar Shalom*, Shar'abi describes the drawing
and enclothement of the five aspects of the soul into the intelligences

(*mohin*) throughout the *kavvanah*, or mystical intention of ritual, as completely vital and the only way to draw down the infinite light: "Without these all of the *kavvanot* are as body without soul." Shortly after this, he describes an exposition closely related to the soul as "almost including all of this wisdom." This crucial methodic statement refers to an elaborate description of the manner in which each configuration (*partzuf*, or countenance, being the Lurianic term) "clarifies" (*mevarer*) aspects of its own realm and raises them to the configuration above it, in order to then receive them anew in form of intelligences and the five aspects of the soul. However, this process cannot occur until these intelligences are "enclothed" or interwoven with all of the intelligences of all of the higher aspects, reaching all the way up to the median spark described above in our exposition of Luria. As we have seen, Luria also describes this spark in terms of enclothing and in terms of the subtle soul.

Thus far, then, we have a very strong reading of a central Lurianic text, leading to the rather radical conclusion that due to the hologramic nature of the divine worlds, every practice radiates up to the infinite in order to draw new psychic intelligence all the way down, especially to the righteous. However, the truly radical move is found later in this text, where Shar'abi describes the sonship of the median aspect as profoundly relative. As he goes on to say, when Luria describes the configuration of *ze'ir anpin* (the Zoharic "restricted face") as a son relative to the aspects above it, or the people of Israel as sons of *ze'ir anpin* and its accompanying feminine aspect, this is all relative. This is the formula underlying the effect of prayer and other rituals: as the practicing communities are the sons of the aspect above them, through the hologramic principle, they can affect any aspect that enjoys the status of sonship through the principle of relativity.[52]

Another way of understanding this highly complex structure is to think in three-dimensional terms: According to Shar'abi, the divine world should be understood not only in a hierarchical, vertical manner, but also through the image of depth. Thus, one can cut through the vertical structure, and each aspect can influence the one occupying the same three-dimensional position. I wish to stress that I am only employing the terminology of the natural sciences as a metaphor here, and not joining the ranks of academics attempting to draw parallels between Kabbalah and physics.

At this point one may wonder whether this incredibly difficult system, which I have greatly simplified here, is intended to have significance for any but the cream of Kabbalists. There is one Shar'abian text that seems designated for a wider audience and has indeed been perceived as such.

This contains words of Mussar preceding the ritual of blowing the Shofar on the New Year. Within a popular discourse in the spirit of Sephardic Mussar (which has not been sufficiently researched), Shar'abi inserts a semitechnical interpretation of the ritual: applying the principles that we have just seen, through awakening repentance in the heart, equivalent to *ze'ir anpin*, related to sonship, the sound of the Shofar reaches the supernal ear, equivalent to the next (and higher) configuration of *imma* (the mother, mentioned earlier in this chapter). As a result, the limbs of the five soul aspects that were dried out and weakened and sleeping are reawakened. Shar'abi describes this reawakening as the desire of repentance (also equivalent to *imma* in the Kabbalistic scheme) drawing the vitality of the soul to its limbs, also drawing down new intelligences. Looking forward to our discussion in chapter 7, one should stress the strong nomian component in this text (as well as Shar'abian Kabbalah in general).[53]

This is not the place to go into the extensive responses to and interpretation of this doctrine in the Sephardic world that have enjoyed only the attention of Kabbalistic authors. One of the most prolific of these is R. Yitzhaq Me'ir Morgenstern, who devoted extensive discussions to the even more complex writings of R. Hayyim de la Rossa (d. 1786), Shar'abi's main disciple (and also named his own Yeshiva after the latter's magnum opus *Torat Hakham*). As Morgenstern has shown, de la Rossa cites numerous esoteric, perhaps even nonverbal teachings imparted by Shar'abi, thus in effect claiming to uncover an entire new layer.

Among these innovations, we should here focus on his use of his teacher's doctrine of relativity in order to resolve the following dilemma within the Lurianic corpus, based on the assumption (presented in a briefer discussion later in the book) that Luria's discussions of the world of Emanation match Vital's term "the quarry of the Sefirot" and nonduality, while his discussions of the world of Creation match the dualistic realm of the "quarry of Souls": at times it appears that the world of Emanation, being part of the "quarry" of the divine Sefirot, does not require any theurgical restoration, this need being reserved only for the "quarry" of souls, while other texts seem to indicate that it does. The answer that de la Rossa extricates is that while the "general" aspect of Emanation is beyond the need for repair, yet the "relative" aspect of Emanation within the "general" aspect of the three lower worlds (i.e., not the absolute aspect but as it manifests relatively within the nondivine worlds) is part of the theurgical project. Again, the later and even more dense text is instructive: Change, as part of duality, exists "from our side," i.e., from the nondivine perspective, even if it is our perspective of the divine.[54]

I believe that even this incredibly limited selection illustrates not just the immensity of the challenge facing academics wishing to enter this vast world, but also the profound discontinuity between the Lurianic reception and pre-Lurianic and certainly premodern Kabbalah, as a result of Luria's corpus (and subsequently Shar'abi's) being transformed, through the sheer weight of interpretation, into the main object of study and reflection in the world of Kabbalistic Yeshivas.

Conclusion

The narrative offered in this chapter described the initial modernization of Kabbalistic psychology in terms of successive waves, divergent schools, cumulative recensions, and formation of centers. One should oppose such an account to the Scholemian and ultimately Zionist attempt to create a unified national history, which also, one might add, blurred the difference between medieval and modern Kabbalah.[55]

We have seen that despite the hegemony of the model of the divine soul that can be partly attributed to the nationalization of Kabbalistic discourse (as described in chapter 4), the elective affinity of the model of soul-making with modern sensibilities as well as its textual base in canonical texts, ensured its preservation. Therefore, to the geographical-historical diversification, one should add a complex internal interplay, that we shall now follow, in ever-proliferating forms, in the next three chapters, as the Safedian models and ideas were repeatedly reworked, often in creative and unexpected manners.

THREE
___

Psychological Theories

The heart falls . . . the heart shouts . . . the heart softens . . . The heart breaks . . .
the heart is torn . . . the heart melts.   *MIDRASH QOHELET RABBA*

Psychological and National Theories in Later Modernity

Although seemingly all of the theories discussed in the book are psychological, the especial proclivity of the Hasidic world to psychological discourse has been repeatedly noted in existing research. However, such discussions usually describe this shift in terms of a new interpretation of Kabbalistic concepts. This is undoubtedly correct, and here I maintain an earlier thesis of mine, namely that psychology and national historiosophy (to be addressed in chapter 4) can be seen as two of the major forms of reception of Safedian Kabbalah. However, Hasidism should be seen not merely as a continuation of premodern and early modern approaches, but rather as situated in a decisive moment in the development of modern Judaism, reaching from the later eighteenth century to the present. As such, it must be understood as occasioning responses by and later responding to parallel movements in the Jewish world. One is the *Haskalah* (Jewish Enlightenment), whose general disdain for mysticism renders it an unsuitable candidate for the present discussion. The other, somewhat later, movement was Mussar, to be discussed towards the end of the chapter.[1]

Generally speaking, both psychological and national interpretations accelerated the turn to the human realm that was already apparent in Safed, especially its Mussar literature. Though this is not our topic, one can refute claims as to an essentialist continuity with premodern Kabbalah by examining progressive increases in discussions of the soul in the present lifetime, this-worldly forms of salvation, and social and historical issues in tandem with the gradual decline of metaphysical discourses (such as the Deed of Creation and the Deed of the Chariot), detailed angelology, apocalyptic imagery and even extensive discussions of reincarnation. By the nineteenth century, the spirit of modern Kabbalah was best captured by the complex treatise *Tal Orot*, a synthesis of Shar'abian Kabbalah and Hasidism. The author of this greatly under-studied work, R. Ya'aqov Me'ir Spielmann, writes that one can understand the supernal world only by first understanding the soul.[2]

Before commencing our discussion of Hasidism, a general sociological distinction between this movement and the slightly later one of Mussar is in order: The former developed from a circle into a mass movement, and as such developed a strong stress on the emotional realm. As we shall see, even more elitist groups, such as the Hasidic dynasties of Habad or Komarno, maintained this characteristic inclination. In contradistinction, the Mussar movement grew out of the rather ascetic circle of R. Elijah Kremer of Vilna and then moved into the Yeshiva world (which it then transformed into an entire society in the second part of the twentieth century). Thus, it focused on what we might term motivational psychology. Its main goal can be described as inspiring its adherents to maintain a very rigorous level of Halakhic observance as well as an intense level of Torah study. As contemporary psychology moves beyond the stress on emotion typical of psychodynamic theory and practice towards a wider understanding of the manifold forms of inner life, one should expect a growing interest in Mussar to balance the disproportionate focus, both scholarly and popular, on certain schools of Hasidism. As we shall see in chapter 5, there are some indications that this process is already underway.[3]

The Schools of Hasidic Psychology

As Pedaya has recently noted, one cannot maintain an overall structure of Hasidism in face of the startling diversification of schools that took place already in the second and third generations. One may go so far as to say that virtually every Hasidic school developed its own psychology, as is also the case for the various schools of Lithuanian Mussar after its second and third generations, though in both instances there is obviously a loose "family resemblance." As the early days of Hasidism, when the movement was somewhat more cohesive, have already been discussed in a disproportionate manner in existing scholarship, I shall move directly to the third generation. However, one should note in passing that according to accounts of the initiations of students by the Besht (R. Israel Ba'al Shem Tov, founder of Hasidism) he revealed aspects of the Torah pertaining to their soul, as did his main disciple, R. Dov Baer Friedman, the Maggid of Mezeritch, to wider audiences. Similarly, while engaging with previous studies when addressing oft-researched later schools, such as Habad and Izbiche-Radzin, I shall also venture beyond the shores of academic exploration and consider lesser-known worlds, especially (continuing earlier work of mine) Komarno.[4]

This choice is part of my ongoing move towards regarding both Izbiche-Radzin and Komarno, together with the writings of the school of Ger (which occupy a median position in terms of academic attention), as part of one encompassing framework—the schools of Lublin, in which mysticism and shamanism played a yet under-recognized role. From this panoramic, yet geographically and historically focused perspective, claims as to the move of the Psischa school (second through fourth generations of Lublin) away from Kabbalah, magic, and messianism should be questioned, especially in absence of significant authentic written material from key figures such as R. Menahem Mendel Morgenstern of Kotzk (an important heir of R. Simcha Bunim Bonhart of Psischa).[5]

One ever-studied school that I shall address briefly and elsewhere in the book (chapters 5 and 7) is that of Bratzlav, although, its founder, R. Nahman, was certainly a specialist in the yearnings of the soul. In my view, granting an excessively central place to a small, marginalized group reflects more on romantic (Martin Buber), existentialistic (Joseph Weiss), psychoanalytic (Arthur Green), and currently New Age projections than on the proper historic context of the nineteenth century. This being said, there is certainly room for a multigenerational study of Bratzlav psychology, drawing on an extensive and well-catalogued corpus as well as important studies of psychological issues (such as the textually well-grounded studies of Zvi Mark, which have certainly contributed towards understanding Hasidic psychology in general).

Before turning to the schools that I have selected, I wish to revisit a general question that could qualify in a sense as being trans-Hasidic, that of redemption: personal or at most communal—i.e., limited to the followers of a specific Hasidic leader ("rebbe" or *tzaddiq*) versus historical, as explored at greatest length by Idel (who critiqued earlier scholarship in doing so). The latter was entirely correct in foregrounding this theme, as it reflects a move towards the individual or Hasidic subsect, rather than the national, and should be strongly contrasted to the national forms of messianism to be discussed in chapter 4, as well as to the near absence of this theme in Lithuanian Mussar. In my view, personal redemption is first and foremost that of the soul, and should thus be seen as a form of psychologization. Statements on this theme are especially prevalent in the nineteenth-century schools of Chernobyl, yet it can be located repeatedly in other streams in the "long nineteenth century" (as we shall now see for Habad).[6]

The Psychological Universe of Habad

Zwei Seelen wohnen, ach! in meiner Brust.
(Two souls alas! are dwelling in my breast)
JOHANN WOLFGANG VON GOETHE, *FAUST*

The motto above reflects a concern with the agonic duality of the soul that can be placed in the turn from the later eighteenth to the nineteenth century. In my view it is no coincidence that Goethe's near-contemporary, R. Shneur Zalman of Lyady (Rashaz), placed this concern in the heart of what is probably the most extensive form of Jewish discourse on the soul—the Habad Hasidism that he founded. Although one can trace his intra-Jewish sources to Safed and Vital (as we shall see soon), one cannot overlook the proximate and general European context, as similar ideas are easily found in non-Jewish texts from the late seventeenth century.[7]

The foundational text for this theme and generally for the vast world of Habad writing is Rashaz's vastly printed and cited work, described by this school as the Bible of Hasidism: *Sefer ha-Tanya*. Naturally, it has been discussed at great length in existing writing on Habad psychology that is large in quantity but of very mixed quality and mostly in Hebrew. In particular, this scholarly enterprise has consciously separated the various generations of the school, focusing almost entirely on the first two and last two of its seven generations. Fortunately, this methodological fallacy has recently been corrected in both theory and in application by Wolfson and Dov Schwartz.[8]

Although I shall revisit well-known texts, such as the *Tanya*, from the theoretical perspective developed here, my main contribution in this section shall be threefold. Firstly, I shall point at a possible textual source for the psychological theory of the *Tanya*. Secondly, I shall present a detailed analysis of *'Avodat ha-Levi*, a commentary on the Torah by R. Aharon ha-Levi Horowitz of Starosselje, an important disciple of Rashaz, who actually contested the succession in rivalry with the latter's son, R. Dov Baer Shneuri. Although Rachel Elior has discussed other works by this master in an important early study, she did not address this hermeneutical work to any significant extent. Finally, in chapter 7, I shall introduce the elaborate psychological theory developed by the fifth rebbe, R. Shalom Dov Baer Schneerson (Rashab), who was probably influenced by Horowitz, despite the general marginalization of the latter in the mainstream of Habad discourse. Although the voluminous and sophisticated texts of Rashab are the core of the contemporary Habad curriculum (together with those of the last rebbe, R. Menahem Mendel Schneerson), they have not been extensively analyzed to date.[9]

It is wise to commence any discussion of heart and soul in Habad theory with a close reading of the texts containing the model of the two souls, one of them divine, found in the opening chapters of the opening section of Tanya, *Likutei Amarim: Sefer shel-Beynonim* (Collection of Sayings: the Book of the Median). Already in the first chapter, Rashaz presents the goal of this part of his classic: Understanding the essence of the *beynoni*, the median person, who although he has no sins, yet is in an existential state of constant agon, unlike the *tzaddiq*, or righteous, whose heart is "hollow" of the Evil Impulse (*yetzer ha-ra'*). In this opening move, Rashaz differentiates himself from much of Hasidic discourse, and especially the Polish school developed by R. Elimelekh Weisblum of Lyzansk, which focuses on the qualities of the *tzaddiq*. The foundation of the theory of the *beynoni* is the profound duality of the soul, which the author immediately presents, in this and the following chapter, as the "interpretation of the matter" of the *beynoni*.[10]

In this psycho-physical model, explicitly based on Vital's *Sha'arei Qedusha*, each and every Jew possesses two souls. One, later referred to as the animal soul, emanates from the three husks (*qelipot*), of the Other Side (*sitra ahra*), or demonic realm, and "enclothes" itself (using Lurianic parlance), in blood, physical vitality, and the four humors of classical physio-psychology.[11] As even positive *middot* stem from the humors, it follows that positive traits (such as mercy and kindness), to the extent that they are natural, must have their source in this inferior soul. The reason for this paradoxical mixture of good and evil is that the natural soul of Jews, although it also emanates from the demonic realm, belongs to the singular and borderline husk of *noga* (brightness), which contains an admixture of good and evil, paralleling the mythical archetype of the Tree of Good and Evil.

Here, Rashaz introduces a sharp national divide, somewhat setting Habad apart from earlier Hasidic writing. The souls of the non-Jews, which are not divine, are entirely derived from those husks that contain no good at all, so that even their seemingly good deeds are based on self-seeking motives. However, unlike the texts to be discussed in chapter 4, and unlike the reading espoused by a contemporary Habad Kabbalist, R. Yitzchak Ginsburgh (as discussed in chapter 5), the thrust of the *Tanya* is still not national but psychological. I shall soon contend that this is not an apologetic reading of mine, but rather that of the successive generations of Habad, and especially that of Horowitz.[12]

Returning to the model itself, the second soul, which Rashaz leaves to the second chapter (in his meticulous construction of the book), is the divine Jewish soul, which as in the Nahmanidean theory emanates from the interior dimensions of the divine, and for Habad specifically from divine thought. Using a trope that is central for the thought of his own teacher, R. Dov Baer Friedman, the author describes the relationship between the soul and its divine origin in terms of the extension of the son from the brain of the father. Furthermore, relatively speaking, the souls of the rebbes (here he inserts a literal reading of the acronym *rosh bnei yisra'el*, "Head of the Sons of Israel") parallel the head, or brain, of the Jewish souls. Thus, the common Jews may connect the various aspects of their soul to that of the *tzaddiqim* and rebbes of their generation, and through this mediation they may obtain a "wonderful and powerful union" with the divine thought. Although this is again not his main concern, Rashaz provides a cosmic-psychic ground for the famous *tzaddiq*-centered social stratification of the Hasidic movement at large, thus significantly mitigating his stress on the *beynoni*.[13]

At this point, one should pause in order to reconnect this model to the main theme of this part of *Tanya*: The existential struggle of the *beynoni* derives from the foundational structure of the Jewish psyche, which is ruled by profound duality of identity. The confrontation between good and evil is between two entire souls, rather than two faculties or inclinations, as earlier theories, rabbinic and philosophical, would have it. As a result, as the author puts it in an epistle printed in the fourth section of the book (*Iggeret ha-Qodesh*, "The Holy Epistle"), there can be no peace in the world until the messianic period, when the powerful revelation of divine luminosity will annul the very reality of evil, restoring the positive aspects of the soul to their divine source, once the latter is openly revealed.[14]

This eschatological aspect of the *Tanya* was developed intensively by the last two rebbes of Habad, R. Yoseph Yitzhaq and R. Menahem Mendel Schneerson; however, in this specific elaboration, the explicit focus is not on "the generality of the world," or the national and cosmic levels, but rather on the individual "small world" (*'olam qatan*), in which the individual may momentarily replicate the messianic process by means of prayer, meditation, or acts of charity. The latter are deemed especially important by Rashaz (here and elsewhere), as they transcend the natural but semidemonic goodness of the Jewish "animal soul," by overcoming the natural limits to one's generosity or capacity for effortful work. By doing so, one may awaken the powerful illumination that brings with it peace, both above and below. While in prayer, as oft-noted in Habad texts on this topic, the forces of evil may immediately and spontaneously reassert themselves once the service is concluded (due to their strong hold on the world at large), charity produces a more lasting effect, producing a calm state that may be broken only by deliberate negative acts on the part of the individual.

My focus here, in attempting to summarize Rashaz's complex theory in the bare-bones fashion necessary for the flow of this chapter, is not on the agonistic theory of psychic life, and its concomitant theory of labor (a theme that shall be addressed further in chapter 4). Rather, I wish to point out the central role of the heart in his elaborate scheme, which has been somewhat understated in the great majority of studies. Generally speaking, Habad writing may be compared to a fugue, constantly repeating while unfolding.[15] In our case, the dual model is elaborated somewhat later in the first part of *Tanya*, where the place of the residing of the animal soul is identified as the space of the left chamber of the heart, which is full of blood, "and therefore all of the desires and glorification and anger and suchlike are in the heart and from the heart they expand throughout the body and also ascend to the brain in the head to think."[16]

On the natural level, the intellect is subordinated to the passions engendered by physical vitality. In contradistinction, the place of residing of the divine soul is in the "intelligences" (*mohin*) in the head, as well as in the right chamber of the heart, which is empty of blood. On this divine level, the heart is clearly subordinated to the brain, as when the flame of love for God is awakened by contemplation, which takes place in the brain. Indeed, as Rashaz writes at length towards the end of this section of *Tanya*, the main revelation of the power and vitality of the soul within the body is in the brain in the head, or in the power of thought of the three upper Sefirot, *Hokhma, Binah,* and *Da'at* (Habad, this also being the acronym of the movement founded by Rashaz).[17]

In other words, the profound duality of the soul is reflected in the dichotomy between the heart and the brain, as well as in a subsidiary division within the heart itself. Rashaz immediately translates this opposition into agonic terms: "The body is called a small city and just as two kings fight over one city that each wishes to conquer and rule . . . thus the two souls . . . fight over the body."[18] What we have here is a form of spiritual warfare, a theme common in early modern Christian writing. This parallel reinforces Shaul Magid's broader thesis as to the echoes of Christian thought in Hasidic writing. This then is the intrapsychic meaning of the eschatological theme of the ultimate transformation of good into evil. In the following chapters, the author returns to the subsidiary theme of the *tzaddiq* and the *beynoni*. The former has either completely subdued or even transformed the evil of the left chamber of the heart, the level of eradication of the natural forces determining the thousands of possible levels of sainthood.

The *beynoni*, on the other hand, only manages to establish the rule of the divine soul over the small city in specific times, after which evil reawakens, just as we just saw. Thus, the *beynoni* is in a permanent stalemate, as it were, between the two souls, neither of which gains complete ascendancy. In these terms, the ongoing task of the *beynoni* is to use the willpower of the brain to overcome the passion of the heart. In an alternative formulation, as soon as an evil impulse ascends from the heart to the brain, it is repelled by the power of cognitive control. However, later on Rashaz softens the sense of stalemate by stressing that God decides the issue by shining his light on the divine soul, giving it a limited advantage.[19]

Rashaz concludes this part of his theoretical presentation by saying that the *beynoni* is everyman, "the measure of all men." Everyone is capable of the cognitive feat of determining that the content of his thought be contrary to the desire of the heart, thus awakening the love for God hidden in every Jewish heart. In practical terms, the "great rule" of worship of God for the *beynoni* is to control and rule the natural impulse of the heart. Perhaps the most central dictum of Habad practice, the rule of the brain over the heart, is described as an innate ability, related to the natural urge of the Jewish soul to adhere to God.

However, sin creates a spiritual death or exile, which occludes the vitality of divine soul, leading to the control of the brain by the (demonic) heart. In other words the national theme of exile is rendered in terms of individual psychology. Here the cure is that of repentance, the subject of an entire section of *Tanya* (the third, *Iggeret ha-Teshuva*, "The Epistle on Repentance"). This process consists of "breaking" the heart in contrition. As Rashaz puts it in a later chapter in the Book of the Median, "the main repentance is in the heart," so that heartedness is required in order for the light of the soul to shine. The psychology of repentance, in Habad and in modern Kabbalah in general (and especially the theme of the broken heart) requires a separate and detailed study.[20]

This opening discussion, which seemingly subordinates the heart to the brain, should be set against a text from the fourth section of the *Tanya* that opposes the fiery enthusiasm of the "externality of the heart" to the "interiority of the heart" (or "point in the inner part of the heart" or "the depth of the heart"), which is actually superior to the mental qualities of *Da'at* and *Binah*, as it stems from the "supernal wisdom," which is none but the divine spark in every Jewish soul. Interestingly, Rashaz relates this trans-rational wisdom to "matters of the world," in which concern for a "very very great matter" on which all one's vitality depends could occasion deeds or speech, which transcend rationality.

However, for many this spark of the interior heart is in an exile that is likened to the biblical "foreskin of the heart." The messianic redemption entails the removal of the subtle layers of this foreskin and the revelation of the inner point, which is at present revealed only in the self-forgetful passion that may awaken during prayer, known already in rabbinic writing as the "worship of the heart." One may see that this discussion seemingly replicates the earlier discourse, yet casts it in different terms, which reestablish the supremacy of the heart.[21]

I believe that even this partial survey suffices to convey the overwhelming importance of the soul and heart in the thought of the founder of Habad, as well as the complexity introduced into the notion of the divine soul once it is joined repeatedly by the animal soul. It must be stressed, however, that this discussion reflects only the authoritative and widespread work, the *Tanya*, and that more nuanced discussions may be found in numerous other volumes (which were usually not written by Rashaz himself, but rather recorded and edited by various members of his family). Here it is a pleasure to mention Naftali Loewenthal's detailed work on the diachronic layering of Habad thought. However, his psychological reading, though highly important, appears to differ from mine, as it stresses self-sacrificial imagery. To enter this question would require an entirely different and less modern contextualization, in the history of Jewish martyrdom, especially in the Ashkenazi world.[22]

Having clarified the general theory of the heart and soul in the *Tanya*, I now wish to briefly turn to an overlooked source, perhaps hinted at in the introduction to the book (where Rashaz writes that his book is based on various "books and writers"). In chapter 2, I briefly discussed R. Aharon Shmu'el of Kremnitz's *Nishmat Adam* and its complex reworking of the model of the divine soul. Pervaded throughout by a sense of agon, this work presents a three-tiered structure: the *hasidim* (confusingly, as in many Jewish texts, identified with the *tzaddiqim*), who are single-heartedly good; the wicked, who are entirely evil; and the median level of the *beynoni*. This obvious similarity to *Tanya* is joined by martyrological discussions (reinforcing Loewenthal's reading of the *Tanya*). R. Aharon Shmu'el's main innovation appears to be his description of the transformation of the worship of God into a natural process on the level of the *tzaddiq*. One should also note his poetic psychological description of the painful yearning of the soul to reconnect to its divine source.[23]

Moving now beyond the *Tanya*, one should bear in mind that Habad, like other Hasidic groups, developed from a more intimate circle (continuing the previous circle of Friedman) into a large movement, a process reflected in ideational shifts traced by Loewenthal. Existing scholarship has already noted the intense debate accompanying this process, between Rashaz's son and ultimate successor, R. Dov Baer Shneuri (the *Mittler* or "middle" rebbe) and his main disciple, R. Aharon ha-Levi Horowitz of Staroselye. At the same time, Wolfson has correctly claimed that one should also bear in mind the affinities between these two thinkers, both after all continuing the thought of Rashaz. For our present purpose, the most important point at issue was that of suspicion towards enthusiasm from the animal soul and "revelation" of emotions in the heart on the part of the former leader. Shneuri forcefully insisted on an extremely difficult process of refinement (described in his manuals on meditation), leading to manifestation of the divine soul, and especially its higher levels, that he actually identifies with the secrets of Kabbalah and Hasidism.[24]

As I have suggested, one may fruitfully compare this dispute to the general debate on enthusiasm in the eighteenth century. On a more theoretical level, one can see such debates as part of the history of the mystical construction of emotion that contains its own unique problematic relative to psychology of religion in general. One may read Horowitz's insistence on the impossibility of the transformation of the heart without the more accessible heartfelt enthusiasm in terms of democratization. According to this reading, in a more panoramic view one could say that it more fully expresses the logic of the divinity of the soul, thus mitigating the duality inherent in Rashaz's psychology. This is most apparent in Horowitz's definition of the very innovation of Rashaz's doctrine as rendering God's unity accessible to every (Jewish) heart and soul according to its attainment. In a historiosophical move, Horowitz subverts the strong sense of hierarchy found in Rashaz (and his sources) by claiming that in the present historical era, all the levels of the soul are "mixed" in each individual.[25]

To some extent following Loewenthal, I feel that Horowitz's view reflects the shift in the later doctrine of Rashaz, especially in the homily *Liqqutei Torah*, towards an appreciation of the attainment of ordinary Jews, as part of the trans-Hasidic doctrine of "personal redemption." This move entailed an effort to render the Habad doctrine accessible even to those lacking "exalted souls," by enclothing or absorbing the "radiance of soul" in the intellect as one of the garments of soul.[26]

Despite such interpretative achievements, studies such as Elior's have not considered the exegetical writing that for Horowitz (as for many other Hasidic writers) is often a better expression of the subtlety of his thought than a systematic work. In his biblical commentary, *'Avodat ha-Levi*, Horowitz describes the essence of the soul as the mysterious point of the heart that like the ineffable name of God requires no emendation. All that is needed is for the powers of the soul to be revealed. Here we find the underpinning of the acceptance of the revelation of emotion in the heart in an essentially passive doctrine, the reverberations of which can be traced in later generations of the main lineage of Habad (especially in the writings of Rashab). In an even more psychological vein, Horowitz writes elsewhere in this work that one should aspire to a desert-like state of abandonment in which "one views all of one's worship as nought." It is precisely through this seemingly hopeless state that one may contemplate the divine essence and awaken a "powerful desire" arising from the "point of the heart."[27]

The Schools of Lublin

A well-known legend recounts that the founder of Polish Hasidism, R. Elimelekh Weisblum, bequeathed his mystical sight, soul in intellect, mind, and speech to various students. This account reflects the self-perception of this highly popular branch of the Hasidic movement, as diversifying into several subbranches, while retaining a "family resemblance." One of these diverse schools, that headed by R. Ya'aqov Yitzhaq

Horowitz, the Seer of Lublin, was characterized by further subdivisions (Psischa, Kotzk, etc.), with successive generations of students rebelling against their teachers. It is tempting to suggest, as some nonacademic writers have, that this atmosphere of "holy rebellion" owes something to the spiritual, social, and political unrest of the nineteenth century and to Romanticism. Be that as it may, the process of constant splitting off has led academic observers to study the various schools of Lublin in isolation, while ignoring their commonalities. In my view, as exemplified in my earlier writing on Hasidism, groups such as Ziditchov-Komarno, Izbiche-Radzin, and Ger should be seen as offering conflicting interpretations of the teachings of R. Elimelekh Weisblum and R. Ya'aqov Yitzhaq Horowitz.[28]

A major example of such a debate is that surrounding the uplifting of "alien" thoughts during prayer, often seen as soul-fragments, and the related question of the criteria for being able to perform *yihudim* (the main meditative technique of modern Kabbalah). While other schools, such as Habad, also took part in this ongoing debate, it reached particular intensity and crystallization of positions in the schools of Lublin. Already the student of the Besht, R. Ya'aqov Yosef of Polony, wrote: "In order for his thought to be worthy to perform *yihudim* without any alien thoughts, one cannot perform them so much unless one has a soul from the world of creation (*beri'a*), and if not then his *yihud* is not a *yihud*." Continuing in this vein, R. Ya'aqov Yitzhaq Horowitz's student R. Qalonymus Qalman Epstein wrote the following reservation regarding the practice of *yihudim*, in the name of Weisblum, whom he describes as the leader of the generation:

[. . .] One should not think thoughts and calculations on the *kavvanah* [mystical intention] of the [divine] names, but rather connect one's revealed and hidden aspects, that is the *nefesh, ruah,* and *neshama,* to the Infinite . . . and one's thought should be so adhering to the pleasantness of God that one should have no leisure even a moment for directing *kavvanot yihudim,* and one who is in this state in his prayer, then his *kavvanot* are performed by themselves through his prayer.[29]

Due to the close connection between study and prayer in virtually all Hasidic worlds, this locution should be read in tandem with the following statement in the name of Weisblum: "Whoever has only the level of *nefesh* should not come to study the secrets of Torah." One should not regard such views as expressing a withdrawal from mystical prayer towards mere emotive awakening, as Moshe Hallamish tends to interpret similar statements by another student of the Seer, R. Tzevi Hirsch

Eichenstein of Ziditchov, nor as a general withdrawal from the Lurianic *kavvanot*, as Idel has claimed. Rather, one should interpret this approach as a restriction of the active and technical practice of intention and *yihudim* to the superior soul-level of the *tzaddiqim*. Thus, their adherents, the Hasidim, are directed towards a more "generic" connection of their soul to its supernal source, so that deeper levels passively and spontaneously manifest.[30]

Eichenstein's student, R. Yitzhaq Yehiel Safrin of Komarno, quotes the original statement by R. Ya'aqov Yosef of Polony (which he attributes to a forgery!) while obviously clearly having more contemporary views in mind as well. He then responds extremely forcefully, drawing on the "democratic" implications of the model of the innate divinity of the soul:

> This is a mistake and complete lie, for even a soul of '*assiya* is from the aspect of divinity, part of the divine from above, unified in divinity . . . my son accustom yourself to be expert in the holy names and *yihudim* . . . for anything of holiness suitable for Moses is suitable for a lesser of the least, such as myself.[31]

Elsewhere I have shown how Safrin's extensive writings on the soul (including his democratization of mystical practice) should be seen as a response to processes of advanced modernization in the nineteenth century. This is well apparent in a text presenting an organic model of the chain of connection between the soul as a "very long branch" extending from the supernal tree of life to the human heart and using the metaphor of new technologies of communication such as the telegraph: "And take a simile from the new invention of the cord that one talks through between countries . . . and this *segula* (magical-like virtue) emanates from the *segula* of the cord in the human heart that reaches to the Throne of Glory." Safrin goes on to describe this connective process in terms of rebirth and transformation of the heart: "And when a person desires to ascend to his source it is easy, for the light of his thought in a heart made joyful by the Torah ascends . . . and he literally becomes a new creature with a broad and joyful heart full of vitality and light."[32]

We see here how the selfsame teachings led to extremely sharp debates revolving around the ongoing questions of restriction of the soul-divine connection to the *tzaddiqim* or its extension to all Jews. While it is possible to read these debates in the narrower terms of personal disputes for succession or reactions to the process of institutionalization of Hasidism as a mass movement, I feel that it is more profitable to place them within a wider vista of intellectual history. Again, it is not necessary to generalize to Hasidism as a whole, yet one can at least identify the unity of various branches of the same tradition. Likewise, in chapter 1 I expressed reservations as to "panoramas" that bridge the modern divide, yet we can observe that it is still possible to follow the evolution of premodern questions regarding the divinity of the soul. In the more general methodological sense, a true "toolbox" approach should enable us to utilize geographical-historical focus and more panoramic, longue durée approaches at different times or even combined, depending on the topic at hand.[33]

One of the most modern forms of Lublinesque psychology is found in the writings of the school to which my own paternal ancestors belonged, that of Izbiche-Radzin. Though the radical nature of the writings of this school has enjoyed some academic attention, the central place of the soul and the heart in this extensive corpus has been largely overlooked. Nonetheless, the profound psychological insights developed by the successive generations of the school have been recognized in the wonderful writings of Avivah Gottlieb-Zornberg, as well as her students (see chapter 5). At first glance, this Hasidic branch adheres to the model of the innately divine soul, in a strongly national manner: Numerous formulations assert that as the deep inclination of the Jewish heart is pure, it ultimately transpires that all actions performed by a Jew are aligned with the divine will. It is these statements that have led to the designation of the school as antinomian.

However, a wider reading discloses a far greater degree of complexity: In a relatively well-known text, the founder of the school, R. Mordekhai Yosef Leiner of Izbiche, reflects on the search of Abraham for the root of his life. Citing the Midrash on this Biblical figure seeing a burning castle and then asking "who is the owner of the castle?" Leiner describes the *tar'omet*, or anguished protest, of the psyche of Abraham. In a radical rereading, Leiner says that revelation occurred when Abraham realized that the very uniqueness of the *tar'omet* of his heart, in an unprotesting world, is the sign of God's presence, in awakening his heart and soul:

God answered him: "You yourself see that for the whole world this is not a question, and no one takes to heart to say: 'who made these?,' and only for you it is puzzling, so from the anguished protest of your heart you can deduce that there must be a God . . . and it was He who awakened your heart and soul to this."[34]

On the immediate or proximistic level, Leiner is responding to the lifelong *tar'omet* of his erstwhile teacher, R. Menahem Mendel Morgenstern of Kotzk, who was famously compared (by the twentieth-century

American writer R. Abraham Joshua Heschel) to Søren Kierkegaard. However, this is also a response to the pain of the modern: In the mid-nineteenth century, in a world already beginning to burn, it is the complaint of the heart and the soul, where deep meaning can be located, just as took place within the psychoanalytic setting at the end of the century.

In a far less known text, Leiner discusses the concept of the "chasm" (shades of his younger contemporary Nietzsche), defining it as a state in which one acts with God's will being hidden, so that one has to be attuned to it in the depths of the heart even in the condition of the hiding of God's face:

'In his knowledge chasms were parted' (Proverbs 3:20): A chasm refers to the matters in which one acts in a state of concealment and is attuned to God's will . . . for from the depths of the heart God builds in the heart of man so that he can perform His will even in hiddenness and it will be clarified [yitbarer] through this that he adheres completely to God.[35]

This is far from a deterministic worldview, as some have interpreted his teaching. Rather, in the secularized situation of modernity, God's will is no longer a given, but must rather be recovered, or built as Leiner has it, through depth psychology. Our reading is reinforced by a third text from this work, in which he writes that even when walking with the words of the Torah one needs to be in doubt, imaged here as darkness, as the will of God is very deep. However, it is precisely through doubt, and especially those doubts that are related to desire, that this shall be ultimately revealed.[36]

In this teaching, the advent of doubting one's faith in the modern era is not to be overcome, as is the essential message of Bratzlav Hasidism. Rather, the way forward is through doubt. Just as in the later thought of R. Abraham Yitzhaq Kook (influenced by this Hasidic school and discussed in chapter 4), redemption proceeds through and beyond secularization. Echoing Bratzlav teachings yet moving in an opposite direction, Leiner is recorded as saying that one is connected to the will of God beyond reason in the depth of the heart and that repentance manifests the power of the soul to reach to depths beyond reason. The latter statement should be read in view of the double and radical claim that one can reach the depths of Torah only when connected to one's soul root, and the roots of some individuals call them to go beyond reason to the depth of Torah.[37] A true depth psychology!

Although I have stated here and elsewhere that a strong antinomian interpretation misses the subtlety of the schools' teachings, one cannot deny that its unique psychology leads at times in this direction. Describing the rules of the Torah as idolatrous "Gods of masks" (Exodus 34:17), Leiner continues: "and the verse tells you that when you have explicit understanding (*binah*) of the heart, then do not look to the rules for your conduct, rather know from the understanding of your heart how to conduct yourself in each detail." Similarly, the formula "I am the Lord your God" repeated throughout the Torah portion "Qedoshim" is interpreted as follows: that God promises man that he dwells in his heart, and this is a great fierceness for the places where one's mind falls in fear that maybe one, God forbid, one retreats from the will of God. And on the verse "If you walk in My statutes, and keep My commandments (Lev. 26, 3)" (*behuqotai*), Leiner commented:

As long as the holiness of God is not engraved and fixed in the heart of Man, he is called "standing" as he needs to restrict himself in all matters . . . and when he turns to the words of the Torah until they are engraved and fixed in him, then he can expand and walk in all the matters that he wills, for God is with him.[38]

These radical teachings, only a fraction of which have been discussed here (many others are to be addressed in a future study), were understandably not cited by the later figures who were influenced by them or debated them, including in my view (besides Kook) R. Shalom Baer Schneerson, R. Yehuda Leib Ashlag, and R. Yitzhaq Hutner. It is true that, following certain tendencies in the school itself (especially the writings of R. Zadoq ha-Kohen of Lublin), its reception often took a national turn, yet I believe that this does not capture the complexity of Leiner's thought. This can readily be demonstrated through the following teaching on the Biblical figure of Jethro:

Even though he was less than the level of the seed of Israel, nonetheless through his great desire he drew very close to God and all the more so one who is from the seed of Israel and desires the light of God . . . and thus the arrival of the convert is a preparation for receiving the Torah [in the "Yitro" portion named after Jethro], for one of the causes that prevent accepting the yoke of Torah is that of weakness that enters the heart in thinking of one's value . . . and therefore it was written before this: 'Jethro heard' (Exodus 18:1) . . . to show how great is the power of Torah in returning to the good, even unto Jethro, who was not from the seed of Israel and was very far . . . still as he truly desired, he merited the mention of the giving of the Torah and this portion . . . and this shows that it is the passion that is the main thing . . . and it is in the power of the words of Torah to return to the best (*mutav*) all the souls that have drawn far.[39]

Elsewhere I hope to discuss at length the playing out of these themes in the successive generations of the schools, most of which have not been researched, despite a recent wave of publication of manuscript materials. However, one must point to the startling psychological teachings of Leiner's grandson, R. Gershon Henokh Leiner of Radzyn (1839–91), who discusses the increase of the soul in the eschatological future through a paradoxical process in which the body rises above the soul and woman above man. At this point, worship itself will be transcended as one reaches one's root (the paradox again being that the root is not innate but increasing), and then one can perforce choose only what belongs to one's soul. It appears that the key to this process, radical in the original etymological sense, is faith in the disclosure of one's root through the dialectical conflict of its forces.[40]

I now wish to turn to the more conservative and demographically far more numerous branch of Ger, founded by R. Yitzhaq Me'ir Alter, who remained faithful to R. Menahem Mendel Morgenstern of Kotzk even after R. Mordekhai Yosef Leiner broke with him. The main text here is *Sefat Emet* by his grandson and student R. Yehuda Aryeh Leib Alter that has enjoyed some academic attention, but has not been published in its entirety. In my view, there are numerous responses to Izbiche thought here, with Alter choosing a far more nomian direction. It is high time for a detailed diachronic analysis of the layering of this work, as it records earlier Ger traditions and dates discourses delivered over many years. For our purposes, I wish to briefly follow the evolution of his teaching on the heart and soul in the direction of growing complexity.[41]

Although the scope of material renders generalization difficult, one can discern two levels in Alter's homilies, each containing a cluster of central terms or keywords: The first level is largely made up of nomian terms, such as circumcision and Sabbath, alongside with national themes such as the Land of Israel and the people of Israel. The second level, which is found in earlier texts yet more prominent in later homilies, is composed of psychological terms such as the "point of the heart," interiority and the soul, together with the central Hasidic doctrine of the Tzaddik. In other words, the general direction of the evolution of Alter's thought is towards abstraction, psychologizing, and individuation (in the sense of focusing on the exalted individuals). However, it should be stressed that the keywords on the second level retain a strong connection to the first cluster of terms.

One striking example, related to the relationship of body and soul, can be found in his interpretation of the Torah portion "Hayye Sarah." In the Hebrew Year 5636 (most likely during 1875), Alter taught that access to the ungraspable divine is through the adherence of the body to the soul, which is equally transcendent and supernatural in nature. This in itself is an interesting teaching, transferring the central Hasidic term of Devequt or adherence, to the body-soul interaction. However, in 5644 (1883), he presents a far more complex structure. The "divine point" in the soul is far too great and vital to be contained in the "vessel of the body." However, on the Sabbath, one is granted some access to this transcendent realm through the "extra soul" that comes with the day of rest according to Talmudic sources (see chapter 7). Drawing on his oft-repeated equivalence between "world," "year" (or time), and "soul" (itself going back to the canonical mystical text from late antiquity, *Sefer Yetzira*), Alter asserts that the righteous can adhere to this "root of the soul," and thus transcend nature.[42]

The understanding of the Sabbath as referring to a form of body-soul relationship is fleshed out, as it were, in a talk on the later portion of "Va-Yetze" in 5661 (1900), where Alter states that the righteous trans- form the vessel of the body and uplift it together with the three main aspects of their soul, while the wicked convert the vitality of the soul into the "darkness of nature." On the next year, Alter returned to this theme and added that the righteous, like the Sabbath, convert the desire of the body into the desire and "thirst", or yearning, of the soul. This subordination of the first level to the second is even clearer in a rela- tively late (5653/1893) talk on the portion "Tazria'," where he discusses the extension of the "shining of the soul" to the body by the righteous. He then states that all the positive commandments are designed for this purpose, while observing the negative commandments prevents the body from obstructing the flow of vitality and power of the soul. The Sabbath, which famously has a positive aspect of *Zakhor* (remembrance) and a negative aspect of *Shamor* (guarding), is simply the "generality of all of the commandments."[43]

A close parallel to the role of the righteous can be found in Alter's late ("Va-Yer'a" 5661/1900) discussion of the ancestors of the nation, here in relation to the heart. He writes of redemption coming about through the children of Israel being drawn after the heart of the an- cestors. While during the period of exile this power is hidden in the souls of the former, it is awakened in the three daily prayers (famously established by the three ancestors: Abraham, Isaac, and Jacob). Here too, collective nomian practice is a means to enter a more psychologi- cal and individual realm. In other words, just as the school of Izbiche should not be categorized simplistically as antinomian, so Ger should not be seen as merely nomian or conservative. When one analyzes the deep structure, the affinity between these two close branches of Lublin emerges.[44]

I wish to conclude this overview of a vast, varied, and rich world with a mention of one contemporary representative, R. Benzion Rabinovitch, the rebbe of Biale-Lugano, who consciously models himself on the "holy Jew," R. Ya'aqov Yitzhaq Rabinovitch of Psischa, the rebellious student of Horowitz. In a volume devoted to this figure, Rabinovitch describes the effect of the souls of the *tzaddiqim*, during and after their lifetime. Writing specifically of "the holy Jew," he differentiates between the lesser challenge of rival faiths (especially Christianity) and the "new method of the devil," namely atheism, which calls for a new method on the side of holiness. He then claims that "for this the soul of 'the holy Jew' . . . came to this world." This exalted soul was able to "draw down" a new method and path in the worship of God, and by doing so to annul the power of the new, demonic method. Again the theurgical effect of the descent of this soul is not limited to his lifetime, but instead he still operates in the supernal world "to draw influx of innovation and holiness to the children of Israel." Elsewhere, Rabinovitch gives this project a specific theurgical focus: The emendation of the souls of the "world of chaos."

These texts, chosen from a voluminous corpus, offer a cosmopsychic, yet modern, framework for the controversial and at times antinomian innovations of the Psischa school, all the while insisting on the continued influence of the soul of its founder. Rabinovitch's definition of the essence of the innovation of the school provides a clue as to its social psychology: "Of course his holy Torah flows from the Hasidic Torah of the holy Ba'al Shem Tov—but it is an innovation in depth, and also so that the 'young sheep' [see, e.g., Jeremiah 59:20], can attain it, and not merely the great ones of Israel, as in the time of the Ba'al Shem Tov."[45] Though it would be correct to interpret this text in terms of democratization, it would also not be far-fetched to see it as continuing the theme of Hasidism as a youthful movement, which can be readily located in the traditions of this particular school.

Psychology in Modern Mussar

A vast and largely untapped resource for Jewish spirituality and psychology may be found in the Mussar movement that flourished in Northeastern Europe in the second part of the nineteenth and the first part of the twentieth century (and later partly reestablished itself in Israel and in the United States). Although several of the early figures of the movement (like some Hasidic masters, including the Besht and R. Menahem Mendel Morgenstern of Kotzk) were somewhat reticent about writing, we do have a large corpus of works devoted to the main goal of the movement—incisive analysis of human character and internal processes. In recent years, new material based on manuscripts and notes taken by students has been published in Mussar circles, together with a greater display of academic interest.

Benjamin Brown, who has done much in teaching and writing to reawaken interest in Mussar, has adopted the earlier assertions of Immanuel Etkes as to the "metaphysical indifference" of the founder of the movement, R. Israel Lipkin (Salanter, 1810–83), which manifested in avoidance of Kabbalah.[46] As a result, the study of Mussar has often been detached from the history of Kabbalah. If this claim were true, it would amount to a striking reversal of a long-term process that began in the thirteenth century and peaked in the sixteenth and seventeenth centuries: The assimilation of the genre of Mussar within that of Kabbalah, while serving as an avenue for popularizing the latter and greatly contributing to the ascendancy of mysticism in the intellectual landscape of modern Judaism. I myself do not believe this disconnect to be the case. I wish to demonstrate the problem with Etkes' thesis through a median position developed by a central scholar of Kabbalah, Mordechai Pachter.

In a short yet important article, Pachter recognized the salience of Kabablah in certain schools in the second and third generations of the Mussar movement. However, he grafted these valuable observations onto the existing theory, asserting that some thinkers in the successive generations of Mussar reversed the earlier reversal by returning to Kabbalistic discourse to some extent. No wider cultural or historical explanation is given for this doubly surprising process. The problem is compounded when we recall that Lipkin himself was a student of the pietistic R. Yosef Zundel of Salant (1786–1866). While one might debate the place of Kabbalah in the practice of R. Yosef Zundel, who presented detailed *kavvanot*, or mystical meditations, one cannot deny its centrality for R. Yosef Zundel's own direct teacher, R. Hayyim Iczkovitz of Volozhin, and especially for his own teacher, R. Elijah Kremer of Vilna (to be described in chapter 4). According to Pachter, Lipkin reversed not merely the general tendency of Mussar literature but also the heritage of his own lineage, only to have his own reversal gradually reversed by his students.

Using Occam's razor (only metaphorically), I wish to offer an alternative and far simpler hypothesis. The leaders of the Mussar movement, like other traditional modern Jewish intellectuals, saw Kabbalah as part of a broad intellectual world, which needs to be mastered by any true *talmid hakham* or Torah scholar. At the same time, the curricular policy of the prototypical Lithuanian Yeshiva, that at Volozhin (founded by the above-mentioned R. Iczkovitz), reserved the study of Kabbalah for the select few. Furthermore, it is entirely correct that the focus of Lipkin and some of his followers was inner change rather than metaphysical knowledge or mystical experience, and thus some Mussar teachers explicitly warned against pursuit of Kabbalistic aspirations not founded on inner change.[47] As a result, Kabbalah was largely removed from the open discourse of the first generation or two of the movement. However, with the exception of a few important scholars, it was never set aside at any point. Hence, it is not surprising that this policy was speedily and increasingly relaxed, as is apparent in the contemporary Mussar world, in which classes on Kabbalistic classics such as the Lurianic *Otzrot Hayyim* or R. Yosef Gikatilla's *Sha'arei Orah* are being delivered to senior students.[48]

I wish to bring but one striking example of the continuity between early modern and modern Mussar with regard to Kabbalah's psychology. As we have seen, Cordovero's *Tomer Devorah* can be seen as representing the modern translation of theosophy into psychological theory. The most central figure of the second generation of the Mussar movement was R. Simha Zissel Ziv of Kelm, who held this work in high regard. Furthermore, in the Mussar fashion, he founded a select fellowship dedicated to intense inner work and named it *hidabeq tov*, or "adhere to good," itself a reworking of the term *devequt* (adherence), so central for Cordovero and other Jewish mystics. This social-psychological structure itself is derivative of the pattern of the Kabbalistic circle. Again in typical Mussar fashion, but also in the wake of earlier fellowships, members of the group committed themselves to follow stringent regulations, including the daily study of *Tomer Devorah*.[49] This critique of existing scholarship, only part of which can be presented here, is vital for appreciating my choice to include the later Mussar literature within this overview of explicitly psychological theories of the heart and soul.

As suggested at the beginning of the chapter, the Mussar movement should be properly seen both as responding to and later influencing Hasidism, as well as the Haskalah. Most of the Mussar luminaries were cognizant of current developments in European thought, including psychoanalysis, and this is also the self-perception of its adherents. Indeed, the halakhist and essayist R. Yehiel Ya'aqov Weinberg, who studied with the third-generation Mussar master R. Nathan Tzevi Finkel, claimed that

Lipkin predated Freud by speaking of the "dark" or unconscious forces. Etkes, who has written the most comprehensive academic book on the movement to date, has claimed that this formulation is indebted to Kant, as well as pointing at the indirect influence of the psychological theories of Benjamin Franklin on Lipkin. More broadly, Mussar should be seen as a modern and to some extent revolutionary movement.

It is no accident that many of its adherents were attracted to Bundist Socialism and Zionism, as competing forms of youthful rebellion against the communal structures and leadership. However, the movement itself, at times sharply apolitical, insisted on inner change as opposed to activism. An oral account that I heard from a close student of the late twentieth-century teacher R. Shlomo Wolbe went as follows: A student of Wolbe's own master, the charismatic third-generation teacher R. Yeruham Leibovitz of Mir, asked for his blessing on joining an Orthodox political party. Leibovitz replied with the characteristic Lithuanian irony: "I give you my blessing, as long as you understand that you are hereby relinquishing your internal development."[50] As we shall see in chapter 4, this choice bifurcates Mussar and the school founded by Kook, who came from the same intellectual world.

A striking example of the extensive interaction of the Mussar movement with contemporary intellectual figures can be found in the following account: In the summer of the Jewish year 5693, or 1933, R. Abraham Isaac Bloch, the rosh yeshiva of Telz in Western Lithuania and (since 1930) successor of the renowned Mussar teacher R. Yosef Leib Bloch, vacationed at a resort on the Baltic seaside. The rabbi acceded to the students' request, and joined a sail from en route to the port of Memel. The author of this biographical account, Rabbi Simha Bunem Stein, states that this outing was to be held a day or two before the elections in which Hitler ascended to power in Germany. The rabbi wished to see the machinery operating the ship, and gazed at a great furnace generating the heat to move the ship. The rabbi then looked out at the sun upon the waves, yet his contemplation of the grandeur of God's works was tinged with concern, as he spoke of the possible rise of *oto ha-'ish* (that man), to power.

A few steps away stood a solitary man leaning on the railing. He asked one of the Yeshiva students if he spoke German, and when the latter identified himself as German-born, the newcomer introduced himself as the famous writer Thomas Mann. The student then disclosed his teacher's worry regarding the approaching elections. Mann leapt and declared: "This will not be. Tell your teacher, I am German. . . . One of the people . . . I know this people and trust it to know how to guard itself, and at the decisive moment to know how to protect the true German culture." He went on to say that he was returning home from the German-speaking provinces of Lithuania to take part in the elections and thus protect German democracy and culture.

Mann then asked the rabbi numerous questions on Judaism. In particular, he asked why the Sabbath is spent in inaction instead of a refreshing outing. The rabbi answered that one cannot enjoy oneself at the expense of another's suffering. He then said that as this was his first boat trip, he looked at the machinery, and since then was troubled by the situation in which some enjoy the sea breeze and some are almost roasted working at the great furnace. The Jewish Sabbath, he concluded, was designed to avoid such situations. One day a week, class distinction is abolished.

As detailed elsewhere, I have some doubts as to the historical exactitude of this tale: At the same time, not being beholden to the fallacy of misplaced rigor—to paraphrase Alfred N. Whitehead—dominating some parts of Jewish studies, I do not wish to dismiss this account outright. Rather we have here some testimony as to a discussion of social, spiritual, and political issues, between the leader of one of the main branches of the Lithuanian Mussar movement and a very prominent European writer who was clearly influenced by Freud.[51]

A second example, also drawn from the third generation, is that of a response to Freudian psychology written by R. Eliyahu E. Dessler, a prominent student in the Kelm Yeshiva. Dessler's crucial years were spent between 1928 and 1947 in London and in Gateshead, near Newcastle-on-Tyne. During this time, Dessler tutored several prominent members of the Anglo-Jewish elite. This exposure to a far less Torah-centered culture required Dessler to formulate a Mussar response to a variety of scientific and social issues. It is in this context that we should read a discussion of Freudian psychology published recently in a memorial volume, which includes previously unpublished talks.

Dessler begins with the failure of the great minds to reveal the true causes of cognition and behavior. He notes recent attempts to uncover such causes, yet—tellingly using Freudian terminology—he states that we now know that these are only minor symptoms and not true causes. In other words, a true depth psychology is still lacking. Thus, the efforts on part of the "great researchers" of the psyche to expose its secrets have failed. The reason for this is that the means are lacking. Just as true microbiology was impossible before the microscope, psychology lacks an instrument that can observe the microbes of the soul. While new analytical instruments in the natural sciences have led to the overthrow of Aristotelian views, psychology has essentially not been modernized, or as he puts it, it "remains as it was." Drawing on his interpretation of Luzzatto's *Mesilat Yesharim*, he claims that the Torah scholars are the specialists of the soul, who possess tools equivalent to the microscope. This science of the soul enables an understanding of the commandments as addressing subtle psychic elements and movements (an interpretation echoed in the writings of R. Yosef Bloch of Telz as well as those of R. Yeruham Leibovitz).

Again implicitly addressing Freud, Dessler moves on to the psychology of sexuality, claiming that the rabbinic view of the *Song of Songs* demonstrates its subtle approach to the psyche and the rabbinical sages' understanding that the holy secret can be conveyed only through sexual imagery, as also found in Kabbalistic works. This is not the place to examine the sources of his views, which clearly include the works of the semisocialist Kabbalist R. Yehuda Leib Ashlag, whom he met in London during the latter's brief English period in the late 1920s. For our purposes, it suffices to note the engagement not only with Freud but also with a host of scientific and social issues.[52]

A further third-generation example, all but completing the array of major schools, is a briefer discourse from the Slobodka school, by R. Yitzhaq Hutner, who studied philosophy in Berlin in the early 1930s before establishing a strong center in the United States. Hutner writes that the prevalent heresy is that of denial of free will in favor of psychological and sociological determinism. However, he reframes this phenomenon positively, as a harbinger of the imminent annulment of free will in the messianic era. He even tantalizingly hints at parallels between these secular views and the teachings of the Izbiche-Radzin Hasidic school that are known to have influenced him.[53] Together, these illustrate the active involvement of Mussar in both European and American culture, including psychology, around the time of the Second World War.

One of the most detailed theoretical discourses on the heart and soul in the third generation is found in *Da'at Torah*, a collection of talks on the Pentateuch delivered (also to numerous American students) by the above-mentioned R. Yeruham Leibovitz (1873–1936, a disciple of R. Simha Zissel Ziv). Leibovitz begins with a strong statement on the centrality of the heart for inner work. In a classical Mussar move, he subordinates seemingly intellectual outlooks to the heart:

[. . .] We observe that we . . . change from moment to moment . . . and imagine that all this is due to our understanding, that first one understands thus, and later comes to understand in a contrary manner . . . but this is a complete mistake, for when we know this secret that there are no things that are external to us, but all depends on the powers of the heart, then when one sees that one has been affected and is changing, this is clear evidence of a spoiling (*qilqul*) of the heart, and all of one's thoughts and understanding now emit from the situation where one is in now, and one has no other advice . . . but to awaken the power of the heart.[54]

This passage relates to other core teachings of Leibovitz, such as stability and the imperative to work within one's own existential "situation." However, for our purposes the stress both on the centrality of the heart and on its powers should be rather familiar by now. In his characteristic fashion, Leibovitz immediately translates this theoretical observation into a practical recommendation, based on a strikingly concrete simile:

[. . .] like a person who lies down on his side, and when he is uncomfortable, then he turns over, and if he is still uncomfortable, then he readjusts his position . . . but one simple thing he knows: that the main thing is to improve his lying posture . . . and thus it is literally with spiritual matters, a person should know for certain that, that if he falls, there is no recourse to wisdom etc. but merely to say to him: turn over; turn yourself to a firmly standing heart, and thus with all powers, restore the heart to its health, and then already all of the wisdoms and thoughts that bother you will dissolve and go away by themselves, and you will remain in your health.[55]

Besides the biographical context, namely the heart disease from which Leibovitz himself suffered, there is also a historical background. According to this text, the rival claims of Enlightenment, Bundism, and Zionism should not be withstood on their own ideological terms, as ideology merely reflects a deviation on the internal, heart level, which should be corrected as such. As he was nonetheless an intellectual, Leibovitz grounded his theory in a theoretical statement, fascinating in itself, by one of the most intriguing of eighteenth-century scholars and mystics, R. Jacob Emden (1697–1776).

The text from Emden's *Birat Migdal 'Oz*, which Leibovitz quotes at great length, presents a Galenic medical model in which various combinations of the humors, founded in turn on the elements, determine one's psychophysical condition in every moment of the day. The conclusion that Emden draws from this structure is that the healing of the soul from ill *middot* is identical with the healing of the body. In typically modern fashion, in sharp contrast to his utilization of a model dating to antiquity, Emden stresses that this "secret" has been overlooked in existing Mussar literature.[56]

Accepting Emden's description of human psychology, Leibovitz poses a bold question: "How do the Torah and its commandments suit each person equally, as one is subject to many kinds of affects caused by unique situations and contingent events?" He immediately responds:

Yet the truth is that this very question contains its answer, as well as the instruction for all of our work, for indeed this is truly the goal of our holy Torah. Precisely because Man, from his very formation, is subject to so many effects, and the slightest deviation has such influence, the Torah was given, with all of its commands and warnings, in order to preserve and to maintain Man from the outset in the proper equilibrium . . . and this is very astonishing, for we see the greatness and severity of the labor incumbent on Man, for he must be literally an expert doctor . . . and we will illustrate this from the awesome matters that a slight deviation from equilibrium entails. The verse says: 'For it came to pass, when Solomon was old, that his wives turned away his heart after other gods; and his heart was not whole with the LORD his God, as was the heart of David his father' (1 Kings 11:4–7). Though of course we have no idea of the healthy heart possessed by Solomon . . . and all the more so no concept of the subtle deviation of this essentially healthy heart . . . a slight deviation in the heart, subtler than subtle . . . and already the result is more terrible than terrible . . . and contrarily on the positive side . . . what is all of our work and purpose if not to effect a change of direction of the heart . . . this is the virtue of all of the Torah and commandments in the proper fashion, to bring about a predilection of the heart.[57]

Seemingly, Leibovitz veers back from a potentially anomian medical discourse to the safe ground of the Torah, as well as classical Mussar ideas such as the subtle deviations of the great men of the past, equilibrium, etc. Although such a reading would be essentially correct, it would miss the manner in which Leibovitz also subordinates the external dimension of the Law to the subtle work of the heart. He reiterates this point when he summarizes the complex picture evoked by Emden by stating that although there are numerous powers of the soul "the root of all and the source of their life is the heart . . . for all is the heart, which includes all." Thus, the heart is the root of all of the *middot* as well as all action, "for there is no more than the heart." So that "in a pure heart all deeds are assumed to be perfected (*be-hezqat metuqanim*), and a pure heart cannot be acquired except through the labor of rectification of the heart."[58]

One must pause to appreciate the polemical context of these statements. Critics of the Mussar movement, most prominently the towering twentieth-century leader R. Avraham Yesha'yahu Karelitz, warned of the anomian potential of its teachings, which relegate study and meticulous performance of the commandments to second place and foreground

instead internal dimensions that are not explicitly formulated in canonical texts. Leibovitz essentially accepts this observation, while insisting that Mussar appeals to a constitutive psychophysical layer that
predates, shapes, and determines religious life, thus echoing his well-
known critique of the ideal of mere religiosity, expressed by the Yiddish
term *frumkeit*.

Leibovitz's teachings were partly preserved from the Holocaust
through the astonishing efforts of one man, Chiune Sugihara (1900–
1986), the Japanese consul in Lithuania, who facilitated the escape of
hundreds of students of the Yeshiva to Shanghai, among thousands of
Jewish refugees. The main Mussar teacher emerging from the exile in
Shanghai was R. Yehezkel Levenstein (1895–1974), who helped to partly
reestablish the movement in Israel. Levenstein develops the medieval
text (R. ibn Ezra's) noted above on the primacy of the heart into a somewhat radical understanding of external deeds as a means for the work of
the depth of heart. Thus, he critiques the common view of the heart as a
mere repository for the internal intention of deeds. He describes this insight as particularly relevant for this generation and startlingly describes
Mussar as a new Torah, as deeds are limited but the heart is limitless.

In postindependence Israel, the teachings of Mir were, and are being,
disseminated mostly through the school of my first spiritual teacher, R.
Shlomo Wolbe (1914–2005), who survived the Holocaust through the
Scandinavian escape route.[59] Although Wolbe never ceased to stress that
he was only exposed to the teachings of Leibovitz for a couple of years,
his academic background enabled him to explicitly formulate the teachings of his mentor in contemporary and especially psychological terms.
This is the reason for his appeal for the returnees to Haredi Judaism in
the late twentieth century, some of whom, such as R. Reuven Leuchter,
have continued to creatively develop the Mir heritage, while others,
such as Yishai Shalif, are practicing psychotherapists.[60]

Elsewhere, I have briefly discussed Wolbe's psychological theory in
the context of twentieth-century anomian approaches.[61] For the purposes of the present discussion, I shall cite a representative anomian
discussion of the relationship between the heart and the textual canon.
In a recently published collection of talks (which has not been addressed
even in the very few academic studies that engage Wolbe), the following
formulation appears:

The manner of study of the holy Torah is not as it appears to the eyes of the flesh,
that one learns Torah from books and writers, but rather the truth is that one learns
from oneself and the words emit from one's heart, except that one requires books and

writers to waken that which has been forgotten . . . [and] open the doorway to the light hidden inside.[62]

Although obviously this stress on the internal and the heart continues along the path of Leibovitz, nonetheless the anomian implications of this approach are somewhat more prominent. This heart-centered approach is the foundation of a strongly individualistic and experiential hermeneutical theory. As Wolbe puts it elsewhere:

The study of Torah is not a mental (intellectualistic) preoccupation alone. If the Torah addresses only the intellect—then everyone would have heard the same thing at Sinai. But the holy Torah speaks to all of man's powers, to the entirety of the psyche (*nefesh*) . . . when a word of Torah penetrates in this manner into the inside of the inside of the person, and a person feels that each word also addresses his basest inclinations that he would be ashamed to even reveal to another person . . . this shows the word of Torah in a light that only he sees . . . this action of the Torah is what teaches the person his interpretation on that word . . . when the person sees how he himself, with all of his powers and inclinations, is clarified by each word of Torah, he apprehends his unique "commentary" on each word . . . . Through the holy Torah a person attains his individuality, which is his identity.[63]

Before concluding our discussion of Mussar, the Mir school should be compared to a rival approach in which the Kabbalah is far more openly present. The writings of R. Yosef Leib Bloch of Telz (father of the above-mentioned R. Abraham Isaac Bloch), an equally charismatic and far more political leader and educator than Leibovitz, are never mentioned in the writings of Mir, a fact that has escaped even those scholars who have briefly written on the movement.[64] The reason for this avoidance is obviously that this rival school, which continued after the Holocaust in the United States, is seemingly close to the path of Mir yet essentially divergent. This is not the place to note the numerous parallels to the discourses of Leibovitz, including that discussed above, in the writings of Bloch. Rather, as in the former case, I wish to exemplify his psychology through one *shmus*, or talk, delivered during the First World War and entitled "The Soul of the Torah." A *shmus*, delivered by the Mussar supervisor (*mashgiah*), who at times also headed the Yeshiva, was one of the performative rituals innovated by the Mussar movement, perceived as one of the peaks of the intense weekly inner work in its Yeshivas.

Bloch begins with the general Mussar idea of unconscious movements of the soul, which he relates to the unconscious effect of extremely subtle influences. One example that he employs is strikingly reminiscent of the hypnotic theory of state-dependent learning, as well as closely related to the rigorous time management inaugurated already by Lipkin (under the mediated influence of Benjamin Franklin). When accustomed to perform an action at a regular time of day, one feels an imperative to repeat it when that time arrives.[65] Bloch then moves rather swiftly from the behavioral-psychological level to the theurgical one:

When a person, whose affairs are infinite and each of which reaches to the worlds of worlds up to his supernal root, adds any level, then all of his affairs, his actions, his movements, and aspects of his soul in all the worlds from their roots till their end-point are somewhat uplifted and beautified: can one then measure a small advantage obtained in his soul? . . . with regard to the levels of the human soul—all that has been until now is incomparable to the slight advantage added now. This small addition is more important than all that was found in the human soul previously and includes this all and is in relation to this [the previous attainment] as a cause to an effect or a soul to a body! Therefore, a slight improvement in Torah, fear of God, delicacy of soul, softness of heart, purity of thought, expands and extends throughout the person, in all his affairs and all of the worlds, and this has no measure or [defined] value.[66]

This text clearly describes a process of soul-making: As opposed to the pseudomedical model of Leibovitz, who describes the restoration of a natural equilibrium, here we are speaking of a completely open-ended process in which each advance is equivalent to a new soul, as in the Lurianic system. Although there is no explicit resort here to Kabbalistic sources, the employment of technical terms such as "infinite," "worlds," and "root" clearly betrays the background of Bloch's thought. Soul-making is not merely a personal path, but intimately linked to a cosmic process. Traditional values such as Torah and fear of God and psychological refinement are entirely fused in this self-fashioning.

This being said, the general frame of the talk is the subtle psychological effects of the commandments of the Torah (e.g., the symbols of the Passover Seder), as also reflected in the subsequent section, in which Bloch raises the question of whether the Torah could not have mandated laws with more obviously powerful effects? He responds that contemplating this question led him to a "great" innovation, namely that subtlety is itself the goal of the Torah, as only such subtle effects reach and awaken the "thin capillaries" of the soul. Based on this reframing, he boldly states that obvious and external effects actually nourish the grosser psychic forces. The contemporary context of this reversal is immediately apparent when Bloch ironically (and somewhat prophetically) exemplifies a gross approach to ritual by imagining the employment of new technologies to create a dramatic pageant in lieu of the restrained celebration of Passover.[67]

He then provides a more explicitly Kabbalistic answer to his question, by claiming in a more classical manner that every detail of ritual expresses cosmic secrets founded on the secrets of the Torah (Kabbalah). However, lest one assume that Bloch's connection to the Kabbalah is of a general and standard nature, one should stress the continuation of the talk, in which he presents yet another innovation, which he describes as awakening and moving him each time he ponders it. Referring also to parallel talks, he emphasizes that the secret and attainable realities are not distinct, but rather represent different expressions of the exact same overall reality. This, according to his presentation of the Kabbalistic worldview, is the answer to the "fools" who critique the anthropomorphic imagery found in this lore. According to his rebuttal, their mistake lies in failing to comprehend that the material and the spiritual are simply divergent perspectives on a continuum. From this vantage point, the apparent and hidden rationales for the commandments are one, the latter being the "soul" of the former and the source of true pleasure in study of Torah.[68]

Here we come to the title of the talk. Following on a Zoharic image to be discussed in chapter 7, the concept of the "soul" of the Torah is central in Bloch's thought. Just as soul-making is an endless process, interpretation leads to discovering the "soul" of a law, or its hidden reason, only to realize that this soul, too, has a soul. He applied this understanding to the immediate concern of his listeners, who as followers of the Telz approach were engrossed in the study of the subtle reasoning underpinning the Halakha. He concludes this talk by describing the goal of Torah scholars as "penetrating to its soul," and rebuking, in typical Mussar fashion, those who do not exert themselves to comprehend this soul.[69]

The dispute between Bloch and Leibovitz is complex, and cannot be encompassed here. To the points of difference already noted above, I wish to add the following observation on overall psychological orientation. Leibovitz's main concern is with the transformation of the self (ha-'adam 'atzmo) from within the individual's concrete existential situation. Bloch was devoted to inspiring a cohort of ideological devotees through offering them cosmic vistas. Despite the continuous influence of the Mir school, within the broader arena of post-Holocaust Haredi society, Bloch's approach, which was dubbed hasqafa (outlook) prevailed. Among purveyors of hasqafa one should note R. Hayyim Friedlander, mashgiah mussari of the highly prestigious Ponovitch Yeshiva in Israel (inheriting R. Levenstein's position), and R. Aharon Kotler, head of the large and prestigious Lakewood Yeshiva in the United States.[70]

I wish to conclude my discussion of Bloch and indeed of Mussar with a methodological coda. The espousal of subtlety couched in the rhetoric of irony should preclude interpretive moves, which search for obvious contemporary influences, clear evidence of disputes, or striking examples of Kabbalistic themes.[71] Such expectations not only go against the grain of the texts but also of the entire cultural atmosphere of the Lithuanian Yeshiva. Rather, the richness of the texts will expose itself, in the language of phenomenology, only to researchers whose tools are fine and whose approach to the text is subtle. Needless to say, ideological agendas, whether apologetic (as in the case of Haredi writing) or Zionist preclude such an approach by necessity. Against this background, I am heartened by the work of Yakir Englander, to be discussed in chapter 4.

FOUR

National Psychology

The development of "national mysticism," even if based
on earlier sources, should be seen as one of the prime expressions of the modernization of Kabbalah. Though this
development had several manifestations, for our purposes
I focus on the vast discourse on the restriction of the divinity of the soul to Jews, and the subsequent doctrine of
the divine national soul. Seemingly, national psychology
mitigates against comparison, yet it should actually be
seen as a sign of the increasing influence of the rise of the
modern nation-state on the Jewish world, as discussed recently by Sorotzkin.[1] Thus, Kabbalistic national psychology
can be traced to earlier modern periods, as I have shown
elsewhere for the sixteenth-seventeenth century center
of Prague. One can even trace some of its theoretical origins, though not its sociopolitical setting, to premodern
texts, such as R. Yehuda ha-Levi's *Sefer ha-Kuzari*, which
had a substantial influence of modern Jewish thought, especially in the twentieth century.[2] However, it developed
most markedly from the eighteenth century through the
twentieth century to the contemporary scene in tandem
with the circles discussed in chapter 3. A comparative view
would not hesitate to include the parallel history of psychology of the Jews in modern anti-Semitic writing. When
considering the relationship between psychoanalysis and
anti-Semitism, a question that weighed heavily on Freud's
mind, one should also include the image of the "soulless
Jew" in anti-Semitic discourse. In such a discussion anti-
Semitism should not be viewed in an ahistorical manner, as

a continuous phenomenon, but rather one must consider its specifically modern forms.[3]

Despite the salience of national psychology, one should not assume that nationalism characterizes all forms of modern Kabbalistic thought. To mention but one example, in chapter 7 we shall examine the case of R. Ya'aqov Abuhatzeira, who wrote extensively on the soul in a far less national vein; this is also true in the earlier case of R. Shalom Shar'abi. Though this might reinforce the hypothesis of the European provenance of nationalistic Kabbalah, it could also simply demonstrate the plurality of forms of modern Jewish mysticism. On a more comparative note, the presence of a strongly political modern Kabbalistic tradition can be seen as a counterexample for Grace Jantzen's assertion that modernity relegates mysticism to the private sphere.[4]

The Politics of the Soul in Modern Italian Kabbalah

National mysticism is associated in a complex manner with an entire system of thought on issues such as the political realm and history. Clearly, modern Italy was an important site for such discourses, as one may see in the works of Niccolò Machiavelli and Giambattista Vico. This is no less true for Italian Jewry, which traditionally maintained a close and bilateral dialogue with extra-Jewish thought. As I have shown elsewhere, the first Kabbalistic discourse on "politics" as a realm may be located in the eighteenth-century circle of R. Moshe Hayyim Luzzatto.[5]

As mentioned in chapter 2, the formation of circle focused on charismatic individuals is one of the characteristics of modern Kabbalah. This pattern continued in the eighteenth century, in the case of groups with formal "contracts," such as those of Shar'abi and Luzzatto. This is also true, in a much less formal fashion, for the circle of R. Elijah Kremer of Vilna in the nineteenth century. In that century, the eighteenth-century circle centered on the founder of Hasidism, the Baal Shem Tov (the Besht), was transformed into a full-fledged social movement. A similar transformation can be seen in the case of the circle founded by the Latvian Kabbalist R. Avraham Yitzhaq Kook in Ottoman Palestine in the early twentieth century. It is no coincidence that Kook's circle, to be discussed at length below, partly modeled itself on that of Luzzatto.

The latter, Luzzatto's highly prolific group greatly developed the historiosophical interpretation of Lurianic Kabbalah. Although full-fledged Italian nationalism that certainly drew in Jewish intellectuals was more evident in the nineteenth century, already in the writings of the circle one can discern the presence of more regional forms of collective identity and reflections on civic history, transcending the Jewish context. The writings of Luzzatto and his Eastern European followers had a formative effect on a fuller development of national psychology in the Lithuanian Kabbalah of Kremer and his students, to be discussed later in this chapter. This is part of a larger history of the rehabilitation of Luzzatto after he was persecuted by numerous rabbinical and communal authorities (as I have discussed in my intellectual biography of Luzzatto).[6] While here I focus on the more theoretically oriented and extensive works of the circle, one should note, though leaving for a future study, the importance of national mysticism in the works of other eighteenth-century figures, especially R. Immanuel Hai Ricci, who also had a marked effect on the Lithuanian Kabbalists.[7]

Prior to setting out Luzzatto's theory of the soul, a characterization of the style of the texts of the circle is in order. These works cannot be regarded as mere containers for theory, as they are deeply rhetorical in nature, in the Italian tradition. Writing as a Baroque intellectual, Luzzatto composed explicit discussions of rhetoric, along with his theatrical and poetic works. Likewise, the work of his close associate, R. Moshe David Valle (who will be addressed soon) is replete with discussions of rhetorical figures, using the appropriate Italian terms. The relationship between rhetoric and psychology is far from external. Hillman has suggested that rhetoric is the natural expression of discourse on the soul, which for him is the discourse *of* the soul. Beyond the craft of his style, Luzzatto was also a master theoretician, bringing order to the vast and rather chaotic world of post-Safedian Kabbalah and Mussar. It is thus highly useful for our discussion of psychological thought to focus on his theory of the soul rather than his experience of communication with exalted souls or his practice of rectification of the souls of his contemporaries (which I have addressed at length in the above-mentioned biography).[8]

As I have shown in the past, as a result of his persecution, including burial and possibly even burning of his texts, Luzzatto's surviving Kabbalistic writings are a mixture of authentic and spuriously attributed texts. Of his authentic Kabbalistic texts, the most extensive is *Adir ba-Marom*, a rereading of part of a Zoharic section. Quite early in the treatise, Luzzatto describes the secret of the body and the soul as "the basis (*'iqar*) of everything." From this work, one should especially note the following fascinating discussion that I believe is autobiographical, while also echoing his semicontemporary, Immanuel Kant:

And you shall see that the soul in itself is not bound by the senses, and in that state it sees and hears everything . . . and knows the things in themselves, not as they are depicted for her by the vessels. And therefore the prophet goes out of his senses in order to receive prophecy.[9]

Fortunately, all of the non-Kabbalistic works from the later period of his life seem to have survived. Understandably, it is these works that have come to enjoy all but canonical status, as a result of the above-mentioned process of rehabilitation. The first of these, printed in Hebrew as *Da'at Tevunot*, was translated as *The Knowing Heart* in the useful bilingual edition by the twentieth-century American Kabbalist R. Aryeh Kaplan. However, its title in manuscript is usually *A Debate between the Intellect and the Soul*. One should compare the resort to this particular genre to the addresses to the heart and soul in *Mar'eh ha-Mussar* ("The Mirror of Mussar") by Luzzatto's close Lithuanian student R. Yequtiel Gordon (found only in manuscript).[10]

Echoing the above-cited text from *Adir ba-Marom*, Luzzatto writes that the "covering of the physical flesh and blood" conceals the vast complexity of the clocklike organization of the universe, so that it is only the soul that is capable of perceiving it. It follows that only one who can exit the physical in a prophetic state is capable of grasping the world-system presented throughout *Da'at Tevunot*. It is fitting that he describes the divine providence pervading this system as the soul of souls.[11]

I shall now turn to the hugely influential Mussar text *Mesilat Yesharim* that though not written in a Kabbalistic key as some claim, naturally expresses Luzzatto's Kabbalistic worldview. In the introduction, he proves that the physical world cannot be the goal of human existence through a reflection on the existential dissatisfaction of the soul. He then enlists the rabbinic parable of the princess who is dissatisfied by a less than royal lifestyle. This oft-quoted passage should be understood in light of a parallel in *Da'at Tevunot*, where he explicitly resorts to the doctrine of the divinity of the soul. I believe that this exposition is also the impetus toward the internalizing trajectory of this extremely well-crafted work, leading towards an increasing stress on the centrality of the desire of the heart and soul in divine worship. Although *Mesilat Yesharim* locates the satisfaction of the heart's desire in the world-to-come, "the world of souls," it is apparent as the book nears its conclusion that this but sets the stage for deeper possibilities of mystical-messianic fulfillment in this world.[12]

The centrality of Luzzatto's own mystical and messianic life in the intense Kabbalistic activity of the circle, before it disbanded following the persecution, is well reflected in his surviving Kabbalistic works. However, it should not obscure the importance of his associate, R. Moshe David Valle, who was at least as central a figure in its messianic vision. Valle composed a remarkably extensive corpus, partly printed recently (and since increasingly quoted in the Kabbalistic world) and partly in manuscripts. As these texts, including numerous autobiographical entries, are presently less known in the English-speaking world, I shall address them here at some length.[13]

The brief examination of Valle's treatment of the heart and soul that will follow shall demonstrate his own sense of superior mystical attainment vis-à-vis Luzzatto, although the extent to which the latter shared this assessment is a complex question. I have proposed a division between Valle's early works, composed while collaborating with Luzzatto, and the more numerous works written in later periods, after the disbanding of the circle and indeed long after the early death of Luzzatto. The earlier cluster reflects far greater concern with Valle's own psychology, while the later works deal more with political issues and with the soul of the nation.

Nonetheless, as we shall see, Valle creates a strong link between the individual and general psyche, with the Messiah, as a "general soul," providing the mediating link. Throughout, the soul is one of his central themes. Although he was far less of a systematic theoretician than Luzzatto, writing mostly in an exegetical mode, he had a clear sense of the important place of the soul within a wider cosmological picture, as evidenced in his presaging the division of the entirety of creation into souls, worlds, and lights, which is customarily attributed to the founder of Hasidism, the Besht. Similarly, Valle accorded the heart an important place in his complex picture of the universe, stating that "all follows the heart."[14]

In Valle's early writing, however, both heart and soul branch off from his central theme in these works, which is that of the "rectifying" *tzaddiq*, who is clearly a foil for his autobiographical discourse. Often he names this figure the "sifter," or "winnower" (*mevarer*), echoing the Lurianic theme of "sifting" the sparks of holiness from among the husks, as a central part of the messianic project of rectification. In terms of the Kabbalistic map, this *tzaddiq* is identified with the Sefira of *Yesod*, adjacent to the *Shekhina*, or the tenth Sefira of "divine kingdom," the uplifting of which is the main task of the rectifier. The *Shekhina* is a central theme in Valle's thought, earlier as well as later, as it "impregnates" the soul of the Messiah.[15]

The redeeming rectifier, as a clearly messianic figure, is described in an early text of Valle's as the "secret of the king," a figure who is "also the heart of the body of the holy nation."[16] Thus, here and in another discussion close by, he writes that the Messiah carries in his heart the sufferings of the body, that is to say the Jewish people, whose tribulations in exile are another important topic of his writing. In a passage that is significant for appreciating his prophetic consciousness, closely related to his messianism, Valle describes the "general soul" of the prophet or *tzaddiq* of the generation, absorbing the sins of the people. Here, as in other places, one may discern the possible influence of Christology. It can also be seen as another example of proto-Hasidic views in Valle's writings.[17]

The identity of the king with the heart is foundational for this understanding of the roles of the two Messiahs, itself perhaps the central theme in the entire discourse of Luzzatto's circle. I have argued elsewhere that Valle identified himself, in his preliminary stage of mystical self-development, as the Messiah son of David, while he regarded Luzzatto as the lesser Messiah son of Joseph. He writes that the root, and thus the rectification of the Messiah son of David, is "literally the heart of the king," referring here to the divine rather than the national monarch. Thus, Valle, as a messianic figure, is indeed both the king and the "secret of the heart." The Messiah son of Joseph, or Luzzatto, is assigned a lower level, on the left arm of the king. Or as he put it elsewhere, "He is literally the secret of the heart, for Messiah son of David is the king, in the paradigm of the heart [*dugmat ha-lev*], which is king of the body's limbs."[18]

More generally, Valle's autobiographical discussions include his reflections on the theurgical-messianic function of the souls of the members of Luzzatto's circle. Thus, he writes that "one needs to follow the importance of souls, and one important soul that is from the root of emanation (*atzilut*), rectifies more than numerous lowly souls from the root of [the world of] action ('*asiya*)."[19] As in the case of Safed, and more clearly in the later Hasidic texts, the discourse on the role of the souls of the righteous should be seen in the social-psychological context of the formation of circles as the main medium of Kabbalistic creativity in the modern period. This being said, even in the period in which he was in close contact with the Luzzatto circle, Valle's main concern was with his own soul.

In his autobiographical phase, Valle described his personal suffering at great length, due to its national and cosmic importance. His tribulations and eventual healing are frequently described in terms of his attainment of the various stages of the soul, which eventually lead him even beyond the identification with David, on the soul-level of *nefesh*, towards a connection with the soul of Moses, on the level of his own *ruah* and *neshama*, transcending and thus unifying the two Messiahs.

As Valle puts it elsewhere, "The rectification of Israel will not be completed except through his soul root," as the soul of Moses impregnates that of the Messiah. The culmination of this process is when the rectifier ascends to the world of emanation, attains his levels of *haya* and *yehida*, and thus fully gains his kingship. As he explains elsewhere, the meaning of the attainment of *yehida* is the transformation of evil into good. In other words, this level corresponds to the revelation of unity (*gilui yihud*), perhaps the most central concept in Luzzatto's historiosophical thought. For Valle, these are far from merely theoretical formulations, as he actually dates the stages of this process month by month. Valle thus joins earlier figures such as Vital (and later figures such as the Hasidic master Safrin) in offering a detailed itinerary of his internal development, demonstrating that the rise of Kabbalistic autobiography was part of a modern process of psychologization.[20]

Despite the eventual transcendence of the Davidic phase, the "pious king" David was a model of identification for Valle, who described the "rectifier" as the descendant of King David. In an all but explicitly autobiographical statement, Valle writes that David predicted, through his Holy Spirit, not only his own tribulations, but also those of the "last rectifier," who is "literally the reincarnation of the soul of David," and thus reenacts his suffering. This is an interpretative key utilized by Valle throughout several volumes of exegesis of Psalms. In a similar vein, he wrote that the power of redemption is drawn down from the soul of the Messiah residing in the world of emanation to "the redeemers of all generations."[21]

Building on the Lurianic theory of impregnation, Valle writes that powerful study of a text can enable such an intimate connection with the soul of the author. I would like to posit that he saw the study of Psalms, a central practice of the circle of Luzzatto, as a means for establishing such a connection with the soul of David, to whom the authorship of this book is traditionally ascribed. Valle's sense of soul-connection with King David led him to regard him as a source of strength during his own periods of despair, which, as he wrote, threaten to overcome the purity of his soul. It is the 'kindnesses (*hasadim*) of David' (Isaiah 55:3), which "[. . .] awaken and renew every morning for the sifting *tzaddiq* . . . , [who] becomes like a new creature every morning through the drawing down (*hamshaka*) of these kindnesses, which give him power."[22] One should especially note the sense of empowerment, transformation, and rebirth as result of the influx from the soul of David, echoing the Lurianic theme of the "new souls" as expressing the advent of the Messianic era (see chapter 2).[23]

More generally, the book of Psalms, which contains numerous descriptions of the condition of the soul, in all its names, served as rich source of psychological commentary in modern Kabbalah starting with the converso work *Kaf ha-Qetoret*, as well as for contemporaneous Christian writings, such as those by Martin Luther, which also contain important political discussions.[24] Towards conclusion of this intensive textual discussion, one should note a markedly autobiographical commentary on the weeping of David's soul during his troubles (Psalm 119:28), which, as Valle writes, reflect the national theme of the suffering of the Jews in Exile as well as his own tribulations (although one should stress that he was not directly exposed to the persecution):

There is such a great blockage and such great tribulations that Man cannot sweeten with the tears of his eyes, but the soul from within cries in an overflow of spiritual tears, which are revealed to God who alone sees all hidden as it is written 'Most devious is the heart; It is perverse—who can fathom it?' (Jeremiah 17:9). And thus the pious king said to Him, blessed be He: you alone know that my soul overflows in tears . . . for there is no disfigurement [*hashata*] as that of the soul, and she cries and weeps in hiding and no man sees and knows her trouble . . . and who can preserve the soul that it shall not be disfigured, except for God alone who made her and sees her spoiling from within. And just like He preserves the general soul during Exile . . . . So He can preserve the private soul of every man from being disfigured by its troubles.[25]

I would see this as an early discussion of the unconscious, which describes a direct relationship between the deeper levels of the individual soul, the collective or national soul, and the mediating soul of the Messiah, and divine awareness. One should also note the comparison with deeper layers of the heart, as reflected in the prooftext from Jeremiah. In Valle's commentary on that verse, he writes that "the heart is more of a cheat than other organs, for the deeds of all other organs are visible, but the thought of the heart is not visible to the eyes of the flesh, rather to His eyes [alone]."[26]

To conclude our discussion, Valle can be seen in post-Jungian terms as tracing a process of soul-making, leading through initial "dark nights" of suffering towards eventual rebirth, culminating in his specific case in the attainment of prophetic and messianic levels. Valle's rhetoric merges several subsidiary images, all of which capture facets of this process. As I have shown elsewhere, labor and effort are central tropes for him. I have also suggested that this theme, which is paralleled, though to a lesser extent, in the writings of Luzzatto, cannot be divorced from the historical context of the early industrial revolution and more generally from the theme of effort as a major facet of the psychology of modernization. In one of his commentaries on Ecclesiastes, the Biblical book which dwells most on labor, Valle writes that the nature of the soul was formed from "the place of rest" and thus it must undergo great pain due to the labor caused by the rule of the husk in the lower world, which for him is the feminine realm. However, the eventual victory over the forces of evil will restore the soul to its rest and heal its pain.[27]

As Valle puts it elsewhere, both the individual and the collective must undergo the process of sifting, which leads through effort to rest. Rest for him is the return to the root of the soul, which is the natural imperative of the heart: "It is already known that the nature and heart of Man bring him to come as close as possible to his root, for there is his rest and not outside of himself." Yet another "root metaphor," to use Owen Barfield's term, is that of the transition from "smallness" to "greatness." The period of "greatness" will be characterized by the expansion of the Holy Spirit among all of the souls rooted in the *Shekhina*. As he wrote in an autobiographical entry on his life stages, "greatness" is that of the soul, and is again identified with the heart of the king.[28]

Lithuanian Kabbalah: from the Political to the National

In an early study (that now requires some amendment), I suggested that national Jewish mysticism proper began with the circle of R. Elijah ben Shlomo Zalman Kremer, the Gaon (genius) of Vilna, the famous opponent of Hasidism. Although we have located elements of national psychology also in some Hasidic schools, I already noted in chapter 3 that this is not a major theme in the thought of the movement as a whole, and thus could be said to be a subtle difference between the two alternatives for spiritual hegemony in Jewish Eastern Europe. As the towering figure of Kremer is the subject of a recent study by Eliyahu Stern (and subsequent critical responses), I wish to focus on the national psychology of his successors (who have barely been discussed in English).[29]

During the nineteenth century, Kremer's school branched out into two main groups. One, devoted to the ideology of the Yeshiva as a total institution (following the heritage of his main disciple, R. Hayyim Iczkovitz of Volozhin), included the early teachers of Lithuanian Mussar who then predictably found a home in the Yeshiva world. The other school that has at times been somewhat exaggeratedly described as proto-Zionist followed the highly independent R. Menahem Mendel of Shklov in emigrating to Palestine.[30] Iczkovitz's major work, composed partly as an anti-Hasidic polemic, is *Nefesh ha-Hayyim*, that has recently enjoyed extensive commentaries, from which I shall choose the one composed recently by the highly creative Lithuanian Mussar teacher R. Reuven Leuchter.

On the one hand, Iczkovitz, probably consciously critiquing the Hasidic movement, severely limits the accessibility of higher levels of the soul: For example, he adopts the Nahmanidean view that the soul is the divine breath, yet precisely because of this he argues that other than Moses (as is perhaps fitting for the recipient of the Torah), no man has had this aspect in his body, as opposed to sparks of light merely shining above his head. Furthermore, this aspect is described in intellectualistic, rather than mystical terms, as the "extra understanding" that enables grasping the inner intellect hidden in the Torah.[31]

I believe that this stance can be related to Iczkovitz's stress on prayer for the state of the national soul root, rather than individual needs (which admittedly has Hasidic parallels) as well as his description of Torah study as focused on intellectual insight, rather than any emotional experience of adherence to the divine, as in Hasidic views. However, the soul still plays a central role in his work, alongside the major image in the book, the more body-centered *tzelem*. Likewise, Iczkovitz describes a technique for connecting the various levels of the soul to each other and to the divine during prayer. However, in the portion of the book devoted to an explicit polemic against Hasidism, Iczkovitz stresses that this process cannot take place merely through the thought of the heart, but must rather ascend through the proper and exact process prescribed by nomian ritual and liturgy.[32]

Alongside his discussions of the soul, Iczkovitz's treatment of the heart affords interesting insight as to the important role of the text in the construction of the above-mentioned ideology of the total Torah institution, mirroring the development of Hasidism as a social movement. Iczkovitz writes close to the beginning of the book that the individual should not "say in his heart . . . what am I and what is my power to act," but rather should "understand and know and impress on the thoughts of his heart, that all the details of his deeds and speech and thoughts at every time and in every moment [. . .] each one rises according to its root to have an impact in supernal heights, in the supernal worlds."[33] Here we have a call for internalization of awareness of theurgical empowerment as individual empowerment. I wish to stress the expression "thoughts of his heart," which is a catchphrase for internalization. This phrase, as well as subsequent references to the heart, should be read in light of Iczkovitz's assertion that the human heart is the axis mundi, which parallels the supernal temple. However, internalization in the sense of awareness is but a prelude for emotive transformation:

Truly, when the wise man truly understands this in truth, his heart will be moved inside him in fear and trembling, when he directs the attention of his heart (be-sumo 'al-libo) to his wrongdoing [. . .] how far it reaches to ruin and destroy by the lightest of sins.[34]

We have here a description of the formation of conscience in the form of what one might term "theurgical guilt." This guilt, not surprisingly, focuses on sexual fantasy:

[. . .] When a person errs to think in his heart, a thought that is impure, in adultery, God preserve us, he is actually introducing a prostitute, the symbolic object of divine zeal (semel ha-qin'a) into the awesome Holy of Holies, in the holy supernal worlds, God forbid, and increases . . . the powers of impurity and the Other Side in the supernal Holy of Holies, much and greatly more than the empowerment of the power of impurity by [the conquering Roman general] Titus, when he consorted with a whore in the Holy of Holies in the lower Temple.[35]

Sexual fantasy, which affects the heart, or the human equivalent to the supernal temple, thus has a far more detrimental theurgic effect than any physical act. The internalization of theurgy enables the empowerment of conscience and the enhancement of guilt. In these texts, theurgy is a means for creating an essentially psychological and heavily sexualized inner world that can easily be compared to that described in nineteenth-century literature, religious and secular. Furthermore, Iczkovitz's discourse on the heart lays the ground for the distrust of individual religious impulses later developed in the Mussar movement. Thus, in a gloss found in the polemical section of the book, Iczkovitz discusses the mobility of the Evil Impulse, which is capable of moving between the chambers of the heart and masquerading as piety.[36]

This stress on the inner sanctum of the individual and on a form of soul-searching seemingly supports Leora Batnitzky, who joins Hasidism and the approach of Iczkovitz, together with the enlightenment of figures such as Salomon Maimon, as varied responses to the rise of a modern, individualistic approach to Jewish religiosity. By now it should be apparent that I certainly concur with her stress on the overreaching compass of modernity. However, Batnitzky somewhat overlooks the intensely communal nature of the Hasidic social movement. Were it limited to the adulation of charismatic individuals, as in previous Kabbalistic circles, Batnitzky would be on firmer ground. However, one must also factor in the complex horizontal relationships between the Hasidim, or followers of the charismatic rebbes. In the case of Iczkovitz, besides the institutional and ideological framework of the Yeshiva as a social world, one cannot overlook the nationalistic thought of Lithuanian Kabbalah as the true context for Iczkovitz's writing.[37]

As mentioned above, national mysticism is especially apparent in the branch of R. Menahem Mendel of Sklov. His own writing is highly dense and replete with numerology and other cryptic allusions; however, his main student, R. Yitzhaq Haver, dedicated extensive theoretical discussions to the soul, following consciously in the footsteps of Luzzatto. Haver's main development of the teaching of Kremer, most clearly presented in his supercommentary, entitled *Or ha-Torah* (on *Ma'alot ha-Torah* by R. Avraham ben Shlomo Zalman, the brother of Kremer), is that as the *neshama* is basically inaccessible, the *ruah* is the main component of humanity. Indeed, being human in a true sense is expressed in the study of Torah, as this is what strengthens the *ruah*. This approach easily extends to national psychology. Haver explains the famous or infamous Talmudic dictum that the nations of the world are not considered *adam*, or "fully human," in national-textual, rather than merely national terms: the nations do not study Torah. As Haver explicitly mentions the Haskala in a central passage in *Or ha-Torah* (and elsewhere), one should regard his construction of national difference as a response to assimilatory tendencies in Eastern Europe in the nineteenth century.[38]

However, like Iczkovitz, Haver also polemically responds to Hasidism, stressing that it is the nation (rather than the exalted individual) who is the sanctum and castigating the "new sects" promoting insufficiently scholarly enthusiasm. However, like Iczkovitz, it is apparent that Haver was influenced either by Rashaz's psychology or else by shared earlier sources (perhaps oral traditions undiscovered by scholarship).[39] In a discussion of "the depths of the supernal wisdom" that are hidden in a cluster of legends in the fifth chapter of the Talmudic tractate *Baba Batra* (that also intrigued Hasidic authors such as R. Nahman of Bratzlav), he wrote as follows:

The main purpose of the creation of man was to emend his animal soul that is beneath his level, and the *ruah* was given to him in order to emend the *nefesh* (animal soul) . . .

when a person sins then the spirit withdraws from him, and then his *nefesh* descends and falls below and parallel to this the spark of his soul (*neshama*) that is fixed in the *Shekhina* descends . . . and this is due to the neglect (*bitul*) of the Torah and command-ments, for the Torah and commandments parallel *ruah* and *nefesh*, male and female, as is known.

Setting aside the gendered aspects of this text, it adds to the emphasis on study and on *ruah* the deeper purpose of emending the animal soul, while also positing a negative theurgy of sin, in which the decline of the lower aspect of the soul creates a chain reaction reaching even to the distant divine spark in the *neshama*. Yet another passage reminiscent of Hasidic doctrine, in this case that of the circle of the Besht, can be found in a far less elitist homily in which Haver writes:

For truly all of Israel are one soul, divided only in their levels, and each needs the other, and each one is divided from the other by his root and the aspect (*behina*) of his soul, like the ladder that one wishes to use to ascend to a high place that one needs the rungs . . . and when one rung is missing then one cannot ascend or descend . . . thus with the order of the souls of Israel, each one in a different level.[40]

No discussion of the soul can be complete without at least briefly addressing the highly complex writings of R. Shlomo Elyashiv that are playing an important role in the current renaissance of Lithuanian Kab-balah. This Kabbalist, formerly of Lithuania and later of Jerusalem, took an independent position (though it has been espoused by some Sephardic Kabbalists), being possibly critical of both Lithuanian sub-schools for interpreting the Kabbalah in terms of the lower world, or in other words in a modern fashion. As we have seen that earlier versions of Lithuanian Kabbalah exhibit commonalities with Hasidic ideas, it is with Elyashiv that this stream truly comes into its own, also in terms of theoretical sophistication.[41]

Elyashiv's austere stance would lead us to expect little psychologi-cal interpretation in his voluminous works, yet several central passages demonstrate that he maintained the centrality of the soul, also for his-toriosophy, while resisting strong psychological moves, as in Hasidism, that he staunchly opposed. Rather predictably, he employs the soul as a central metaphor for the indwelling of the divinity within the supernal world of emanation that again is the main arena of Kabbalistic narra-tive and practice. In a more innovative fashion, Elyashiv anticipated Karl Mannheim by more than half a generation in presenting what one should term an intergenerational social psychology. In this system, each successive generation consists of the "soul ancestors" for the next one. In a somewhat national manner, he adds that each generation has one shared "general root," drawn from the general root of the previous generation, thus establishing the psychological fraternity inside the same generation.[42]

Elyashiv was certainly aware of the scientific advances of his time, and this topic was part of his recently published correspondence with another immigrant from the Lithuanian world [Bialystok] to Palestine, R. Naftali Hertz ha-Levi Widenbaum. After an opening missive presenting his view of kindness and restriction as two basic psychoid powers that operate in the supernal world (developed throughout his works), Elyashiv apparently received a response from Hertz. The latter identified the manifestation of the two supernal powers in the lower world with physical forces such as magnetism. Elyashiv then responded that this is certainly a pure teaching, yet stressed that the overall goal should be to expose the higher roots of material forces (rather than reducing the supernal to the mundane).[43]

In concluding this section, I would like to note a characterization of the Lithuanian approach to the soul that may reflect oral tradition as much as any specific written text. The twentieth-century Mussar teacher R. Shlomo Wolbe, commenting on a manuscript sent to him by a younger scholar, wrote: "You wrote that the soul is complete divinity. As I was taught, this is an error. The soul is the first separate power."[44] Though one should be cautious as to such an oral tradition, it at least reinforces the sense that the Lithuanian world was less sanguine about the doctrine of the divinity of the soul than other schools, while still developing a rich psychological doctrine. As we have seen, in both branches of this school, national mysticism played an important role, though less pronounced than in the school that we shall now turn to, founded by no other than an erstwhile student of Elyashiv—the famous and ever-researched R. Avraham Yitzhaq ha-Kohen Kook.

R. Avraham Yitzhaq ha-Kohen Kook's Naturalistic National Mysticism

The soul is cast down and suffers its pains inside, but at last it shall win.
R. AVRAHAM YITZHAQ HA-KOHEN KOOK

Of all of modern Jewish mystics, Kook and his school, strongly influenced by Lithuanian Kabbalah, provide the clearest example of the nationalization of psychological theory. So much so that his son and main editor, R. Tzevi Yehuda ha-Kohen Kook, wrote approvingly of the early twentieth-century theory of *Völkerpsychologie* (psychology of race and ethnicity).[45] Generally speaking, Zionism represents the strongest influence of a modern ideology on both modern Kabbalah and its research. Besides the very large number of texts penned by Kook and his disciples, more of which are being published on an annual basis, there is a vast and ever increasing body of writing on this figure, which I cannot do justice to here. This being said, one must note that there are few explicit studies of Kook's psychology, and especially of his theory of the soul and heart. In the following discussion, I wish to reformulate my earlier analyses of Kook, firstly in order to relate them explicitly to our topic, secondly in order to acknowledge several important studies published since my own monograph on twentieth-century Kabbalah was completed, and most importantly, in order to integrate texts published in recent years.[46]

In my earlier book, *The Chosen Will Become Herds*, I interpreted Kook's writings according to the following general principles, all of which have been confirmed by recently published texts and studies. Firstly, his theories almost always express his personal mystical, as well as poetic, experience, which partly accounts for the centrality of psychology in his work. Secondly, despite this salience, psychology is subordinated to national mysticism. Thirdly, as in the case of Luzzatto, Kook cannot be studied in isolation, but should be seen as part of an interactive and ongoing circle, as posited originally by Dov Schwartz and now strongly argued also by his student Uriel Barak. Finally, Kook, as a practicing Kabbalist, should be seen within the tradition of modern Kabbalah, and especially that of Luzzatto and its Lithuanian reception.[47]

Shlomo Fischer, in his important discussion of the Romantic elements of Kook's thought, has described it as "expressivist." He has parsed this characterization into several "core idea-patterns," one of which is "embodiment" of the spiritual in the material, another being "expression," or the unfolding of the subject from within. In this context, he describes the Kookian notion of the "inner will" of creation that realizes its true nature by returning to the divine source. This cosmic movement dialectically complements that of embodiment. However, this scheme is not merely metaphysical, but immediately translates into national terms. As Fischer correctly summarizes this aspect of Kook's thought, "The individual realizes his authentic self by identifying with the 'universal generalness' or the general will of the collective-cosmic entities outside of him: the Jewish People, humankind, or the cosmos." Although there are various strands within Kook's own corpus and subsequently in his school, each emphasizing one of these entities, again following Barak I believe that the national collective was the most central for him.[48]

Fischer has emphasized the striking similarity between this approach and expressivist Romanticism with regard to holistic-organic integration with nature. Through relating this insight to our topic, I wish to reformulate and actually reinforce Fischer's argument: Kook's theories, as well as his personal practice (which Fischer does not greatly discuss) should be seen as focusing on the integration of the individual and national soul, which dialectically realizes and expresses the authentic nature of both. In other words, Kook's psychology can be described as naturalistic national mysticism. As I have suggested elsewhere in a more preliminary fashion, his privileging of the natural volition of the soul is partly responsible for his tolerance for secularism as well as his own anomian and even antinomian tendencies.[49]

At the same time, one must correct the tendency found in Fischer's study as well as my own earlier work towards overemphasizing these non-nomian implications. Kook's approach, in a characteristically dialectical manner, contains numerous controls and restraints to the freedom of self-expression, individual or national. As Yehudah Mirsky has briefly noted, the influence of the early modern Maharal of Prague precludes a completely naturalistic approach, as this earlier thinker developed a strongly antinaturalistic thought. More generally, Kook as a leading halakhist, was inherently inhibited from giving full rein to his expressivist inclinations.[50]

An explicit formulation of this dialectic is found in a very late and somewhat overlooked essay, where Kook writes of the voice of God, which calls in the depth of the soul, and manifests in the heart in two ways: the voice of the natural psychic desire for the closeness of God and the voice which refines and purifies this desire. The "great giants" of the Jewish people bring vitality to the soul of Man and especially the soul of Israel precisely by joining these two voices in their hearts. Such a soul was that of Maimonides (the official subject of the essay), and one presumes that Kook saw himself as belonging to this exalted company. Be that as it may, this source clearly expresses the need to balance the natural desire of the soul through a process of critical refinement.[51]

Although I shall soon focus on newly published texts, I wish to illustrate the approach formulated here through translations of a dozen of many better known passages from the canonical works edited by Kook's disciples, which will amply demonstrate the complete centrality of the soul and heart in his mystical life and thought. The first of these has been cited and translated by Fischer, yet not fully analyzed, certainly not in the terms employed here:

Israel as a singular nation is blessed in the profundity of its sanctity, and its divine aspiration influences the entire circumference of the entire range of peoples; to refine the national soul of every people, and in its power, to bring them closer to a more exalted and noble rank.

In other words, the national soul of the Jewish people is distinguished by the power of influencing that of other nations, thus establishing a clear hierarchy of influence, which accounts for Kook's rejection of absorption of non-Jewish culture, as I have shown elsewhere. Generally speaking, Fischer's emphasis on national embodiment, though correct in and of itself, has led him to overlook, like most other scholars, the centrality of the soul in Kook's thought.[52]

A second well-known text refers to prayer, as one of Kook's central mystical practices:

The constant prayer of the *neshama* always strives to emerge from concealment to disclosure, to expand in all of the life powers of the *ruah* and *nefesh* . . . so that we find that the work of the entire Torah and its wisdom is the constant revelation of the hidden prayer of the soul . . . prayer cannot be in its correct form except through the thought that the soul really constantly prays . . . at the time of prayer in practice the constant soulful prayer is openly revealed.[53]

In this slightly anomian formulation, prayer as a concrete practice is a secondary expression of the deeper movement of the yearning of the soul. Similarly, in a text published in *Orot ha-Teshuva*, the edited collection of his writings on repentance, Kook describes repentance as being present at all times, even during sin, in the soul and heart, the "most healthy sensation" of the psyche, in which the healthy soul feels the greatest natural pleasure.[54] In a vision, rare in the canonical corpus of texts published by members of his school, he describes the salvation that the soul experiences even through the mere thought of repentance, and its complete redemption when it realizes this potential. This is a clear description of the individual redemption of the soul (reminiscent of the internalized messianism of the Hasidim mentioned in chapter 3).

However, one should not think that for this thinker the understanding of external action as an unfolding of psychic desire is merely an individual phenomenon. As we find elsewhere in *Orot ha-Teshuva*, the repentance of the individual soul emerges from a depth in which it is indistinguishable from the whole.[55] The interplay of the individual and national process of *teshuva* as redemption of the soul is clearly described in another passage from *Orot ha-Teshuva*, discussing the *anima mundi*. Passages such as this reflect the near-final triumph of the model of the divinity of the soul in later modernity:

When one forgets the essence of the selfful soul (*neshama 'atzmit*), when one ignores looking at the core (*tokhiut*) of one's inner life, then all becomes confused and doubtful . . . and the main repentance, which immediately lights up the darknesses, is that Man should return to himself, to the root of his soul, and immediately return to God, the soul of souls . . . and this matter holds for individuals, an entire people, all of humanity, and the rectification of the entire cosmos . . . and this is the secret of the light of the Messiah, the manifestation of the soul of the world.[56]

Indeed Kook's national views, both political and cultural, which have greatly preoccupied scholarship in Israel, should be interpreted mainly by means of this psychic key. The very superiority of the Jewish people, the cornerstone of these ideas, is explicitly described in psychic terms:

From the point of view of the virtuous individuals (*yehidei ha-segula*), we know no difference between nations . . . but what we speak in praise of the congregation of Israel (*knesset yisra'el*) as a whole refers to the matter of the divine virtue (*segula ha-'elohit*) found in the soul of the nation as a whole.[57]

A further and central implication of the distinction between the national and individual soul is that in other nations the former is connected directly to the divine soul, while for the Jews the national soul is the direct source of the individual soul, the medium of connection being the commandments. Kook's famous tolerance for secular Jews should be ascribed to his visionary experience of the light of their soul, as he hints in a messianic-mystical passage on the natural merits of the Jewish nation, containing a rare combination of visual and olfactory experience:

We are refined and filled [with] the Holy Spirit, sparks of the light of the Messiah enter our soul . . . and whoever has within him the pure odor of the fragrance of the paradise of the Messiah sees no debit in anyone of Israel, and his love for each one of Israel is infinitely great. He beholds the great light in their soul, the virtue (*segula*) of their glory and the brightness of repentance that hovers over them always.[58]

The rarity of those vouchsafed with such experiences led Kook to develop a theory of the Kabbalistic vanguard entrusted with perceiving and thus guiding the national soul. In a letter of guidance sent from abroad to a leading member of his elite circle, the Jerusalemite Kabbalist R. Ya'aqov Moshe Harlap, Kook wrote:

[. . .] The exaltedness or baseness of the movement of salvation depends on the depth of the holy-thought of the nation, which is revealed by its remnants, who bear the general thought of the soul of Israel, the general thought that is flourishing in the souls of the thinkers . . . it itself prepares for redemption, it itself brings the spirit of the king, the Messiah . . . and these sons of the Torah in its inner soul, their entire character is dedicated and connected and dependent on the soul of the Torah . . . but to prepare the hearts for such a supreme and encompassing vision of salvation, which shall up-lift nature itself from its fall, and crown all the worlds, all the *nefashot* and *ruhot* and *neshamot*, which have been born and which shall be created and born in the future, this salvation shall come from the light of Israel, which shall shine from the light of the supernal Torah, from a regular study of the secrets of Torah.[59]

The importance of this letter lies in its positioning of the role of the Kabbalist within this cosmic vision. Thus, the second part of the letter, which I cannot discuss here, provides a technical Kabbalistic exegesis of the place of the secular ideal in the Lurianic system. It is precisely because the holiness of the nation is hidden in its soul-depths that its manifestations in Zionist political and cultural processes can be perceived only by Kook and his close associates. The counterpart consists of the anti-Zionist Kabbalists and scholars, who he regarded as failing to grasp this connection. In his prophetic self-perception, he saw his circle as seeing through the secular façade of Zionism to its eventual return to its religious sources:

The settlement in the Land of Israel should develop, the national building be built, from within it a great spirit will blow, the soul of the nation will awaken in revival, from the depth of its nature it shall recognize all of its essence . . . the softness and withering of power, which rules now delays the living move of the practical commandments and the tie of faith in the divine from manifesting . . . but the inner power will break out . . . and this natural character will bring the great repentance . . . an inner repentance flowing from the depth of truth in the living light of the soul. There is no cause for distress at the currents of the stormy natural national spirit.[60]

Indeed, the messianic process as such is described by Kook as the transformation of the secular and the bodily into the holy and the soulful:

The light of the Messiah illuminates the entire world, transforms the entire creation to the radiance of Torah. We are called from the depths of our soul to feel this greatness, even now when it sends out but tiny lines of light. We must immediately grasp the measure of the great radiance, which gradually seeps in from the light of redemption, even at the beginning of its minor manifestation. And the quality is the appearance of the Torah in the light of the entire world, the manifestation of the holy in the light of all of the profane, the appearance of the refined spirituality amidst all of materiality, the appearance of the psyche (*nefesh*) in all of the flesh.[61]

This internalizing view of the processes of renewal of Jewish nationhood extended to numerous specific interpretations of social and cultural processes. To cite but one example, in a letter from his Jaffa period discussing the Zionist "revival" of the Hebrew language, Kook writes, "The very natural soul itself, whose waves break on the heart of all the good ones of our nation . . . forces us to revive our language together with the revival of our people and land."[62]

I now wish to turn to several previously esoteric texts recently published, which strongly reinforce the thesis presented here. These are derived from Kook's personal diaries, which reflect the increasingly autobiographical tendency of modern Kabbalists. The first of these appears in one of the rare collections of personal writing during his last period (1929–35):

All is ruined in Man when his natural desire for exaltedness and holiness is withered inside him. The entire foundation of great structures, of the worlds of emanation in the soul of Man, should be naturally imprinted (*tavua'*) on the basis of the natural desire of the soul, which never ceases to yearn for the ultimate good, which is treasured within all aspirations of exaltedness and holiness.[63]

Although there are some echoes of Mussar thinking here (as in the stress on *romemut* or "exaltedness"), this entry is clearly imprinted with Kook's original thought, which stresses the natural and ceaseless positive desire of the soul and attributes cultural decline to repression of this desire.[64] A more technically Kabbalistic text from his early period in Jerusalem equates the "growing" of the soul, a form of soul-making, with the theme of the *tzelem*:

When the divine image (*tzelem elohim*) is revealed in Man then is also revealed in him the matching (*hat'ama*), the twinhood (*to'emiut*), of Man in his higher spiritual soul with the divine greatness. And the more the divine matter (*ha-'inyan ha-'elohi*)

97

increases greatness in him, and shines on his inner *tzelem*, thus the soul also grows in its inwardness and is filled with life.

It is striking that this evocative passage fluidly blends rabbinic views of the divine image, technical Lurianic phraseology, personal poetics, and the above-mentioned premodern mystical psychology, which greatly influenced Kook and his circle; That of R. Yehuda Halevi and his use of the Arabic term "divine decree" (or order, or matter, *'amr ilahi*), also alluded to in the discussion of *segula* above to describe the superiority of the Jewish soul. In terms of Kook's personal experience of the process of writing, which I have discussed at length in the past, it is interesting that the next entry elaborates on the ineffable "divine shining," for which one's soul prepares several "small branches" that then become entire libraries.[65]

It must be stressed in the face of various scholarly descriptions that Kook's statements are not merely poetical, Kabbalistic, or ideological. Rather they express his intimate experience as a practicing mystic. Some selected passages from recently released material should suffice to demonstrate this crucial point. In the first of these, he writes,

The soul finds its power-increasers and power-reducers, through its self-sensing. Sometimes we will sin greatly if we oppress our noble spirit by burdening it with studies and images that in themselves are good and holy but do not suit one's situation in a given hour. And we need to constantly discern what the suitable channel (*tzinor*) is for the exact time and event, for it to pour the sap of life into our yearning soul.[66]

In existential terms that somewhat recall formulations found in the Izbiche-Radzin corpus, Kook is in effect criticizing the contemporary heteronomic religious culture, opposing it to attunement to existential situation, as the primary means of sensitivity to the needs of the individual soul. This can be described as a form of "situation ethics," similar to later moves in the Christian world.[67] It is striking that a few passages later, in the same vein, he contrasts the "psychic discoveries that reveal the courage and purity of the soul" (perhaps a reference to Nietzsche) that emanate from the Holy Spirit, with those that reveal the "weakness and ugliness of life" (a possible reference to Freudian theory), which dialectically enable the refinement of repentance.[68]

At this point one should consider the relationship between Kook's psychological theory and that of the Lithuanian Mussar movement (which he went on record to support in the face of some criticisms in its locale). Mirsky has significantly advanced the diachronical study of

Kook's thought by examining in depth his early period—before his immigration to the Land of Israel. In doing so, he placed Kook within the context of the strong Jewish centers of learning in the Baltic states. Mirsky correctly described Kook as responding to both the Mussar movement as well as the Haskalah, which gained momentum in this area in the fin-de-siècle. In this context, Mirsky provides a thoughtful close reading of Kook's own Mussar work, *Mussar Avikha*.

However, I differ from Mirsky in pinpointing the precise point of Kook's difference with Mussar. Kook describes the emotionally intense reading of Mussar texts recommended by Lipkin (with the end result of influencing the unconscious mind) as "the rousing of the heart to storms" and "the soul's ecstasies." However, although this method "rouses the forces of the soul a bit," it has a merely passing effect. Mirsky's interpretation is that Kook provides as an alternative the writing of Mussar texts, such as his own, that will challenge the intellect as well as nourish the soul. However, based on the original text, only part of which is naturally cited by Mirsky, my own interpretation is that Kook assigns emotional awakening to prayer while Mussar study, like all study, should be accompanied by calm. In other words, he differed with Mussar on the desired construction of emotion.[69]

Mirsky goes on to oppose the Kookian microcosmic and macrocosmic dialectic of constriction and expansion of the soul-as-self with the "post-Salanter" "repression of the self" within the Mussar movement. I believe that the texts cited in the previous chapter show that this binary opposition (like most of its kind) does not capture the full complexity of the issue, and thus one must search for a far more subtle difference between Kook and the Mussar school, especially Leibovitz, through perusing later, and thus more developed, discussions by the former.[70]

Although my intention here is not to further develop the diachronic reading of Kook, which would also entail some form of psychobiography, I do wish to take Mirsky's move further and suggest that Kook, who spent several years in Europe during the First World War, did not disconnect from his intellectual origins after his move to the Land of Israel. To mention but one example, his predecessor in the rabbinate of Jaffa was R. Naftali Hertz ha-Levi, who maintained strong ties with R. Shlomo Elyashiv, with whom Kook also studied, just like certain Mussar teachers. A far more significant fact is that in 1927 a large Mussar Yeshiva moved to Hebron near Jerusalem, headed by none less than the "old man" of Solobodka, R. Nathan Tzevi Finkel, whom Kook visited and whose students visited him! As I hope to show elsewhere, Finkel's view of the greatness and exaltedness of man goes far beyond a stress on dignity and approaches an expressivist and expansive view of the self. In other words, the prevailing tendency in Israeli scholarship to study Kook in an entirely Zionist context is more a reflection on the nationalist agenda of such studies than on their illustrious subject.

From this point of view, Kook's later writings, written in periods not covered in Mirsky's work, reflect his response to the third generation of the Mussar world. Don Seeman has briefly suggested that an important passage on natural morality by Kook should be read in light of a discussion by Leibovitz. This insight should be extended as follows: Kook's psychological writing should be seen as a complex critique of Mussar, in which Kook adopts certain elements of Leibovitz's thought, while clearly rejecting others, as part of his general tendency to balance between various extremes. Like his famous contemporary, R. Avraham Yesha'yahu Karelitz (the "Hazon Ish"), Kook warned against the excessive introspection and cultivation of fear of God on the part of the adherents of Mussar, writing in the Jaffa period that "the moral inclination (*ha-netiah ha-mussarit*) . . . when it greatly increases in the heart of Man, can sometimes become a kind of illness, which constantly pecks at the inwardness of emotions, and finds faults . . . and threatens Man too much, and becomes a dividing partition between him and the light of God."[71]

In a parallel text from his final years, Kook opposes the detailed examination of the *middot* (as conducted in the Mussar school) to the uplifting of the soul in the light of God, automatically uplifting the *middot* as well. Although he acknowledges the need for careful observation of the details of the latter, "the main power of purity" emanates from the second path, which is obviously his own. It is possible that Kook attributed the superiority of his path to the prophetic insight that he attained by moving to the Land of Israel. More generally speaking, Kook's nationalist psychology stands in clear opposition to Leibovitz's apolitical and strongly individualistic thought. Finally, his writing, especially in the private and recently released works, is far more openly Kabbalistic than any Mussar text.[72]

I wish to conclude this somewhat lengthy discussion of Kook by briefly describing the recent and current embellishments of naturalistic national mysticism in the third generation of the mystical vanguard established by him (as the second generation has been quite thoroughly covered by Barak). Foremost in this context is R. Yehoshua' Zuckerman. A central figure in the Har ha-Mor faction (which is most devoted to continuing Kook's path among the multiple factions splitting Religious Zionism today), Zuckerman has written little. However, based on the numerous and widely circulated recordings of his highly influential classes, one can conclude that the central aspect of his teaching is the naturalness of the Torah, interpreted in national mystical terms.[73]

In terms of writing, the most prolific author in this circle is R. Tzevi Yisra'el Tau of Har ha-Mor Yeshiva in Jerusalem, who regards himself as preserving the purity of the Kookian vision. This thinker has been briefly surveyed by Fischer and will be discussed in detail in a forthcoming dissertation by Udi Abromovitz, so that I shall merely highlight his cultural and political applications of the Kookian views of the national soul. Generally speaking, Tau's texts combine a close, if at times strong, reading of numerous Kookian texts, which glosses over their mystical-Kabbalistic aspects, aiming rather, in the tradition of his own teacher, R. Tzevi Yehuda ha-Kohen Kook, at contemporary and ideological applications.[74]

Tau's writing, dialectical and polemical in nature, has two protagonists. One is universalistic secular culture, which he regards as corrupting the souls of the Israelis, and especially the youth. In one place, he describes secular popular culture and media as leading to a forgetting of the divine soul and heart of the nation through imitation of the mores of other nations. In a wider sense, he ascribes the "national sadness," or the current social and cultural crisis in Israel, to this forgetting, while the very escape to popular entertainment is a manifestation of this sadness.

Interestingly for Jewish studies scholars, Tau accuses academic teaching in this field of impressing upon students knowledge that is alien to their souls, as opposed to the Kookian method, which engages the soul of the students so much as to give birth to a "new spirit" in them.[75] A related opposition is that between the "purity of heart" required in order to critically engage the canonical Jewish texts and the career-oriented psychic constitution of the academic critics, who project their own negative *middot* on the texts under the guise of objectivity. He goes on to say that secular psychology can by no means provide a resource for the power of the pure heart, as the universities are not at all oriented towards ethical development.

At the same time, Tau opposes his Haredi and right-wing contemporaries who speak ill of the secular Jews as such, as well as the political leadership of the nation. He insists on the greatness of the "soulful light" of the generation, and that the negative phenomena that he himself diagnoses are dialectical expressions of this very greatness, the external seemingly masking but actually revealing the internal. Tellingly, at times he refers to the soul of the generation as "new." It is thus the very power of the souls of the Israelis of today that causes such anguish when its proper and full manifestation is delayed. I believe that the phrase "psychic pain," coined by the Kleinian psychoanalyst Betty Joseph to describe similar states in individual psychology, is appropriate here.[76]

However, in Tau's dialectic, this acute crisis will cut through superficial forms of national self-perception and restore Israel to recognition of its "supernal Self." The more the light of the soul draws closer to its birth, the rejection of impoverished forms of nationalism will grow, as manifested in the increase of post-Zionist tendencies. Therefore, in a statement revealing his own self-consciousness, he writes that those who perceive and understand the soul of the nation strongly feel its pain at this junction. However, in a radical reversal, he goes so far as to say that one should rejoice in the current sadness more than in the joy of the establishment of the state, for the latter event was "a small thing," while the sadness today is an expression of the "great soul inside us," a preliminary message from the greatness of the soul due to break out.[77]

Conclusion

The close connections between the psychological and the political found most prominently in Tau's writings, as those discussed throughout this section and indeed the entire chapter, reflect the rise of the political in modern Kabbalah. As I have suggested elsewhere, the political model of power is its unique contribution to the diverse models of power found in earlier period (and discussed in my first book, on power in premodern and very early Kabbalah). Following our discussion in chapter 1, one can place the development of this model in the context of the increasing destabilization of Jewish existence in the modern period, as part of the general phenomena of what Zygmunt Bauman has termed "fluid modernity." In other words, the more the violence of modernity impacted on the Jewish worlds (a major turning point being the unprecedented scope and cruelty of the 1648–49 massacres in Poland), the more Kabbalists needed to address the political.[78]

The circle of R. Avraham Yitzhaq Kook, like the other recent and contemporary streams to be discussed in the next chapter, contended with the need to relate the often virtual, at times otherworldly, forms of political imagination developed in modern Kabbalah with the growing concretization of spiritual realities called for by the return to the Holy Land. Here the thought of Yaron Ezrahi is highly pertinent. Following Vico, Ezrahi underscores the foundational role of the imagination in the formation of modern politics. In doing so, he points at the great importance of the imagination of the soul as the "inner core" of the concrete individual self. As he argues, the specifically modern ideas of the soul were part of a process that "enabled poetry and art to increasingly influence the imaginaries of modern individualism in the sociopolitical context." Ezrahi himself, kindly responding to my earlier writing, describes Kabbalist imaginaries as generating resources from which later political imaginaries could draw. However, as he stresses, the dangers of the gap between the fantasies of power of a powerless-stateless minority and the constraints of actual political experience can be seen in "the contemporary role of the Jewish political imagination in Israeli politics." In this context, he alludes to the complex relationship between the individualizing impetus entailed in the stress on the power of the righteous (the psychological aspects of which were discussed in chapter 3), and its troubling implications for the egalitarian imagination of democratic societies. The dangers evoked by Ezrahi will be addressed now in chapter 5 (especially in my discussion of R. Yitzchak Ginsburgh), while one of the comparative questions raised by our discussion of twentieth-century national mystical psychology will be addressed in chapter 6.[79]

FIVE

The Soul and the Heart in Twentieth-Century Kabbalah

The Kabbalistic Social Psychology of R. Yehuda L. ha-Levi Ashlag

Following a distinction developed in an article of mine, the very structure of this chapter is founded on the distinction between continuous forms of recent and current Kabbalah, namely those maintaining a strong connection to what I term "classical" Kabbalah, or earlier forms of modern Kabbalah, and discontinuous forms, explicitly or implicitly weakening this connection. Thus, I am here updating and expanding the research expressed in my monograph *The Chosen Will Become Herds: Studies in Twentieth-Century Kabbalah*, which included a chapter on psychology. The very need to update this recent book (published in its Hebrew and English editions in 2005 and 2009 respectively) as we move into a new century reflects the accelerating proliferation of contemporary Kabbalistic discourse.

In my article, I defined continuous Kabbalah using the following six interrelated criteria: relationship, in exegesis as well as in self-modeling on biography, to the classical modern Kabbalists; connection to other branches of traditional Jewish life and learning; conversely, the disengagement from non-Jewish discourse (reflecting the nationalization of modern Kabbalah); strong emphasis on theurgical practice related to the traditional liturgy; a marked tendency towards esotericism; and a limited, usually negative response to current historical events. Although some of these characteristics are also true of premodern Kabbalah, it is usually classical modern Kabbalah, especially the Safedian and eighteenth-century writings, that recent or current Kabbalah breaks with or develops. Simply put, discontinuous Kabbalah (to some extent including the Kook circle) weakens or opposes some or all of these tendencies. I also suggested utilizing this distinction in the study of other mystical traditions. As we are speaking of a fluid combination of elements, not all of which need to be present simultaneously, this is not a binary distinction, of the kind I as a rule avoid, but rather a spectrum.[1]

Like the central distinction between premodern and modern Kabbalah that lies in the heart of this book, my distinction between continuous and discontinuous forms of late modern Kabbalah is part of a break theory. My claims as to the repression of the religious sources of twentieth-century psychology constitute a more complex example of this form of analysis. All reflect my Foucauldian predilection for locating fissures, dislocations, and displacements, rather than assuming smoother processes that proceed heedless of the turbulence of history.

One should contrast this account to Peter Homans' highly creative interpretation of the relationship between twentieth-century psychology and religious thought. Homans situates this issue within the context of a long-term process (going back to the seventeenth century and even earlier) of mourning over lost religious symbols and the social cohesion they enabled. The most poignant representation of this atmosphere in popular culture is REM's 1991 song "Losing My Religion." Parsons, in expanding Homans' thesis towards the contemporary situation, describes "spiritual" or "unchurched" mysticism as what I would term a discontinuous project of mourning for traditional forms of mysticism. Parsons then extends this move to include certain elements in the academic study of mysticism. The theoretical power of Homans' argument is that he joins Weberian social analysis, such as a powerful critique of standard secularization theory, with a detailed exploration of the psychical processes of the founders of psychoanalysis and especially their search for healing for their alienation from their religious traditions. As Homans argues, while these figures adopted a break theory, they "failed to recognize how tightly the hand of the past continued to grip" their lives. Homans' theoretical joining itself is a psychoanalytical move, drawing on Winnicot's theory of transitional space, in this case between the social and the psychological.[2]

If one were to follow Homans (as well as writers such as Eigen, clearly influenced by Kabbalah, yet largely detached from both is original texts and daily practice), one could read the forms of discontinuous Kabbalah discussed below as a manifestation of "mourning religion." Indeed, some of the scholarship critiqued throughout for reinterpreting Kabbalistic texts in order to suit contemporary imperatives (also in the very choice to favor discontinuous streams) can be seen as a third manifestation of the same process. However, one should stress one crucial difference between the figures described by Homans, or even later thinkers such as Eigen, and both discontinuous Kabbalists and their adherents in academia. While Homans' theory, befitting the well-known link between mourning and melancholy, stresses loss (even if joined by creativity), absence, and disenchantment, discontinuous Kabbalah is suffused with the optimism of messianic fervor.

Even when contemporary society is roundly critiqued in such texts, it is because its critics envision the imminent dawning of utopia. Moments of acute loss, such as the death of the seventh rebbe of Habad, R. Menahem Mendel Schneerson, were almost instantly overcome, in broad Habad circles, by messianic responses that render the absent even more strongly present. Psychoanalytically speaking, the appearance of discontinuous Kabbalah, together with substantial elements in the Zionist ideology with which it is at times allied, can be interpreted as denial of the massive losses incurred by the Jewish people throughout the twentieth century, including the displacements and pogroms around the First World War, soon overshadowed by the Holocaust, the subsequent displacement of Middle Eastern Jewry as result of the Arab-Israeli conflict, and the victims caused by the conflict itself. In this sense, it is a manifestation of "inability to mourn," or as Homans (following Winnicot) parces it, denial of loss and inability to be depressed.[3]

Thus, it is not surprising that Kabbalah is increasingly hailed today as a form of positive psychology (critiqued in chapter 1), as in highly popular seminars by R. Laibl Wolf (who is affiliated with Habad). One can easily trace earlier similar processes in the Christian world. The most striking example is the 1952 classic *The Power of Positive Thinking*, whose author, Norman Vincent Peale, was a minister. Peale began to propagate his approach in highly popular radio talks in the 1930s, against the backdrop of the Great Depression and the looming threat of war. At the same time, one should note that there was a strong Jewish branch of New Thought, the immediate ancestor of positive psychology, known as the Society for Jewish Science.[4]

I shall devote the first part of this chapter to these highly popular discontinuous streams, yet around half of it shall be reserved for continuous forms of contemporary Kabbalah. It should be clear from my comments above that the latter are far more important from the point of view of text-centered scholarship. These manifestations are mostly to be found in the astoundingly text-centered Haredi (so-called ultra-Orthodox) world. The depth of the continuity of Haredi discourse with the classic age of Jewish modernity has recently been demonstrated in a panoramic manner by Sorotzkin.[5] This being said, I wish to commence the current chapter with a study of the place of the soul in a highly discontinuous form of Kabbalah, as it is not only the most popular of schools of twentieth- and twenty-first-century Kabbalah, but also the most psychological—the school founded by in Jerusalem in 1921 by R. Yehuda L. ha-Levi Ashlag (1885–1954). One should add that this form of Kabbalah is currently being rehabilitated by certain continuous Kabbalists, at the cost of obscuring its originality.

Already in my above-mentioned monograph, I claimed that the international appeal of Ashlagian Kabbalah derives from its favoring the psychological over the national, and I might add here, the nomian. There, I summarized Ashlagian psychology as a description of the strife between two psychic powers—egoism and altruism, or the will to receive and to influence (lehashpia'), including a method of transforming the former into the latter. Thus (here thinking beyond my earlier writing) this is essentially a social psychology, focused on interpersonal relationships. As the school became more institutionalized, the arena for these interrelationships was none other than the circle itself. An important issue that I cannot go into here is the influence of extra-Jewish sources on Ashlag's psychology. However, it seems rather clear that the very terms "will to receive" and "will to influence" respond to Nietzsche's "will to power" as well as its own sources in Schopenhauer.[6]

The most explicit discussions of modern psychology appear in Ashlag's articles that also contain important statements of Kabbalistic self-identity. The first text from this corpus examines the question of "spirituality," which is often adjacent to that of the psyche. He critiques what he describes as the philosophical view of spirituality as greatly divergent from materiality, and yet mysteriously also its source. He then states that as the philosophers lack direct experience of spirituality, it can be apprehended and described only by the true Kabbalists. From their point of view, spirituality is a bodiless, pure power, identical with the aspect known as "vessels" in classical Kabbalah, to be carefully distinguished from the "lights," as the latter are identical with the utterly indescribable essence of the divine.

He then goes on to make the surprising and somewhat discontinuous claim that the Kabbalistic texts do not really describe the lights, but merely the manner in which the vessels are impacted by them. In other words, we are dealing with interactions rather than with substances. This impactedness (*hitpa'alut*) is the "form" of the vessel, while the "immaterial power" of spirituality is, confusingly, its "matter." However, love of God, which is born from the "gift" of this matter, is itself abstracted from any concrete gift and thus is form without matter. In the experience of love, the gift itself is erased from the heart, just as the attention expressed in a material gift is of far greater significance than any object.

Thus, love is born of the gift, yet greatly transcends it (as part of the general imperative of going beyond selfish receiving). This love can be studied only by "the Kabbalah of forms," the more important part of this wisdom and not by "philosophy of forms," presumably Platonic idealism. I cannot dwell on the rich echoes of this text in the current theology of the gift (addressed within Kabbalah studies in a tour de force by Wolfson), as I wish to follow the dialectical unfolding of Ashlag's own theory.[7]

The latter goes on to overlap this structure with the four worlds theory, so that the Kabbalah of forms is identical with the world of creation and the dialectical resolution of this entire problematic takes place in the world of emanation, in which love is reunited with the gift of the light, or "matter" (as the will to receive, after all, needs to be transcended rather than negated). I believe that one should interpret all mentions of the light as referring to the interaction of the light with the vessel and the latter's impactedness (in light of the opening caution). At this point, Ashlag begins to unravel the confusion created by his idiosyncratic terminology by disclosing that the seemingly immaterial spiritual power is truly "matter," although it is not apprehended by the senses. The semiscientific simile that he employs is that of hydrogen and oxygen, that cannot be sensed, yet in their interaction become accessible to the senses as water.

Thus (here recalling the text from Dessler, probably influenced by Ashlag), the pure power that is the greater part of the material, may yet be discovered by science, just like the recent (at the time of his writing this) discovery of the chemical elements. This is the reason for rejection of idealistic philosophy that barely catches up with the march of scientific discovery. In contradistinction, the clear and direct perception of the Kabbalists leads to the conclusion that the perception of humans, as material entities, is always of a composite of form and matter, or of the will to receive (and, I would again add, to be affected by receiving) and what is actually received.

Thus, Ashlag continues, the spiritual and the material are as "two drops of water," except that the spiritual is "spiritual matter" and the material is "material matter." In my view, this conclusion should be seen in the context of his oft-mentioned attraction to Marxist dialectical materialism that also informed his theory of altruism. Nonetheless, when he goes on to praise the destruction of idealistic philosophy by "materialistic psychology," and proclaim the indebtedness of Kabbalah to this psychology, I believe that he is actually referring to Freudian theory.[8]

Although the rest of the text, describing "philosophical theology" as a demonic impostor displacing the exiled wisdom of Kabbalah which takes twenty or thirty years of study to grasp, is fascinating, I shall conclude by quoting his final and amazing statement that "there has not been a salvation for Israel like the time when materialistic psychology was disclosed and dealt a devastating blow to philosophical theology," thus paving the way for the return of true Kabbalah from its exile. I think that the firm placement of this article in the discourse of the twentieth century (scientific, philosophical, and especially psychological), rather than that of the Kabbalistic tradition, sidestepped through the trope of disruption of transmission in exile, cannot be denied, especially upon reading this last section.[9]

Seemingly, Ashlag's extensive interpretative corpus, including detailed exegesis of both premodern and modern classics, should show a greater degree of continuity than his articles. However, the degree to which the Ashlagian school breaks with the main body of modern Kabbalah is evidenced precisely there, in the former's sharp criticism of the doctrine of one of its paragons—Shar'abi, found in his *Beit Sha'ar ha-Kavvanot*, a commentary on the Lurianic intentions of prayer overlooked in the rapidly expanding scholarship on Ashlag. The latter rejects local commentaries by Shar'abi on a Lurianic text as extremely forced, disproves the textual supports that the latter adduces for certain of his tenets, and expresses his wonder at others, but more generally states that the entire three-dimensional structure of Shar'abi's system should have been provided with some kind of support from within the Lurianic corpus. In doing so, he overlooks the pressing question of the extent to which his own innovative theory can be reconciled with the Lurianic corpus.

More importantly for our specific concern, Ashlag goes on to say that the discussion of the soul-level of *yehida* in the Shar'abian *Hasdei David* (by R. David Majar) mixes the authentic Lurianic tradition (which Shar'abi himself confined to the transmission of Vital) with unreliable transmissions (that are similar to those of Menahem 'Azaria da Fano and other European traditions). Although the last critique seemingly frames Ashlag as "conservative," his sharp rejection of a highly authoritative form of modern Kabbalah signals his extremely independent self-awareness (which I have also discussed in the past). In light of this text, it may well be that he would not see Shar'abi's school as included among the "true Kabbalists" mentioned above.[10] Although I am disinclined to use the overly general adjective "fundamentalist," it is true that innovative modern readings are often cloaked in a purist rhetoric.

Discontinuous Kabbalah thus significantly predates the alleged move from modernity to postmodernity. Although this periodizing distinction has been employed by Boaz Huss, a central researcher of contemporary Kabbalah, I myself feel more comfortable with the position of Shmuel Noah Eisenstadt and others who hold that postmodernity is but a later form of modernity, thus contained within the theory of multiple modernities that guides my research.[11] This being said, the degree of discontinuity in the Ashlag school certainly accelerated in the second part of the twentieth century, after Ashlag's death, especially in the teachings of his son, R. Barukh Ashlag, and even more so in the current popular rendition by the latter's most influential student, Michael Laitman, who will be discussed anon.

R. Barukh Ashlag was central in transforming his father into what Foucault has termed a "founder of discourse," while downplaying the latter's sources. However, he still manifests imprints of classical Kabbalah, even if not always explicitly. While this is far from the only recent line of transmission and interpretation of R. Y. L. Ashlag's teachings, I choose to focus on it, as it is at the same time widespread and reasonably text-based, being at the very least somewhat continuous with the first generation of the school (while Laitman's school does not greatly consider parallels and influences, they made some steps towards comparison with the teachings of Kook, and certainly both R. Barukh Ashlag and Laitman offer numerous close readings of R. Y. L. Ashlag's texts themselves).[12]

Having begun to establish the discontinuous nature of R. Y. L. Ashlag's Kabbalah, I shall now continue with a sample from his exegetical writings, which are by far the greater part of his published oeuvre. It is important to briefly visit his commentary on the *Zohar*, *Ha-Sulam* ("the ladder"), for which he is known as *ba'al ha-sulam* ("author" or "owner" of the ladder). As Meir has shown, Ashlag was instrumental in developing the twentieth-century ideology of the centrality of the *Zohar* that is still prevalent in various academic as well as popular circles (though far less among Haredi Kabbalists). Ashlag reinterprets the premodern rabbinic-Zoharic myth of divine weeping (usually over the exile) in terms of the lower "branch" of human weeping, described as fundamentally interpersonal and related to the friction between the altruistic desire to give and love and the psychological screens or barriers that it encounters. This interpretation contains psychological riches that can be again compared to Joseph's description of psychic pain (and working through defenses against psychic change); however, it entirely covers up the force of the premodern narrative of divine pathos and Eros, as well as any national-historical dimension. In this sense, the already sharp divide between modern Kabbalah and its somewhat nebulous premodern roots is greatly accentuated.[13]

The way in which canonical texts, premodern and modern alike, are transformed into the uniform shape of Ashlagian Kabbalah marks the beginnings of twentieth-century discontinuity, setting this century apart within the much wider frame of modernity. As a result, the Ashlagian commentaries are studied within his school entirely within the framework of his thought and subsequent interpretation, almost denuded of any reference to the texts that Ashlag himself commented on and their wider textual and cultural context. This is apparent in the numerous and widespread writings of Laitman, which greatly emphasize the psychological, as indicated in their very titles (such as *The Point in the Heart: A Source of Delight for My Soul*).

I shall conclude here by turning to a recently published collection of very important statements on social psychology and its effect on the political arena of the mid-twentieth century. There, Ashlag makes strong claims that natural religion is the only cure for collective egotism, ingrained in the subconscious, claiming that Nazism could not have taken hold in a religious society and that it is the ultimate logic of socialism and democracy without religion, rather than an aberration specific to Germany. These texts contain strong messianic and rather antinomian statements, equating Ashlag's psychological doctrine of altruism with the messianic Torah, this in the context of an apocalyptic warning on the danger of a nuclear third world war if this new "law" is not accepted by humanity. As in the case of Kook's circle, when conjoined with external influences, messianism can certainly galvanize discontinuity.[14]

Popular Discontinuous Kabbalah

I am not greatly inclined to discuss neo-Kabbalah, which may be better termed "marketing Kabbalah," seeing it as part of the history of late capitalism rather than that of Jewish mysticism. However, one cannot entirely ignore the massive turn to psychology, and specifically the extensive employment of the word "soul" in this literature. Philip Berg, who studied briefly with a student of Ashlag (R. Yehuda Tzevi Brandwein) before establishing a famous empire of neo-Kabbalistic marketing and celebrity recruiting, devoted one of his early books to the "wheels of the soul" or reincarnation, and this tendency continues in the works of his sons and heirs. Again, psychologization has been an effective device in selling the Kabbalah to the non-Jewish world. Although the current diffusion (and hence dilution) of Ashlagian Kabbalah in the non-Jewish world is a seemingly natural progression due to its universalist nature, it still can be seen as internally discontinuous, as the original Kabbalah of Ashlag still contains elements of national psychology, as in the description of the Jews as the internal aspect of the world, and thus eligible to study the soul of the Torah or the Kabbalah (of course this view is reversed today, with the Jews being rather redefined as those studying in Kabbalah Centers).[15]

More generally speaking, the blend of psychology and "Judaism" and especially Kabbalah enjoys an increasingly broad appeal. Due to my focus on the soul, I shall just mention the more comparatively interesting out of many examples. Among them are the use of the Enneagram method in the Jewish context by Miriam Adahan and the so-called "Jewish psychology" of Yair Caspi, which is very similar to Eric Johnson's Protestant project, to be described in chapter 6. One should also mention the prominence of the heart and soul (in the sense of "experience" discussed in chapter 1) in the titles or contents of popular books and anthologies written by academics. All of these materials are mostly of quantitative sociological interest. However, once I shall join them with comparative findings, they support the following important insight of Peter Homans: "Popular psychology is most popular when it is blended with religion," and—I might add—especially with popular religion.[16]

In view of my discussion of Izbiche-Radzin doctrine in chapter 3, one should note the strongly antinomian interpretation in contemporary popular Kabbalah, and especially the Jewish Renewal movement. One of the founders of this movement, R. Zalman Schachter-Shalomi (1924–2014), offered an original interpretation of Hasidic psychology already in his doctoral dissertation. Despite his antinomian views, it is hard to regard Schachter-Shalomi as entirely discontinuous, due to his deep roots in the pre-Holocaust Hasidic world. However, one cannot say the same for the transformation of Leiner's ideas and other Hasidic teachings, blended with some Christian ideas, into a New Age–type "self-help" method by the controversial Marc (Mordekhai) Gafni, who was disowned by his former mentor, Schachter-Shalomi.[17]

It is important to note at the end of this deliberately brief section that together with such psychologistic readings of Kabbalistic sources, there are also some nonacademic, yet profound and continuous blends, of psychology and Jewish writing, including mystical writing. Most prominent among these is the teaching, oral and written, of Avivah Gottlieb-Zornberg, who joins deep readings of Midrashic and Hasidic texts (especially from Izbiche-Radzin) with psychoanalytic theory, as well as with psychological insights drawn from belles lettres. Although her work is clearly part of the wider and ongoing revolution of women's Torah learning, Gottlieb-Zornberg does not have an explicit feminist agenda and certainly not an apologetic agenda. As Gottlieb-Zornberg has an emerging generation of students, it is to be hoped that this far more learned discourse will eventually receive more attention than some of the others.[18]

The Discontinuous National Psychology of R. Itzchak Ginsburg

Continuous national psychology was discussed briefly in chapter 4 in the context of the Kook circle (roughly contemporaneous to that of Ashlag), which was rapidly transformed by the overwhelming effect of the Zionist revolution into a discontinuous form of Kabbalah and thus critiqued, at times sharply, by central Kabbalistic and Hasidic figures. Today, the main non-Haredi (in spite of their name) continuous form of spirituality and mysticism is the growing *haredi-le'umi* (ultraorthodox-National) stream that primarily continues the thought of Kook and his disciples, while mitigating its more radical implications in a process of "routinization of charisma." However, one should mention, following Fischer, the strong interest in psychological and poetical self-expression in the more modernistic religious-Zionist Yeshivas, often accompanied by the study of works such as Leiner's.[19]

In the ever-growing borderland between this group and the contemporary, rather mutated and thus post-Haredi (at least since the death of the last rebbe, R. Menahem Mendel Schneerson) Habad school, one finds the influential and highly prolific discourse, oral and written, of R. Yitzchak Ginsburgh (whom I briefly discussed in my book on the twentieth century). Though not greatly influenced by Kook or any other central writer on national psychology (such as Luzzatto or the Lithuanian

Kabbalists), Ginsburgh's extreme right-wing stances have accorded him some favor among *haredi-le'umi* circles disenchanted with Zionism, especially after the 2005 disengagement from Gaza (the latter event addressed in two of Ginsburgh's books, which incorporate debates with the Kook school, while also debating Haredi positions). Ginsburgh's distance from the Haredi approach to the Zionist state is reflected in his dubious reception in more continuous circles, including the more traditional of Habad Hasidim.[20]

Ginsburgh certainly cannot be seen as merely continuing Habad thought, (to note but one example, Ginsburgh does not extensively engage R. Shalom Dov Baer Schneerson, one of the two psychological masters that I have focused on, although talks branching off from the teachings of the latter can be found on the internet). Thus I shall not enter the question of the debt of his psychological theory to that of the seventh and last Habad rebbe, R. Menahem Mendel Schneerson, though it is undoubtedly considerable, as evidenced in Ginsburgh's recently published commentaries on some of the latter's talks. However, Schneerson's thought is far wider than its reception on the part of Ginsburgh, as it also relates to a large extent to the American experience (rather than Ginsburgh's Israeli interpretation that has been influenced by the West Bank settler movement just as much as it has influenced it).[21]

Ginsburgh delivered series of classes on several other Hasidic works, most notably on *Mei ha-Shiloah*. The evidence of Bratzlav Hasidism is especially apparent in his works reflecting, yet also enhancing, the ever-growing popularity of these texts in the liminal groups attracted to him.[22] He also has a multivolume commentary on the above-mentioned Shar'abian *Hasdei David*, which displays far less knowledge of Ottoman Kabbalah than is evident in the Haredi works to be discussed below. However, I have heard a testimony from one of his close students, according to which Ginsburgh's *hasagot* or mystical attainments are derived from his early training with Sephardic Kabbalists in Jerusalem. This joins a testimony that I have already cited and attempted to textually support as to his studies with the circle of R. Barukh Ashlag.[23]

In spite of all of these signs of apparent continuity, Huss is undoubtedly correct in asserting that Ginsburgh's writing betrays a strong affinity to the New Age discourse (despite a rhetoric of opposing it), as evidenced in his emphasis on psychology (including that of dating and marital sexuality) and, one might add, more recently parapsychology. Thus, his earlier writings and some of his later ones are qualitative Kabbalistic texts (for all of their reprehensible bigotry towards the non-Jewish world and especially the Palestinians), indeed at times so esoteric in style as to require a companion volume of commentary. However, some of the English-language works, as well as later Hebrew works edited by students (and often reflecting their own worldview), are closer to the merely quantitative "marketing Kabbalah" described above. Indeed, lately Ginsburgh's school has become the "dynamic corporation" that he himself describes, including the establishment of a "School of Jewish Psychology." Therefore, methodologically speaking, it is the earlier works, and verbatim transcriptions of recordings of early classes that will be most rewarding for researchers of Kabbalah who have not yet extensively addressed them for understandable reasons.[24]

Continuous Streams: Lithuanian Kabbalah

In moving to the central concern of the chapter, one should note at the outset that despite the constant proliferation described in my earlier studies of the "Haredi worlds," the Haredi community still maintains some self-conscious and deliberate coherence and can thus be still easily divided into a few main streams. The first of these, the "Lithuanian," has already been discussed to some extent in chapters 3 and 4, and is in any case the least explicitly mystical. However, one must note the increasing interest in the works of the Luzzatto circle, in this world and to a lesser extent outside it. R. Hayyim Friedlander, who was briefly mentioned in chapter 3, began the extensive project of publishing their works (continued today by his American-born associate R. Joseph Spinner of Sha'ar ha-Shamayim Yeshiva in Jerusalem) and included them in his Mussar talks. Elements of the psychology of Luzzatto are apparent not only in popular books such as that penned by Binyamin Efrati, but also in more interesting writings inspired by Luzzatto's works, such as *Adir bi-Melukha* by R. Avraham Ya'aqov Pritzky, which betrays influence of Ashlag and is laden with strong sexual imagery. Elsewhere I have discussed the entire shelf of Kabbalistically oriented supercommentaries on Luzzatto's *Mesilat Yesharim*, a true psychological classic in its own right.[25]

From the extensive literature, covered in my earlier discussion in Hebrew, I shall select but two further texts. The first, written by R. Avraham Tzevi Kluger, a controversial ex-student of R. Yitzhaq Me'ir Morgenstern (who will be discussed below), places the central modern Kabbalists in a Lurianic map of the levels of the soul. Kluger assigns Luzzatto to the level of *ruah* (or spirit), with Shar'abi occupying *nefesh*, Kremer the level of *neshama*, and the higher levels of *haya* and *yehida* assigned to the Besht. Recently, among more popular transcriptions of Kluger's talks, we can find a work, *Qarva el Nafshi*, devoted to the soul and the inner life and including an attack on the growing influence of Western psychotherapy in the Orthodox world.

The second was written by Nir Stern, a former dean of a Yeshiva, who for several years wrote subversive and profound critiques of the mainstream Haredi approach in his blog under the alias Nir'eh Likhora [it apparently seems] and has now moved out of the Haredi world in order to develop a form of existential psychotherapy. The core of his psychological approach, drawn from the teachings of Leibovitz, is respect for the "psychic forces" (*kohot ha-nefesh*); the only one of them that should be "killed" is that of "alienation . . . estrangement . . . guilt, self-hatred, and emotional blocks." This approach, which follows Leibovitz in seeing the Torah as a commentary on the soul, leads to a series of bold Halakhic conclusions. One of these, found in this specific article, is that there is no room of compulsory heterosexuality, as it "kills" the natural forces and vitality of the psyche. The distance between these two writers, neither of whom belongs to the Haredi mainstream, demonstrates the exciting ferment of ideas taking place in this world after the weakening of central authority and uniform ideology.[26]

The most explicitly Kabbalistic of recent and contemporary "Lithuanian" writers, consciously continuing the tradition of Kremer, is the American-born R. Israel Elijah Weintraub, whom I discussed in one of my articles on Haredi mysticism. There, I described his radical critique not only of Zionism (including its religious forms) but also of Haredi society itself, a critique that recently aroused the dismay of a central Religious-Zionist Rabbi, R. Aharon Lichtenstein, an heir of the Lithuanian-American Modern Orthodox leader R. Joseph B. Soloveitchik (who like Weintraub, studied with R. Yitzhaq Hutner). As many more of Weintraub's writings have now become available (including highly valuable detailed documentation of his mentoring in Kabbalah studies), this is a good opportunity to delve further into the work of the last of a tradition of deep Haredi critics of Zionism that includes the rebbe R. Yo'el Teitelbaum of Satmar (whose general approach has been admirably covered by Sorotzkin). For our present purposes, I shall focus on Weintraub's psychology, which is best described as "antinational."[27]

Writing in an apocalyptic vein, Weintraub identifies Zionism as the rule of the heresy of the "mixed multitude," allied with the power of Gog (from the apocalyptic prophecy in Ezekiel, chapters 38–39). Due to this harrowing change, any sense of the Jewish collective, or *kelal yisra'el* has been nullified, relegating the Jews to the guidance (*hanhaga*) that God grants to the other nations, a diminished form of providence that refers only to the merits of individuals. Using the very texts from the circle of Kremer that were previously drawn on in the Kook circle, Weintraub identifies this tragedy with the Talmudic myth of the killing of the Messiah, the son of Joseph. This radical change is indeed described as a form of total desolation and death (and thus the eventual salvation is resurrection). He then escalates by saying that heresy actually destroys not just the nationhood of Israel but the very human image, turning mankind into just another species. Thus, his psychology is not only antinational, but posthuman. In discussing this view, R. Tzevi ha-Kohen Glick, a student of Wolbe's heavily influenced by Weintraub, quotes Wolbe as describing the mixed multitude as "anti-*mensch*," the Yiddish term *mensch* having much richer connotations than the translation as "human."

Although I have described Weintraub as a paragon of ultimate conservatism, and thus as a continuous Kabbalist, he paradoxically asserts a more radical discontinuity in history than any other Haredi thinker. To cite just one other telling example, in a fascinating historiosophical discussion of the death of the soul of the Jewish collective (accompanied by damage to the Kabbalah as the soul of the Torah) after the destruction of the Second Temple, he describes this tragic process as the source of current crises, as it is the source of the power of the souls of the ruling "mixed multitude," who threaten the remnants of the Jewish collective body through their hostility to the Haredi scholars. This highly pessimistic view of the state of the collective, both in body and in soul, in the Zionist era is in complete opposition to the view of the Kook circle. Weintraub is well aware of this and describes the latter's views as the result of the damage to the soul of the Torah, which leads to interpretations of the Kabbalah based on the "blurring of the intelligences" (*tishtush ha-mohin*).[28]

Continuous Streams in the Hasidic world

In turning to early twenty-first-century Hasidic psychological mysticism, one should say that the central figure to be described here, R. Yitzhaq Me'ir Morgenstern, while maintaining a strong Hasidic identity, also somewhat dissolves the distinction between Hasidic, Lithuanian, and Sephardic forms of Kabbalah. I have written elsewhere of the rapid rise of this Kabbalist, head of the Torat Hakham Yeshiva in the new center of the ever-growing Haredi part of Jerusalem (known officially as Giv'at Moshe but usually called Gush Shemonim). Born in 1966 in England,

Morgenstern (who like other English Jews grew up in a decidedly unmystical setting) gravitated towards Kabbalah already in his teens. According to media reports, he prayed with the Shar'abian meditations already at the age of seventeen. Certainly, from the turn of the current century he published increasingly lengthy yearly treatises known as *Yam ha-Hokhma* ("Sea of Wisdom"). Morgenstern's profound contact with the Kabbalah of Shar'abi is expressed not only in close readings of his texts, but also in a weekly ritual of "removing curses" according to the system of this Kabbalist and late-night study sessions (*havruta*) with Sephardic Kabbalists.[29]

Even in the age of the Internet (which he strenuously opposes, identifying Google with the above-mentioned figure of Gog), Morgenstern is one of the most highly recorded of contemporary Kabbalists. Besides his works, which already extend to many thousands of pages, several weekly classes are both broadcast and archived on the Qol ha-Lashon radio, and extensive e-mail lists convey further video, audio, and text recordings and renditions at least weekly. While his ever-growing written and oral teaching has barely been touched in academic writing and deserves a much longer treatment, for our purposes I shall focus on the more explicit consideration of the soul as one of the most central themes in his thought, as well as mystical practice. It is no coincidence that the weekly collections of virtually every Torah statement that he made in the preceding Sabbath are given the Aramaic title *Nishmatin Hadatin*, or new souls.[30]

Morgenstern's writings should be seen as reflections of the self-awareness of what elsewhere I have described as the Haredi spiritual-mystical renaissance, and as also stated by the American Kabbalist R. Yehiel Mikhel Hendler, an associate of Morgenstern, in a messianic context: "The secret doctrine is revealed and explained more and more . . . and every day new books and manuscripts appear and reveal its hidden treasures, which previous generations have not seen, and the light constantly spreads and increases."[31] This is most apparent in the treatise *Derekh 'Etz Hayyim*, dedicated to the special innovation of Hasidism.

Morgenstern begins with the statement that the soul of the Besht was dispatched to our world in order to remove barriers in the understanding of Lurianic Kabbalah. Following R. Aharon Horowitz (one of his main sources) he describes the Besht's main innovation as employing the metaphor of the body-soul connection for the relationship to the divine, all this so that the sole existence of God can be grasped in each heart and soul. Morgenstern then goes on to describe Hasidism as the revelation of the Torah of the future, whose onset is the move from body imagery to soul imagery. Here he ties the various themes together by stating that this removes the danger of anthropomorphism inherent in Lurianic Kabbalah while enabling the soul to contain the paradoxes inherent in the claim of God's sole existence.[32]

Continuing to follow Morgenstern's somewhat circuitous argumentation, one should especially note his declaration of Hasidic independence. As the psychological discourse is the unique innovation of the movement, it cannot be regarded merely as a superior interpretation of the Kabbalah. In this sense, he is claiming that a new era began in the eighteenth century, in a manner similar to Luzzatto (regarding his own teachings). This bold move is even more apparent when Morgenstern writes that every exalted soul brings a new revelation, with those of the Besht and R. Nahman of Bratzlav being superior to those of Luria. Although Morgenstern engages in a complex and extensive scholastic move in order to preserve the dictum that earlier generations are superior, the force of his argument is hardly diluted for the keen reader.

This becomes apparent when he unfolds the heart of his argument. As the soul is now the metaphor for the divine, the metaphor becomes that which it denotes. Therefore, the psychological discourse is not merely explanatory but transformative (with the details of the transformation, in his typically synthetic mode, being derived from Shar'abi). In other words, metaphor is not a matter of language or symbolism, but rather ontological and theurgical in its implications. It is here, as in many other places, that Morgenstern deploys the Lurianic doctrine of the median psychic spark (see chapter 2), radically describing the Besht as the divine aspect and R. Nahman of Bratzlav as the created aspect, so that when one joins these two teachings one unifies soul and divinity.[33]

This is a launching ground for a discourse that for all of its originality typifies the divinization of R. Nahman, who is described as the *tzaddiq* who succeeds in mediating between souls and divinity, especially by uplifting fallen souls. Indeed, this is part of Morgenstern's own self-awareness, as often reflected in his talks, probably reflecting the fact that they attract non-Haredi intellectuals. Moving to the textual level, he describes Nahman's magnum opus *Liqqutei Moharan* as a revelation of exalted soul levels, this being an interpretative key that informs his own discourses, written and oral, on this work. This exposition concludes with an intriguing introduction to the respective soul levels of modern Kabbalists (including Luzzatto, Kremer, and Ashlag), the greater part of which remains secret, reflecting both its importance and its radical nature.[34]

Immediately following in the same volume, we have a companion teaching, entitled "Worlds, Souls, Divinity," drawing on the Besht's tripartite structure. As I have addressed this essay elsewhere, I shall only summarize it briefly here. Again reflecting on the trajectory of Kabbalah after the eighteenth century, Morgenstern describes the real path of adherence to the divine as moving from "worlds," or the Lurianic-Shar'abian system of meditation on divine names, to connection to the souls of the righteous as mediating divinity. Moving into messianic language, he describes this as the personal redemption of the soul. I believe that we have here the culmination not only of the logic of Hasidism, but also of Safedian Kabbalah. Clearly echoing the previous discourse, he emphasizes the special imperative of connecting to the righteous who revealed the inner aspect of the Torah.[35]

He personalizes this teaching by describing innovations in Torah, as a form of prophecy, as manifesting an awakening inside the soul. Somewhat radically, he writes that Halakhic innovations are only a vessel for innovations along the path of seeking unification with the divine. Describing the alternative to this path, he critiques the dry study of divine names without involving the heart, probably referring to specific schools within Sephardic Kabbalah. In a later volume, Morgenstern ties together these two discussions in an important footnote in which he writes that every aspect in the cosmological scheme of *Sefirot* and divine names has an exact parallel in the quarry of souls, so that every aspect in the Lurianic system has a parallel in the soul of one of the righteous. However, he adds, it is easier to grasp the latter, and this is the foundation of the Hasidic path of adhering to the righteous, so that actually one can attain divinity only through the souls of the righteous.[36]

One should avoid the Stalinist fallacy of "counting the Pope's divisions" and should rather approach Morgenstern's influence with the same tools that one would use in studying the equally small circles of Luria or Luzzatto. Such an investigation would reveal the steadily growing influence of Morgenstern on Kabbalistic circles in both Israel and the United States, as evidenced in his voluminous correspondence (including extensive discussions of the soul) with leading Haredi experts on Hasidic doctrine, a small part of which has been recently published.[37]

As I wrote elsewhere, the first circle that one must consider is that of the above-mentioned elite Ashkenazi Kabbalistic Yeshiva Sha'ar ha-Shamayim, which was established in the early twentieth century. An internal document written in 1925 places the activity of the Yeshiva in the context of the danger of the Kabbalah as "the soul of the Torah" becoming incomprehensible and removed, as well as the absence of this very soul in the new Zionist movement. The latter statement, coupled with the ties of the Yeshiva to Kook and one of his main students (as described by Meir) testifies that the new geopolitical context of increased immigration to Palestine encouraged the incorporation of the national model.[38]

The current place of the soul in the life of this elite institution can be learned from the eulogy delivered by the popular Hasidic teacher R. Tzevi Me'ir Zilberberg (himself a close associate of Morgenstern's) for the veteran Kabbalist R. Yehiel Fischel Eisenbach, longstanding dean of the Yeshiva:

The great soul is here with us and especially in this holy place . . . a place where the great soul taught Torah for decades. . . . And certainly the great soul together with all of the great souls of all of the righteous of the world that he received Torah from. . . . Certainly these righteous are here with his soul . . . we ask the great soul to ask all of the souls that are here and all of the souls in whose Torah he labored to be advocates first of all for the students and friends and the *rebbetzin* [the rebbe's wife] . . . and all of the Jewish people . . . for a soul that was entirely self-sacrifice and entirely the prayer of the soul is able to ask.[39]

Another associate from Sha'ar ha-Shamayim is R. Yitzhaq Moshe Erlanger. Erlanger, who devoted a booklet to the *tzelem*, merges the emotive rhetoric of the Hasidic classics with excursions and commentaries on premodern and modern Kabbalah, including texts usually studied only by academics. In his self-perception, he is responding to the "cry of soul" among contemporary Haredim, searching for mystical inspiration. In a manner that we shall see echoed by Morgenstern, Erlanger sees himself as invoking the psychic influence of the Besht as "the precious of our heart, the point of our soul."

A second circle important for understanding Morgenstern's thought and influence is of course that of contemporary Bratzlav, and especially his mentor R. Nisan David Kivak. For reasons explained in chapter 3, I prefer not to enter the ever-increasing and already vast literature of this generally discontinuous movement that is brought closer to the Haredi mainstream through the efforts of Morgenstern and other respected figures such as R. Ya'aqov Me'ir Shechter, whose psychology I have discussed briefly elsewhere. Morgenstern is joined here by his associate R. Yehuda Sheinfeld, author of the multivolume series *Osri la-Gefen* that, inter alia, offers a highly psychological reading of Bratzlav texts (intermixed with Halakhic discussions). To mention one instance, Sheinfeld discusses the medical model of the heart as a pump and contrasts it with a more spiritual one that retains the central role of the circulation of blood. According to his view, the *middot* are the "movements of the soul," determined by the heart as center of circulation of vitality.

However, he adds an aesthetical dimension to this somatic interpretation, according to which the heart is the "painter" of the *middot*, with the *yetzer*, or "impulse," being the result of this painting.[40]

Morgenstern serves a similar function for other discontinuous figures that are now arousing interest in more conservative circles, such as Ashlag, as well as (though never explicitly) Ginsburgh and Kook. The latter connections may explain the attraction of some *haredi-le'umi* Kabbalists and Yeshiva students to his Hebrew-language talks. In this context, it is worth mentioning the American-based R. Moshe Weinberger, an admirer of Morgenstern, who has composed a Haredi-oriented (and thus "standardizing") commentary on one of Kook's central works, *Orot ha-Teshuva* ("Lights of Repentance"), described by him as the inner essence of the author's soul, which he "poured onto its every page and into its every word" and of which we can thus barely understand "the tiniest drop."[41]

At the same time, Morgenstern espouses strongly nomian positions, and much of his creativity is expressed in a pioneering Kabbalistic exegesis of the tractates of the Talmud, reflecting his view that Talmudic insights should be a vessel for mystical pursuits. Furthermore, he begins some of the *Yam ha-Hokhma* volumes with a strong critique of alternative medicine, responding to its recent inroads in the Haredi worlds. However, at one point one could detect a momentary change in tone (probably due to the support of such practices by the vastly esteemed, charismatic and hypernomian figure R. Ya'aqov Aryeh Milikovsky, the rebbe of Amshinov and a mentor of Zilberberg). As this stance is accompanied by frequent attacks on the Internet and smart phones, one should interpret it as continuous with the discourse of Haredi isolation that Sorotzkin has traced back to much earlier modern periods. Of course, Morgenstern is attempting to establish an enclave culture in a far more diffuse world, his antagonist being not European but rather global modernity.[42]

A third circle is that of American-born Kabbalists, especially Morgenstern's mentor R. Moshe Schatz (for many years in Jerusalem). In his recently reprinted *Ma'ayan Moshe*, Schatz provides an unusually candid description of finding his unique path in Kabbalah scholarship, with the decisive event being a contradiction regarding soul levels in Luria's *'Etz Hayyim*, which led him to near-despair after ten or fifteen attempts to resolve it. This impasse led him to the realization that pursuing the customary path will not lead anywhere even after twenty more years. His new start in Kabbalah study, led him inter alia, to the formulation,

traced through Shar'abi to premodern sources, that the Kabbalistic structure concerns perfection and lack, each level being lacking in comparison to that above it and perfect relative to those below. For our purposes,
it is significant that he applies this insight to the notion that each level
needs to acquire the higher three levels of the soul in its "growth" in
order to aspire to the perfection of the level above it.

This is a striking synthesis of Shar'abian relativity, soul-making, and
the central modern theme of perfection and lack, to which I hope to
devote a separate study. In terms of influence of modern psychology, it
is highly important that Schatz attributes such insights to the realization that Kabbalah studies needs to be approached through rendering
the right brain dominant. One can regard this as the onset of the era
of the dialogue of Kabbalah and neuroscience, reflecting parallel trends
in the Buddhist world and in scholarly research on mysticism. Schatz
was also the mentor of the New York–based R. Ephraim Goldstein, whose
virtuosic classes have done much to make Shar'abi's Kabbalah accessible to Haredi scholars, while offering a somewhat simplified version
of Schatz's teaching. Indeed, a Kabbalist from this New York circle, the
above-mentioned Hendler, recently composed a popular commentary
on Shar'abian techniques, *Barukh u-Mevurakh*, that extensively quotes
Morgenstern.[43]

A final circle to consider is that of Morgenstern's students or ex-
students. I have already mentioned Kluger, who has written in a mystical vein of seeing people as souls and on drawing souls from the world
of emanation through relaxation.[44] However, here as elsewhere, I shall
focus on the most explicitly psychological of contemporary Kabbalistic
writers, R. Itamar Schwartz, a young Lithuanian-trained writer whose
hypernomian tendencies led to a split with Morgenstern. Schwartz, who
has influenced an emerging generation of *ba'alei teshuva* or "newly ob-
servant" writers (especially Ran Weber), has composed extensive commentaries on classical Kabbalistic texts, as well as several books on psychology aimed explicitly at non-Haredi audiences. Recently, the former
part of his activities has been curtailed following pressure from senior
rabbinical leaders in the Lithuanian world.

As I have discussed Schwartz elsewhere as a trans-Haredi figure, I
should just note his explicit critique of Western psychotherapy, reminiscent of Kluger (and of Morgenstern on alternative medicine), for
advocating unbridled expression of psychic forces, as opposed to the
quieting, balanced, and moderate expression of these (inter alia through
requesting the assistance of the soul) cultivated through the practice

that he himself describes. Unpublished lectures of his on alternative healing also reflect his critical engagement with Far Eastern psychology, albeit based, according to his own testimony, on very limited exposure. Throughout, his insistence on the superiority of Jewish approaches to both psychological and somatic problems reflects a strong national psychology, reflecting the increasing effects of Zionism on the Haredi world. Schwartz's techniques for quieting the forces of the soul probably reflect the influence of the early twentieth-century R. Qalonymus Qalman Shapira of Piasecszna (whose hypnotic practice I have addressed elsewhere).[45]

Kabbalistic Psychology and Kabbalah Scholarship in the Second Decade of the Twenty-First Century

Though addressing numerous sources that have not yet been researched, this survey is by no means exhaustive, and due to the rapid proliferation of Haredi Kabbalah it will be outdated as soon as published. Among the materials not discussed here, one should mention the phenomenon of extensive collections of sources on the soul and heart that also include some original commentaries.[46] One development worth addressing in conclusion (and alluded to in chapter 1) is the increasing exchange between Kabbalistic and academic writers. While the first generations of Kabbalah scholars, both in Israel and the United States, were markedly secular, since the 1960s the worldwide phenomenon of "identity studies" has also affected Jewish studies and Kabbalah scholarship in particular. Thus, it would be highly artificial to separate the proliferation and popularization of Kabbalah in the latter half of the twentieth century and the first years of this century from the expansion of scholarly centers at the same period. As a result, the growing interest in research on Kabbalah's psychology is closely related to the processes described here. The same is probably true of Mussar, as the slight scholarly revival described in chapter 3 echoes a certain revival of Mussar, in and beyond the Haredi world.[47]

Although there is some fruitful interchange between Haredi and academic scholars, as I can testify from personal experience, the nature of the identity politics is that it is mostly the noncontinuous forms of Kabbalah that attract academic attention and influence scholarly positions. This is the reason for the fact that numerous figures and texts, even those dating to previous decades, were discussed here (or in my other writings) for the first time. I have remarked above on the similarity between popular expositions within discontinuous circles and popular portrayals of Kabbalah penned by academics.

There are several other manifestations of this ongoing development, including the disproportionate stress on Bratzlav in the study of Hasidism and the ideology surrounding the *Zohar* and its importance, which is clearly related to the culture of joint secular-religious *batei midrash* (study halls)—the joining itself being an arena for celebration of Zionist identity. Most colorfully, we have the conscious attempt by Abraham Elqayam to transform academia into a "school for prophecy" (which I have discussed elsewhere).[48]

These developments are especially apparent in graduate training in Israel; many dissertations are being dedicated by graduates of the educational systems of the ever-fragmenting branches of the religious world to their particular sectors, at times their personal teachers, as in the case of R. Yehuda Leon Ashkenazi ("Manitu") or R. Shime'on Gershon Rosenberg (Shagar), whose works are the subjects of research. As a result, there has been a rapid reversal of the situation described in my book on twentieth-century Kabbalah: while at the time of writing the Hebrew version this field was relatively undeveloped, it has now become the area of choice for graduate theses, resulting in neglect of entire centuries of Kabbalistic writing. As I have noted in the past, this type of writing is usually devoid of interest in wider concerns of religious studies, and one can expect this insularity to increase due to the growing nationalization of Israeli society.

These centrifugal forces will undoubtedly make it even harder to acquire any overall sense of Jewish civilization within the context of the study of religion or of intellectual history, already a challenge in overspecialized and constantly downsized humanities departments. The increasing privatization of academia, against the background of the financial crunch of the universities and the accompanying collapse of confidence in the value of humanistic study, further breeds special courses and subsidized publications serving identity politics rather than scholarship in any recognizable sense.[49] I shall take up this issue again in the concluding chapter, focusing on the role of the nomian in Kabbalah studies, while pointing towards some hopeful signs of reevaluation and cross-fertilization.

SIX

Modern Mystical Psychology: A Comparative View

Modern European Kabbalah and Comparative Contextualization

I desire to know God and the soul. Nothing more? Nothing at all.
AUGUSTINE OF HIPPO

Harold Berman, a leading authority on law and religion, put it well: "It is the tragedy of 'scientific' history that it was invented in the nineteenth century, in the heyday of nationalism. . . . History was to be primarily national history." In much of Jewish studies, certainly in Israel, intellectual history is part of *historia shel 'am Yisra'el*, or the history of the Jewish people. Curiously, the intellectual history of Jewish mysticism is usually separated from even this parochial enterprise, as it treated in an even more particularistic framework, that of *mahshevet Yisra'el* (translated as Jewish thought). However, a more comparative approach should not lead to an opposite extreme of sweepingly ahistorical and translocal statements, also quite common in current Kabbalah scholarship, perhaps in reaction to the limitations imposed by the prevailing academic culture.

Restricting our investigation to the modern period is one preventative measure, along with addressing only the geographical contexts relevant to this period, as described immediately. This method, integrating the method of intellectual history, as opposed to the ahistorical "history of ideas," can be described, following April DeConick, as "contextual comparative." This method resonates with Fred Eggan's anthropological method of "controlled comparison," in which one isolates a limited set of cognate case studies and then creates various sets of relationships or Wittgenstenian "family resemblances," depending on the investigation at hand. Actually, an argument can be easily made that all contextualization should be comparative, as focusing only on the Jewish context, for example, is really a form of essentialism.[1]

When considering the evolution of modern Kabbalah's psychology, one must constantly bear in mind that this development took place, at least until the middle of the twentieth century, mostly in Christian countries. This in and of itself is one of the main differences between premodern Jewish mysticism, which evolved in a variety of settings— Christian, Islamic, Zoroastrian, and classical-pagan—and modern Kabbalah. The Jewish demographic revolution in modern Europe suffices to locate the main scene of Jewish life in Catholic, Protestant, and Eastern Orthodox settings. Furthermore, the Eurocentered printing revolution also dictates the ratio of textual material available in Christian versus Islamic locations (the ambivalence about this technology in Islamic and even Jewish circles in the Middle East in earlier periods is well-known). Even in the case of the Safedian revolution, one must consider the effect of immigration from Iberian, Byzantine, and Italian centers, as has been pointed out already by several scholars, especially Idel. Finally, the later Kabbalistic renaissance in Ottoman (soon to become mandatory) Palestine also was shaped to a large extent by European immigrants, such as Kook and Ashlag.[2]

Here it should be said that following the close relationship between Jewish and Christian religiosity is not only my own goal over the last few years, or that of other younger scholars in Israel (as acknowledged here throughout). It can in fact be said to be one of the classical projects of Jewish studies in Israel (as in the work of Yitzhak Baer, David Flusser, Ephraim E. Urbach, Shlomo Pines, Moshe Idel, Yehuda Liebes, Yosef Kaplan, Menahem Kister, Ora Limor, Israel Yuval, and others), which has been somewhat neglected in recent years (especially in teaching and advising), while actively pursued elsewhere, especially by Daniel Boyarin and Wolfson. The striking increase of mutual interest among Jewish and Christian scholars, echoed in the work of senior theologians such as Walter Brueggemann and Michael Wyschogrod, assists us in providing an apt balance to the growing particularism in both Israeli society and American Jewish Orthodoxy, as well as certain conservative Christian forces.[3]

The contact with Christianity, as a religion of the heart from its out-set, testifying early on (Tertullian) *animae naturaliter christianae* (of a soul naturally Christian), undoubtedly facilitated the development of modern Kabbalah's psychology, as part of a modern religious culture shaped in a foundational manner by this interaction. It is also for this reason that at least until very recently, Christian themes were the main influence on Western psychology, and especially on streams more open to mysticism (despite Freud's well-known turn to Greek mythology, as continued by Hillman). It is for these reasons that even within the Western context, I have focused on the Christian worlds, although I am well aware of the ongoing impact of Gnosticism, as well as the re-sidual impact of classical psychological thought, especially Stoicism, not to mention neo-Platonism. Indeed, this is not just a matter of intel-lectual history, as Gerhard Oestreich has pointed out the role of Neo-Stoic writings in the development of the governmental and disciplinary practices of the modern state.[4] All the same, I cannot enter the com-plex history of the multistaged transition from premodern to modern Christian psychology (in which the relationship of soul and spirit seems to be pivotal), as this examination requires considerable expertise in the latter two traditions, together with the entire history of Christian thought.[5]

Although in principle, comparison with Sufi psychology, in which the *nafs* (soul) and the heart (under various names) also play a central role, should also be part of the history of modern Kabbalah, in practice it is hard to locate even hints of influence of Sufi ideas on Ottoman Kabbalah. Generally speaking, the latter does not betray the kind of openness to extra-Jewish thought that one may readily locate in cases such as the Luzzatto circle or the later ones of Kook and Ashlag, due to the different trajectory and timing of Jewish modernization in the Middle East. In chapter 2, I called for further critical examination of the claim that the ascent of psychological discourse, ideational as well as poetic, in Safed was related to the popularity of these themes in contemporane-ous Ottoman Sufism. Such an investigation should also rightly include the possible impact of manifold and unique views of the heart and soul in Hesychasm on the Byzantine sources of Safedian Kabbalah. Again, to the best of my knowledge, none at all have made any reverse claim as to an influence of Kabbalah on Ottoman Sufism even remotely compa-rable to the effect of Kabbalah on German Romanticism (as described below). Although in a more phenomenologically oriented and less his-torically "controlled" analysis other Islamic forms of psychological thought would have their due place, this would be equally true of the extensive Buddhist discourse on the heart, not to mention a wealth of Hindu views of the *atman*.[6]

Enduring an "embarrassment of riches" in selecting consciously from the vast corpus of modern mysticism and esotericism, this chapter will take up four case studies, of which the first three are the Protestant mystical tradition leading from the radical Reformation through German Romanticism, the Catholic "religion of the heart," and and at greater length (thus continuing chapter 5) the global mystical culture of the second half of the last century (and the first decade of this one), in which the confines of geography and even of religious culture were largely breached. This breach reflects the triumph of the psychological, in which the inner life of the individual is increasingly privileged over traditional forms of identity and sociality, while it is increasingly saturated by the commercial conditioning of the late capitalist world system replacing these forms.[7] A further departure from controlled comparison will be found in my fourth case study, that of the nationalization of Zen Buddhism in the twentieth century (complementing the discussion of national psychology in chapter 4). Obviously, this scheme leaves for the future or for other researchers several central promising avenues of investigation, to be alluded to throughout, and most notably the Greek and Russian Orthodox worlds (accompanied by Balkan Sufism).[8]

My choice to commence with the case of Protestantism stems not only from the greater recent and contemporary effect of this religious culture (due to the American hegemony of the last century or so), but also from an attempt to balance the stress on Catholicism among the few scholars who have examined modern Kabbalah through a comparative lens. To note one striking example, when discussing reformatory tendencies in the Kabbalah of the sixteenth and seventeenth centuries, Weinstein (drawing on his Italian expertise) focused on the Catholic Revival (or counterreformation) rather than on the earlier Protestant Reformation. This reconsideration of the role of largely Protestant Central European thought is reinforced by the important (Hebrew) studies of Liebes on modern Ashkenazi Kabbalah and the ongoing exploration of the history of Kabbalah in this geographical context by Kahana, as well as other recent textual findings (as discussed in chapter 2). Finally, while not the only instance of the influence of Kabbalah on modern European culture, the Protestant tradition provides the most striking evidence for my overall thesis as to Kabbalah being a source of modern psychological theory and not merely another domain in which it may be applied.[9]

Mystical Psychology from the Radical Reformation to German Romanticism

The Reformation is often associated with an impoverishment of psychological religiosity, as in the disappearance of an entire world of discourse and practice on rescuing souls from purgatory. Indeed, in several ways the Protestant revolution set the stage for the decline of discussions of the soul around the eighteenth century. Nonetheless, recent scholarship is painting an increasingly multifaceted picture of this deeply and foundationally modern movement, which is in many ways still with us. For example, I accept Brad Gregory's thesis as to the role of the Reformation in the genealogy of modernity. However, I diverge from his description, although it is as complex as he formulated it, of this effect in terms of secularization. Rather, I opt for a "postsecular" approach that sees the Reformation as a continual source of certain forms of mysticism. Although there are certainly rich lodes of mystical psychology among the most dour of Protestant Reformers, such as John Calvin, I chose to focus on more radical traditions, due to their lasting influence, also on popular culture, and their explicit interaction with Jewish and Christian Kabbalah.[10]

In her fascinating account of the manifestations of the Gothic tradition in popular culture, Nelson has pointed at the subtle influences of the radical Reformation on the development of individualistic "personal gnosis," allied with an "almost Gnostic emphasis on the primacy of the spiritual."[11] This case leads towards chapter 7, as it illustrates the antinomian (also in the political sense) paths opened by heart- and soul-centered religiosity. One striking sixteenth-century case study is that of Thomas Muenzer, who was influenced by the German mystical tradition in stressing the inner knowledge of God. For our inquiry, one should especially note his development of the Paulinian notion of hearts of men as paper and parchment on which God writes his will, as opposed to "book religion." Again leading towards the discussion of the place of the text in chapter 7, we find the conclusion that one may find God even without Scriptures, as the Elect have the spirit already in their heart, or "bubbling" from it. Thus, as Muenzer put it, even one born a Turk may have the beginning of this faith. The mention of Turks is far from coincidental, as his period paralleled the ascent of the Ottoman Empire, the implications of which for the history of modern religion have yet to be thoroughly examined. From a more phenomenological point of view, the heart here is joined less with the soul and more with the concept of the internal and with the spirit.[12]

The radical Reformation was but the first of a series of wavelike effects of the bold German mystical writings. As Carter Lindberg has
written, the pietist theologians, operating in Germany and elsewhere
in Northern Europe, "are the bridge from the Reformations of the sixteenth century to the Enlightenment and beyond." As the term "pietism" is used in Jewish studies scholarship to describe both medieval
Ashkenazi and modern Eastern European Hasidism, it is surprising that
the relationship of this movement to Kabbalah has not been more thoroughly examined. For a start, such an examination should investigate
instances of the influence of Christian Kabbalah on the antinomian,
or "radical," wing of the movement. This being said, one should recall
the strong presence of Catholic thinkers among Christian Kabbalists, in
both the Renaissance and early modernity.[13]

One of the better known sources for pietistic psychological thought
was the very large corpus penned by Jacob Boehme, who will be the
major textual case study for this chapter. Miklos Vassányi has placed
this fascinating figure in a very wide intellectual context in his account
of the return of world soul in German romantic philosophical reflection
on the self. He emphasizes, for a start, the internal continuity with the
German mystical tradition, especially that of Meister Eckhart, famous
for his insistence on the unity of the soul and God, as well as the continual "birth" of God within the soul, which can be understood as a
form of soul-making. However, Vassányi goes on to foreground the
"most significant impact," namely the revival of "Cabbalistic" (i.e.,
Christianized Kabbalistic, as denoted by the spelling of the term) literature in Germany in the late seventeenth and nineteenth centuries.
Following his account, one should emphasize the role of Cabbalistic
ideas in Boehme's theory of the world soul. My interest here is less with
the psychological theories of Christian Cabbalah, which require a separate and lengthy study, but rather with the overall place of the Kabbalah in a modern movement that was also an important influence on
psychoanalysis.[14]

The case of Boehme is of particular importance, as unlike the other,
philosophical, authors covered at length by Vassányi, his views of the
world soul emerged from an ever-developing experience, in a state of
trance (as Evelyn Underhill already noted), of gazing into the very heart
of things, as part of contemplation of the "great deep of this world." Not
surprisingly, his many writings enjoyed the attention of depth psycholo-
gists from Jung through Norman O. Brown to Kathryn Wood Madden, in
her *Dark Light of the Soul*. Madden has importantly noted the impact of
Boehme on twentieth-century Russian mysticism and philosophy, whose

connections to Kabbalah and other Jewish developments have been explored by Hamutal Bar-Yosef.[15]

One should especially note Boehme's treatise, *Forty Questions of the Soul*. His lengthy exposition of the divine origin of the soul, replete with geometrical and letter symbolism that readily betrays Kabbalistic influences, together with specifically Christian cross-symbolism, is especially noteworthy for its stress on the fiery nature of the soul's vitality and power. In this manner, it joins our theme of the soul with the Shamanic imagination of blazing power, appropriate for a mystic of the depths. It is highly likely that this work, consciously employing the metaphor of keys, makes up an entire esoteric dimension, focusing on the secret of the breathing in of the soul into the heart on the sixth day of creation. While identified with the archetypal crucifixion, this day also contains the secret of the eschatological end, and thus can be said to be a subtle form of messianic mysticism.

A second dimension of esotericism relates to the magical-alchemical applications of the sulphurous power of the soul; Boehme explicitly writes of this that he erected a thick wall in order to protect the meaning of the book from the false of spirit, from whom the power of the soul is the ultimate defense. As Jung and his followers have especially emphasized, alchemy should be seen as yet another modern psychological tradition, with known premodern sources, such as Gnosticism. Its place in modern Jewish thought, including medical and scientific discourse, is gaining increasing recognition, as in a seminal study by Kahana. There is also a treasure of references to alchemy in unpublished manuscripts by Valle. However, the esoteric nature of modern messianism is more important for the present discussion.[16]

One should join here the known correlation of messianism with modernity, with an understanding of the intimate link between messianism and the secrecy implicit in a sense of spiritual and magical warfare against the dark forces attempting to obstruct the eschaton. One of many keys distributed throughout the treatise and indeed throughout Boehme's entire corpus is the description of the Kingdom of God as the magical power of the soul becoming the divine child by feeding on the body of God. I believe that this can help decode the thirty-sixth question, which (not coincidentally) is devoted to the victory of the messianic soul of Christ, which is also our soul, leading into the explicitly esoteric thirty-eighth question on the end of the world. I also find a connection between the messianic nature of Boehme's thought and his prophetic concern for social justice and his critique of earthly warfare and "outward might," obviously affected by the horrors of the Thirty Years' War.[17]

Of course, there are numerous additional lines of influence between Kabbalistic thought and German romanticism, such as that noted by Vassányi, namely the revival of Italian psychological ideas, particularly those of Giordano Bruno, who is known to have been greatly influenced by Jewish mysticism. However, as the latter's sources essentially predate modern Kabbalah, he shall not concern us here. As briefly noted in chapter 3, there has been a rudimentary attempt to relate certain facets of Hasidism to the later poetic, philosophical, and political expressions of the Romantic movement in the nineteenth century. Needless to say, proceeding further with this insight requires a consideration of the numerous competing definitions of "Romanticism" as well as its own history. Furthermore, Romanticism must be placed within the broader context of the development of religious psychology in the transition from the eighteenth to the nineteenth century.[18]

For understanding the place of the soul in this transition, Roy Porter's extensive *Flesh in the Age of Reason* is an invaluable guide, though focused on the British context, which has very rarely been directly relevant for the study of Kabbalah (while very important for understanding the contemporary case of America that I shall address below). Porter has correctly placed the Romantic return to the soul and heart as locations of creativity against the background of the Industrial Revolution and its accompanying mechanization of the psyche. His analysis of romantic poetry, such as that of Lord George Gordon Byron, supports my thesis as to the migration of soul from authoritative discourse to the realm of poetics in this period: "It is qua poet that Byron resurrected the exploded and discarded immortal Christian soul by bodying it forth through the notion of soul conceived as poetic imagination. Verse itself could assume immortality, could be a proof of the 'soul.'" Precisely because the "Byronic soul" is expressed primarily in poetry, it is not "Christian and Orthodox but personal and idiosyncratic." Again, the full cultural implications of this radical shift shall be explored in a separate study.[19]

The Religion of the Heart and the Modern European State

The question of the soul troubles many people, and I confess that I am among them.
AUGUSTINE OF HIPPO

One of Sorotzkin's important contributions was to remind us of the centrality of the state for the modernization of European Judaism. Indeed, the differential political structure of European nation-states and Islamic empires is one of the main divides between the two main contexts of

Jewish modernization. From the perspective of periodization, I have already alluded to the possible genesis of modern Kabbalah in the response of conversos and Spanish exiles to the rise of the Catholic State in late fifteenth-century Spain. Therefore, in differentiating the Catholic and Protestant mystical worlds, it would be wise to follow the classical approach of Weber in considering the different socioeconomic and political structures in these two cultures.[20]

One of the most striking examples of the role of religious psychology in the development of the modern state can be found in the case of what is usually seen as a manifestation of secularization—the French Revolution. As part of a "postsecular" reexamination of the role of religion in the pivotal eighteenth century (as also seen in previous chapters), Raymond Jonas has shown that the seventeenth- and eighteenth-century visions of the sacred heart of Jesus were accompanied by messages related to the election of France among the nations and the need to express this connection by placing the sacred heart on national symbols. Furthermore, the failure of King Louis IX to do so was regarded in Catholic circles as the cause for subsequent setbacks in the national arena. Thus, the sacred heart came to be a rallying symbol for counterrevolutionary elements, who regarded it as what I would term apatropaic, or defensive, magic against the demonic forces of the French Revolution. Through most of the nineteenth century, the sacred heart condensed, in my psychoanalytic rephrasing, the desire to reunite France with its king and God, in a discourse reminiscent of that of the Luzzatto circle.[21]

The political dimension in this history is joined by important observations pertaining to the relationship between psychology and spirituality in the movement of devotion to the sacred heart. The blending of private and spiritual life, as succinctly captured by Jonas, included intensive journaling and conversations with spiritual directors, all in order to chronicle the "development of the soul." The writings of Alphonsus de Liguori, whom I shall discuss soon, and especially his *Direction of Souls to Spiritual Life*, are of great importance for this history. This personalized religion both parallels that found in Kabbalistic Mussar and Hasidism and presages much later Christian developments surveyed later in the current chapter. One should at least mention the very extensive current literature, especially in the United States, on spiritual journaling and spiritual direction.[22]

The French tradition was part of a wider movement of "religion of the heart" in Catholic Europe, as covered generally, yet admirably, in the monograph under this title by Ted Campbell. While comparing this movement to contemporary Protestant and Orthodox parallels, Campbell has pointed out the continuity between this form of intense piety and the *devotio moderna* movement that presaged modern personal religion in the fourteenth and fifteenth centuries. Based on the materials that he adduces from the formative works of Jean Eudes, one can describe devotion to the sacred heart as a form of *unio mystica*, in which the heart of Jesus becomes that of the believer, a mode similar to Hasidic mystical psychology. I would also add that this move radicalizes the discourse on *imitatio dei* in *devotio moderna* books such as the famous *Imitation of Christ* by Thomas à Kempis. However, Campbell brushed aside the geographically plausible comparison (currently being developed by Idel) between Hasidism and the spirituality of the heart developed around the publication of the hesychast collection *Philokalia* in the eighteenth century in Russian Orthodox circles.[23]

As is frequently the case in history of European religion, Campbell does not discuss the fascinating Italian branch. De Liguori, whose possible influence on the circle of Luzzatto I have discussed elsewhere, campaigned (in his *Novena to the Sacred Heart*) for the centrality of the sacred heart in Catholic ritual, explicitly mentioning the theories of William Harvey (a graduate of the medical faculty in Luzzatto's Padua!) in support of the centrality of the heart. De Liguori's text also provides a firsthand account of the extremely rapid proliferation of the movement in Italy. From a phenomenological point of view, de Liguori's importance lies in his descriptions of a highly reciprocal personal relationship between the human and divine hearts: God's heaven is the human heart, while devotion pleases God's heart.[24]

The Emergence of Global Psychospirituality

Anima est quodammodo Omnia.
(The soul, in a certain way, is all things)
THOMAS AQUINAS, PARAPHRASING ARISTOTLE

When attempting to encompass the vast recent and contemporary literature on the soul and heart, it is best to resort to the distinction between continuous and discontinuous mysticism. One of the most powerful mechanisms of rendering mysticism (as well as its "elder relative" shamanism) discontinuous is that of reframing it as "spirituality." This concept is so closely allied to the psychological that the term "psychoanalytic spirituality," used in Parsons' analysis, is apt. In many ways, the ever-increasing proliferation of spirituality represents the triumph of the spirit over the soul. Therefore, though it is again tempting to think of spirituality as a form of mourning for mysticism, the upward, upbeat tendency of the spirit, allied with popular psychology, moves against such an interpretation.[25] As in its Paulinian sources, this move also ensures the globalization of mysticism, most evident in the New Age movement, as mentioned at the beginning of the chapter. This development forces a loosening of the geographical constraints that have hitherto guided my investigation. Indeed, at this point one should not even be overly beholden to the term "mystical," that has become but one of a "family" of terms within a self-consciously loose and fluid discourse.

These observations also lead into chapter 7, as universalization and psychologization are almost always allied with anomian or antinomian tendencies. In a sense, discontinuous, anomian mysticism, detached from cultural and geographical context, should not be seen merely as a result of secularization (although in some contexts, such as post-Christian Europe, it could be said to be such). Rather, it expresses the internal logic of the connection between interiorized and worldly forms of religion that may be traced from the Reformation through Romanticism, as noted by Kirschner. National mysticism, for all of its relationship to geography and culture, should be viewed within this overall context, together with, and not in opposition to, universalistic expressions of the move of modern mysticism to the "world" as a general category. In referring to the category of worldliness, I invoke not only Weber's analysis of inner worldly mysticism, but also the philosophical investigation of this theme in the phenomenological tradition, which has itself had both universalist and nationalistic branches. In other words, discontinuity should be seen as an imminent development within the history of modern mysticism. The exposure of twentieth-century mystics to psychoanalytic theories certainly accelerated the psychologization of mystical life in a discontinuous direction.[26]

Due to the ongoing effect of the Reformation, notwithstanding the globalization of spirituality, I shall nonetheless focus this section mostly on the Christian context of this chapter, though in the American rather than the European context, as this is currently the more vibrant location of Western Christianity. Though already somewhat dated, the powerful intuitions in Harold Bloom's *American Religion* are highly useful for appreciating the blend of mysticism and psychology in what is— perhaps more than ever—one of the most religious of modern cultures. Especially, Bloom has alerted us to the close relationship between the development of the "religion of the self" in America and the role of poetry in American culture. Moving from Bloom's "religious criticism" (as in "literary criticism") to historical narrative, one should insert here the complex continuities between the Radical Reformation and romanticism and both religious and poetic (as in the writings of Walt Whitman and Ralph Waldo Emerson) treatments of the soul in American culture.[27]

The case of America is especially interesting, as it is a thoroughly modern context, almost devoid of residual premodern traces. However, I shall not expand here on parallels between early modern Kabbalah and spiritual sects (such as the Shakers) active in America in this period, as these are more of phenomenological than of historical interest (despite the obvious European roots of the latter). I shall but mention the stress on the direct authority of the individual soul as divine in circles that are still part of American religious culture, a position that obviously has marked antinomian potential, also in the political sense.

The recent context is also the appropriate site for addressing Sufism, contrasting European and American developments with Middle Eastern and American "control cases" in light of the above-mentioned need for further exploration of the relationship of Sufism to Kabbalah throughout modernity. While in the past I have critiqued the psychologization of the Buddhist tradition in America, I do not consider myself equipped to describe the global development of the Buddhist discourse on the heart.[28]

Turning first to the Christian world, one must warn that the scope of relevant material is overwhelming, as evidenced by the sheer number of recent books with heart and/or soul in their titles. Therefore, I shall but point at a few striking case studies.

The psychology of the ever-spreading evangelical world within American Christianity has been wonderfully covered in a comprehensive study by Tanya M. Luhrmann. This work has shown that "heart is a near-sacred word for Evangelical Christians," an event happening in the heart being "private, personal, deeply felt, and spontaneous" yet God-given. Based on her findings, one may deduce that in these circles, the heart has largely overshadowed the soul, this itself being a marked sign of discontinuity. While Luhrmann's anthropological or social psychological orientation has led her to focus on churched groups, one should also note the vast outpouring of writing on the heart penned by independent authors, some of whom, such as Wayne Jacobsen and Dave Coleman in *So You Don't Want to Go To Church Anymore*, take the antinomian stance of challenging the very need for a church, a view common among "emergent" writers.

Among the many popular authors of this kind, one should mention John Eldredge, whose gendered writing on the masculine soul, "the wild heart," and the heart of the warrior is reminiscent of the post-Jungian men's movement (to be discussed further towards the end of this chapter). Though not explicitly couched in these terms, the language of wildness also arouses antinomian associations. At the same time, as in the case of the men's movement, one can see the image of the warrior, together with talk of the heart as the "first line of defense" in spiritual warfare, and indeed the prayer warrior phenomenon (also discussed by Luhrmann), as an internalization of a strong and long-standing militaristic trend in American social psychology. Here too, the political intrudes on what appears to be individualistic, inner-oriented soul-searching.[29]

Eldredge's wild male spirituality is echoed in the soul-centered works of Richard Rohr, a Catholic contemplative teacher who is open to influence by non-Christian psychospiritualities, especially the Enneagram typological system, whose roots lie in the post-Sufi system of G. I. Gurdjieff, though I can also detect the influence of Jung's famous typology. Indeed, the Catholic-based "Contemplative Prayer" movement, and especially the set of practices revolving on "Centering Prayer," are in loose alliance or affinity with the "emergent" movement within evangelical Protestantism. Here (especially in the works of Thomas Keating), the heart is described in a contemporary spiritual (also literally, as in the focus on "prayer in the spirit") parlance reflecting Far Eastern adaptations as well as in psychotherapeutic terms.[30] Like much of contemporary mystical Christianity, this psychospiritual trend strongly reflects the influence of the fascinating figure of Thomas Merton. The latter joined a continuous connection to monastic Catholicism and a pioneering interest in global spiritual culture (including Eastern Christianity and its prayer of the heart), as well as psychoanalysis.

Merton's influence, as well as his imagining of the heart as center, are both well apparent in the highly psychological (also in the professional and autobiographical senses) works of another Catholic figure, Henri J. M. Nouwen, who has also greatly influenced the Protestant emergent movement. Nouwen reframed psychotherapy as a modern form of soul-care, although his favored term was "heart," especially in its wounded, restless, and broken states. In doing so, and in his troubled spiritual biography, he became an important inspiration for many in the growing field of pastoral counseling (Jewish as well as Christian). Nouwen is one of the major sources for the ever-growing current discourse on spiritual formation, which he described as "formation of the heart" (understood as the meeting of body, mind, and soul), thus moving from spirit to heart and soul. Generally speaking, figures such as these reflect the ongoing rendering of recent spiritual teachers as psychological archetypes as well as spiritual models. This process is enabled by the radical openness of the spiritual culture evolving outside the mainstream churches to human imperfection and "brokenness," creating a rather different set of images from Kabbalistic hagiography, or even the Hasidic hagiography that I have pursued elsewhere. One major exception is the troubled soul of R. Nahman of Bratzlav, which is still seen as an inspirational figure for the restless spiritual seekers of today.[31]

In chapter 5, I mentioned the similarity between Yair Caspi's "Jewish psychology" and the Society for Christian Psychology. Within this framework, Eric Johnson's *Foundations of Soul Care* explicitly places the "upbuilding" and healing of the soul at the center of his Christian psychology. Joining religious ideas and developmental psychology, Johnson offers a model similar to that of soul-making, in which the soul develops throughout life into a more complex and dynamic structure. However, like many religious systems, it subordinates the growth of the soul to the empowering and energizing activity of the indwelling (Holy) Spirit. Unlike Caspi's highly selective relationship to the Jewish sources (focusing on the bible), Johnson's approach is self-described as "canonical," and founded on the classical texts of the Christian (mostly Protestant) tradition. In this and in its strong critique of liberal Protestant circles for being overly influenced by secular psychology, it can be viewed as strongly continuous. This being said, Johnson, like Caspi, is bibliocentric by virtue of being a rather conservative Protestant. Thus, "the Holy Spirit works within us by convincing us of Scripture's primacy . . . it is the supremely valuable . . . soul-guide." Obviously, each of the two figures prefers a different Testament.[32]

Perhaps the most interesting continuous Christian thought that I know of is the multiyear corpus of John S. Dunne (1929–2013), which can be seen as an extended autobiographical meditation on the gospel of, not surprisingly, John. The heart is perhaps the most central theme in his beautiful writing, focused on the triune core of mind, heart, and soul, reversing a common modern trend by moving back from the idea of the self to that of the soul. His rich and numerous works cannot possibly be summarized briefly, so I shall just touch on a few select themes. Dunne's *The Homing Spirit: A Pilgrimage of the Mind, of the Heart, of the Soul,* a turning point in his spiritual trajectory, is based on his visits to Israel and not surprisingly contains illuminating discussions of R. Nahman of Bratzlav.[33] Indeed, like the romantics, Dunne describes his travels to various countries, in which he responded to various religious cultures with great openness as journeys of the soul. However, his reframing of this travel as pilgrimage moves it away from the context of globalization and connects it to an ancient tradition, in which the journey of the soul and physical travel were seen as both complementary and oppositional in various texts. Thus, although Dunne acknowledged debts to the thought of Merton and personal contact with Nouwen, he should be placed much closer to the continuous side of the continuum that I have created here than these writers and their followers. I see Dunne's writing as a major inspiration for scholarship attuned to both the continuous and the comparative and universal in reading spiritual writing.[34]

One can conclude that it is in contemporary Christian America that the Christian natural soul, or naturally Christian soul, returns, yet in a form somewhat similar to that of the soul of the Romantics, which emerged in reaction to the discarding of the Christian soul. Yet even in the Christian context, the influence of globalized, antinomian, "unchurched" New Age spirituality is apparent. Giegerich has recently addressed simulations of soul phenomena that require "a logically highly sophisticated, devious, cunning soul that has lost its innocence." For him, a "particular important example" of such phenomena can be located in the area of religion and spirituality. In his critical reading, the new spiritual movements "are not of soul significance because they . . . belong to the sphere of the ego, its emotional needs, and cravings. They are . . . phenomena that can certainly be the legitimate study of sociology, but not of psychology. The soul has no stake in them," as "they are occurrences on the modern *market of meanings* [italics in the original] where 'anything goes.'" For Giegerich, "the soul has left that innocent level" that once made concrete religions etc. be true expressions of the soul's truth "at its respective historical locus." Rather, it has risen, or fallen, to the abstraction of the market, as the one single phenomenon of modernity.[35]

Sharp though it is, this critique possesses power, and indeed resonates with Nikolas Rose's somewhat dated, yet acute, description of holistic therapies as part of the "governing of the soul," or Jeremy Carrette and Richard King's description of "the commodification, packaging and selling of one's soul" as an expression of "the emerging values of capitalist spirituality." Giving their argument some historical depth, they add that "the Faustian dilemma takes on a new dimension of novelty in a consumerist context." Certainly, Giegerich is acutely aware of the deep gap between premodern and modern sensibilities of the soul, as part of his acceptance of the historicity of the expressions of the soul, diverging from the common wisdom of the New Age and most of Jungian thought. However, upon reading someone like Dunne, or his Jewish continuous equivalents, I cannot accept in toto Giegerich's claim that even traditional phenomena, such as the Catholic Church, are only simulations, only seeming to possess a higher dignity but really "mere competitors on [sic] the modern market of meanings."[36]

Indeed, Leigh E. Schmidt's genealogy of American spirituality traces its antecedents to nineteenth century liberal, democratic religion, described as emancipation of the soul. Here religious eclecticism signifies not the abstraction of the market but rather a search for the likeness of the soul that transcends religious and cultural difference. Similarly, Courtney Bender's ethnography of New Age spiritual circles in Massachusetts is a very serious representative of a positive (far more than Giegerich or even my own) approach towards the New Age and contemporary spirituality based on a strong claim as to its continuity with nineteenth century American thought. Such accounts force us to recognize that due to its very globalized nature, contemporary spirituality is an extremely complex phenomenon, containing an extremely wide range of sources and motivations and weaving together strands of continuity (of varied lengths) with strong forms of discontinuity. As in Schmidt's apt image, we are speaking not so much of a family tree than a family thicket.[37]

One of the striking effects of the globalization of mysticism is the gap created between the ongoing development of the Sufi tradition in Islamic countries and the far more psychological, universalistic, and anomian Western forms. As Schmidt shows, this development can also be traced back to the nineteenth century. It is well known that the dominant voices in contemporary Western Sufi discourse are those of the thirteenth-century Muḥyī ad-Dīn Ibn 'Arabi and Jalāl ad-Dīn Muhammad Rūmī. The choice to conjoin these two figures reflects an aspiration to merge spiritual and poetic concerns in contemporary culture. I have already noted the psychoanalytic reverberations of Corbin's Western, yet essentially continuous "thought of the heart," based on Ibn 'Arabi as well as other Sufi mystics. One should note the reciprocal influence between Corbin and R. Abraham Joshua Heschel, who made similar moves in inserting Hasidism into American spirituality in the mid-twentieth century. Corbin's oeuvre is part of what Patrick Laude (in a move similar to Margolin's account of internalization in Jewish mysticism), referred to as the "inner Islam" of the twentieth century, as an answer to the challenge of modernization. When considering the ratio of continuity and disjuncture, one should note that at least two of the figures discussed by Laude (René Guénon and Frithjof Schuon), along with other propagators of Sufism in the West, were self-described "traditionalists." However, more recent manifestations are weighted more towards discontinuity. In

California, heartland of psychological spirituality, Western Sufis have published several books popularizing Sufi psychology (and focusing on the heart and soul) in a decontextualized manner reminiscent of popularizations of Kabbalah. As I have frequently argued, the more discontinuous, the more the same.[38]

In view of the prominent place of Jungian psychology in twentieth-century discourse on the soul, it would be instructive to demonstrate this process within two generations of a school attempting to synthesize it with Sufism. One of the most striking attempts to develop a Sufi-Jungian psychospirituality, can be found in the teachings of the Russian-born Naqshbandi teacher Irina Tweedie (1907–99), who also wrote a fascinating autobiographical account of her spiritual path, composed at the request of her teacher at their first meeting. Tweedie writes in this vein, employing the terminology of Gurdjieff together with the Jungian notion of individuation: "From the moment that my Teacher [Radha Mohan Lal] took me seriously in hand, it became increasingly clear to me that the spiritual training was a continuation of the Jungian integration process, but on a higher octave, if I may put it this way." As Sara Sviri, Tweedie's student and a leading researcher of Sufi psychology, has argued, Tweedie's diary reflects the psychological concern at the heart of the Sufi tradition, in this case a process of fiery transformation (see further below on this theme). The result of this process is the revelation of pure light in "the heart of hearts."[39]

The Golden Sufi Center, based in California but with global reach, continues to develop her teachings. Tweedie's designated heir Llewellyn Vaughan-Lee has brought this synthesis into the area of dreamwork, described by him as an area in which the spiritual transcends the psychological, despite the usefulness of Jungian thought for Westerners seeking to understand Sufism. In her introduction to his *Catching the Thread: Sufism, Dreamwork and Jungian Psychology*, Tweedie writes that it uses dreams "to illustrate the inner happenings of the soul." However, Vaughan-Lee does not significantly avail himself of the rich resources of Naqshbandi psychological thought that his teacher received from her own teacher, nor of the extensive Sufi literature on dreams (addressed in fact throughout Sviri's own writing). This being said, Tweedie's own discussions of her dreams with her teacher are mentioned, as are other aspects of her biographical "drama of the soul," as she put it. Generally, Vaughan-Lee bases his discussion on classical and well-known Sufi texts, mostly stories. Similarly, the discussion of Jung does not refer to most of his collected works and the vast treasury of interpretation and exegesis of his writings. Rather, we have short quotes from a few of his works, so that both Sufism and Jungian psychology are a general frame for Vaughan-Lee's own work with dreams of members of his group or participants in his workshops. In other words, within one century we have discontinuous Jungian psychology.[40]

Choosing from a very wide contemporary literature on Sufi psychology, I now wish to focus on two authors, one Palestinian and one American.

Elsewhere, I have briefly noted the somewhat antinomian teachings of Muhammad Sa'id al-Jamal ar-Rifa'i as-Shadhili a contemporary Sufi teacher operating in Jerusalem and with some following in the West, recorded in *The Music of the Soul*. As we have seen in the Christian context, as-Shadhili equates the realm of the secret to the "heart of the soul," echoing classical Sufi discourse on the secret heart (*as-sirr*). In describing the process of psychic transformation, he talks of placing one's heart in the fire of the heart of God, in order to converse directly from one's own soul to the divine soul (as the language of the soul speaks only with the divine voice). This discourse of intimacy, while echoing classical Sufi statements on friendship with God (*wilaya*) probably also reflects the current spiritual climate, evident in Luhrmann's findings as well as the spiritual vocabulary of popularized Bratzlav Hasidism.

At the same time, the particularistic and thus continuous nature of these teachings is evident in the stress on the heart of Muhammad as the eye of the soul, typical of the Shadhili order (centered in Egypt and with branches of which Schuon and Guenon also belonged) with which he associates himself. The practice accompanying these teachings is centered on a litany known as *al-wazifa al-mashishiyya* (described as a deep prayer for opening the soul). Besides the book, his website "sufiheart.com" contains recordings, as is to be expected due to the centrality of the image of music in this school, including a song of Jerusalem, recorded in 2003 and accompanied by a description of this city as "the heart of the world." The political impact of the Israeli-Palestinian conflict is apparent here.[41]

My second example exemplifies the blend of academia and spirituality in the contemporary world of Sufi scholarship in the West. James Morris combines erudite translation and textual analysis with a system of developing "the universal process" of "spiritual intelligence" (in turn a prevalent extension of the current theory of multiple intelligences) focused on the image of the heart. For Morris, the interpretation of the heart as "the spiritual reality" of each person is the key for a hermeneutic that extracts Quranic and other Islamic texts from their immediate cultural context and enables a universalistic, psychospiritual reading. As

Morris emphasizes (in terms presaging our own discussion in chapter 7), interpretation of Scripture is founded on the "preparedness and receptivity of the heart."[42]

Psychology and the Nationalization of Zen

Our final case study takes us to the Far East, in other words beyond traditions that were in historical contact with the Jewish world. As noted above, the accelerated globalizing forces of the twentieth century force one to somewhat relinquish controlled comparison. Specifically, it is highly instructive to compare the nationalization of the psychology of Zen in Japan to developments in the Kook circle. I rely here on the compelling studies by Robert H. Sharf, rather than the later, less judicious pronouncements of Brian Daizen Victoria.[43] Sharf's analysis matches my own, in that he traces the development of Japanese Zen since the Meiji period (1862–1912) to the accelerated modernization of Japan. In other words, the development of Zen in Meiji Japan can be seen as a more condensed parallel to the more protracted processes that occurred in Europe. Sharf's critique of romanticized ideas of Zen in Western scholarship is also greatly relevant for my critique (in chapter 7) of denomianizing tendencies in Kabbalah scholarship. As Sharf writes, "Classical Zen ranks among the most ritualistic forms of Buddhist monasticism."[44]

It is fascinating that Sharf locates the formation of nationalistic ideas of the uniqueness of the Japanese and exaltation of bushido, or "the way of the warrior" in Nitobe Inazō's *Bushido: The Soul of Japan*, translated at the very beginning of the twentieth century. The parallel to the works of Kook, especially those written after his immigration to Palestine in 1904, is obvious. And indeed Kook wrote (in response to a suggestion that an article of his be translated into English for the Japanese audience) of great admiration of the Japanese people and the awakening of its powers.[45] It is also striking that the statements on the superiority of Japanese Buddhism propagated by cultural transmitters such as D. T. Suzuki include its anticipation of modern psychology, unlike "the dogmatic superstitions" of "all other religious and philosophical systems," with "Jewish traditionalism" being a special example of such dogmatism. The discourse on the national soul is joined by the fiery, upward-rising tropes of spirituality (as in Suzuki's work *Japanese Spirituality*), as critiqued here throughout. Here is Shaku Sōen, author of the first writing on Zen published in English, on Japanese military action in Manchuria: "Many material human bodies may be destroyed, many humane hearts be broken, but from a broader point of view these sacrifices are so many phoenixes consumed in the sacred fire of spirituality, which will arise from the smoldering ashes reanimated, ennobled, and glorified."[46]

While contemporary Israeli scholarship and New Age writing tends to join in the romanticization of Buddhism (just as the Buberian romanticization of Hasidism is enjoying somewhat of a vogue and as Jung's political shadow is surprisingly overlooked in much of Kabbalah scholarship), Sharf correctly notes that a founding figure of Religious studies in Israel, R. J. Zwi Werblowsky, cautioned against the western reception of Suzuki's writings already in the Festschrift published in honor of Scholem's seventieth birthday.[47]

So that here, as in the comparison with Christianity, I am attempting to restore an earlier scholarly heritage. Although this sampling, focused as it is on psychology, leaves out several promising areas of comparison (including aesthetics, views of language etc.), it suffices to show that as one moves into late modernity, the globalization of intellectual history, including the proliferation of translation, necessitates a move beyond the European context. Paradoxically, as Sharf argues, twentieth-century nationalism, European or Asiatic, is itself a response to globalization, as indicated by the similarity between its various forms.[48] It is no coincidence that both Japanese nationalist thinkers and the Kook circle responded to what we know as the world wars. More generally, Sharf's incisive interpretation of Zen, as understood in the West, as a twentieth-century construct, tallies well with my stress on the discontinuous nature of much of twentieth-century Kabbalah. I call especial attention to Sharf's critique of the role played by the Jamesian category of experience within this construct, again fortifying my critique (in chapter 1) of the place given to experience in Kabbalah research.[49]

The Psychological Politics of Spirituality

These comparative reflections have demonstrated that the interplay of the two main models of the uncreated divine soul and of soul-making extend beyond Kabbalah. More specifically, the realm of the political is prominent at several junctures. This is only to be expected, as the increasing politicization of both society and psyche should be seen as one of the central processes within modernization. Though related to the rise of the nation-state, as we have seen, the political is also closely related to globalization, and thus globalization of spirituality, together with the commodification typical of late capitalism.[50]

At this point it is well worth reflecting on the political role of psychoanalysis. In a fierce polemic, Hillman (together with Michael Ventura) castigated the movement for abandoning its initial critical and even revolutionary potential and impulse and becoming a device for increased adaptation to the sociopolitical order.[51] Here I must add that for all of my reservations as to the utility of the Freudian system for the study of mysticism, one cannot deny the liberating power of his critique of religion and of repressive social discourse. Though coming from a very different place, Hillman's understanding of the disappointing trajectory of psychoanalysis echoes similar voices in the neo-Marxist Frankfurt School, especially that of Marcuse, whose use of Orphic myth (which itself is shamanic in my reading) in bringing out the radical implications of Freud's thought has been under-recognized.[52]

However, one should also consider the "shadow" of the Jungian tradition from which Hillman emerged (his close reading of Jung's texts in his book *Anima* resembling a medieval Jewish commentary on the Talmud), even beyond the known question of Jung and the Nazis, that is often dealt with an apologetic manner. Although Hillman himself was certainly a progressive thinker in the best possible sense, the popularization (and thus commodification) of his thought in the mythopoetic men's movement has troubling sides that are also rather well known. However, one does not wish to be in a position of casting the first stone. As we shall see further in chapter 7, the combined forces of nationalism and hyper-capitalism conspire to render academia politically ineffective (especially as it retreats into technical specialization) and often compliant.

Against this background, I find inspiration and hope in Bernard Brandchaft's vision of an emancipatory psychoanalysis that is constantly aware of the dangers of "pathological accommodation," also of the patient towards the analyst (and theory itself). Brandchaft sees the goal of psychoanalysis as empowerment of patients in privileging their own thoughts and feelings. As such, this is a balanced expression of the valuable work on validating the individual's self-esteem and even grandiosity in Heinz Kohut's school of self-psychology (as opposed to the ineffectively hyper-radical polemics of Alice Miller). I see this approach that also contains an incisive critique of a theory whose foundations are "embedded in the authority of another day," as has having liberating implications for academic, spiritual and political life.[53]

Likewise, Andrew Samuels has offered a thoughtful analysis of the psychoanalytic dimensions of "the political," resembling Hillman in proposing a therapy for the world. Tellingly, he has warned of "an inward politics of self-righteous ineffectuality, full of rhetoric about soul and meaning but lacking any weight with the electorate or with the corridors of power," this being a good description of the New Age movement, in Israel and elsewhere. Samuels is rather unique among the "left wing" of psychoanalysts in joining political critiques rooted in clinical practice (based on the bold move of analyzing the patient's political, as well as personal history) with an aspiration to resacralization of politics, inspired also by Hasidism. However, Michael Vannoy Adams' writing, especially his latest book *For Love of the Imagination: Interdisciplinary Applications of Jungian Psychoanalysis*, applies the more general thought of Hillman in specific political arenas, such as the economic crisis of 2008 and post-Soviet Russia. Yet one must note that the term "application" is consciously modeled on a current technology that is almost entirely commodified.[54] It is theorists such as these who give rise to the hope that Jewish mysticism may also have a progressive potential, as I shall attempt to show at the end of chapter 7.[55]

SEVEN

The Soul of the Nomian

Der Sitz der Seele ist da, wo sich Innenwelt und Außenwelt berühren.
(The Seat of the Soul is there, where outer and inner worlds meet.)
NOVALIS

Having explored the place of the soul in numerous texts, it is now time to examine the understanding of the relationship of text and soul in modern Kabbalah and its surroundings. As Abrams has written, "Perhaps no subject is more central to the study of Kabbalah . . . than the status and function of text." In Jewish writing, the text is usually conceived of in terms of "Torah," a term that often refers to the law. So this chapter is also a good place to examine the relationship of the soul to Jewish practice, continuing my earlier investigations of the central role of the nomian realm in modern Kabbalah. However, as we shall see, study was the heart of the Jewish nomian realm, even in the modern area. Although R. Elijah de Vidas, around the beginning of Kabbalistic modernity, attempted to reverse the priority of study over practice, the sheer proliferation of texts in this period mitigated against this move.[1]

As the number and complexity of texts exponentially increased, fueled by the advent of print and by a sheer demographic explosion, the centrality of Torah study and the scope of discourse devoted to it, Kabbalistic as well as Halakhic, grew. Torah study became not only the main form of Jewish thought, but also the supreme ritual, in a reflexive mode in which one performs a constantly accessible rite mostly by studying the laws and narratives of rituals. Therefore, I shall devote the greater part of the chapter to several ways in which the soul is expressed or made in the practice of Torah study, while setting aside more theoretical, yet fascinating questions (such as the relationship between the soul and the letters of the Torah and other graphic and semantic elements of the text).

Turning to the nomian requires breaking down disciplinary boundaries, and especially the containment of the study of normative Jewish life under the Zionist designation *Misphat 'Ivri* (officially translated as "Jewish law" yet literally "Hebrew law") within law faculties. This methodological move is part of a wider commitment to integrating comparative legal history and legal theory into the intellectual and religious history of the modern West, thus joining with pioneering work being conducted today, especially by David Flatto, Moshe Halbertal, Kahana, and Sorotzkin. Doing so would counteract the growing denial of the nomian in some scholarly circles, motivated in the United States by New Age discontinuity, joined by a desire to cater to the majority culture, and in Israel by secular Zionist ideology.[2]

A striking example of the former tendency can be found in a recent all-American collection (edited by Frederick E. Greenspahn), which includes a chapter on neo-Kabbalah and pop Kabbalah, and one on Christian Kabbalah, but none on the commandments. The Hebrew term *"mitzvoth"* appears seven times in the book and "Halakhah" twice, together with Madonna, while customs merit one mention less than that celebrity (this being said, Wolfson's article and monograph on the thirteenth-century Kabbalist R. Abraham Abulafia emphasize nomian themes such as circumcision). It is instructive to compare this process to similar developments in the popular and popular-academic reception of Tantra, as critiqued incisively by Hugh Urban.[3]

As for the second-mentioned bias, I have suggested elsewhere in this book and in other writings that the prominence of the nomian in modern Kabbalistic discourse on the soul should give pause when depicting Hasidism in terms of "inner religion" or overemphasizing antinomian aspects of the path of worshipping God in the material in this movement, as well as describing the thought of Luzzatto as antinomian. It is true that one can discern progressive waves of internalization, characterized by strongly psychological discourse, from Safed through the eighteenth century up to recent years. Kabbalah shared this development with other spiritual genres, such as devotional songs (as in the *baqqashot* genre and the later universe of Hasidic *nigunim*, which are often related to states of the heart and soul, either in the lyrics chosen or in the meanings attributed to them). However, these exact junctures also saw intensifications of ritualization that played a major role in the spread of Lurianic Kabbalah.[4]

The very Rabbi Kook who waxed poetic and somewhat transgressive on the soul wrote numerous responsa (she'elot u-teshuvot), founded a Yeshiva, and initiated important Halakhic projects, while his Lithuanian contemporaries developed Mussar in tandem with a revolution in Talmudic analysis, including numerous sophisticated discussions of legal psychology (especially in the Telz school). Novardok, the one Mussar circle which did not sufficiently stress talmudics, had a brief heyday and aroused strong opposition in Lithuanian scholarly circles. Therefore, Margolin's focus on this school and his description of it as a response to secularization epitomizes the tendency in much of contemporary scholarship to interpret nomian positions as reactions, while regarding secularization as the primary process.[5]

In other words, the centrality of the nomian in Jewish religious life, joined with its intrinsic complexity, certainly leave room for antinomian and certainly hypernomian manifestations, including moves that subordinate the commandments to the root of the individual soul. These should by no means be covered up as they are by some factions of Orthodox scholarship (also in universities), yet one cannot occlude the immense importance of the law in both life and learning. Claims to the contrary usually reveal anachronistic projections from the current situation, in which the law is less central for the life-world of large parts of the Jewish public.

The Soul of the Torah and the Torah as Soul

One of the most important statements of Kabbalistic self-identity is the description of this lore as the "soul of the Torah" (nishmeta de-'oraita). As phrased in the Zohar, traditionally associated with the tannaitic period, actually dating from medieval Spain and truly canonized only in the sixteenth century and onwards, the wise servants of God look only at the soul. In other words, their visionary mystical experience is directed towards perceiving the soul of the text. The Zohar goes on to voice the eschatological expectation that they will see the soul of the soul in the future. As Wolfson has emphasized, one should not regard such formative statements as an abandonment of the plain sense of the text for an internal, spiritual one. Rather, the mystical or spiritual sense is comprised within the literal one, just like the soul dwells in the body. This approach should be compared to a statement found in a later stratum of the Zoharic literature, according to which "the Torah is subsidiary to the soul" (*oraita tflea la-neshama*). It is also significant that a major aspect of the largely modern process of the canonization of the *Zohar* was the claim that the study of the *Zohar* (even without understanding) is highly beneficial for the soul.[6]

With the advent of the Safedian revolution, this canonical approach was substantially embellished. In the Lurianic *Sha'ar Ma'amarei Raza"l* (devoted to Kabbalistic exegesis of the rabbinic corpus), the secret is described as the soul, the interior aspect (*penimiyut*) and the spirituality (*ruhaniut*) of the plain sense, joining the soul to the concept of the internal, in a move that we have observed at several junctures.[7] With the major development of Lurianic Kabbalah in the school of Shar'abi, which devoted the greater part of its voluminous writing to the details of the intentions of prayer and commandments, the idea of Kabbalah as the soul of Torah was further refined.

Following on a detailed discussion of each of the 613 commandments of the Torah as matching a "great and complete soul root," or "great rootly (*shorshiot*) souls", Shar'abi writes that the typological number of six hundred thousand commentaries emanate from the "light of the body of the Torah" to the minute subaspects of the five soul aspects of each configuration. This forms the basis for the theory of the fellowship of scholars. The soul roots of the commandments parallel the 613 leading scholars of the generation (with the rest of the generation paralleling the six hundred thousand interpretations). As each of these great souls includes all of the others in a hologramic fashion, they are responsible for each other in this world and in the world of souls (as detailed in the charter of Shar'abi's fellowship).[8]

Remaining outside of Europe, we may find an overlooked enhancement of the relationship of the Torah and the soul in nineteenth-century Maghreb. In the writings of R. Ya'aqov Abuhatzeira, whose writings are much admired to this day (including among Ashkenazi Kabbalists), the soul is a major topic of Torah commentary. Abuhatzeira's exegesis is often directed towards showing that the text is actually concerned with the soul. In his various lengthy commentaries on the Torah, this Kabbalist repeatedly interprets thematic and numerical structures within the text as referring to the levels of the soul and stages of their acquisition, reaching all the way to the shining (*he'ara*) of *yehida*. He especially tends to interpret nomian structures, such as the priestly blessing or the laws of nonobligatory war, in this fashion. Concomitantly, the heart is a central player in Abuhateizra's exegesis: To adduce one example, when he interprets Noah's ark (*teiva*) as the body, or as a vessel for the three major aspects of the soul, like the *teiva* holding the Torah scrolls, he describes the emendation of the body through Torah study as dependent on the heart as the "mainstay (*'iqar*) and root" of the Torah.[9]

If, as Kimberly Patton has claimed, reflexivity is a crucial element of the divine in religious thought as well as of ritual, then Torah study, as the supreme Jewish ritual, is an exemplar of reflexivity. However, in the texts discussed here, the reflexivity is that of the divine soul, which reads itself in the text that is also divine. In other words, as in a famous saying, probably formulated in the school of Luzzatto, "Israel, the Holy One, blessed be He, and the Torah are one," we have a triangular relationship between text, soul, and God. Comparatively speaking, the dynamic of reading the text as soul recalls Marguerite Porete's *Mirror of Simple Souls*. According to Amy Hollywood's reading, Porete describes the soul of the author and that of the reader being transformed by writing a text describing it, the process of transformation thus bridging the gaps between author, text, and reader familiar from literary theory. However, as opposed to the Jewish texts discussed here, Porete's writing had clear antinomian implications (which led to her execution on the charge of heresy in 1310). Once the unification of God and the soul is accomplished, the latter thus realizing its deepest freedom, the book is no longer necessary and the text thus annihilates itself. Such a conclusion is all but impossible in the world of Kabbalah, due to the premodern inheritance of the identification of God and Torah.[10]

When considering the theme of Torah as soul one cannot forget the essential duality of the Written and Oral Torah. One should recall the extensive discourse around the identity of the Hebrew letters of *neshama* and Mishna (the foundation of the Oral Torah) that fueled the development of Mishna study as a mystical practice in Safed. Within the schools of Lublin, the Oral Torah was accorded a natural affinity with the soul. Thus, Alter writes that it represents the totality of the good *middot* that have been imprinted (*hutbe'u*) in the hearts of Israel and in their souls. This theme was especially developed by his contemporary R. Zadoq ha-Kohen of Lublin; for this writer, the Oral Torah emanates solely from the hearts of the people of Israel, although, in a complex dialectic, he often identifies the Oral Torah with the brain and the heart with the Written Torah (that in one place he identifies with soul-making). Rather radically, he writes elsewhere that the text is merely the "engraving" (*haqiqa*) of the power of the soul.[11]

Eliezer Baumgarten has made an interesting comparison between ha-Kohen's views and similar ideas in the second and third generation of the Kabbalah of the circle of Kremer. Indeed, the former's works have enjoyed a positive reception in the Lithuanian world, perhaps due to such instances of resonance. However, I believe that the overall framework of Lublin is more relevant for appreciating ha-Kohen's doctrine, not only due to the comparison with Alter but because of similar and more innovative statements on the Torah of the heart in the Komarno school, though not referring specifically to the Oral Torah. Thus, commenting on the verse "I will put my Teaching into their inmost being and inscribe it upon their hearts" (Jeremiah 31:32), Safrin writes that all of the Torah can be seen in the heart, going on to say that certain individuals can already realize a state in which their soul itself becomes Torah.[12]

The special psychic connection to the Oral Torah described in these texts, often phrased in the by now familiar national terms, should moderate the stress on the text in the recent study with which we opened this chapter. Rather, one should think in terms of an extremely complex interplay between a more shamanic oral culture familiar from numerous global contexts and a more modern text-centered scholastic culture. The complexity of this interaction lies in the fact that although these cultures roughly overlap with the Hasidic/Lithuanian distinction, diverse Hasidic schools also differ in this respect.[13]

Interpretation as Finding One's Soul in the Text

As we have seen in chapter 2, the manifold creative impulse of the Safedian revolution was expressed in the view that the Torah and the Kabbalah itself should be interpreted according to the "root" of the soul of the interpreter. During the eighteenth century, this pluralistic psychological understanding of hermeneutics received several innovative interpretations. Elsewhere, I have adduced a lengthy text, probably from the East European branch of the school of Luzzatto, on interpretation as extending from the fire of the soul of the reader and awakening the latent power of the text. Clearly, such approaches subordinate any literal sense of the text to the psychic processes of the reader.[14]

Such views of the text as a reflection of the soul can partly explain the known impact of Kabbalistic ideas on modern Hebrew literature (on which Luzzatto is considered by some to be a major influence). This is an important, yet under-studied chapter in the oft-addressed history of the encounter of literature and psychology, in which again psychoanalysis continues to hold an exaggerated place of pride. To note but one recently researched example, Elchanan Shilo has pointed at the innovative idea, absent in Kabbalistic writing, of "souls of the heart" in the works of the Israeli Nobel laurete S. Y. Agnon, who received the "secret of his soul" from the Jerusalemite Kabbalist R. Mas'ud Kohen.[15]

Indeed, alongside the notion of interpretation by the soul, there is an entire lode of modern Kabbalistic texts on interpretation depending on the heart. Many of these can be found in the writings of R. Nahman of Bratzlav, one of the prime inspirations for Agnon and other Israeli writers. Despite my reservations as to the inflation of the historical significance of this corpus, its phenomenological value and especially its literary beauty cannot be denied. While Idel has focused on the pneumatic interpretation of the Torah in these writings related to the trope of the spirit, R. Nahman was actually more concerned with the heart, just as his contemporary followers often declare.

As I have written elsewhere, one of the texts central for Idel's interpretation describes a process of drawing down fire from the supernal heart in order to revive the soul from the coldness and death of the modern era. This coldness can be compared to the death of the heart and soul in his famous story of the heart and the fountain, which, as Dunne has suggested, refers to the human heart just as much as to the heart of the world, or one could say the heart of the human world. In what one can describe as the theory behind his famous tales, R. Nahman describes the spoiling of the heart, leading to the spoiling of the face and to a form of negative sleep, from which one can only be awakened by tales.[16]

More generally, R. Nahman's self-consciously innovative, indeed modern approach should be understood chiefly through his description of the "generality" (*kelaliut*) of the Torah as the heart. R. Nahman saw himself as drawing down his "hearty" Torah in order to awaken the modern soul, as is evident in the following and autobiographical description:

And this is the Aspect of the revelation of the Torah of the future . . . whoever possesses the aspect of Moses-Messiah, can receive Torah and can draw down the shining of the Torah to teach other people, for the revelation of the Torah comes from the union of the Holy One, blessed be He and his *Shekhina* . . . and their union is through uplifting the souls of Israel . . . and the wise one can take the souls and uplift them and through this union the Torah is born . . . and *nefesh* is the aspect of will, as all these people come to the wise one of the generation, each and every one has some kind of will, and the *tzaddiq* takes all of the wills and ascends with them . . . in the aspect of 'And the living creatures ran and returned' (Ezekiel 1:14). "Ran" in the ascent of the souls and "returned" in the return of the souls together with the revelation of the Torah.

This passage is placed within a description of the messianic process of warming up the heart through cooling down the negative warmth of passion for money that scatters the soul and darkens the will, as R. Nahman seems to put it later in this Torah (see the concluding remarks of this chapter for the political and cultural implications of this move). Despite the radical flavor of the stress on the new, messianic revelation imparted to R. Nahman, I would not describe this text as antinomian, as at most it is neo-nomian, in the sense of revitalization, described here in terms of rebirth.[17]

Torah Study and Soul Making

Lurianic Kabbalah describes the rectification of one's soul root in the macro-anthropos (*adam qadmon*) as the main *kavvanah* or "intention" of Torah study, which is the very purpose of creation. This key statement is found, inter alia, in a volume devoted to the rationales of the commandments (*Sha'ar ha-Mitzvot*). This formative view of the very purpose of study was canonized in an important seventeenth-century commentary, *Beit Hadash* by R. Yo'el Sirkis, on the fourteenth-century legal code *Arba' Turim* (by R. Ya'akov ben Asher, 1270–1343). Sirkis, an important early modern Halakhic authority, wrote as follows on the importance of the blessing ordained before Torah study at the start of the day (commenting on the striking Talmudic statement on its absence being the cause of the destruction of the Second Temple): "His intention, blessed be He, in the world was that we should study the Torah in order that our soul become essentialized (*tit'atzem*) by the essence (*'atzmut*) and spirituality and holiness of the source of the origin of the Torah." While his language of essence and spirituality is Cordoverian, this statement echoes the view of Torah study as soul-making that is more often identified with Luria.[18]

The relationship of the soul and Torah study was probably most fully developed in the school of Habad. Neither in two books devoted to Rashaz (R. Shneur Zalman) published by academic presses, nor in previous general studies of Habad, nor even in the recent studies that finally bring into account all of the generations of Habad thought, do we find an integration of Rashaz's work on Halakha and Kabbalah. However, one must recall that Rashaz was the author of the influential *Shulkhan 'Arukh ha-Rav* legal code, Halakhic responsa, and liturgical discussions (in his commentary on the prayerbook) together with his oft researched mystical texts.[19]

In my view, the very bibliographical fact that Rashaz's first printed work was his treatise on the laws of Torah study points towards the salience of an integrated concept of Torah study for his intellectual character. In an above-noted recent discussion of the nomian in modern Kabbalah, I began a section on study and experience in Hasidism by referring to this highly formative text, in which Rashaz writes that attaining all that the soul can in terms of knowledge of the Torah, in all of its parts, is the only way that the soul can be rectified and purified in its divine source. I immediately noted the parallel in his best-known work, the *Tanya*, known as the Bible of Hasidism. I shall address the *Tanya* text and its neighbors soon; however, I first want to note an exception to my observation on the history of scholarship.

The important location of the laws of Torah study in Rashaz's trajectory has been addressed in Naftali Loewenthal's important study of early Habad. This is one of his two brief comments on the importance of the interrelationship between the Halakha and the Kabbalah—known in Habad and other Hasidic schools as the revealed and concealed aspects of the Torah—not only in Rashaz's own writing, but also in its editing by his son and successor, R. Dov Baer Shneuri. These comments are part of Loewenthal's general thesis, according to which the integration of the esoteric and exoteric was part of Habad's increasing effort to communicate the infinite to wider audiences. In doing so, Loewenthal echoes, as elsewhere in his book, the Habad tradition itself, in which Rashaz's first name, Shneur, was read in an illuminatory vein as *shnei or*, "two lights," those of the revealed and concealed Torah.[20]

Having laid some methodological ground, I wish to move to a more sustained textual analysis, beginning with *Tanya*. In chapter 5 of the first and main section, *Liqqutei Amarim*, Rashaz writes:

When someone understands and grasps a Halakha . . . clearly, then his intellect grasps and encompasses it, and his intellect is also enclothed in it at that moment. And indeed this Halakha is the wisdom and will of God that . . . when, for example, so and so claims such and such, and so and so such and such the decision shall be such and such, so when a person knows and grasps this verdict with his intellect . . . then he grasps and encompasses with his intellect the will and wisdom of God that are ungraspable . . . except through their enclothement in the Halakhot . . . and this is a wonderful union unmatched . . . and this is the great and wonderful advantage of the commandment of the knowledge of the Torah over all practical commandments, and even commandments performed by speech and even the commandment to speak the words of Torah . . . for by means of all the commandments performed in action and speech God enclothes the soul and encompasses it head to toe . . . and with the knowledge of the Torah . . . also the wisdom of God is inside one . . . and since through the knowledge of the Torah it is enclothed in the soul and intellect of the person . . . it is sustenance for the soul and indwelling life from the life of the life, the blessed Infinite.[21]

Though this text is relatively well known, it is worth decoding. It moves from a more technical theory of encompassing and inner lights derived from Lurianic Kabbalah into a double move. The first of these deliberately uses the example from the laws of *to'en ve-nit'an*, or "claims," precisely because this is a seemingly "unspiritual" part of the law. This is the very example used by Rashaz's contemporary and antagonist, R. Hayyim Iczkovitz, when he demonstrates the supreme value of Torah study devoid of any pietistic or overtly spiritual intent in his *Nefesh ha-Hayyim*. It is through the knowledge of the manifestation of the divine in the seemingly mundane, yet not in any anomian mode, but rather in a Halakhic frame, that the ungraspable infinite is made intimately accessible to the soul.[22]

At the same time, Rashaz chooses an entirely theoretical case to demonstrate the supreme value of knowing the entire Torah, just as he wrote in the laws of study. The heart of the text is the claim that the knowledge of the Torah is superior even to the study of the Torah. My comments cannot substitute for a sustained effort to uncover the deep structure informing the entirety of Rashaz's writing, whether Kabbalistic or Halakhic. However, they demonstrate both the vitality of Halakha for his theory of vitality, as in the end of the text, and the need to view his oeuvre in its Lithuanian context, confounding facile distinctions between Hasidim and their opponents.

Later in this section, Rashaz connects these themes to the overall psychological theory set out in this portion of the *Tanya*, based on the distinction between the two souls, as well as a theory of the three garments of the soul (deeds, speech, and thought): when thinking of words of Torah, the innermost garments of the divine soul, and all the more so the divine soul itself, are all united in the utmost unification with God.[23] As the only barrier to utter unification can be concealment, as in the general ontological system of Habad (as explicated in depth by Wolfson), the state of complete disclosure of God to the divine soul, without any concealment "at all at all" is in fact God's own self-revelation through his wisdom and will. In other words, revelation, rather than being an external event, as in the plain sense of the Biblical account of revelation at Sinai, is actually an internal occurrence within the divine. This leads to Rashaz's conclusion, which has radical ramifications for the relative place of Halakha and Kabbalah. The union of the divine soul and the infinite source is:

far more intensive and powerful than the union of the light of the infinite in the supernal worlds, as the divine will is in complete disclosure in the divine soul and its garments that are engaged in the Torah, for He himself is the Torah itself, and all of the supernal worlds receive their vitality from the light and vitality of the Torah . . . and from this the enlightened person (*maskil*) can draw upon himself great awe while studying the Torah.[24]

In other words, the supernal worlds, the concern of a great deal of Kabbalistic writing, are derivative of the vitality of the law as the will of God, which is one with the essence of the divine, as explained throughout this and the following chapters. The *maskil* (intellectual) can draw down some of this vitality in the form of awe, while studying, as opposed to the separation of awe and study in Iczkovitz's *Nefesh ha-Hayyim*, as the awe is drawn from the same ontological source.[25]

We can observe here the beginnings of the sociological divergence between two ideal types in subsequent generations of Habad: the *maskil*, or pure scholar of Hasidic thought, and the *'oved*, "worker" or "pietist." This text seems to champion the former type, but now we shall see one final text as a counter. As Wolfson has shown, the theory of Habad is almost infinitely complex, truly in an awe-inspiring manner, so that approaching it with an eye to summarizing an ideology, as it were, is doomed to failure. Thus, I wish to balance the upshot of the texts that we have just seen by a countertext from Rashaz's later *Liqqutei Torah*, embedded in a discussion of disclosure and awe:

By Israel we denote two aspects: the first is the part of the soul enclothed in the human body . . . that Israel are below the level of Torah . . . but the second is the soul above on the encompassing level . . . that Israel is the beginning and the source of the Torah . . . that the entire Torah is founded on the aspect of Israel.[26]

If we follow the implications of this text (whose distant source is found in the late pietistic Midrash *Tana de-Bey Eliyahu*), then while Torah study is above ontology, true depth psychology is above the text. Again, this should be seen as a hypernomian rather than an anomian or antinomian move, if only because of the strong emphasis on the people of Israel, whose merit derives precisely from being the source of the

Torah.[27] At the very least it deconstructs the sense of total disclosure that one may have possibly derived from the previous quote.

The disembodied encompassing soul is revealed in the heart and soul through prayer, as Rashaz continues, yet by definition it remains ultimately inaccessible, just as Heraclitus said of the soul, in a saying oft quoted by Hillman: "You could not discover the limits of the soul (*psyche*), even if you traveled every road to do so, such is the depth (*bathun*) of its meaning (*logos*)." It may well be that the divergence between these texts by Rashaz supports the diachronic proposal in Loewenthal's book as to the gradual unfolding of the Habad system, though in order to establish this properly one would need to go into complex questions of layered editing. In any case, I think that this is not the only possible resolution to such quandaries that may also be addressed through onto-logical dialectic.[28]

If one follows the correct method of studying the universe of Habad as a whole, one can cast light on these issues by delving into the intri-cate and vast works of the fifth rebbe, R. Shalom Dov Baer Schneerson (Rashab, 1860–1920). As elsewhere I have suggested, based on the tradi-tion of Habad itself, that in this thinker's later writings there was a shift, possibly due to his encounter with Freud or one of his followers, I shall select his magnum opus from 1912, *Be-Sha'a she-Heqdimu*, commencing with a text claiming that the special power of the soul to connect to the *'atzmut*, or "essence" of divinity is through the Torah.[29]

Here, Rashab makes a crucial move in describing the revelation of the Torah at Sinai not only as the onset of the era of Torah but also as pre-saging the messianic era. He compares the known Midrashic accounts of the resurrection of the souls in this event to the future eschatological resurrection. In both cases, it is the Torah that enables the souls to be connected to the essence yet without being totally annihilated when this world-negating essence is revealed. A further interpretative key is that the internal connection of the soul with the Torah is through the *sha'ashu'im* or "playful pleasure" when studying. This enables the soul to paradoxically remain a separate entity while completely unified and connected. In other words, it is pleasure that is the guarantor of identity, recalling Ronald Barthes' portrayal of the role of *plaisir* in reading.[30]

A slightly earlier discussion should flesh this theme out in a satisfac-tory manner. Rashab contrasts regular pleasure that is but a "shining" (*he'ara*) outwards with the "selfy" (*'atzmi*) pleasure of Torah, compared to which all pleasures are as nothing. In detailing this move, Rashab discusses the pleasure revealed by the "clarifications" (*birurim*) that take place in the lower world, as in the process of difficulties and resolutions through studying topics such as monetary laws (in a move similar to that of Rashaz, as discussed above). Strikingly, Rashab relates this scholastic pleasure to the divine self-pleasure (*sha'ashu'im 'atzmiyim*), the joy of God's heart in the soul of the soul of the Torah. The higher aspiration is to have "tangible pleasure (here using the Yiddish term *geshmak*)," in God's pleasure in his own Torah study. Again, the context of the Lithuanian Yeshiva world is instructive, as *geshmak* in study is a major value in that world, yet lacking the mystical-theurgical dimension added here.[31]

In a talk delivered in 1913, Rashab directs this move to a remarkable turn:

The advantage in the connection of the light of the Infinite (*ein sof*) below being effected by the souls of Israel is that through the connection of the souls to divinity and the Torah they draw down (*mamshikhim*) the revelation of a new light in the Torah, and this is what it says [in Deuteronomy 29:28] 'to make all the words of this Torah': that the souls of Israel make the Torah in drawing the light of the infinite into the Torah . . . that it is drawn from the aspect of pleasure above wisdom. And heel (*'eqev*) connotes the heels of the Messiah, that in this time most of the souls are from lower levels that come from the aspect of enclothing and utmost reification (*tefisa be-geshem be-yoter*) . . . and precisely through this a revelation of new light in the Torah is drawn down.[32]

Here we go beyond connection to creation, as the drawing down of the essence by embodied souls through study, especially of laws related to the material world and precisely by means of the human intellect, renews the Torah from its infinite source, its infinity being expressed precisely in the capacity for renewal. Again, this echoes the Lithuanian value of innovation through the *geshmak* of subtle learning and in the nonutilitarian play of Torah.[33]

Later in the work, in a messianic context, Rashab raises the question of the annulment of the commandments in the future, explaining that they are not literally cancelled but won't take up any place relative to the selfy light of the future, the selfy pleasure that is even more internal than the selfy will. Thus, both will and law will be as a candle near a sun, using an image found in countless Habad texts. Here he refers to the verse 'only God had a delight in thy fathers' (Deuteronomy 10:15), understood as the divine pleasure in souls of Israel from their intrinsic viewpoint (*mi-tzad 'atzmam*). Rashab somewhat cryptically relates this level of the relative nullification of will and law to the seeming change in God's will effected by repentance from the depth of the soul, described here as the cry of the heart.[34]

I believe that Rashab did not want to expand too much on this sensitive issue in a public discourse, rather doing so in the undelivered and later written teachings (published within the same work). Firstly, in a discussion of *teshuva*, where he writes that in their root in the essence the souls are above the Torah, the proof being that even if one transgresses the whole Torah nothing withstands repentance: "And this is due only to the exaltedness of the souls." He then adds that even though *teshuva* is also mentioned within the Torah, it is still above the Torah as in the famous Midrash that God on this matter contradicts what the Torah itself says on punishment of sin, God interpreted here as the essence to which the souls connect. Again, this is not an antinomian move, but rather a hypernomian move in which the law excesses or transcends itself.[35]

This is stated more explicitly in a slightly later discussion of the superiority of souls to Torah:

But we have found that the sages have the power to act even not in accordance with the Torah . . . and sometimes because 'there is a time to act for God' (Psalms 119:126), the sages can rule according to the minority . . . and actually the court is empowered to change even something accepted and undisputed, even a positive or negative commandment of the Torah . . . and one must say that this is because Israel indeed precede the Torah.[36]

Slightly further on, Rashab relates this bold move to our previous theme of pleasure, and in the gendered and sexual terms that should only be expected. The root of the powers of the court is that the souls of Israel are the male aspect that influence the feminine Torah, drawing into it the pleasure of the essence that is even above the *sha'ashu'im* of the Torah and thus constantly draw down influence to the commandments, as limited articulations of the divine will, from their limitless source. One should compare this formulation to an earlier discussion in this work, concerning the famous disregard of heavenly voices in Talmudic decision making: "This is the matter of not taking heed of a *bat qol* [daughter of a voice], for the true supernal will is known only to the souls."[37]

The relative length of this discussion reflects the centrality of Torah study in modern Kabbalah, and indeed in modern Jewish religiosity in general. One cannot conclude it without further developing our comparison to views of Torah study as soul-making extant in Lithuanian

Kabbalah. For authors such as Iczkovitz, the ultimate ideal is neither knowledge nor study itself, but innovation, or *hiddush*. As he writes in his *Nefesh ha-Hayyim*, "There is nothing that can measure against the awesome wonderful matter and effect" of innovations, as the innovators renew not only the world but the Torah itself. This stress, that easily lends itself to views of Torah as soul-making, both reflected and further reinforced the creative Talmudic culture of Lithuania, as is also apparent in the twentieth-century synthesis of philosophy and Kabbalistic motifs in the American writings of R. Joseph Baer Soloveitchik.[38]

Earlier in that century, in a rather radical development of the Lithuanian understanding of Torah study as soul-making, R. Shlomo Elyashiv wrote that the goal of innovation in Kabbalah study is to reveal and shine the supernal aspect that one is studying according to one's specific soul root, though always in connection with the national soul of Israel. In this view, Torah study blends the individuation of the soul with the theurgic effect of the very act of studying Kabbalah. Rather than being an isolated example, Elyashiv's statement reflects the continued value of in-depth study of Kabbalah in Lithuania, also reflected in quotes from Kabbalistic works from the circle of Luzzatto found in the classic of Lithuanian Talmudics, *Sha'arei Yosher* by R. Shime'on Yehuda ha-Kohen Shkop.[39]

The Sabbath as Soul-Time

The claim that the rectification of the soul is a central rationale (*ta'am*) and "intention" (*kavvanah*) of the commandments extends beyond Torah study to the totality of the complex structure of Jewish law. I shall focus on two major case studies, while hoping that the recent and praiseworthy increase of interest in Kabbalah and Halakhah will lead to further investigations.[40] One of the themes that the Kabbalah clearly inherited from rabbinic Judaism and thus from "normative Judaism" is that of the "extra soul" granted on the Sabbath. While Elliot Ginsburg has admirably covered this theme, his study is focused on medieval or at latest early modern material. As Idel has shown, mystical discussions (especially Hasidic) of the Sabbath point towards a nomian, cyclical realm of recurring experiences of plenitude created through ritual. Idel notes that these experiences include that of the return of the soul to its source—another cyclical move. In a strongly, though not explicitly, psychological or internalizing move, he shows that in some texts, the very category of time is a projection of inner experience. When considering the modern development of this theme, one should focus on the Lurianic tradition. There, the receipt of the extra soul is described as a form of soul making (the acquisition of extra levels of soul) as well as transformation and renewal of the soul as part of a cosmic process of the naked, unsheathed disclosure of a "great and powerful light" throughout the world during the prayers welcoming the Sabbath.[41]

Following the development of Lurianic Kabbalah in the early modern period, one should note a striking text found in the under-studied seventeenth-century Lithuanian commentary on the Zohar, *Aspaklaria ha-Me'irah*, by R. Tzevi Hirsch ben Yehoshua Moshe ha-Levi Horowitz (an important rabbinical figure who should not be confused with others with a similar name). Horowitz writes that the extra soul is accorded in a differential manner, with the recipients meriting one of the three main soul-levels (*nefesh, ruah, neshama*), apparently based on the level of their preparation for the Sabbath and the quality of their prayers welcoming the day of rest. Here too, the extra soul is described as a nomian form of soul-making. This picture is supplemented by an earlier text by R. Menahem 'Azaria da Fano, according to which the "extra" Sabbath soul can somewhat restore the fourth level of *haya* that together with the even higher *yehida* removes itself from sinners.[42]

The theme of the extra soul was especially developed in the Hasidic world, whose social life centered on the talks of the spiritual leader delivered at various points during this day. Besides numerous earlier texts, one should point again at the wealth of material in the schools of Lublin. For example, characteristically reading the soul in terms of the heart, R. Zadoq ha-Kohen writes that on the Sabbath God dwells in the heart of Israel. True to his illuminatory discourse on the soul, Alter wrote of the extra soul on Sabbath as the shining of the soul, drawing down in its root in the light of the Torah, where it is annulled in divinity (to be compared with his view of the Sabbath as described in chapter 3).[43]

One can find a rather different understanding of the "extra soul" in Lithuanian sources. In a characteristically elitist move, Haver writes that the extra soul is given only to the *tzadiqqim* in secret. However, in another passage, Haver writes in an experiential mode, in what could be read either as an autobiographical testimony or as a general observation, that "as we can see in Man that every Sabbath he receives an extra soul and breadth of heart for rest and pleasure, and his senses greatly expand and enjoy, and also the spirit of holiness in him greatly increases, with breadth of heart to understand and cogitate." The reference to spirit should be understood as follows: in keeping with his general psychology, he describes the extra soul in terms of a relatively modest ascent from *nefesh* to *ruah*, establishing a lower peak than most Hasidic texts. Although gender imagery is not my main concern here, the text indicates that he understands this process as the assimilation of the feminine aspect in the male (a move often pointed out by Wolfson).[44]

R. Eliyahu E. Dessler records a somewhat similar tradition in the name of his teacher, R. Simha Ziv of Kelm, according to which, however, one who does not sense extra sanctity of the Sabbath is devoid of the extra soul (while whoever feels no sanctity at all has lost his soul completely). Dessler describes this test as very useful, as usually one tends to delude oneself regarding ones' spiritual level. Here, the extra soul is not a given but an achievement, reflecting at least to some extent a wider discrepancy between the more passive approach of the Hasidic world, according to which the extra soul descends from the root or another supernal entity, and the more activist Lithuanian doctrine.[45]

The Soul of the Tefillin

Due to the general neglect of the nomian in academic teaching and research on Kabbalah, the centrality of the near-daily rite of laying tefillin (themselves containing portions of the Torah and often associated with it) in Kabbalistic thought has been overlooked. In Lurianic texts such as R. Ya'aqov Tzemah's *Nagid u-Metzave*, the tefillin are associated with the internal aspect of souls, the sole site of the cosmic coupling (*zivug*) and thus of revelation of unity in the exilic reality. As the head tefillin is placed on the forehead, it is possible that the Lurianic method of diagnosing the state of the individual's performance of the commandments and the state of his soul levels by gazing at the forehead, as discussed in the same book, is also related to the tefillin. Even if this connection is somewhat far-fetched, we have here a strong sense of the imprinting of the soul on the body in direct relation to nomian practice.[46]

As in the case of the Sabbath, the tefillin rite can be understood as a nomian form of soul-making. For example, the anonymous hypernomian (despite being Sabbatean) work *Hemdat Yamim*, composed in the eighteenth century, stresses that through the tefillin, placed on the head and heart—the two classical sites of the soul— one not only amends the soul but acquires a new one. Therefore, the tefillin contain four biblical passages, corresponding to the four accessible soul-levels.[47]

Here too, the writings of Haver are highly instructive. He equates the tefillin with the level of revelation of holiness and prophecy that is presently accessible only slightly, through the commandments and the

Sabbath (echoing the discussion we saw above). Later in this discussion, he explains that the head tefillin parallel the open revelation in the time of the Temple, while the hand tefillin parallel the residual and hidden connection to the divine in exile, which is even more of a miracle, as the Jews have managed to preserve every letter of the law in the most difficult circumstances. Although these particular discussions refer more to the "intelligences" (*mohin*) than to soul-levels (as is often the case in modern Kabbalistic treatments of this issue), one should read them in view of an earlier discourse on the revelation of the *Shekhina* in the Temple paralleling the manifestation of the soul in the body, leading into a text of which he wrote, "Indeed, I should have abstained from going into the place of the flame"; however, he felt compelled to reveal the depths of the Torah in face of the rejection of Kabbalah by the followers of the Haskala.[48]

The tefillin rite is also a major theme in the writings of Kook, who devoted his first printed book, *Havash Pe'er*, to the details of its laws. His previously censored diaries are replete with discussions of his experiences while donning the tefillin, including the yearning of souls such as his to wear them all day. He associates this impulse with the constant revelation in his soul through its *segula* and the thirst of such souls for redemption through seeing the sparks of goodness in the souls of the Zionists. We should avail ourselves of such texts when interpreting his descriptions of the tefillin as building the national soul on a daily basis.[49]

A Comparative Excursion

Following on chapter 6, one should consider the themes discussed here also from a comparative viewpoint. In a truly interdisciplinary study, *The Book of the Heart*, Eric Jager traces the history of this metaphor for selfhood from antiquity (including the Bible) to modernity. For our purposes, Jager's discussion of the *Book of Man's Soul* is particularly important. I found especial interest in his description (following Michael Tresko) of the system of the late fourteenth-century English theologian John Wyclif. In a five-level layering of Scripture reminiscent of the Judeo-Christian (and Kabbalistic) fourfold system, Wyclif describes the fourth level (the one before the physical text, and thus almost furthest removed from the Trinity) as the book of "the natural man, which is his soul." From my perspective, Jager did not sufficiently emphasize the discontinuity between this premodern view, in which the emphasis seems to be on the book of the soul as distant from the divine, and its fifteenth-century reception (including the *devotio moderna* work *The Imitation of Christ*), where the antinomian focus is on the subordination of the sense arising from the "outward book of holy Scripture" and on the "verdict of reason written in man's soul and heart."

Indeed, Jager posits a basic continuity between premodern and modern uses of the metaphor of the self-text, locating the real change in the relocation of the self from heart to head in the seventeenth and eighteenth centuries, accompanying the post-Harvey mechanization of the heart. At the same time, he does recognize that Protestant authors reconceived the book of the heart in legal or financial, and thus worldlier, terms. He also describes the early modern move away from the biblical context to a secularized Romantic image that is still with us (as in Valentine cards, as Jager notes in an on-line follow-up).[50] In any case, once one accepts Jager's main argument, one may note here another instance of the way in which modern Kabbalah generally had greater preservatory power in maintaining the centrality of the heart, although our discussion of Rashaz in chapter 3 does point at a migration to the brain in the very end of the eighteenth century.

Questions of periodization aside, reading Jager's findings in tandem with those contained in this chapter is highly rewarding from a phenomenological point of view. One should particularly note the Christian texts describing contemplative reading of Scripture as transcribing divine truth in the book of the reader's heart. Here, one should mention the felicitous formulation within Robin Bower's discussion of transformation through reading in the monastic tradition: "*Lectio divina* thus becomes a writing that inscribes the text of scripture upon both the body and the soul The fruitful engagement of reading and memory reconstitutes human interiority and desire." I believe that a rich phenomenology of reading and writing around religious and mystical themes is of great value for all, inside academia and outside, who share this endeavor. For the more archetypically oriented among us, part of this would be an understanding of the book as archetype, as Meredith Sabini has written in the shamanic context.[51]

The antinomian possibilities in the Christian material on the book of the heart and soul echo the more general instances of antinomianism discussed in this book, despite my reservations as to overuse of this category. On the one hand, this is not surprising, as at least from the time of Paul antinomian discourse has had a firm place in Christian religious culture. However, the movement of devotion to the sacred heart not only reinterpreted the Eucharist as the feeding of the soul, but also established numerous rites concretizing this form of devotion. This is but one example of the artificiality of a sharp distinction between internal-psychological and nomian manifestations of personal religion.[52]

Epilogue: Themis and the Soul

I'm a rebel, soul rebel.
BOB MARLEY

As stated at the beginning of the *Hoshen Mishpat* section of the *Arba' Turim*, the purpose of the most extensive and most analyzed part of Halakha, monetary and economic law, is to guide the judge in "breaking the arms" of the wicked, and returning the spoils that they took to their just owners. In doing so, the judge becomes God's partner in creation. Following along the path of Hillman, Ann Shearer has devoted an in-spiring book to Themis as goddess of justice and as archetype of *thymos*, the blood-soul or heart-soul (as opposed to psyche or the breath-soul that she describes as spirit-soul). This blood soul seems to resemble the "animal soul," and as we have seen, various modern Kabbalists regard the transformation of this soul as the key to the redemptive process. Drawing on Renaissance thinker Ficino, Shearer identifies this archetype with justice as the "common soul" of society. In her vision, redemptive descriptions such as that in Isaiah draw on a primal conception of justice that transcends the later division between the human and the divine realm. In the later chapters of her book, she studies restorative justice, such as the Truth and Reconciliation process in my own country of birth, South Africa, as examples of this archetypal manifestation.[53]

Shearer's analysis blends well with the somewhat neglected thought of Jan Patočka, who described the soul as the center of philosophy and defined the latter as the care of the soul. Moreover, European history "cannot be understood except from this point of reference that we call the care of the soul." For this original (and politically persecuted) thinker, a student of Edmund Husserl, the model for "the soul in its ac-tion" is not "a mystical look into oneself," but rather "where justice and injustice are visible—*in the community*." Thus, society is a picture of the soul and the question of the *polis* is that of the soul.[54]

The current time of mass demonstrations for social justice worldwide is an appropriate time to conclude with this archetypal invocation of Themis, and with it, the book. Though it may seem strange to conclude a Jewish studies book (and a chapter on the nomian at that) with a Greek goddess (especially in light of my self-distancing from Hillman's return to Greece), this is part of what I see as one of Zionism's main cultural contributions, the return to Greek myth. Quite close to the beginnings of political Zionism and of psychoanalysis, an almost prayer-like return to Greece was manifested in Saul Tchernichovsky's poem *Le-Nokah Pesel Apollo* ("Before a Statue of Apollo"), written in 1899. However, one should remember that Apollo was the God whose worship pushed aside that of Themis at Delphi, so that perhaps the healing of Israel, more than a century later, requires going back even further.

The plural psyche of modern Kabbalah can well meet what Miller has described, long before the return of the gods, old and especially new, in popular culture (most recently Neil Gaiman's *American Gods*, Rick Riordan's many books, Scott Mebus' *Gods of Manhattan*, etc.), as "the new polytheism." Indeed it is Miller who wrote an overlooked call for a revolution in the understanding of mysticism: "The notion of Dike (righteousness and justice) lies at the root of mystical thinking." As Michael Davis has recently shown, the Greek world saw the questions of law and justice in society as deeply intertwined with those of the soul, in a manner often lost in the contemporary divide between individual psychology or spirituality and collective politics. As he summarizes his close reading of the Socratic *Cleitophon*, "Justice is a sign that there are such things as souls in the world." Again, recourse to Greek religion may jar; however, the polytheistic perspective can join the Kabbalistic-theurgical approach, based on linking the almost endless aspects of the Godhead, in dethroning what Hillman termed "monotheistic psychology."[55]

Miller's close associate, James Hillman of blessed memory, to whom this book is dedicated, placed the lines on the soul clapping hands and "sing and louder sing" in William Butler Yeats' "Sailing to Byzantium" at the beginning of *Re-Visioning Psychology*. The image of sailing to Byzantium is itself a form of return to the Greek world, as evoked in Yeats' expression "Grecian goldsmiths." As academia becomes increasingly soulless and dominated by Weber's "specialists without spirit, sensualists without heart" (sensualists in the sense of market-driven materialists), all the more does the soul need to sing in joy, as the Hasidim, singing-masters of the soul, have exhorted us. It is my hope that the readers had a heartfelt sense of the joy of writing this book.[56]

Appendix: The Soul in the Work *Binyan Shmu'el*

One lesser known text currently arousing some interest in Haredi circles is *Binyan Shmu'el* by R. Shmu'el ben Qalonimus Landau of Galicia. This work, as its title (the building of Shmu'el) indicates, follows the convention of an architectural structure, and one of its four sets of "buildings" is that of the soul. Already in his introduction, Landau describes the book as redressing the decline of Kabbalistic lore, due to the rise of the Haskala and Zionism and despite the prevalent belief that the year 1840 would enable an increase in its dissemination. It is interesting that in this brief survey of the history of Kabbalah, he uses the modern term "Middle Ages" to describe the period prior to Luria. Rarely for his time (yet like his contemporary Kook), Landau describes both the Besht and R. Kremer of Vilna as continuing and expanding R. Luria's path. Besides the Hasidic teachings (such as those of Komarno) and those of Kremer, Landau also includes texts from R. Menahem 'Azaria da Fano in his argumentation. Therefore, one can see his writing as providing a panorama of modern Kabbalah, and this is the reason for the interest in this book in our times, when several Kabbalists are searching for just this synthesis.[1]

Towards the beginning of the opening section "the houses of the soul" (*batei ha-nefesh*), Landau innovatively describes Kremer as innovating a "new world" in describing the *nefesh* or lowest aspect of the soul as one's personal time and destiny (*mazal*), and also as the feminine aspect of Malkhut (of the world of Emanation). He then goes on to ponder how one can reconcile this view with the Lurianic teaching on gradual acquisition of all of the three main parts of the soul through the process of reincarnation. Through a lengthy juxtaposition of texts by Luria and Kremer, Landau concludes that one must distinguish between the feminine garb of the soul, which is the personal time not subject to the process of reincarnation, and the primordial essence and root of the soul, which does takes part in this process. In other words, the singular aspect of the *nefesh* that accompanies the body in one lifetime is its feminine time.[2]

Having placed this idea within the framework of modern Kabbalistic writing, Landau then integrates it with teachings of the Besht in order to show that the number of one's days, as well as the quantity of one's possessions, is determined by this personal destiny. Merging this view with that of the school of Kremer described in chapter 4, he distinguishes between this level and that of worship, which belongs to the sphere of *ruah*. Here he offers an interesting distinction regarding the senses, a topic that cannot be addressed here yet is important in modern Kabbalistic psychology. The senses refined in worship, belonging to *ruah*, differ from those described in the premodern classic *Sefer Yetzira*, which belong to destiny. In other words, we have two separate sets of body-soul relationships. And here, reflecting his keen historical consciousness, Landau returns to his earlier discourse in a surprising manner. Luria omitted to mention this entire distinction revealed by Kremer and others, as he focused only on matters relevant to divine worship. Similarly, Luria did not discuss the aspects revealed by his student R. Yisra'el Sarug (not discussed in the present study), as they too do not pertain to worship. It is tempting to interpret this bold statement as follows: from the eighteenth century, Kabablah begins to move away from the self-enclosed domain of worship and discuss aspects of life—economic, existential, and psychological—usually addressed by the materialistic doctrines that it now competes with.[3]

Like many others in the book, this brief discussion of *Binyan Shmu'el* is designed towards arousing interest in further research. At the same time, I believe that it wonderfully demonstrates one of our main claims. Especially after the eighteenth century, and in an ever increasing manner, modern Kabbalah becomes its own autonomous realm. The vast number of modern texts rendered accessible through print (and more recently by computer technology) enabled elaborate discourses to be constructed through navigating in this scholastic universe. As we see in Landau's book, medieval texts, such as Zoharic writings, are addressed only to the extent that they are discussed by modern authorities. As

Kabbalah scholarship discards the illusion that it can operate in isolation from modern Kabbalah itself, the brief attempt to always address modern Kabbalah in a premodern context will give way to the relentless advance of modernity. While I regard this as a positive process, I can empathize with those who see it as a failure of the project of scholarship, yet feel compelled to say that this is so only if one attempts to remove academic study from the course of the very history that it investigates.

Notes

1. For a nuanced reading of the series, quite sensitive to the presence of religious themes yet somewhat downplaying Christian elements, see Shira Wolosky, *The Riddles of Harry Potter: Secret Passages and Interpretive Quests* (New York: Palgrave Macmillan, 2010), esp. 168–69, 211n1, and 212n8. For a Jungian reading see Christine Gerhold, "The Hero's Journey through Adolescence: A Jungian Archetypical Analysis of 'Harry Potter'" (Ph.D. diss., University of Chicago, 2010). It is surprising that such studies have overlooked the role of Gnosticism (a major concern of Jung's): for example, Dumbledore's command to Severus Snape to betray him may well reflect what is often seen as a Gnostic reinterpretation of the betrayal of Christ by Judas (though of course I cannot enter the question of the scholarly exactitude of this perception).

2. See Jeffrey J. Kripal, *Mutants and Mystics: Science Fiction, Superhero Comics, and the Paranormal* (Chicago: University of Chicago Press, 2011) (on the soul, see esp. 294, 320, 331–32); Joseph Grange, *Soul: A Cosmology* (Albany: State University of New York Press, 2011), 41–51, 56, 63–65, 104–9.

3. Julia Kristeva, *New Maladies of the Soul*, trans. R. Guberman (New York: Columbia University Press, 1995), 64–66, 116. On Kristeva and Kabbalah, see Elliot R. Wolfson, "Suffering Eros and Textual Incarnation: A Kristevan Reading of Kabbalistic Poetics," in *Toward a Theology of Eros: Transfiguring Passion at the Limits of Discipline*, ed. V. Burrus and C. Keller, 341–65 (New York: Fordham University Press, 2006).

4. Erich Fromm, *Psychoanalysis and Religion* (New Haven: Yale University Press, 1950). Dawson is quoted in John S. Dunne,

A Journey with God in Time: A Spiritual Quest (Notre Dame, IN: University of Notre Dame Press, 2003), 28.

5. Martha Nussbaum, *Not for Profit: Why Democracy Needs the Humanities* (Princeton and Oxford: Princeton University Press, 2010), 6.

6. Victoria Nelson, *The Secret Life of Puppets* (Cambridge: Harvard University Press, 2001), 144, 146, as well as 31, 44, 51–52, 57, 128–29, 258, 268. On the pole theme in more recent mystical literature, see Kripal, *Mutants and Mystics*, 33–38. A recent popular fantastic representation of the golem theme is Jonathan Stroud, *The Golem's Eye* (New York: Disney-Hyperion, 2004). On travel in imaginal or mythical geography, see Jonathan Garb, *Shamanic Trance in Modern Kabbalah* (Chicago: University of Chicago Press, 2011), 27–29, 55, 67. See also on the journey of the soul in chapter 6.

7. See Sarah Rivett, *The Science of the Soul in Colonial New England* (Chapel Hill: University of North Carolina Press, 2011), and Edward S. Reed, *From Soul to Mind: The Emergence of Psychology from Erasmus Darwin to William James* (New Haven: Yale University Press, 1997), and compare to Raymond Martin and John Barresi, *Naturalization of the Soul: Self and Personal Identity in the Eighteenth Century* (London: Routledge, 2000). Milner is quoted in Roy Porter, *Flesh in the Age of Reason* (New York: W. W. Norton & Co., 2004), 27, who writes of "the demise of the soul" at this time. See also my discussion of German romanticism in chapter 6. On psychoanalysis as mythology, see James Hillman, *The Myth of Analysis: Three Essays in Archetypal Psychology* (Evanston: Northwestern University Press, 1972), as well as idem, *The Dream and the Underworld* (New York: Harper & Row, 1979), 23. Stewart Goetz and Charles Taliaferro, *A Brief History of the Soul* (Oxford: Wiley-Blackwell, 2011), 65–151, provide a useful overview of treatments of the soul in modern philosophy. See also the more focused discussion of the early modern decline of the classical notion of the world soul in Miklós Vassányi, *Anima Mundi: The Rise of the World Soul Theory in Modern German Philosophy* (Dordrecht and Heidelberg: Springer, 2011), 13–81, 164–67.

8. Chaim Potok, *The Chosen* (London: Penguin, 1970); Fischel Schneersohn, *Chaim Gravitzer,* trans. A. Shlonsky (Tel Aviv: Miskal, 2013) [Hebrew].

9. Gershom Scholem, *On the Possibility of Jewish Mysticism in Our Time and Other Essays*, trans. J. Chipman (Philadelphia: Jewish Publication Society, 1997), 6 (compare to idem, *Major Trends in Jewish Mysticism* [New York: Schocken Books, 1961], 8, on the soul as the scene of mysticism and its path as its main preoccupation).

10. William James, *The Varieties of Religious Experience* (New York: Mentor and Plume, 1958), 112–39. For good overviews of the field see Diane Jonte-Pace and William B. Parsons, *Religion and Psychology: Mapping the Terrain* (New York: Routledge, 2001); Andrew R. Fuller, *Psychology and Religion: Classical Theorists and Contemporary Approaches* (Lanham, MD: Rowman and Littlefield Publishers, 2008); James M. Nelson, *Psychology, Religion and Spirituality* (New York: Springer, 2009), and most recently William Parsons, *Freud and*

Augustine in Dialogue: Psychoanalysis, Mysticism and the Culture of Modern Spirituality (Charlottesville: University of Virginia Press, 2013), esp. 69–96. For a discussion foregrounding the soul, see Graham Richards, *Psychology, Religion, and the Nature of the Soul: A Historical Entanglement* (New York: Springer, 2011). For a fairly recent overview of psychology of mysticism, see Anton Geels and Jacob A. Belzen, "A Vast Domain and Numerous Perspectives: Introduction to the Volume," in *Mysticism: A Variety of Psychological Perspectives*, ed. J. A. Belzen and A. Geels, 7–15 (Amsterdam: Rodopi, 2003).

11. See Michael Eigen, *The Psychoanalytic Mystic* (Binghamton, NY: ESF Publishers, 1998), 27; Gary Lachman, *Jung the Mystic: The Esoteric Dimensions of Carl Jung's Life and Teachings* (New York: Tarcher & Penguin, 2010), 1; Peter Homans, *Jung in Context: Modernity and the Making of a Psychology* (Chicago: University of Chicago Press, 1995), xvii, xxviii–xxxi; Otto Rank, *Psychology and the Soul: A Study of the Origin, Conceptual Evolution, and Nature of the Soul*, trans. G. C. Richter and E. J. Lieberman (Baltimore: Johns Hopkins University Press, 1998), 7, 8, and see also 61, 94. For an illuminating discussion of Rank's relationship with Judaism, see Peter Homans, *The Ability to Mourn: Disillusionment and the Social Origins of Psychoanalysis* (Chicago: University of Chicago Press, 1989), 152–71. On Jung and James, see Somu Shamdasani, *Jung and the Making of Modern Psychology: The Dream of a Science* (Cambridge: Cambridge University Press, 2012), 33–37, 57–61, 65–66, 298–99 (11–18, as well as 89–90, 165, 200, 244–49 [on the soul], are also relevant for my argumentation here). Eigen, Rank, and other writers addressed here have been discussed from a rather different angle in Dan Merkur, *Explorations of the Psychoanalytic Mystics* (Amsterdam: Rodopi, 2010).

12. See John Kerr, *A Most Dangerous Method: The Story of Jung, Freud, and Sabina Spielrein* (New York: Alfred A. Knopf, 1993), 9, 105, 185.

13. See Stephen Frosh, *Hate and the Jewish Science: Anti-Semitism, Nazism, and Psychoanalysis* (New York: Palgrave Macmillan, 2005), 1 (and cf. the balanced comments of Homans, *Jung in Context*, xlv–xlvi); Frank Tallis, *Darkness Rising* (New York: Random House, 2009); Bruno Bettelheim, *Freud and Man's Soul* (New York: Random House, 1984), esp. 12, 70–78; William Parsons, "Freud's Last Theory of Mysticism: The Return of the (Phylogenetic) Repressed," in *After Spirituality: Studies in Mystical Traditions*, ed. P. Wexler and J. Garb, 173–86 (New York: Peter Lang Publishing, 2012), that also cites a rare text on the soul.

14. See Carl Jung, *Psychology and Religion* (New Haven: Yale University Press, 1966), 3, 11, 18 (see also 57); idem, *Psychological Types*, vol. 6 of *The Collected Works of C. G. Jung*, ed. H. Read et al., trans. H. G. Baynes (London: Routledge and Kegan Paul, 1971), 463, 465–71. For the importance of these works for understanding Jung's development, see Homans, *Jung in Context*, 91–93 (on "Psychological Types"), 187–92 (on *Psychology and Religion*). On dreams and Jewish texts in Jung's lecture, see Elliot R. Wolfson, *A Dream Interpreted within a Dream: Oneiropoiesis and the Prism of Imagination* (New

York: Zone Books, 2011), 173. For a fine distinction between the "fantasy of opposites" in Jung's text and the independent phenomenology of anima as "our individualized becoming" or "soul-making" (see below), see James Hillman, *Anima: An Anatomy of a Personified Notion* (Dallas: Spring Publications, 1985), 14–15. Hillman also traces the cultural and historical origins of Jung's locution (ibid., 41–42). For a Jungian-oriented history of the interrelationship of the terms "soul" and "psyche," see Victor White, *Soul and Psyche* (New York: Harper and Brothers, 1960), 11–31.

15. Hillman, *Anima*, 45, 160–61 (and cf. Homans, *Jung in Context*, 82–86, 106, 109; Lachman, *Jung the Mystic*, 121). For an extensive discussion of psyche and the feminine, see Erich Neumann, *Amor and Psyche*, trans. R. Manheim (Princeton: Princeton University Press, 1971), which includes some Jewish parallels (74, 101—part of his propagation of Jungian psychology in Israel). One should note that there is an entire book of Neuman's on Hasidism in a German-language manuscript possessed by his family, the publication of which is a prerequisite for an informed discussion of the place of Jewish mysticism in his thought. On Kabbalah in Jung's visions, see my comment in Jonathan Garb, *The Chosen Will Become Herds: Studies in Twentieth-Century Kabbalah*, trans. Y. Berkovits-Murciano (New Haven: Yale University Press, 2009), 111, and the slightly more extensive treatment in Wolfson, *A Dream Interpreted*, 426n156. For gender and Kabbalah's psychology, see the numerous works of Elliot R. Wolfson, and esp. his *Through a Speculum That Shines* (Princeton: Princeton University Press, 1997), 306–17; the body-centered approach of Daniel Abrams, *The Female Body of God in Kabbalistic Literature: Embodied Forms of Love and Sexuality in the Divine Female* (Jerusalem: Magnes Press, 2004) [Hebrew], his more psychological *Ten Psychoanalytic Aphorisms on the Kabbalah* (Los Angeles: Cherub Press, 2011), and the discussions of body-soul interaction from a gendered perspective in Charles Mopsik, *Sex of the Soul: The Vicissitudes of Sexual Difference in Kabbalah* (Los Angeles: Cherub Press, 2005), esp. 38–47. See also Dvorah Bat-David Gamlieli, *Psychoanalysis and Kabbalah: The Masculine and Feminine in Lurianic Kabbalah* (Los Angeles: Cherub Press, 2006) [Hebrew] (cf. Hava Tirosh-Samuelson, "Gender in Jewish Mysticism," in *Jewish Mysticism and Kabbalah: New Insights and Scholarship*, ed. F. E. Greenspahn [New York: New York University Press, 2011], 229n110). See also the reservations regarding psychoanalytic interpretation of Kabbalistic gender imagery in Moshe Idel, *Kabbalah and Eros* (New Haven: Yale University Press, 2005), 96–101 (and compare to idem, *Ascensions on High in Jewish Mysticism: Pillars, Lines, Ladders* [Budapest: Central European University Press, 2005] 5, 8–10). For a critique of the "dogma of gender" in archetypal psychology, see Patricia Berry, "The Dogma of Gender," in *Echo's Subtle Body: Contributions to an Archetypal Psychology*, 35–51 (Dallas: Spring Publications, 2008).

16. James Hillman, *Re-Visioning Psychology* (New York: Harper and Row, 1975), xv (for the Keats citation), 67 (and 39), xvii.

17. See Wolfgang Giegerich, *The Soul's Logical Life: Towards a Rigorous Notion of Psychology* (Frankfurt am Main: Peter Lang, 1998); David L. Miller, *Christs: Meditations on Archetypal Images in Christian Theology* (New York: Seabury Press, 1981), e.g. 81, 124; idem, *Three Faces of God: Traces of the Trinity in Literature and Life* (New Orleans: Spring Journal Books, 2005), e.g. 7, 155; Robert Sardello, *Love and the Soul: Creating a Future for Earth* (Berkeley: North Atlantic Books, 2008), 11, 17–30 (see also Robert D. Romanyshyn, *The Wounded Researcher: Research with Soul in Mind* [New Orleans: Spring Journal Books, 2007]). The mytho-poetic approach was largely developed in the school of Yehuda Liebes (see Garb, *Shamanic Trance*, 5–6; Jonathan Garb, "Yehuda Liebes's Way in the Study of the Jewish Religion," in *And This Is for Yehuda: Studies Presented to Our Friend, Professor Yehuda Liebes*, ed. M. Niehoff, R. Meroz, and J. Garb, 11–16 (Jerusalem: Mossad Bialik, 2012) [Hebrew]), the current exemplar of which is Jonatan Benarroch, "Sabba and Yanuqa, 'Two That Are One': Allegory, Symbol and Myth in Zoharic Literature" (Ph.D. diss., Hebrew University of Jerusalem, 2011) [Hebrew] (see esp. 345–52).
18. I find Randall Collins, *The Sociology of Philosophies: A Global Theory of Intellectual Change* (Cambridge, MA: Belknap Press of Harvard University Press, 1998), 24–28 to be the most useful social psychology of academic ritual. For mysticism in the Hillman Festschrift (which is also a good representation of the current map of his network), see Stanton Marlan, "Mystical Light: Dream Images and the Alchemy of Psychic Momentum," in *Archetypal Psychologies: Reflections in Honor of James Hillman*, ed. S. Marlan (New Orleans: Spring Journal Books, 2008), 341–49.
19. Tom Cheetam, *The World Turned Inside Out: Henry Corbin and Islamic Mysticism* (Woodstock: Spring Journal, 2003), 9 (see also 80–81 and n58 for an important distinction between Hillman and Corbin). For the soul and modernity at Eranos, see John von Heyking, "From a Wooded Summit: Learning to Love through Augustinian Meditation at Ascona," in *Pioniere, Poeten, Professoren: Eranos und der Monte Verità in der Zivilisationsgeschichte des 20. Jahrhunderts*, ed. B. Elisabetta, M. Riedl, and A. Tischel (Würzburg: Königshausen & Neumann, 2004), 83–96. For a politicized reading of the interaction of Scholem and Corbin (as well as Eliade, of whom see below), see Steven M. Wasserstrom, *Religion after Religion: Gershom Scholem, Mircea Eliade, and Henry Corbin at Eranos* (Princeton: Princeton University Press, 1999). For Wolfson and Corbin, see esp. Wolfson, *Through a Speculum*, 8, 61–63 (as well as my discussion below of his *A Dream Interpreted*). For the soul-heart link, see also Sardello, *Love and the Soul*, 275–304.
20. James Hillman, *The Thought of the Heart and the Soul of the World* (New York: Spring Publications, 2007), 7–8, 9, 13, 22; Jonathan Garb, "The Circle of Moshe Hayyim Luzzatto in Its Eighteenth-Century Context," *Eighteenth Century Studies* 44/2 (2011): 189–202; Thomas Fuchs, *The Mechanization of the Heart: Harvey and Descartes*, trans. M. Grene (Rochester: University of Rochester Press, 2001).

21. Hillman, *The Thought of the Heart*, 30, 28, 35. On emotions and *middot*, see for now Garb, *Shamanic Trance*, 92, 122–25. The most quoted psychobiographic study of a Jewish mystical figure is Arthur Green, *Tormented Master: The Life and Spiritual Quest of Rabbi Nahman of Bratslav* (Tuscaloosa: University of Alabama Press, 1979). On psychobiography and Jewish studies, see Zev Eleff, "Psychohistory and the Imaginary Couch: Diagnosing Historical and Biblical Figures," *Journal of the American Academy of Religion* 80/1 (2012): 94–136. For a Foucauldian analysis of psychotherapeutic practices as the "offspring, however distant" of modern transformations of "medieval systems for the administration of the soul," see Nikolas Rose, *Governing the Soul: The Shaping of the Private Self* (London: Routledge, 1989), esp. 213–20. See also Abram De Swaan, "On the Sociogenesis of the Psychoanalytic Setting," in *Human Figurations: Essays for Nobert Elias*, ed. P. Gleichmann, J. Goudsblom, and H. Korte, 381–413 (Amsterdam: Stichting Amsterdams Sociologisch Tijdschrift, 1977).

22. Hillman, *The Thought of the Heart*, 91–92, 107–8; Moshe Idel, *Hasidism: Between Ecstasy and Magic* (Albany: State University of New York Press, 1995), esp. 11–12, 218–21.

23. James Hillman, *Suicide and the Soul* (New York: Harper & Row, 1972); idem, *Insearch: Psychology and Religion* (New York: Scribner, 1967); idem, *The Soul's Code: In Search of Character and Calling* (New York: Random House, 1996) (for Kabbalah see 43–44). For an alternative periodization of Hillman, see Marcus Quintaes, "Hillman Revisioning Hillman: Polemics and Paranoia," in *Archetypal Psychologies: Reflections in Honor of James Hillman*, ed. S. Marlan (New Orleans: Spring Journal Books, 2008), 79–89, and the essays quoted there.

24. For the heart in previous research on Jewish mysticism, see, e.g., Haviva Pedaya, *Name and Sanctuary in the Teaching of R. Isaac the Blind: A Comparative Study in the Writings of the Earliest Kabbalists* (Jerusalem: Magnes Press, 2001) [Hebrew], esp. 238–39 (and see also 90–91); idem, "Text and Its Performance in the Poetry of R. Israel Najjara: Banishing Sleep as a Practice of Exile in the Nocturnal Space," in *The Piyyut as a Cultural Prism: New Approaches*, ed. H. Pedaya (Jerusalem: Van Leer Institute; Tel Aviv: Hakibbutz Hameuchad, 2012) [Hebrew], 46–49; Wolfson, *Through a Speculum*, 63, 145–47, 170–80, 184–85, 290–95, 308–9; idem, *Language, Eros, Being: Kabbalistic Hermeneutics and Poetic Imagination* (New York: Fordham University Press, 2005), 233–35, 308–9; idem, *Open Secret: Postmessianic Messianism and the Mystical Revision of Menahem Mendel Schneerson* (New York: Columbia University Press, 2009), 44–51, 201–2; idem, *Venturing Beyond: Law and Morality in Kabbalistic Mysticism* (Oxford: Oxford University Press, 2006), 67–73, 96–97; Ron Margolin, *Inner Religion: The Phenomenology of Inner Religious Life and Its Manifestation in Jewish Sources (From the Bible to Hasidic Texts)* (Ramat Gan: Bar Ilan University; Jerusalem: Shalom Hartman Institute, 2011) [Hebrew], 49, 273–75, 358.

25. See Garb, *Shamanic Trance*, 7–11, and also 145–47 on the influence of Freudianism on Kabbalah.
26. Hillman, *Thought of the Heart*, 102, as well as 33; idem, *Revisioning Psychology*, esp. 167–83; Jonathan Garb, "Mystics' Critique of Mystical Experience," *Revue de l'histoire des religions* 21 (2004): 293–325; Martin Jay, *Songs of Experience: Modern American and European Variations on a Universal Theme* (Berkeley: University of California Press, 2005). Jay's discussion of William James' psychology of religious experience and its earlier Pietistic roots is most pertinent (102–10). Cf. Melila Hellner-Eshed, *A River Flows from Eden: The Language of Mystical Experience in the Zohar*, trans. N. Wolski (Stanford, CA: Stanford University Press, 2009), esp. 67, 212, 218, 286–88.
27. Eigen, *The Psychoanalytic Mystic*, 24, 39, 38, 162 (and see 41 for a striking erotic experience of the opening of "a vagina in my soul," compared to 49, 89 on the "psychic invagination" of the biblical figure of Jacob and 105, 168 on "soul orgasms"; for the meeting with the rebbe of Habad, see 185); idem, *The Sensitive Self* (Middletown: Wesleyan University Press, 2004), 44, 45, 48, 60; idem, *Ecstasy* (Middletown: Wesleyan University Press, 2001), 4, 10. See also my comments on Bion and Winnicot in Garb, *Shamanic Trance*, 8–9, 92, 135.
28. Michael Eigen, *Kabbalah and Psychoanalysis* (London: Karnac Books, 2012), xi, 59. Eigen draws heavily on the psychobiography by Green mentioned above.
29. And thus clearly distinguished from imaginary premodern fellowships that lack such historical documentation. Cf. the 'near dissolution' of the place of fellowships in the history of Kabbalah in Daniel Abrams, *Kabbalistic Manuscripts and Textual Theory: Methodologies of Textual Scholarship and Editorial Practice in the Study of Jewish Mysticism*, 2nd rev. ed. (Los Angeles: Cherub Press, 2014), esp. 379–80, 535, 714, 720.
30. On the centrality of circles for intellectual history, see Collins, *The Sociology of Philosophies*, which in my view does not sufficiently emphasize the modern enhancement of this process. Cf. Jonathan Garb, "The Psychological Turn in Sixteenth Century Kabbalah," in *Les Mystiques juives, chrétiennes et musulmanes dans L'Egypte médiévale (VIIe–XVIe siècle): Interculturalités et contextes historiques*, ed. G. Cecere, M. Loubet, and S. Pagani (Cairo: Institut français d'archéologie orientale, 2013), 109–24. At the end of the eighteenth century, one can discern an attempt to synthesize Kantian philosophy with Kabbalah as in Pinchas Horowitz's *Sefer Ha-Brit*. On psychology in this work see Resianne Fontaine, "The Immortality of the Soul in Pinchas Hurwitz's 'Sefer ha-Berit': Philosophers versus Kabbalists," *Jewish Studies Quarterly* 13 [2006]: 223–33, esp. 230. The book and its context are discussed in David Ruderman, *A Best-Selling Hebrew Book of the Modern Era: The Book of the Covenant of Pinhas Hurwitz and Its Remarkable Legacy* (Seattle: University of Washington Press, 2014).
31. See De Swaan, "On the Sociogenesis"; cf. Homans, *Jung in Context*, xxiv–xxvii, xxxvii–xxxix, 135–44. For an important sociology of knowledge

analysis of the conditions for the emergence of modern psychology in general, see Joseph Ben-David and Randall Collins, "Social Factors in the Origins of a New Science: The Case of Psychology," *American Sociological Review* 31/4 (1966): 451–65. The comment of Tirosh-Samuelson, "Gender in Jewish Mysticism," 221, though from a different direction, matches my own thinking.

32. Suzanne Kirschner, *The Religious and Romantic Origins of Psychoanalysis: Individuation and Integration in Post-Freudian Theory* (New York: Cambridge University Press, 1996), esp. 26–27, 45–46, 56–60, 192, 194 (see also 19–20, 28, 206–8 on Foucault, as well as my further discussion in chapter 6); cf. the description of Freudian psychoanalysis as antithetical to the religious tradition of cure of souls in Philip Rieff, *The Triumph of the Therapeutic: Uses of Faith After Freud* (Chicago: University of Chicago Press, 1987), esp. 89–92.

33. Joel Whitebook, "Freud, Foucault and 'the Dialogue with Unreason,'" *Philosophy and Social Criticism* 25/6 (1999): 29–66. For a critique of my indebtedness to Foucault based on a surprising claim as to the irrelevance of this major theorist even to the study of early twentieth-century Kabbalah, see Ron Margolin, "Review of Garb, *The Chosen Will Become Herds*," *Journal of Modern Jewish Studies* 10/3 (2011): 441–44. Cf. Jeremy R. Carrette, *Foucault and Religion: Spiritual Corporality and Political Spirituality* (London: Routledge, 2000). I do not wish to ignore the roots of psychoanalysis in Greek thought, as discussed throughout Hillman's writings. For a nuanced discussion, see Giovanni Vassalli, "The Birth of Psychoanalysis from the Spirit of Technique," *International Journal of Psychoanalysis* 82/3 (2001): 3–25.

34. Wolfson, *A Dream Interpreted*; idem, *Open Secret* (see my discussion in chapters 4 and 5).

35. Garb, *Shamanic Trance*, 152n27; Wolfson, *A Dream Interpreted*, esp. 51–52, 56–57, 64–71, 90–99, 171–76, 182–87, 198–99, 390n60 (for dreams and the soul and heart, see 190–93, 195–96); Sigmund Freud, *The Interpretation of Dreams*, trans. and ed. James Stratchey (New York: Basic Books, 2010), 570.

36. Sanford L. Drob, *Kabbalistic Visions: C. G. Jung and Jewish Mysticism* (New Orleans: Spring Journal Books, 2010), 61–67 for Wolfson, and 51–52 for Scholem. See also, one example of many, 105, where the second volume of a translation of the *Zohar* is tellingly referred to as the second book of the *Zohar*! (see however 39, 46, 59, 91, 111 for interesting Jungian quotations on the soul and Kabbalah); see also Steven M. Joseph, "Jung and Kabbalah: Imaginal and Noetic Aspects," *Journal of Analytical Psychology* 52 (2007): 321–41. There are a few special issues of Jungian journals devoted to Judaism, esp. Kabbalah (most recently issue 55 (2012) of *Psychological Perspectives* and volume 7/1 (2005) of *The Journal of Jungian Theory*, the latter volume containing important critiques of Drob's writing). For earlier treatments of Jungian theory in Kabbalah, see Wolfson, *Through a Speculum*, 56–57n21, 66–67; Avraham Elqayam, "To Know the Messiah: The Dialectic of Sexual Discourse in the Messianic Thought of Nathan of Gaza," *Tarbiz*

NOTES TO PAGES 13–14

65/4 (1996): 646–58 [Hebrew]; Idel, *Hasidism*, 135; idem, *Kabbalah and Eros*, 55–57; 236–37; idem, *Ascensions on High*, 226; Shimon Shokek, *Kabbalah and the Art of Being* (New York: Routledge, 2011), 68–76; Haviva Pedaya, *Vision and Speech: Models of Prophecy in Jewish Mysticism* (Los Angeles: Cherub Press, 2002) [Hebrew], 39–41; idem, *Expanses: An Essay on the Theological and Political Unconscious* (Tel Aviv: Hakibbutz Hameuchad, 2011) [Hebrew], 283; Daniel Abrams, "Knowing the Maiden without Eyes: Reading the Sexual Reconstruction of the Jewish Mystic in a Zoharic Parable," *Daat* 50/51 (2003): esp. LXI; Margolin, *Inner Religion*, 433–34. For critical assessments of studies of Kabbalah's psychology beyond my previous overview, see my notes above on gender and mytho-poetics. Roni Weinstein, *Kabbalah and Jewish Modernity* (Tel Aviv: Tel Aviv University Press, 2011) [Hebrew], 157–76, addresses psychological issues without considering modern psychological theory (see however my more positive assessment of other parts of the book in chapter 2). This is certainly the case for the numerous important studies of Liebes (see esp. Liebes, "Myth vs. Symbol in the Zohar and in Lurianic Kabbalah," in *Essential Papers on Kabbalah*, ed. L. Fine [New York: New York University Press, 1995], 212–42; idem, "Mysticism and Reality: Towards a Portrait of the Martyr and Kabbalist R. Samson Ostropoler," in *Jewish Thought in the Seventeenth Century*, ed. I. Twersky and B. Septimus [Cambridge: Harvard University Press, 1987], 221–55). For brief critical discussions of psychology and phenomenology in the study of religion, see Margolin, *Inner Religion*, 20, 27–31, 433–34. As we shall see, while Margolin's extensive treatment of interiorization (as in his previous book *Human Temple*) touches on many psychological issues, he does not greatly address psychological theory, not even classic studies of interiorization (e.g., Roy Schafer, *Aspects of Internalization* [Madison: International Universities Press, 1990]).

37. Peter Berger, *A Rumor of Angels: Modern Society and the Rediscovery of the Supernatural* (Harmondsworth: Penguin, 1971), 10. For my earlier studies see Jonathan Garb, "The Modernization of Kabbalah: A Case Study," *Modern Judaism: A Journal of Jewish Ideas and Experience* 30/1 (2010): 1–22; idem, "Circle of Moshe Hayyim Luzzatto"; idem, "The Political Model in Modern Kabbalah: A Study of Ramhal and his Intellectual Surroundings," in *'Al Da'at ha-Kahal—Religion and Politics in Jewish Thought: Festschrift in Honor of Aviezer Ravitzky*, ed. B. Brown et al., 13–45 (Jerusalem: Zalman Shazar Center and Israel Democracy Institute, 2012) [Hebrew]; idem, *Kabbalist in the Heart of the Storm: R. Moshe Hayyim Luzzatto* (Tel Aviv: Tel Aviv University Press, 2014) [Hebrew], esp. 91–93, 321–22; idem, "Shamanism and the Hidden History of Modern Kabbalah," in *Histories of the Hidden God*, ed. A. DeConick and G. Adamson (Durham: Acumen Publishing, 2013), 175–92. For a similar argument on gender, see idem, "Gender and Power in Kabbalah: A Theoretical Investigation," *Kabbalah* 13 (2005): 87–93 (and compare to Moshe Idel, "Ascensions, Gender, and Pillars in Safedian Kabbalah," *Kabbalah* 25 (2011), 74–75, 105).

38. Guy G. Stroumsa, *A New Science: The Discovery of Religion in the Age of Reason* (Cambridge, MA: Harvard University Press, 2010).

39. See David Sorotzkin, *Orthodoxy and Modern Disciplination: The Production of the Jewish Tradition in Europe in Modern Times* (Tel Aviv: Hakibbutz Hameuchad, 2011) [Hebrew], esp. 149, 163–66.

40. François Jullien, *The Silent Transformations*, trans. M. Richardson and K. Fijalkowski (London: Seagull Books, 2011), 67–69.

41. For Ottoman Kabbalah, see the comments of Weinstein, *Kabbalah and Jewish Modernity*, 197, 567, 591, and see also my review in *Zion* 80 (2015): 148–53. On empires in Jewish historiography, see the important discussion by Jacob Barnai, "Nationalism and Jewish Historiography," in *Zionism and Empires,* ed. Y. Shenhav (Tel Aviv: Hakibbutz Hameuchad; Jerusalem: Van Leer Institute, forthcoming) [Hebrew]. I shall discuss the relationship of Ottoman Kabbalah and modern European Kabbalah in chapter 2. On Eliade, see Moshe Idel, *Mircea Eliade: From Magic to Myth* (New York: Peter Lang Publishing, 2014), esp. 171, 243–45.

42. On Mussar and hypnotic states see Garb, *Shamanic Trance*, 122–25. For my critique of commercialized neo-Kabbalah, see idem, *The Chosen*, 7, 16, 74. See also idem, "Contemporary Kabbalah and Classical Kabbalah: Breaks and Continuities," in *After Spirituality: Studies in Mystical Traditions*, ed. J. Garb and P. Wexler (New York: Peter Lang Publishing, 2012), 19–46.

43. See Margolin, *Inner Religion*, 365–418 (on avoiding periodization) and 10, 54 (on Far Eastern religion). See 24, 35 for an evaluation of the role of myth similar to mine.

44. The overview of Kabbalah studies in Israel in Moran Gam-Hacohen, "Trends in Kabbalah Research in Israel, 1929–2010" (Ph.D. diss., Ben Gurion University of the Negev, 2010), reveals the centrality of the premodern in both research and teaching. Likewise, the popular chapter on the soul in Pinchas Giller, *Kabbalah: A Guide for the Perplexed* (London: Continuum International Publishing Group, 2011), 84–100, barely mentions developments after the sixteenth century. This is not the place to present my opinion of the suitability of the scholarly construction "medieval" (which unlike the term "modern" has no reflection in the self-consciousness of thinkers in this period) for the study of Kabbalah. See for now the complex argument in Norman F. Cantor, *Inventing the Middle Ages* (New York: Morrow, 1991).

45. David B. Ruderman, *Early Modern Jewry: A New Cultural History* (Princeton: Princeton University Press, 2010); Maoz Kahana, "An Esoteric Path to Modernity: Rabbi Jacob Emden's Alchemical Quest," *Journal of Modern Jewish Studies* 12, 2 (2013): 253–75; Sorotzkin, *Orthodoxy and Modern Disciplination;* Yaacob Dweck, *The Scandal of Kabbalah: Leon Modena, Jewish Mysticism, Early Modern Venice* (Princeton: Princeton University Press, 2011); Pawel Maciejko, *The Mixed Multitude: Jacob Frank and the Frankist Movement, 1755–1816* (Philadelphia: University of Pennsylvania Press, 2011); Ada Rapoport-Albert, *Women and the Messianic Heresy of Sabbatai Zevi 1666–1816* (Oxford:

Littman Library of Jewish Civilization, 2011). For Sabbatean psychology, see my note below on Elqayam, and the important comments of Haviva Pedaya, *Walking through Trauma: Rituals of Movement in Jewish Myth, Mysticism and History* (Tel Aviv: Resling, 2011) [Hebrew], 216–17; idem, *Expanses*, 66–67.

46. Jonatan Meir, *Rehovot ha-Nahar: Kabbalah and Exotericism in Jerusalem (1896–1948)* (Jerusalem: Yad Izhak Ben-Zvi and the Mandel Institute of Jewish Studies, 2011) [Hebrew] (see also Pinchas Giller, *Shalom Shar'abi and the Kabbalists of Beit El* [Oxford: Oxford University Press, 2008]); Daniel Abrams, *Kabbalistic Manuscripts and Textual Theory*, esp. 331, 386; Jonathan Garb, "The Authentic Kabbalistic Writings of Moshe Hayyim Luzzatto," *Kabbalah* 25 (2011): 214–16 [Hebrew] (and my earlier remarks cited in 215n263).

47. See Charles Taylor, *Sources of the Self: The Making of the Modern Identity* (Cambridge: Harvard University Press, 1989) (and cf. Dror Wharman, *The Making of the Modern Self: Identity and Culture in Eighteenth-Century England* [New Haven: Yale University Press, 2004]); Martin and Barresi, *Naturalization of the Soul*; idem, *The Rise and Fall of Soul and Self: An Intellectual History of Personal Identity* (New York: Columbia University Press, 2008) (for Locke, see 142–51); Shmuel N. Eisenstadt, *Comparative Civilizations and Multiple Modernities* (Leiden: Brill, 2003); Sorotzkin, *Orthodoxy and Modern Disciplination*. For important discussions of the soul and other psychological issues in the eighteenth century, see Jonathan Sheehan and Dror Wharman, *Invisible Hands: Self-Organization in the Eighteenth Century* (Chicago: University of Chicago Press, 2015).

48. Wolfson, *Venturing Beyond*, esp. 107–28 (also covering twentieth-century materials); Jonathan Garb, "Rabbi Kook and His Sources: From Kabbalistic Historiosophy to National Mysticism," in *Studies in Modern Religions, Religious Movements and the Babi-Bahai Faiths,* ed. M. Sharon, 77–96 (Leiden: Brill, 2004); idem, "'Alien Culture' in the Thought of Rabbi Kook's Circle," in *Study and Knowledge in Jewish Thought*, ed. H. Kreisel, 253–64 (Beer Sheva: Ben Gurion University of the Negev Press, 2006); idem, "Kabbalah Outside the Walls: The Response of Rabbi Hadayah to the State of Israel," in *Rabbi Uziel and His Peers: Studies in the Religious Thought of Oriental Rabbis in 20th Century Israel*, ed. Z. Zohar, 13–27 (Tel Aviv: Tel Aviv University Press, 2009) [Hebrew].

49. See Garb, *Shamanic Trance*, 53, 64; idem, "Contemporary Kabbalah," and cf. Idel, *Hasidism*, 11–12, 218–21; Idel, *Kabbalah and Eros*, 85, 190, 194, yet see idem, "Ascensions, Gender," 95–97, in which Idel correctly describes Safedian treatments of the soul as a move away from Ficino's neo-Platonism. For a formulation of Idel's complex overall stance on this issue, see his relatively recent "Metamorphoses of a Platonic Theme in Jewish Mysticism," *Jewish Studies at the Central European University* 3 (2002–3), 67–68, 86. On residual philosophically oriented psychology in dialogue with the sixteenth century, see Hava Tirosh-Samuelson, "Jewish Philosophy on the Eve of

Modernity," in *History of Jewish Philosophy*, ed. D. H. Frank and O. Leaman, 536–39 (London: Routledge, 1997).

50. Brad S. Gregory, *The Unintended Reformation: How a Religious Revolution Secularized Society* (Cambridge: Harvard University Press, 2012), 3. I loved his formulation: "Graduate training tends to condition young historians to serve as new inmates in the inherited cells of periodization constructed by their forebears" (7).

51. Michel Foucault, *Discipline and Punish: The Birth of the Prison*, trans. A. Sheridan (New York: Vintage Books, 1995), 30 (and 29); Kristeva, *New Maladies of the Soul*, 4, 28–29.

52. For studies on reincarnation, see Alexander Altmann, *Essays in Jewish Intellectual History* (Hanover, NH: published for Brandeis University Press by University Press of New England, 1981), 37–38; Gershom Scholem, *On the Mystical Shape of the Godhead* (New York: Schocken, 1991), 197–250; idem, *Devils, Demons, Souls: Essays on Demonology*, ed. E. Liebes (Jerusalem: Yad Ben Tzvi, 2004) [Hebrew], 186–214; Michal Oron, "The Doctrine of the Soul and Reincarnation in the 13th Century," *Studies in Jewish Thought*, ed. S. O. H. Willensky and M. Idel, 277–90 (Jerusalem: Magnes Press, 1989) [Hebrew]; Bracha Sack, " 'Me-'Eyin 'Nusah Rishon' shel Tomer Devorah le-Rabbi Moshe Cordovero," *Asufot* 9 (1995): 161–88 [Hebrew]; Mopsik, *Sex of the Soul*, 38–49; Rachel Elior, "The Doctrine of Transmigration in *Galya Raza*," in *Essential Papers on Kabbalah*, ed. L. Fine, 243–69 (New York: New York University Press, 1995); Lawrence Fine, *Physician of the Soul, Healer of the Cosmos: Isaac Luria and His Kabbalistic Fellowship* (Stanford: Stanford University Press, 2003), 94–95, 192–93, 321–22, 338–39; Moshe Idel, "The Secret of Impregnation as Metempsychosis in Kabbalah," in *Verwandlungen: Archäologie der literarischen Kommunikation*, ed. A. and J. Assman, 341–79 (Munich: Wilhelm Fink, 2006); Mor Altshuler, "'Revealing the Secret of His Wives': R. Joseph Karo's Concept of Reincarnation and Mystical Conception," *Frankfurter Judaistische Beiträge* 31 (2004): 91–104; Shaul Magid, *From Metaphysics to Midrash: Myth, History, and the Interpretation of Scripture in Lurianic Kabbala* (Bloomington: Indiana University Press, 2008), 169–70, 188–95, 223–25; Brian Ogren, *Renaissance and Rebirth: Reincarnation in Early Modern Italian Kabbalah* (Leiden: Brill, 2009). On soul retrieval, see Garb, *Shamanic Trance*, 29–31, and the literature cited there. It is tempting to speculate that the exceptional development of the doctrine of reincarnation in sixteenth-century Safed has something to do with the proximity to the Druze, whose esoteric religion centers on this belief.

53. Hillman, *Re-Visioning Psychology*, esp. 70–73 (on soul and symptom); Yoram Bilu, *Without Bounds: The Life and Death of Rabbi Ya'akov Wazana* (Detroit: Wayne State University Press, 2000), 54, 57; Avraham Elqayam, "The Horizon of Reason: The Divine Madness of Sabbatai Sevi," *Kabbalah* 9 (2003): 7–61; Zvi Mark, *Mysticism and Madness: The Religious Thought of Rabbi Nachman of Bratslav* (London: Continuum, 2009); David Assaf, *Untold Tales of*

the Hasidism: Crisis and Discontent in the History of Hasidism, trans. D. Ordan (Waltham: Brandeis University Press, 2010), 40–64, 115, 119, 220; Idel, *Saturn's Jews: On the Witches' Sabbat and Sabbateanism* (New York: Continuum, 2011), 85–97 (on melancholy); Barbara Ehrenreich, *Bright Sided: How the Relentless Promotion of Positive Thinking Has Undermined America* (New York: Metropolitan Books, 2009), 147–76. For trauma, see chapter 7.

54. Daniel Abrams, "Chapters from an Emotional and Sexual Biography of God: Reflections on God's Attributes in the Bible, Midrash and Kabbalah," *Kabbalah* 6 (2001): 263–86 [Hebrew]; Wolfson, *A Dream Interpreted*, 426n159; Rudolph Otto, *Mysticism East and West: A Comparative Analysis of the Nature of Mysticism*, trans. B. L. Bracey and R. C. Payne (New York: Meridian Books, 1959); Idel, *Hasidism*, 227–38 (and see also idem, "On the Theologization of Kabbalah in Modern Scholarship," in *Religious Apologetics—Philosophical Argumentation*, ed. Y. Schwartz and V. Krech, 123–74 [Tübingen: Mohr Siebeck, 2004]); Nissim Yosha, *Myth and Metaphor: Abraham Cohen Herrera's Philosophic Interpretation of Lurianic Kabbalah* (Jerusalem: Magnes Press, 1994) [Hebrew], 285–88; Garb, *The Chosen*, 52–59.

55. Philip Wexler, "Mystical Education: Social Theory and Pedagogical Prospects," in *Teaching Mysticism*, ed. W. Parsons (Oxford: Oxford University Press, 2011), 277, as well as idem, *Holy Sparks: Social Theory, Education and Religion* (New York: St. Martin's, 1996); idem, *Mystical Interactions: Sociology, Jewish Mysticism and Education* (Los Angeles: Cherub Press, 2007); idem, *Mystical Sociology: Toward Cosmic Social Theory* (New York: Peter Lang, 2013), esp. 102, and cf. Mordechai Rotenberg, *Dialogue with Deviance: The Hasidic Ethic and the Theory of Social Contraction* (Philadelphia: Institute for the Study of Human Issues, 1983), and the work by his student Barukh Kahane (*Breaking and Mending*), who is slightly more au couraunt with Hasidic primary texts, though not with current research in the field. The literature on Buddhist psychology is already vast. See, e.g., Jeffrey B. Rubin, *Psychotherapy and Buddhism: Toward an Integration (Issues in the Practice of Psychology)*; P. Young-Eisendrath and S. Muramuto (eds.), *Awakening and Insight: Zen Buddhism and Psychotherapy* (New York: Brunner-Routledge, 2002); Dale Mathers, Melvin E. Miller, and Osamu Ando (eds.), *Self and No-Self: Continuing the Dialogue Between Buddhism and Psychotherapy* (London: Routledge, 2009); Paul C. Cooper, *The Zen Impulse and the Psychoanalytic Encounter* (London: Routledge, 2010); William Parsons, "Psychoanalysis Meets Buddhism: The Development of a Dialogue," in *Changing the Scientific Study of Religion: Beyond Freud?*, ed. J. A. Belzen, 179–209 (Dordrecht: Springer, 2009).

56. Wexler, "Mystical Education," 284.

CHAPTER TWO

1. For a good general overview of premodern views of the soul in the West, see Goetz and Taliaferro, *Brief History of the Soul*, 6–64, as well as Martin and

Barresi, *Rise and Fall of the Soul*, 39–108, and the more specific study, Jennifer Rapp, "From the Self to the Soul: Platonic Religious Thought" (Ph.D. diss., Stanford University, 2006). For philosophy, see the semiacademic David Bakan, Dan Merkur, and David S. Weiss, *Maimonides' Cure of Souls: Medieval Precursor of Psychoanalysis* (Albany: State University of New York Press, 2009), as well as, for instance, Sarah Stroumsa, "Soul-Searching at the Dawn of Jewish Philosophy: A Hitherto Lost Fragment of al-Muqammas's 'Twenty Chapters,'" *Ginzei Qedem* 3 (2007): 137–61. A sophisticated discussion merging philosophical and mystical texts is Adam Afterman, *Devequt: Mystical Intimacy in Medieval Jewish Thought* (Los Angeles: Cherub Press, 2011) [Hebrew], esp. 119–25, 189–94, 213–16. On Egyptian pietism and Kabbalistic psychology, see Garb, "Psychological Turn" and the studies discussed there. See also Haviva Pedaya, *Vision and Speech*, 173–76, 191–203, for comparisons between Judeo-Sufi psychology and medieval Spanish Kabbalah. For the heart and soul in medieval philosophy and poetics, see, e.g., Dov Schwartz. *Central Problems of Jewish Medieval Philosophy* (Leiden: Brill, 2005), 61–66, 233–47; Adena Tanenbaum, *The Contemplative Soul: Hebrew Poetry and Philosophical Theory in Medieval Spain* (Leiden: Brill, 2002), esp. 132–59; Menachem Lorberbaum, *Dazzled by Beauty: Theology as Poetics in Hispanic Jewish Culture* (Jerusalem: Ben Zvi Institute and Hebrew University of Jerusalem, 2011) [Hebrew], 176–87. See Gershom Scholem, *Major Trends in Jewish Mysticism*, 249, for his comment. The most extensive psychological discussions in premodern Mussar are to be found in two anonymous works from the thirteenth and fourteenth centuries respectively: *Sefer ha-Yashar* and *Orhot Tzaddiqim*.

2. For rabbinic thought, see the excellent overview by Ishay Rosen-Zvi, *Body and Soul in Ancient Jewish Thought* (Ben Shemen: Modan, 2012) [Hebrew], as well as a beautiful discussion of the rabbinic poetics of the soul in David Stern, "*Vayikra Rabbah* and My Life in Midrash," *Prooftexts* 21/1 (2001): 23–38. For the soul in the mysticism of late antiquity, see Andrew Philip Smith (trans.), *Gnostic Writings on the Soul: Annotated and Explained* (Woodstock, VT: Skylight Paths, 2007); April D. DeConick, *Recovering the Original Gospel of Thomas: A History of the Gospel and Its Growth* (New York: T&T Clark International, 2005), 206–11. For the Gnostic nature of Kabbalistic psychology, see Scholem, *Major Trends*, 239, 279–80, 286. For Idel's theory, see his *Kabbalah: New Perspectives* (New Haven: Yale University Press, 1988), 30–32; idem, *Old Worlds, New Mirrors: On Jewish Mysticism and Twentieth-Century Thought* (Philadelphia: University of Pennsylvania Press, 2010), 133–46, 149–53. See also the discussion of the role of Gnosticism in Hasidic psychology in Leah Ornet, *"Ratzo va-Shov, Running and Returning": Ethical and Mystical Perspectives in the Teaching of R. Shneur Zalman of Liadi: A Study* (Tel-Aviv: Hakibbutz Hameuchad, 2007) [Hebrew], 278–79. For the literature on Jungian psychology and Gnosis that is of rather mixed quality, see, e.g., Roberts Avens, *The New Gnosis: Heidegger, Hillman, and Angels*

(Dallas: Spring Publications, 1984); June Singer, *Seeing through the Visible World: Jung, Gnosis, and Chaos* (San Francisco: Harper & Row, 1990); Alfred Ribi, *The Search for Roots: C. G. Jung and the Tradition of Gnosis* (Los Angeles: Gnosis Archive Books, 2013). For a different approach to the premodern relationship between Jewish mysticism and philosophy see Jonathan Dauber, *Knowledge of God and the Development of Early Kabbalah* (Leiden: Brill, 2012).

3. Moshe Idel, "'Nishmat Eloha': The Divinity of the Soul in Nahmanidies and His School," in *Life as Midrash: Perspectives in Jewish Psychology*, ed. B. Kahana et al. (Tel Aviv: Yediot Aharonot, 2004) [Hebrew], 338–82, esp. 350–76.

4. *Zohar* II, fol. 128a–b; Isaiah Tishby, *The Wisdom of the Zohar: An Anthology of Texts*, trans. D. Goldstein (Oxford: Oxford University Press, 1989), e.g. 698–703, 713; *Zohar* III, fol. 70b (and see also III, fol. 25a, and cf. I, fol. 179a); Margolin, *Inner Religion*, 251. See also, e.g., Joel Hecker, *Mystical Bodies, Mystical Meals: Eating and Embodiment in Medieval Kabbalah* (Detroit: Wayne State University Press, 2005), 7–8; Shifra Asulin, "Midrash ha-Ne'elam Bereshit—Between Hebrew and Aramaic," in *And This is for Yehuda: Studies Presented to Our Friend, Professor Yehuda Liebes, on the Occasion of his Sixty-Fifth Birthday*, ed. M. R. Niehoff, R. Meroz, and J. Garb (Jerusalem: Mandel Institute of Jewish Studies and the Bialik Institute, 2012), 238–40; Michal Oron, *Window to the Stories of the Zohar: Studies in the Exegetical and Narrative Methods of the Zohar* (Los Angeles: Cherub Press, 2013) [Hebrew], 174–78. For the soul in premodern Kabbalah, see also Gershom Scholem, *Kabbalah* (Jerusalem: Keter Publishing House, 1974), 152–64; Wolfson, *Through a Speculum*, 185; idem, *Luminal Darkness: Imaginal Gleanings from Zoharic Literature* (Oxford: Oneworld, 2007), 30–35; Nahmanides on Gen. 2:7; Haviva Pedaya, *Nahmanides: Cyclical Time and Holy Text* (Tel Aviv: 'Am 'Oved, 2003), 220–23, 442; Moshe Halbertal, *By Way of Truth: Nahmanides and the Creation of Tradition* (Jerusalem: Hartman Institute, 2006) [Hebrew], 143–48; Eitan P. Fishbane, *As Light Before Dawn: The Inner World of a Medieval Kabbalist* (Stanford: Stanford University Press, 2009), 167–77, as well as the general overview in Rachel Elior, "Soul—Nefesh: The Jewish Doctrine of the Soul," in *Contemporary Jewish Thought*, ed. A. Cohen and P. Mendes-Flohr, 887–96 (New York: Scribner, 1987). On spirit and soul, see James Hillman, "Peaks and Vales: The Soul/Spirit Distinction as Basis for the Differences between Psychotherapy and Spiritual Discipline," in *On the Way to Self-Knowledge*, ed. J. Needleman and Dennis Lewis (New York: Knopf, 1976), 114–47, which is overly dichotomous (on soul and spirit in Kabbalah, see Garb, *Shamanic Trance*, 39–44, and the studies discussed there).

5. On *tzelem* in Nahmanides, see Yair Lorberbaum, "Nahmanides' Kabbalah on the Creation of Man in the Image of God," *Kabbalah* 5 (2000): 287–326, esp. 296–304, 312–19 [Hebrew]. More generally, see Scholem, *On the Mystical Shape*, 251–73; on the four worlds, see Moshe Idel, *Studies in Ecstatic Kabbalah* (Albany: State University of New York Press, 1988), 73–89.

6. See Garb, "Psychological Turn" (that also discusses North Africa) and idem, "Sixteenth-Century Kabbalah," in *The Cambridge Companion to Kabbalah*, ed. E. R. Wolfson (Cambridge: Cambridge University Press, forthcoming), for an overview of the century. On the soul and Italian Renaissance Kabbalah, see Idel, *Kabbalah in Italy*, esp. 166. For Jerusalem in the sixteenth-century context, see Garb, *Shamanic Trance*, 60–65 (discussing several texts on the soul). On Prague, see Garb, "On the Kabbalists of Prague," *Kabbalah* 14 (2006): 362–72. One should especially note Maharal's "path of the good heart" in his under-studied Mussar treatise *Netivot 'Olam* (and see for now Elchanan Shilo, *The Kabbalah in the Works of S. Y. Agnon* [Ramat Gan: Bar Ilan University Press, 2011] [Hebrew], 263); Meir ibn Gabbai, *'Avodat ha-Qodesh* (Jerusalem, 2004), 30 (and Roland Goetschel, *Meir Ibn Gabbay: Le Discours de la Kabbale Espagnole* [Leuven: Peeters, 1981], 216–71). On various topics in Safedian psychology see, e.g., Joseph H. Chajes, *Between Worlds: Dybbuks, Exorcists and Early Modern Judaism* (Philadelphia: University of Pennsylvania Press, 2003); Menachem Kallus, "Pneumatic Mystical Possession," in *Spirit Possession in Judaism: Cases and Contexts from the Middle Ages to the Present*, ed. M. Goldish (Detroit: Wayne State University Press, 2003), 159–85, 385–413; Idel, "The Secret of Impregnation"; Mordechai Pachter, *Roots of Faith and Devequt: Studies in the History of Kabbalistic Ideas* (Los Angeles: Cherub Press, 2004), 235–65; Jonathan Garb, "The Cult of the Saints in Lurianic Kabbalah," *Jewish Quarterly Review* 98/2 (2008): 203–29; Elliot Wolfson, "Weeping, Death, and Spiritual Ascent in Sixteenth-Century Jewish Mysticism," in *Death, Ecstasy, and Other Worldly Journeys*, ed. J. J. Collins and M. Fishbane (Albany: State University of New York Press, 1995), 209–47; idem, *Language, Eros, Being*, 80–81, 179–86, 386–88; idem, "Woman—the Feminine as Other in Theosophic Kabbalah: Some Philosophical Observations on the Divine Androgyne," in *The Other in Jewish Thought and Identity*, ed. L. Silberstein and R. Cohn (New York: New York University Press, 1994), 177; Daniel Abrams, " 'A Light of Her Own': Minor Kabbalistic Traditions on the Ontology of the Divine Feminine," *Kabbalah* 15 (2006); 20–23, as well as my earlier comments on gender in chapter 1 and further studies cited below.

7. Avraham Elqayam, "Nudity in Safed in the Sixteenth Century: Between Hasidism and Deviance," *Kabbalah* 30 (2013): 315–19, 310–14 (and see also idem, "Azamer bi-Svahin: On Ars Poetica of the God-Intoxicated R. Itzhak Luria," in *The Piyyut as a Cultural Prism: New Approaches*, ed. H. Pedaya [Tel Aviv: Van Leer Jerusalem Institute and Hakibbutz Hameuchad Publishing House, 2012], 115–16); R. J. Zwi Werblowsky, *Joseph Caro: Lawyer and Mystic* (Oxford: Oxford University Press, 1962), 138–39 (for Karo's psychology, see 75–83, 234–56). As Werblowsky notes, it is far from sure that this incident took place in Safed. Furthermore, in lectures to be published in book form, Idel has cast serious doubt on the accepted scholarly account of Karo's

revelations and especially their angelic nature. For now see http://www
.youtube.com/watch?v=MApzihqtE-Y (as well as Mor Altshuler, "Prophecy and Maggidism in the Life and Writings of R. Joseph Karo," *Frankfurter
Judaistische Beiträge* 33 (2006): 81–110 (esp. 89–90 on the soul). Fenton's
work on the subject has been discussed at length in Garb, "The Psychological Turn," and see also his general overview, "Judaism and Sufism," in *The
Cambridge Companion to Medieval Jewish Philosophy*, edited by D. H. Frank
and O. Leaman (Cambridge: Cambridge University Press, 2003), esp. 214–15
for Safed.

8. Haviva Pedaya, "Text and Performance," 38, 61–62 (and Chajes, *Between
Worlds*, 110–12); Moshe Idel, "R. Israel Ba'al Shem Tov 'In the State of Wallachia': Widening the Besh't's Cultural Panorama," in *Holy Dissent: Jewish
and Christian Mystics in Eastern Europe*, ed. G. Dynner (Detroit: Wayne State
University Press, 2011), 76–77. For a critique of earlier views of Safedian
messianism (clearly formulated by Rachel Elior, "Messianic Expectations
and Spiritualization of Religious Life in the 16th Century," *Revue des études
juives* 145 [(1986]: 35–49), see Idel, *Messianic Mystics* (New Haven: Yale University Press, 1998), 162–75. On messianism in the sixteenth-century Islamic world, see Cornell Fleischer, "The Lawgiver as Messiah: The Making
of the Imperial Image in the Reign of Süleymân," in *Soliman le magnifique
et son temps*, ed. G. Veinstein (Paris: La Documentation Française, 1992),
159–77; Shahzad Bashir, *Messianic Hopes and Mystical Visions: The Nurbakhshiya between Medieval and Modern Islam* (Columbia: University of South
Carolina Press, 2003), 40–41.

9. See Garb, "Psychological Turn," 115 (and the studies adduced there); Garb,
"The Cult of the Saints," 210, 219–20; Chajes, *Between Worlds*, 49–51, 93.
For similar methodological reservations, see Idel, *Kabbalah and Eros*, 163,
254n28. Elqayam, "Nudity in Safed," 320, writes of "Ottoman Sufi spirituality in all of its aspects" and then relates the tearing of the clothes to
"antinomian spirituality in the spirit of the anarchistic orders in the Ottoman Empire," yet I failed to locate reference to specific texts or studies
along these lines.

10. See Eyal Davidson, "Safed's Sages between 1540–1615: Their Religious and
Social Status" (Ph.D. diss., Hebrew University of Jerusalem, 2009), as well
as Moshe Idel, "On Mobility, Individuals, and Groups: Prolegomenon for a
Sociological Approach to Sixteenth-Century Kabbalah," *Kabbalah* 3 (1998):
159–62, 169.

11. Weinstein, *Kabbalah and Jewish Modernity*, 73–93 (for an example of a soul-
centered Lurianic text analyzed in terms of the body, see 83–84, as well as
431), 420–49, 453–77 (see also his important comment on the *alumbradismo* and *devotio moderna* in 518); Magid, *From Metaphysics to Midrash* (on
the soul see esp. 37–38, 208–13). Magid places psychology and cosmology
on an equal plane (43, and cf. the view of Liebes, closer to my own, discussed

below in the section on Luria). For a psychological reading of the art of memory, see Hillman, *Re-Visioning Psychology*, 91–95. On the converso circles, and their impact, see Jonathan Garb, *Manifestations of Power in Jewish Mysticism: From Rabbinic Literature to Safedian Kabbalah* (Jerusalem: Magnes Press, 2005) [Hebrew], 163–66, where I did not sufficiently stress Catholic influence; Garb, "Shamanism and the Hidden History." For a somewhat different framing of the transition to the sixteenth century, cf. Moshe Idel, "Revelation and the 'Crisis of Tradition' in Kabbalah: 1475–1575," in *Constructing Tradition: Means and Myths of Transmission in Western Esotericism*, ed. A. B. Kilcher (Leiden: Brill, 2010), 255–92, and cf. idem, *Messianic Mystics*, 127–32 (and the earlier studies cited in both of these discussions). For an incisive critique of an attempt to describe the *converso* phenomenon as the start of modern subjectivity, see Yitzhak Melamed, review of Yirmiyahu Yovel, *The Other Within: The Marranos; Split Identity and Emerging Modernity*," *Journal of Religion* 83/1 (2011): 198–200.

12. Pedaya, *Walking through Trauma*, 30–35, 46, 100–101, 262n205 (on the exile of the soul, see 105, 177–80) as well as the essay-style Lacanian treatment in idem, *Expanses*, 66–67, 271. Cf. Andrew Samuels, *Jung and the Post-Jungians* (London: Routledge & K. Paul, 1985); idem, *The Plural Psyche: Personality, Morality, and the Father* (London: Routledge, 1989); Garb, *Shamanic Trance*, 3, 26. The question of the earlier sources of Safedian Kabbalah has been discussed at great length. Nonetheless, none would deny either the originality of the vast Safedian literature nor the sense of this originality in future generations, so this question shall not detain us here.

13. Yosef Avivi, *Kabbala Luriana*, 3 vols. (Jerusalem: Ben-Zvi Institute, 2008) [Hebrew], esp. vol. 1 (*The Lurianic Writings until 1620*), 58–67, and vol. 2 (*The Lurianic Writings after 1620*), 599–605, 673–78. See also Abrams, *Kabbalistic Manuscripts*, 607–9. An important study of seventeenth-century Kabbalah, comparing Safed and Italy, is Isaiah Tishby, "The Confrontation between Lurianic Kabbalah and Cordoverian Kabbalah in the Writings and Life of Rabbi Aaron Berechiah of Modena," *Zion* 39 (1974): 8–85 [Hebrew], containing a lengthy English abstract. Weinstein, *Kabbalah and Jewish Modernity*, also felicitously extends the discussion into the seventeenth century. On the interactive history of Safed and Italy, see Moshe Idel, "Italy in Safed, Safed in Italy: Toward an Interactive History of Sixteenth-Century Kabbalah," in *Cultural Intermediaries: Jewish Intellectuals in Early Modern Italy*, ed. D. Ruderman and G. Veltri, 239–69 (Philadelphia: University of Pennsylvania Press, 2004).

14. Morris M. Faierstein (trans. and ed.), *Hayyim ben Joseph Vital and Isaac Judah Jehiel Safrin: Jewish Mystical Autobiographies: Book of Visions and Book of Secrets* (New York: Paulist Press, 1999), 233–35. Weinstein, *Kabbalah and Jewish Modernity*, 284–85, discusses this text in purely social terms.

15. Hayyim Vital, *Sha'ar ha-Kavvanot* (Jerusalem, 1985), fol. 1a–b. Assaf Tamari, "Human Sparks: Readings in the Lurianic Theory of Transmigration and

its Concept of the Human Subject" (M.A. thesis, Tel Aviv University, 2009) [Hebrew], 90, has devoted a sophisticated thesis to Lurianic ideas of the soul, and has stressed the construction of the fellowship as "soul family" (see also 106–10 on "networks of souls"). On power struggles in Luria's circle, see Ronit Meroz, "Faithful Transmission versus Innovation: Luria and His Disciples," in *Gershom Scholem's Major Trends in Jewish Mysticism—50 Years After: Proceedings of the 6th International Conference on the History of Jewish Mysticism*, ed. P. Schäfer and J. Dan (Tübingen: Mohr Siebeck, 1993), 257–74, as well as the analysis in terms of rhetoric in Tamari, "Human Sparks," 88.

16. See Garb, "The Cult of the Saints." For Karo's psychology, see Werblowsky, *Joseph Karo*, 75–83, 234–56.

17. Moshe Cordovero, *Pardes Rimonim* (Jerusalem, 1962), gate 32, chapter 1 (vol. 2, fol. 78a); gate 31, chapter 3 (vol. 2, fol. 73a); idem, *Or Ne'erav* (Jerusalem, 1990), 8. For his possible sources see Idel, "Nishmat Eloha," 367 (tracing the influence of Nahmanides); Joseph Gikatila, *Shaare Orah*, ed. J. Ben Shlomo (Jerusalem, 1970), 203–4, 211. For the Cordovero circle's predilection for chain-of-being imagery, see Moshe Idel, *Enchanted Chains: Techniques and Rituals in Jewish Mysticism* (Los Angeles: Cherub Press, 2005), 47–48 (for the soul, see 185).

18. Cordovero, *Pardes Rimonim*, gate 31, chapter 3 (vol. 2, fol. 73a). On action, spatial imagery, and modernity in Cordovero's psychology and theurgy, see Garb, *Manifestations of Power*, 202, 208–17, 221–24, 271–72 (where I cited numerous other texts). On sonship in Cordovero's writings and their reception, see Moshe Idel, *Ben: Sonship and Jewish Mysticism* (London: Continuum, 2007), 440–46, 531–34. On the theme of becoming a chariot in Safed, see Eitan Fishbane, "A Chariot for the Shekhinah: Identity and the Ideal Life in Sixteenth-Century Safed Kabbalah," *Journal of Religious Ethics* 37/3 (2009): 385–418. On the encyclopedic enterprise of Safed in comparative perspective, see Weinstein, *Kabbalah and Jewish Modernity*, 48–73. Surprisingly, Weinstein focuses on the far less convincing case of Luria. Cf. the discussion, utilizing a theory of models, in Idel, *Hasidism*, esp. 22, 31.

19. Avraham Azulai, *Hesed le-Avraham* (Jerusalem, ca. 1991), 123. The theme of the righteous in Cordovero has been extensively discussed (also in the studies cited just now). See most recently Bracha Sack, *"Ben Ga'agu'im*: The Righteous in Some Unpublished Chapters of R. Moshe Cordovero's *Elimah*," in *And This Is for Yehuda: Studies Presented to Our Friend Professor Yehuda Liebes on the Occasion of his Sixty-Fifth Birthday*, ed. M. R. Niehoff, R. Meroz, and J. Garb, esp. 348–49 (Jerusalem: Mandel Institute of Jewish Studies and Bialik Institute, 2012) [Hebrew]; this also includes a discussion of sonship (and updates her earlier discussions of Cordoverian psychology in *The Kabbalah of R. Moshe Cordovero* (Beer Sheva: Ben Gurion University Press, 1995) [Hebrew], 103–9, 205–11.

20. See Cordovero, *Pardes Rimonim*, gate 32, chapter 3, 79A; idem, *Tefillah le-Moshe* (Ashdod, 2004), fol. 336a–b, fol. 358b–359a (and see also fol. 340b),

fol. 352a (and cf. fol. 353a). On soul and heart in prayer, see Bracha Sack, "Some Remarks on Siddur *Tefillah Le-Moshe*," *Daat* 44 (2000), 71, 73, 76, 78 [Hebrew]. For the "organic model," see Garb, *Manifestations of Power*, 282–85.

21. Moshe Cordovero, *Or Yaqar*, vol. 11 (Jerusalem, 1981), 26–27; vol. 14 (Jerusalem, 1986), 194–95. For an analysis of another text from this commentary that deals with the subtle transformation of the soul and its garb through intention as the thought of the heart, see Garb, "Psychological Turn." On *nefilat appayim*, see Garb, *Shamanic Trance*, 31–36, 79–81 (and see 65–67 for ascent and descent in *Or Yaqar*). As I noted there, this rite parallels the descent of Jesus into hell, which was *in anima*; see David L. Miller, *Hells and Holy Ghosts: A Theopoetics of Christian Belief* (New Orleans: Spring Journal Books, 2004), esp. 19. Here one should add the Catholic theme of rescue of souls from purgatory. The theme of soul descent complements that of ascent, highly prevalent in Safed, as discussed (within the appropriate context of reception of supernal knowledge from the soul) by Wolfson, "Weeping," 210–12, 230–33 (and see also the imagination-centered interpretation in idem, *Through a Speculum*, 296–99, 320–24); Idel, "Ascensions, Gender," esp. 61–65, 85–92. I shall address the theme of virtual reality and its premodern sources in a separate study.

22. Cordovero, *Or Yaqar*, vol. 14, 231–32, as well as Sack, *Kabbalah of Cordovero*, 103, 116–17, 145–48, 180–85; Zohar Raviv, *Decoding the Dogma within the Enigma: The Life, Works, Mystical Piety and Systematic Thought of Rabbi Moses Cordoeiro (Aka Cordovero; Safed, Israel, 1522–1570)* (Saarbrücken: VDM, Verlag Dr. Müller, 2008), 317–18. More generally see Scholem, *On the Kabbalah and Its Symbolism* (New York: Schocken Books, 1965), 64–65, and the recent discussion (also citing an early study of mine) in Shay Wozner, Hanina Ben Menahem, and Neil Hecht, *Controversy and Dialogue in the Halakhic Sources— Sources and Commentary* (Jerusalem: Institute for Research in Jewish Law, Faculty of Law, 2002) [Hebrew], 2, 320. See also Moshe Idel, *Absorbing Perfections: Kabbalah and Interpretation* (New Haven: Yale University Press, 2002), 94–100, 104–5, 467–69; Sharron Shatil, "The Doctrine of Secrets of Emeq ha-Melech," *Jewish Studies Quarterly* 17 (2010): 369, 380–84.

23. See Elijah de Vidas, *Reshit Hokhma*, ed. H. Y. Waldmann (Jerusalem, 1984), vol. 1, 343, 384–407, 463, 753; vol. 2, 136–40; Idel, *Kabbalah and Eros*, 157, 170; Patrick Koch, "Cultivating the Emotions: Asceticism in R. Elijah De Vidas' Reshit Hokhmah" (M.A. thesis, Hebrew University of Jerusalem, 2007), 60–61, 75–84; idem, *Human Self-Perfection: A Re-assessment of Kabbalistic Musar-Literature of Sixteenth-Century Safed* (Los Angeles: Cherub Press, 2015), 59–66 (and 146–50), 156–57, 207–9. Regarding Cordovero's own opinion of these matters, see his *Or Yaqar*, vol. 3 (Jerusalem, 1964), 248–49, where it is stated that the heart is the main site for the residence of the soul, compared to that of the *Shekhina* (and see also de Vidas, *Reshit Hokhmah*, vol. 1, 154–55).

24. For Cordovero's Mussar, see, e.g., Louis Jacobs (trans.), *Rabbi Moses Cordo-vero: The Palm Tree of Deborah: Translated from the Hebrew with an Introduction and Notes* (London: Vallentine Mitchell, 1960); E. Fishbane, "A Chariot for the Shekhinah," 400–404. On modern Mussar and Kabbalah, see Garb, *Shamanic Trance*, 122–25, as well as Roni Weinstein, *Juvenile Sexuality, Kabbalah, and Catholic Reformation in Italy: Tiferet Bahurim By Pinhas Barukh Ben Pelatiyah Monselice* (Leiden; Boston: Brill, 2009), 101–10, 210–17. On intercorporal connections, see Moshe Idel, "On Some Forms of Order in Kabbalah," *Daat* 50–52 (2003), pp. xxxi–lviii. On Sufism and Kabbalah, see Sara Sviri, "Spiritual Trends in Pre-Kabbalistic Judeo-Spanish Literature: The Cases of Bahya ibn Paquda and Judah Halevi," *Donaire* 6 (1996): 78–84.

25. Hayyim Vital, *Sha'arei Qedusha* (Jerusalem, 1986), part 3, gate 2, 117–20, 132; gate 1, 116, and compare to the exoteric and very different structure in part 1, gate 1, 11–12 that is based on the trope of *diyuqan*, the more Lurianic discussion in Vital (*Sefer ha-Liqqutim* [Jerusalem 1913], fol. 57a), and see also Tamari, "Human Sparks," 20–21, 43. For recent reception of this theme, see chapter 5. For my earlier discussion of his psychology, see Garb, *Shamanic Trance*, 51–60. For *mahtzavim*, see m. *Shevi'it*, 3:5–6. For the Mishna in Lurianic Kabbalah, see for now the pioneering study of Dalia Hoshen, "*Zimzum* and R. Akiva's School: Kabbala and Midrash," *Daat* 34 (1995): 34–60 [Hebrew]. I cannot enter the complex question of the place of the "quarry of souls" in Vital's transmission of Luria's teachings, as opposed to his independent writing (yet see my discussion of R. Hayyim de la Rossa below).

26. Liebes, "Myth vs. Symbol" (and one should also mention his Hebrew studies in the same vein, and see esp. idem, "'Two Young Roes of a Doe': The Secret Sermon of Isaac Luria before His Death," *Jerusalem Studies in Jewish Thought* 10 [1992]: 114–15, 125, 146 [Hebrew], all pertinent to issues discussed below); Isaiah Tishby, *The Doctrine of Evil in Lurianic Kabbalah*, trans. D. Solomon (London: Kegan Paul, 2002); Pachter, *Roots of Faith*, 185–233, as well as Shokek, *Kabbalah and the Art of Being*, 47. On "smallness" and "greatness" see also Wolfson, *A Dream Interpreted*, 169–70; Garb, "Shamanism and the Hidden History." One should note that the triune structure has a prominent place in the very limited exposure to Kabbalah in the Israeli educational system, and has an equally dominant presence in other popularizations. See, however, the popular James D. Dunn (ed.) and Nathan Snyder (trans.), *Window of the Soul: The Kabbalah of R. Isaac Luria* (San Francisco: Weiserbooks, 2008). One should also note the unpublished doctoral dissertation of Ronit Meroz, "The Teachings of Redemption in Lurianic Kabbalah" (Ph.D. diss., Hebrew University of Jerusalem, 1988) [Hebrew], esp. 267–327, as well as her rich unpublished M.A. thesis (idem, "Hebetim be-Torat ha-Nevu'a ha-Lurianit" [M.A. thesis, Hebrew University of Jerusalem, 1980]).

27. Fine, *Physician of the Soul*, 96, 150–67, 265–75, 315–21; Wolfson, *Language, Eros, Being*, 180–81.

28. Yosef Avivi, *Binyan Ariel* (Jerusalem: Misgav Yerushalayim, 1987), esp. 111; idem, *Kabbala Luriana*, esp. vol. 3 (*The Lurianic Doctrine*), 1275, 1304–6, 1311–12, 1413–14 (and see the methodological discussion in 1190–1202). For a further treatment of Avivi's position, see Garb, "The Psychological Turn," 113–14. On the role of the diagnostic-therapeutic practice in the "cult of the saints," see my above-cited study and the references wherein. Practice-centered studies include the unwieldy yet highly erudite unpublished doctoral dissertation of Menachem Kallus,"The Theurgy of Prayer in the Lurianic Kabbalah" (Ph.D. thesis, Hebrew University of Jerusalem, 2002), which also includes comparisons to Buddhism, esp. 114–29, and Amiel Vick, *Through Which All of Israel Can Ascend: On R. Shneur Zalman of Lyady's Composition of Nusah ha-Ari* (M.A. thesis, Hebrew University of Jerusalem, 2012) [Hebrew], 7–12 (and the earlier studies cited there). On complexity in the human sciences, see, e.g., Jeffrey Johnson, "The Future of the Social Sciences and Humanities in the Science of Complex Systems," *European Journal of Social Science Research* 23/2 (2010):115–34.

29. *Shivhei ha-Ari ha-Shalem ve-ha-Mevo'ar* (Jerusalem: Ahavat Shalom,1991), 10–11, and compare to Hayyim Vital, *Sha'ar Ruah ha-Qodesh* (Jerusalem, 1999), vol. 1 64; Faierstein, *Hayyim ben Joseph Vital and Isaac Judah Jehiel Safrin*, 90.

30. Vital, *'Etz Hayyim* (Jerusalem, 1990, reprint of Jerusalem, 1910), part 1, introductory text, fol. 3b–5a; Naftali Bakhrakh, *Emeq ha-Melekh* (Amsterdam: Emanuel Benbenishti Press, 1648), fol. 6b, 7a (and compare to fol. 11a–b, on the soul of Vital and on thousands of souls coming to Luria to receive their emendation). On soul revelation versus angelic revelation, see Werblowsky, *Joseph Karo*, 75–83. On respect for hagiographical writing, see Garb, *Shamanic Trance*, 77–78, and the earlier studies cited there.

31. Moshe Cordovero, *Sefer Eilima* (Jerusalem, 2013), 69. See also Esther Liebes, "A New Examination of the Myth of the Kings of Edom: Cordovero and Luria," in *Ma'yan 'Ein Ya'acov,* ed. B. Sack (Beer Sheva: Ben Gurion University of the Negev Press, 2009) [Hebrew], 53–55. Although the notion of the world-soul is not our main concern, such texts should be placed in contrast to statements such as the following, qualified, one: "Jewish Cabala, in the sources investigated in the present study, never describes God as the universal soul." Vassányi, *Anima Mundi*, 279. As evidenced there in n248, Vassányi has adopted the views of Scholem. For an obvious historical error, see 282.

32. Avivi, *Binyan Ariel*, 423–24. See also Elliot Wolfson, "Divine Suffering and the Hermeneutics of Reading: Philosophical Reflections on Lurianic Mythology," in *Suffering Religion*, ed. R. Gibbs and E. R. Wolfson (New York: Routledge, 2002), 124–25. On the theme of new souls from Luria to the twentieth century, see Elchanan Shilo, "Rabbi Kook's Interpretation of Lurianic Kabbalah, the Appearance of New Souls and *Tikkun ha-Olam*,"

Iyunim Bitkumat Israel 18 (2008): 55–77 [Hebrew], as well as Tamari, "Human Sparks," 29.

33. Vital, *'Etz Hayyim*, part 1, gate 3, chapter 3, fol. 17a.

34. See the description of this model as "mechanical" by Weinstein, *Kabbalah and Jewish Modernity*, 60 (In my view, this is a retrojection of later stages in modern psychology, discussed in chapter 1). On the five-part and four world structures, see Fine, *Physician of the Soul*, 139. On the "isomorphic model" in pre-Lurianic Jewish Mysticism, see Garb, *Manifestations of Power*, 30–36, 122–32, and see Idel, *Kabbalah. New Perspectives*, 112–18, for additional Rabbinic and gnostic sources, thus supporting my broad designation as premodern. For a powerful discussion of Heraclitus, see Hillman, *Re-Visioning Psychology*, xvii. Although I fully concur with Liebes, "Myth vs. Symbol," 226, that previous scholarship bypasses the critical phase of the soul in the Lurianic depiction of emanation, his statement that the rest of Lurianic ontology is a mere introduction to the psychic discourse is perhaps too strong. According to our text, there is no need for such binary dichotomies.

35. Vital, *'Etz Hayyim*, part 2, gate 42, chapter 1, fol. 89a (the connection to the previous text on the infinite can be found in chapter 2, fol. 89b); idem, *Sha'ar Ruah ha-Qodesh*, vol. 1, 39 (and see Liebes, "Myth vs. Symbol," 227). For sonship and the soul see also *'Etz Hayyim*, part 2, gate 50, chapter 10, fol. 117b, as well as Idel, *Ben*, 446–54, who, true to his earlier writing, focuses on the *morphe* rather than the soul.

36. Vital, *'Etz Hayyim*, part 2, gate 50, chapter 10, fol. 117b. For an interesting discussion of the last part of the text, see Weinstein, *Kabbalah and Jewish Modernity*, 535–36. The premodern history of the four worlds has yet to be comprehensively studied; for now see Idel, *Studies in Ecstatic Kabbalah*, 73–89. On Vital's dreams of Rome (which was also central in Freud's dream life; see David Meghnagi, "From the Dreams of a Generation to the Theory of Dreams: Freud's Roman Dreams," *International Journal of Psychoanalysis* 92/3 [2011]: 675–94), and his experience of Damascus, see Idel, *Messianic Mystics*, 167–69. For imaginal geography, see Garb, *Shamanic Trance*, 27–29 (and 57 on Vital). I believe that this Corbinian framing is more successful than that of mere spatiality.

37. Vital, *Pri 'Etz Hayyim*, fol. 39b.

38. Vital, *'Etz Hayyim*, part 2, gate 47, chapter 3, fol. 106b. A very important text integrating the theory of soul and other psychological theories with practice can be found in ibid., part 1, gate 26, chapter 1, fol. 15a. More on souls of the righteous in Luria, see Meroz, "Hebetim," 50. On the concept of the internal in Safedian Kabbalah, see Margolin, *Inner Religion*, 45–48. See also Tamari, "Human Sparks," 40, on the soul and nomian practice.

39. Vital, *Sha'ar ha-Kavvanot*, fol. 24a; Yehiel Mikhel Hendler, *Barukh u-Mevurakh* (Jerusalem, 2011), 165; Vital, *'Etz Hayyim*, part 2, gate 39, chapter 1,

fol. 66b–67a. On Safedian martyrology, see Michael Fishbane, *The Kiss of God: Spiritual and Mystical Death in Judaism* (Seattle: University of Washington Press, 1994), 110–17. See also in chapter 3, on the soul and martyrdom and Garb, "Shamanism and the Hidden History," 178–81, on the failed Lurianic attempt to hasten the redemption (compare the sources and studies adduced here and there to *Sha'ar ha-Kavvanot*, fol. 91b).

40. Shmuel Vital, *'Olat Tamid* (Jerusalem, 1872), fol. 46a–b [reprint]. For the theme of purity in Safedian practice, see Garb, *Shamanic Trance*, 125–26. The rise of modern medical discourse was the provenance of Foucault, yet it is worth citing later studies such as those in Waltraud Ernst (ed.), *Plural Medicine, Tradition and Modernity, 1800–2000* (London: Routledge, 2002). At the same time, the idea of penitential systems as medicine for the soul is premodern, just as are the sources of the details of Luria's penitential system of mortification. See the important discussion in Harold J. Berman, *Law and Revolution: The Formation of the Western Legal Tradition* (Cambridge, MA: Harvard University Press, 1983), 71.

41. Moshe of Prague, *Va-Yakhel Moshe* (Zalkov, 1741), fol. 2a, 3b.

42. For R. Menahem 'Azaria's relationship to the doctrines of Cordovero and Luria, see Isaiah Tishby, "The Confrontation between Lurianic Kabbalah and Cordoverian Kabbalah in the Writings and Life of Rabbi Aaron Berechiah of Modena," *Zion* 39 (1974): 9–13, 79–81 [Hebrew].

43. Menahem 'Azaria da Fano, *Pelah ha-Rimon* (Jerusalem, 2000), 6; Yosef Avivi, "The Kabbalistic Writings of R. Menahem Azaria of Fano," *Sefunot* 4 (1989): 347–76 [Hebrew]; Menahem 'Azaria da Fano, *Ma'amar ha-Nefesh*, ed. Hanina H. Karfman (Jerusalem, 2011), 3, 9, 11–12, 35–36, 54, 96–97, 99.

44. Menahem 'Azaria, *Ma'amar ha-Nefesh*, 8 (and compare to 4). For the soul in R. Menahem 'Azaria's writings, see Alexander Altmann, "Notes on the Development of Rabbi Menahem Azariah Fano's Kabbalistic Doctrine," *Jerusalem Studies in Jewish Thought* 3 (1983/4): 252 [Hebrew].

45. Shabbetai Sheftel Horowitz, *Shef'a Tal* (Jerusalem, 1971 [reprint of Warsaw, 1974]), 3a; Bracha Sack, *Shomer ha-Pardes: The Kabbalist Rabbi Shabbetai Sheftel Horowitz of Prague* (Beer Sheva: Ben Gurion University Press, 2002) [Hebrew], esp. 158–67 (yet see 182 on increasing the soul); Isaiah Horowitz, *Shnei Luhot ha-Brit ha-Shalem* (Haifa: Machon Yad Rama, 1997), 251–54; Dalia Krisspel, "The Concept of Man in 'Shenei Luhot ha-Berit' ('The Two Tablets of the Covenant') by Rabbi Isaiah Horowitz" (Ph.D. diss., Ben Gurion University of the Negev, 2004) [Hebrew], 62–92. See also my discussion of the stress on the heart, soul, and other psychological issues in Garb, "On the Kabbalists of Prague," 353–58; Avivi, *Kabbala Luriana*, vol. 1, 433–87; vol. 2, 831, 1034–35. For later periods in Prague, see Sharon Flatto, *The Kabbalistic Culture of Eighteenth-Century Prague: Ezekiel Landau and his Contemporaries* (Oxford: Littman Library of Jewish Civilization, 2010), esp. 172–203 (I cannot enter here into the current controversy surrounding her conclusions). The takeover of the idea of the divine soul in this period

is apparent even in non-Kabbalistic exegesis on the Bible or Aggadic texts. See, e.g., the sources cited in Leibel Y. Altein et al. (eds.), *Chassidus Mvueres: Tanya* (New York: Kehot Publication Society, 2009), vol. 1, 80.

46. Aharon Shmu'el of Kremnitz, *Nishmat Adam* (Hannover, 1617), esp. fol. 5a, 8b. The doctrine of the divinity of the soul is also strongly present in another influential synthesis from this period, R. Naftali Bakhrakh's *Emeq ha-Melekh* (Jerusalem, 1994).

47. Menashe Ben Israel, *Nishmat Hayyim* (Jerusalem, 1998 [reprint of Leipzig, 1862]), ful. 1a–4a, 40a–b (first treatise, chapter 1, second treatise, chapter 9).

48. For Luzzatto, see Garb, *Kabbalist in the Eye of the Storm*, 39–41, 46–52. For Kremer, see Avivi, *Kabbalat ha-Gr"a* (Jerusalem: Makhon Kerem Eliyahu, 1993), 29–31; Baumgarten, "The Gra and His Disciples' Attitude towards the Authority of the Ari," *Daat* 72 (2011): 53–74 [Hebrew]. For Hasidism, see, e.g., Idel, *Hasidism*, 33–43, who in my view slightly overemphasizes the influence of Cordovero and thus occludes the extent of the break that took place in this century. See also Idel, *Messianic Mystics*, 318–19.

49. On Shar'abi as a reincarnation or soul spark of Luria, see the sources collected in Ya'aqov Moshe Hillel, *Ahavat Shalom* (Jerusalem: Ahavat Shalom, 2002), 5–7; Shmu'el Arenfeld, *Tevu'ot Shemesh* (Jerusalem, 2012), 157–62 (who also adduces numerous sources on Shar'abi's students as reincarnations of those of Luria).

50. Frederic William Maitland, *The Collected Papers of Frederic William Maitland, Downing Professor of the Laws of England*, ed. H. A. L: Fisher (Cambridge: Cambridge University Press, 1911), vol. 1, 484

51. Maitland, *The Collected Papers*, 1:484; Giller, *Shalom Shar'abi and the Kabbalists of Beit El* (for the soul see 49). See also Jonatan Meir's review in the *Journal of Religion* 89 (2009): 448–50. Meir's own study, *Rehovot ha-Nahar: Kabbalah and Exotericism in Jerusalem (1896–1948)*, will be discussed in chapter 5. See also Shmu'el Arenfeld, *Yira'ukha'im-Shamesh* (Jerusalem, 2012)—for the soul, see, e.g., 582–88; idem, *Tevu'ot Shemesh* (Jerusalem, 2012)—esp. 157–60; idem, *Ke-Tze'et ha-Shemesh* (Jerusalem, 2014), esp. vol. 2, 168–69, 218–19, 632–38; Assaf Nabarro, *Tikkun: From Lurianic Kabbalah to Popular Culture* (Ph.D. diss., Ben-Gurion University of the Negev, 2006) [Hebrew], 162–66. For an explicit statement on the wish to distribute Shar'abian writings in a manner that avoids academic attention, see the unpaginated introduction of Yehezq'el Bing, *Nequdot ha-Kesef*, vol. 1 (Bnei Brak, 2008).

52. Shalom Shar'abi, *Nahar Shalom*, fol. 33b–34a in the oft-used version appended to Vital, *'Etz Hayyim* (Jerusalem, 1990, reprint of Jerusalem, 1910), and see also fol. 2b and 9b (as well as a shorter, but more explicit discussion of the median spark as soul and son in fol. 11a, and the application in practice in fol. 23a–b). For an illuminating discussion, in relatively contemporary language (including genetics), of hologramic relativity and the soul in Shar'abian Kabbalah (to be briefly discussed in chapter 5), see Moshe Schatz, *Ma'ayan Moshe* (Jerusalem, 2011), 17–18, 24–36. See also Yitzhaq

Me'ir Morgenstern, *Yam ha-Hokhma* (Jerusalem, 2009), 341–45, who describes the innovative nature of this intention involving the five parts of the soul (as well as idem, *Yam ha-Hokhma* [Jerusalem], 2010, 437, where he goes so far as to ask why the Hasidic masters did not take up this practice, and idem, *Yam ha-Hokhma* [Jerusalem], 2014, 633–40). See also the discussion, in the context of details of practice, by Yaniv Mezuman, "Rabbi Shalom Shar'abi's Kabbalistic Intentions of Prayer for the Morning Blessings" (M.A. thesis, Bar-Ilan University Ramat Gan, 2000), esp. 39–41, as well as 71–75. For an early, brief discussion, see Louis Jacobs, "The Uplifting of Sparks in Later Jewish Mysticism," in *Jewish Spirituality from the Sixteenth-Century Revival to the Present*, ed. A. Green (New York: Crossroad, 1987), 112–13.

53. Shar'abi, *Nahar Shalom*, fol. 39a, and see also a parallel discussion in fol. 9b that utilizes the theme of the soul quarry.
54. On the esoteric layers see the statements by de la Rossa collected in Arenfeld, *Yira'ukha'im-Shamesh*, 47 (as well as Shar'abi's strong statement on "deep deep" secrets, prefacing a discussion of the soul, in *Nahar Shalom*, fol. 8b). For the dilemma and resolution, see Hayyim de la Rossa, *Torat Hakham* (Jerusalem, 1999), fol. 144b, 73a respectively (and see also 49b). Cf. Shar'abi's own gloss on the discrepancy between Vital's independent writing and his rendition of Luria's teaching printed in '*Etz Hayyim*, part 1, gate 17, chapter 2, fol. 84b.
55. See Amnon Raz-Krakotzkin, "The National Narration of Exile: Zionist Historiography and Medieval Jewry" (Ph.D. diss., Tel Aviv University, 1996) [Hebrew], esp. 107–44. However, see Scholem, *On the Mystical Shape*, 272, on the increasing intricacy of Kabbalistic psychological theory.

CHAPTER THREE

1. See, e.g., Scholem, *Major Trends*, 340–41; Idel, *Kabbalah: New Perspectives*, 146–53; idem, *Hasidism*, 227–38; Esther Liebes, "The Novelty in Hasidism according to R. Barukh of Kossow," *Da'at* 45 (2000): 75–90 [Hebrew]; Garb, *The Chosen*, 39–40. On the turn to internalization in the eighteenth century, see Margolin, *Inner Religion*, 419–21.
2. Ya'aqov Me'ir Spielmann, *Tal Orot* (Lemberg, 1876), part 1, fol. 3a (though barely mentioned in academic scholarship, this work has been addressed in contemporary Kabbalistic discourse by R. Moshe Schatz, as in his *Ma'ayan Moshe*). Compare to Kirschner, *Religious and Romantic Origins*, esp. 165–66. For a dissertation on Hasidism and psychoanalysis, based on very partial exposure to Hasidic texts, see Dana Beth Wasserman, "Chasidic Antecedents to the Psychoanalytic Theory of Sigmund Freud: A Biographical and Textual Analysis" (Ph.D. diss., Wright Institute Graduate School of Psychology, Berkeley, 2004).

3. See Allan Nadler, *The Faith of the Mithnagdim: Rabbinic Response to Hasidic Rapture* (Baltimore: Johns Hopkins University Press, 1999), for ascetic tendencies in the circle of Kremer. For a brief comparison between the founders of Mussar and Habad Hasidism, see Immanuel Etkes, *Ba'al ha-Tanya: Rabbi Shneur Zalman of Liady and the Origins of Habad Hasidism* (Jerusalem: Zalman Shazar Center for Jewish History, 2011) [Hebrew], 185.

4. See the important, essay-style comments of Pedaya, *Expanses*, 256–57, 272. On the Besht's initiations, see Dan Ben-Amos, and Jerome R. Mintz, *In Praise of the Baal Shem Tov: The Earliest Collection of Legends About the Founder of Hasidism* (Shivḥei ha-Besht) (Bloomington: Indiana University Press, 1970), 83–84; Moshe Idel, "'The Besht passed his Hand over his Face': On the Besht's Influence on His Followers: Some Remarks," in *After Spirituality: Studies In Mystical Traditions*, ed. Ph. Wexler and J. Garb (New York: Peter Lang Publications, 2012), 88–93. My approach towards the study of Hasidism was introduced in Garb, *Shamanic Trance*, esp. 75–118 (and see the critique of shore hugging in 7).

5. Cf. the semiacademic study Michael Rosen, *The Quest for Authenticity: The Thought of Reb Simhah Bunim* (Jerusalem: Urim Publications, 2008), 85–104.

6. Idel, *Messianic Mystics*, esp. 221–40, 245–46, 286–88; Morris M. Faierstein, "Personal Redemption in Hasidism," in *Hasidism Reappraised*, ed. A. Rapoport-Albert (London: Valentine, Mitchell, 1996), 214–24; Menahem Nahum Twersky, *Ma'or 'Enayyim* (Ashdod, 2008), 246–47. The schools of Chernobyl are beginning to enjoy focused academic attention. See Gadi Sagiv, *Dynasty: The Chernobyl Hasidic Dynasty and Its Place in the History of Hasidism* (Jerusalem: Zalman Shazar Center, 2014) [Hebrew], esp. 255–58, 303–19. For similar formulations in other schools, see Yitzhaq Yehiel Safrin, *Heikhal ha-Brakha* (Lemberg, 1866), vol. 1, fol. 37a. For the highly complex question of the personal and national elements in Habad thought, see Wolfson, *Open Secret*, esp. the soul-centered discussions in 183–90, 231–40, 272–76, as well as the more heart-centered and recent discussion in idem, "Revealing and Re/Veiling: Menahem Mendel Schneerson's Messianic Secret," *Kabbalah* 26 (2012): 63–78.

7. See Porter, *Flesh*, 56–60. This topic has been addressed repeatedly in scholarly writing on Habad. See, most recently, Pedaya, *Expanses*, 283. Cf. Idel, *Kabbalah: New Perspectives*, 269, who, true to his "panoramic" approach, compares Faust to a figure at the very beginning of Kabbalistic modernity. For still earlier parallels, see Guy G. Stroumsa and Paula Fredriksen, "Two Souls and the Divided Will," in *Self, Soul and Body in Religious Experience*, ed. A. I. Baumgarten, J. Assman, and G. G. Stroumsa (Leiden: Brill, 1998), 198–217.

8. The internal and scholarly literature on Habad psychology is too vast to list here: See, e.g., Rachel Elior, *The Theory of Divinity of Hasidut Habad* (Jerusalem: Magnes Press, 1982) [Hebrew] 134–77, 215–20; idem, *The Paradoxical*

Ascent to God: The Kabbalistic Theosophy of Habad Hasidism, trans. Jeffrey M. Green (Albany: State University of New York Press, 1993), 103–24; Yoram Jacobson, "The Rectification of the Heart: Studies in the Psychic Teachings of R. Shneur Zalman of Liadi," *Teudah* 10 (1996): 359–409 [Hebrew]; Wolfson, *Open Secret*, esp. 20–26; idem, "Revealing and Re/Veiling," 77; Dov Schwartz, *Habad's Thought from Beginning to End* (Ramat Gan: Bar-Ilan University, 2011) [Hebrew], esp. 197–238, 258–68, 272–84, 331–40. Schwartz's student, Ariel Roth, "The Habad Literary Corpus, Its Components and Distribution as the Basis for Reading Habad Text" (Ph.D. diss., Bar Ilan University, 2012) [Hebrew], has recently written a pioneering discussion of the textual basis of the Habad corpus, while contributing an updated survey of scholarship. The Habad journal *Heikhal ha-Ba'al Shem Tov* contains several valuable discussions. See also Ornet, *"Ratzo va-Shov, Running and Returning": Ethical and Mystical Perspectives in the Teaching of R. Shneur Zalman of Liadi: A Comparative Study*, esp. 75–90, 111–13, 126–30, 164–73; Sheli Goldberg, *The Spiritual Voyage of the Soul: The Soul of the Zaddik and the Eternity of the Spirit in Habbad's Doctrine* (Jerusalem: Rubin Mass, 2009) [Hebrew], esp. 18–60, as well as Etkes, *Ba'al ha-Tanya*, esp. 149–50, 153–55, 167–71, 207–8, 443–45.

9. On the influence of Horowitz on Rashab, see the oral tradition received by Morgenstern and his textual support for this testimony quoted by Arenfeld, *Yira'ukah 'im-Shamesh*, 790n27.

10. Shneur Zalman of Lyady, *Tanya* (New York: Kehot Publication Society, 1985), part 1, chapters 1–2, fol. 5a–7a. Following on my earlier discussions of Hasidism, I should mention here the extensive Hasidic discourse on the soul of the *tzaddiq*, his transmission to the heart and soul of his followers, etc. One should esp. note the trope of the granting of a new soul by the *tzaddiq*, as in Nahman of Bratzlav, *Liqqutei Moharan*, part 1, siman 35, par. 2–5, and the striking text on the *tzaddiqim* rebirthing themselves in the Tzanz branch of Lublin in Hayyim Halberstam, *Divrei Hayyim*, vols. 1–2 (New York, 2003), vol. 1, 10.

11. Vital, *Sha'arei Qedusha*, part 1, gates 1–2, 14–22.

12. For the souls of non-Jews in Habad, see Wolfson, *Open Secret*, 45, 235, 239. The disturbingly chauvinistic plain sense (*peshat*) of the text may be slightly mitigated through a gloss by the grandson of the author, the third rebbe of Habad, also named R. Menaham Mendel Schneerson, who explains that the divine good is in exile and thus hidden in the souls of the Gentiles. See this quote and others in the valuable collective commentary on the *Tanya* published in New York in 2009 (as part of the *Hasidut Mevu'eret* series), 71n60. For parallels in other Hasidic writings, see Margolin, *Inner Religion*, 218n147. For more universalistic tendencies in early Hasidism, see Menachem Kallus, *Pillar of Prayer: Teachings of Contemplative Guidance in Prayer, Sacred Study, and the Spiritual Life from the Baal Shem Tov and his Circle* (Louisville, KY: Fons Vitae Publishing, 2011), 68n370.

13. Shneur Zalman of Lyady, *Tanya*, part 1, chapter 2, fol. 6a–b (and cf. chapter 42, fol. 59a–b). For sonship in the context of the exile of the soul, see part 4, fol. 32a–b. On sonship in Hasidism, see Idel, *Ben*, 531–84 (and esp. 551–52 for the soul); Garb, *Shamanic Trance*, 200–201n103. For the psychology of Friedman, which deserves a separate study (including comparing its development among his many disciples), see for now Netanel Lederberg, *The Gateway to Infinity: Rabbi Dov Bear [sic], the Maggid Mesharim of Mezhirich* (Jerusalem: Rubin Mass, 2011) [Hebrew]; Menachem Lorberbaum, "'Attain the Attribute of *'Ayin'*: The Mystical Religiosity of *Maggid Devarav Le-Ya'aqov*," *Kabbalah* 31 (2014): 169–235. For parallel descriptions (yet containing subtle differences) of the unitative effect of Torah study, see *Tanya*, part 1, chapter 5, fol. 9a–10a, chapter 41, fol. 58a–b. For a parallel discussion of the commandments, see Shneur Zalman of Lyady, *Ma'amarei Admor Hazaqen: Parshiot ha-Torah ve-haMo'adim*, vol. 1 (New York: Kehot Publishing, 1983), 239. For a parallel in the process of repentance, to be described below, see chapter 8 of *Iggeret ha-Teshuva* ("Epistle on Repentance," section 3 of *Tanya*), fol. 98a–b.

14. Shneur Zalman of Lyady, *Tanya*, part 4, chapter 12, fol. 117a–119a. For a similar pessimistic portrayal of the present state of the world, see ibid., part 1, chapter 6, fol. 10b–11a. For the Messiah as the depth of the heart, see Shneur Zalman of Lyady, *Torah Or* (New York: Kehot Publication Society, 1987), fol. 55b.

15. My choice of a musical analogy is deliberate. In Habad theory one may find numerous parallels between the articles (*ma'amarim*) and melodies (*niggunim*) composed by each rebbe, which together with personal (*yehidut*) and collective (*farbrengen*) encounters are seen as granting access to the various levels of his soul. See for now the introduction to the canonical S. Zalmanov (ed.), *Sefer ha-Niggunim* ("Book of Melodies"), commissioned by Yoseph Yitzhaq Schneerson (New York: Ninah [Nigunei Hasidei Habad], 1985), as well as the talks by the last rebbe, Menahem Mendel Schneerson, on the subject collected in *Heikhal ha-Negina*, ed. Zusha Wolff (Jerusalem, 2007).

16. Shneur Zalman of Lyady *Tanya*, part 1, chapter 9, fol. 13b.

17. Ibid., and chapter 51, fol. 71b. The desire of the soul to ascend in a flame-like manner is addressed throughout chapter 19 of this portion (fol. 24a–25b)

18. Ibid., chapter 9, fol. 13b–14b. For more on this constant internal strife, see chapter 27, fol. 34a–35a. For the image of the city in modern Kabbalah, see chapter 4. See also Wolfson, *Open Secret*, 140–41, 161–62. On Christian thought and Hasidism, see Shaul Magid, *Hasidism Incarnate: Hasidism, Christianity and the Construction of Modern Judaism* (Stanford: Stanford University Press, 2014). For views of spiritual warfare within the psyche in premodern Kabbalah, see Moshe Idel, "The Battle of the Urges: Psychomacia in the Prophetic Kabbalah of Abraham Abulafia," in *War and Peace in Jewish*

Culture, ed. A. Bar-Levav (Jerusalem: Zalman Shazar Center; Haifa: Center for Jewish Culture in Haifa University, 2006) [Hebrew], 99–143.

19. Shneur Zalman of Lyady, *Tanya*, part 1, chapters 10–13, fol. 14b–19b.

20. See respectively ibid., chapters 14 (fol. 19b), 16 (fol. 21b, and see also chapter 47, fol. 67a), 17 (fol. 23a), 19 (fol. 24b–25a), and 29 (fol. 35b–37b). A detailed exposition of the exile of the soul and the breaking of the heart can be found in chapters 6–7 of section 3 (*Iggeret ha-Teshuva*, "The Epistle of Repentance"), and see also chapter 11 of this section for the paradoxical union of joy and contrition in this process. See, however, the statement by Rashaz's student R. Hillel Halevi Malisov, *Pelah ha-Rimon: Exodus* (New York, 1956), 7, on exalted souls for whom the destruction never occurred, and who are thus apparently beyond exile. On repentance in Habad, see, e.g., Wolfson, *Open Secret*, 280–81 (and 55–56); Schwartz, *Habad's Thought from Beginning to End*, 319–55 (and see also Wolfson, *A Dream Interpreted*, 203–8 on the exile of the soul). For a more general discussion of repentance in Kabbalah, see Shokek, *Kabbalah and the Art of Being*, 127–45. For a very rich text on *teshuva* ("repentance") and the mystery of the heart see R. Dov Baer Shneuri, *Derekh Hayyim* (New York: Kehot Publishing Society, 1986), 44–46, and see at length in Tsiri Levanoni, "The Concept of Repentance in R. Dov Ber's Thought and Its Sources in R. Shneur Zalman of Liady's Thought" (Ph.D. diss., Bar Ilan University, 2009) [Hebrew]. Compare also to R. Nahman of Bratzlav, *Liqqutei Moharan*, 1, siman 49, par. 6: "The main repentance depends on the heart."

21. Shneur Zalman of Lyady, *Tanya*, part 4, chapter 4, fol. 105a–106b, and see also chapter 38, as well as idem, *Liqqutei Torah* (New York: Kehot Publishing Society, 1986), part 4, fol. 56b, 82b; Wolfson, *Open Secret*, 51; Reut Glassman, "The Magical Meaning of the Commandments in the Philosophy of Rabbi Shneur Zalman of Liady" (M.A. thesis, Bar-Ilan University Ramat Gan, 2009) [Hebrew], 31, 32n72. This reworking is framed within an even greater stress on the role of charity. On the irrational (*shelo be-da'at*) in Hasidism and its sources, see Mark, *Mysticism and Madness*, 115–34. On fire and the heart, see the poetic elocution in Gaston Bachelard, *The Psychoanalysis of Fire* (Boston: Beacon Press, 1964), 7.

22. See esp. Naftali Loewenthal, *Communicating the Infinite: The Emergence of the Habad School* (Chicago: University of Chicago Press, 1990), 55–56, 62. Though not explicitly citing Weber, this analysis emphasizes other-worldly asceticism. This layer is indeed apparent in two chapters (18, 25) in part 1 of the *Tanya* (fol. 23b–24a, 31a–32b respectively).

23. Aharon Shmu'el of Kremnitz, *Nishmat Adam*, fol. 12b–14a.

24. Wolfson, *A Dream Interpreted*, 210–11.

25. See Loewenthal, *Communicating the Infinite*, 57, 117, 122–29; Elior, *Theory of Divinity of Hasidut Habad*, 134–77; Garb, "Mystics' Critique of Mystical Experience," 314–24 (and the scholarly discussions cited there, as well as

Nahman of Bratzlav, *Liqqutei Moharan*, part 1, siman 49, pars. 1, 4); Aharon
Horowitz, *Sha'arei 'Avoda* [printed with *Sha'arei Yihud ve-Emunah*], fol. 8b,
and idem, *Sha'arei Yihud ve-Emunah* (Jerusalem, c. 1987, 11th ed. of reprint
of Shklov, 1820), fol. 3b respectively (and compare to the unpaginated letter by R. Tzevi Hirsch of Tchashnik printed at the beginning of the dual
edition). On mystical construction of emotion, see Grace Jantzen, *Power,
Gender, and Christian Mysticism* (Cambridge: Cambridge University Press,
1995), 94, 131, 139. For more general discussions see David Lynch, ed., *Divine Passions: The Social Construction of Emotion in India* (Berkeley: University of California Press, 1990); John Corrigan, *Business of the Heart: Religion
and Emotion in the Nineteenth Century* (Berkeley: University of California
Press, 2002).

26. See Aharon Horowitz, *Sha'arei 'Avoda*, fol. 55a–b (on *tzaddiqim* versus the
heart of the repentant); Loewenthal, *Communicating the Infinite*, 132, 60
(and see esp. n112), 69–70, 72–73.

27. Aharon of Staroselye, *'Avodat ha-Levi* (Jerusalem, 2004), vol. 2, part 1,
fol. 1a–2a, part 2, fol. 8a–b and see there fol. 9a–10a (see also idem, *Sha'arei
'Avoda*, fol. 68a, on the level of *Da'at* as the site of disclosure in the "point
of the heart"). A nonacademic yet useful English work on Horowitz is Zalman Schachter-Shalomi and Netanel Miles-Yepez, *A Hidden Light: Stories
and Teachings of Early HaBaD and Bratzlav Hasidism* (Santa Fe: Gaon Books,
2011), 143–209.

28. See the analysis of the legend in Garb, *Shamanic Trance*, 11. For Romanticism and the general cultural context, see Rosen, *The Quest for Authenticity*,
330–48 (and esp. 343 on the soul); Glenn Dynner, *Men of Silk: The Hasidic
Conquest of Polish Jewish Society* (New York: Oxford University Press, 2006),
34. For themes traced from Lublin to Izbiche, see Rachel Elior, "The Innovation of Polish Hasidism," *Tarbiz* 62 (1993): 381–432 [Hebrew], and cf.
Yehuda (Jerome) Gellman, "Hasidic Existentialism?" in *Hazon Nahum: Studies in Jewish Law, Thought, and History Presented to Dr. Norman Lamm on the
Occasion of His Seventieth Birthday*, ed. Y. Elman and J. Gurock (New York:
Michael Scharf Publication Trust of the Yeshiva University Press, 1997),
393–417.

29. Ya'aqov Yosef of Polony, *Toledot Ya'aqov Yosef* (Jerusalem, 2011), vol. 1, 456;
Qalonymus Qalman Epstein, *Ma'or va-Shemesh* (Jerusalem, 1992), vol. 2,
646 (for a different translation and interpretation, in a study generally
attentive to the theme of the soul, see Jacobs, "The Uplifting of Sparks,"
123–24).

30. Epstein, *Ma'or va-Shemesh*, vol. 1, 230 (and see also vol. 2, 487–90 on transmission of soul levels from leaders who have attained the souls of *atzilut*);
Moshe Hallamish, *Kabbalah: In Liturgy, Halakhah and Customs* (Ramat Gan:
Bar-Ilan University Press, 2000) [Hebrew], 99–104; Idel, *Hasidism*, 149 (and
the appraisal closer to my own in 154). For the psychology of Eichenstein,

see Avraham Segal, *The Path of Worship: Topics in the Hasidic Kabbalah of Rabbi Tzvi Hirsch of Zydachov* (Jerusalem, 2011) [Hebrew], 84–85, 154–57.

31. Ya'aqov Yosef Safrin, *Zohar Hai* (Jerusalem, 2006), fol. 112a, and compare to idem, *Heikhal ha-Brakha* (Lemberg, 1866), vol. 3, fol. 170b, yet cf. vol. 2, fol. 304a, which is less democratically formulated (as noted by Yitzhaq Me'ir Morgenstern, *Yam ha-Hokhma* [Jerusalem, 2010], 448). See also the sources adduced in Yehuda Yifrach, "The Elevation of Foreign Thoughts in the Traditions of R. Israel Baal Shem Tov as Transmitted in the Works of His Students" (M.A. thesis, Bar-Ilan University Ramat Gan, 2008), 125–41 [Hebrew]; Kallus, *Pillar of Prayer*, 126–29.

32. Safrin, *Heikhal ha-Brakha*, vol. 5, fol. 173b; Garb, *Shamanic Trance*, 140, 87.

33. See Idel, *Kabbalah: New Perspectives*, 22–25; idem, *Ascensions on High*, 1–13, and cf. idem, *Hasidism*, 6–17. For a panoramic discussion of the theme of the uplifting of "soul sparks" by the Tzaddiq, see Moshe Idel, "The Tsadik and His Soul's Sparks: From Kabbalah to Hasidism," *JQR* 103/2 (2013): 196–240. Idel's discussion of Hasidism mostly focuses on the Besht.

34. Mordekhai Yosef Leiner, *Mei ha-Shiloah* (Bnei Brak, 1995), vol. 1, 22 (see also 109).

35. Ibid., vol. 1, 137.

36. Ibid., vol. 1, 243. For recent English-language studies on psychology in Izbiche-Radzin, see Shaul Magid, *Hasidism on the Margin: Reconciliation, Antinomianism, and Messianism in Izbica and Radzin Hasidism* (Madison: University of Wisconsin Press, 2003); Ora Wiskind-Elper, *Wisdom of the Heart: The Teachings of Rabbi Ya'akov of Izbica-Radzyn* (Philadelphia: Jewish Publication Society, 2010), esp. 6; Don Seeman, "Martyrdom, Emotion and the Work of Ritual in R. Mordecai Joseph Leiner's *Mei ha-Shiloah*," *AJS Review* 27/2 (2003): 253–80, as well as the interesting Hebrew-language psychological discussions in Aviezer Cohen, "Self-Consciousness in the Book Mei Hashiloach as the Nexus between God and Man" (Ph.D. diss., Ben Gurion University of the Negev, 2006) [Hebrew], 56–57 (on Jung), 108–11, 135–40, 218–20, 252–79, 309–22, 445–56; Yehuda Ben-Dor, "A Study in R. Mordekhai Yosef of Izbicha's Mei ha-Shiloah" (Ph.D. diss., Hebrew University of Jerusalem, 2008) [Hebrew], 86–89, 131–65, 220–26.

37. M. Y. Leiner, *Mei ha-Shiloah*, vol. 2, 170, 179, 163 (and see also 158), 184, as well as the hagiograpy by R. Hayyim Simha Leiner, *Dor le-Yesharim* (Jerusalem, 1999), 36. These themes are repeated many times in the writings of Leiner's student R. Zadoq ha-Kohen of Lublin (see, e.g., *Resisei Laila*, [Jerusalem, 2002], 15 [vol. 3 of his collected works]). In my view, the uniqueness of ha-Kohen's psychology lies in his focus on the growth of the soul, again undermining a simplistic understanding of its innate divinity (see, e.g., idem, *Dover Zedeq*, 1, 13 [volume 4 of his collected works]).

38. Leiner, *Mei ha-Shiloah*, vol. 1, 96, 121, 135. See also, e.g., vol. 1, 231.

39. Ibid., vol. 2, 49, and cf., e.g., vol. 2, 79, 121. The theme of the souls of converts shall be addressed in a separate study.

40. Out of very many texts, see Gershon Henokh Leiner, *Sod Yesharim* (Jerusalem, 2002), 40–45, 155–56.

41. See the general introduction of Arthur Green (trans.), *The Language of Truth: The Torah Commentary of the Sefat Emet, Rabbi Yehudah Leib Alter of Ger* (Philadelphia: Jewish Publication Society, 1998), and the publication of unknown portions by Daniel Reiser and Ariel Evan Mayse, "The Last Sermon of R. Judah Leib Alter of Gur and the Role of Yiddish in the Study of Hasidic Sermons," *Kabbalah* 30 (2013): 127–60. For an example of a response to Izbiche, see the tradition on the sin of Samson recorded in Yehuda Leib Alter, *Sefat Emet* (Jerusalem, 2006), vol. 4, 77. I have not discussed here the *Liqqutim* volume of *Sefat Emet*, which belongs to a yet earlier period and deserves a separate study. The responses to Leiner's thought in *Sefat Emet* will be discussed in a forthcoming MA thesis by my student Yifat Lev.

42. Alter, *Sefat Emet*, vol. 1, 82, 87 (and see also 16). On Sabbath, the heart, and the soul in his thought, see Michael Fishbane, "Transcendental Consciousness and Stillness in the Mystical Theology of R. Yehudah Arieh Leib of Gur," in *Sabbath: Idea, History, Reality*, ed. G. Blidstein et al., 125–28 (Beer Sheva: Ben Gurion University Press, 2004). The theme of nature in Alter's writing was discussed at length in Yoram Jacobson, "Exile and Redemption in Gur Hasidism," *Daat* 2–3 (1978–79), esp. 199–201 [Hebrew].

43. Alter, *Sefat Emet*, vol. 1, 175, vol. 3, 132 (and compare to the very similar discussion of circumcision, 133).

44. Ibid., vol. 1, 175. On ancestral psychology, see vol. 1, 48–49 and my comment in chapter 4. Compare to vol. 2, 24, on only the Tzaddik possessing a heart.

45. Benzion Rabinovitch, *Mevaser Tov: Ma'amar ha-Yehudi ha-Qadosh* (Jerusalem, 1996), 333, and compare to 71 (the book is entitled volume 1, yet no further volumes of this work have been printed to date), 261 (see there on the lights of the Messiah and the holy Jew's soul), 334 respectively. On the postmortem effect and presence of the souls of the righteous in Hasidism, see Wolfson, *Open Secret*, 5–9. The parallel between this effect and that of Moses, prominent in the texts discussed by Wolfson, also figures prominently in Rabinovitch's thought and elsewhere in Polish Hasidism.

46. See the sources and studies cited in Benjamin Brown, "'It Does Not Relate to Me': Rabbi Israel Salanter and the Kabbalah," in *And This Is for Yehuda: Studies Presented to our Friend, Professor Yehuda Liebes on the Occasion of his Sixty-Fifth Birthday*, edited by M. R. Niehoff, R. Meroz, and J. Garb (Jerusalem: Mandel Institute of Jewish Studies and Bialik Institute, 2012) [Hebrew], 420–39, who notes my disagreement with his analysis.

47. See Mordechai Pachter, "The Musar Movement and the Kabbalah," in *Let the Old Make Way for the New*, ed. D. Assaf and A. Rapoport-Albert, vol. 1, 223–50 (Jerusalem: Zalman Shazar Center for Jewish History, 2009) [Hebrew]; Eliezer Rivlin, ed., *HaTzaddik Rabbi Yosef Zundel from Salant* (Jerusalem, 1983), 54–58; Garb, *The Chosen*, 15, 34–35.

48. See also Zeev Gries, "The Hasidic Managing Editor as an Agent of Culture," in *Hasidism Reappraised*, ed. A. Rapoport-Albert (London: Valentine, Mitchell, 1996), 152.

49. Dov Katz, *The Musar Movement: Its History, Leading Personalities, and Doctrines* (Tel-Aviv: Orly Press, 1900), vol. 2, 64, as well as the testimony as to high regard for *Tomer Devorah* as the "Code of Law of *middot*" by the senior fourth-generation teacher R. Yehezkel Levenstein, printed in his talk "Nothing Is More Effective Than Judgment," *Yeshurun* 27 (2012): 571.

50. Yehiel Ya'aqov Weinberg, *Seridei Esh* (Jerusalem: Mossad Harav Kook, 1977), vol. 4, 333; Etkes, *Israel Salanter*, 123–33, 304–12; and cf. Hillel Goldberg, *Israel Salanter: Text, Structure, Idea: The Ethics and Theology of an Early Psychologist of the Unconscious* (New York: Ktav Publishing House, 1982), 170–76, 300–310 and n110. For a diachronic analysis of Lipkin's psychology, see Yohanan Silman, "Psychology in the Teachings of R. Israel Lipkin (Salanter)," *Bar-Ilan* 12 (1973): 288– 304 [Hebrew]. See Shlomo Tikochinsky, "The 'Musar Yeshivot' from Lithuania to Israel: 'Slabodka Yeshiva,' Its Education, Emigration and Establishment in Mandate Palestine" (Ph.D. thesis, Hebrew University of Jerusalem, 2009), 95n171, on the possible influence of the theories of Alfred Adler on the Slobodka stream (cf. ibid., 94, on the existence of a proper psychological theory in this school being doubtful). For more general discussions of Lithuanian Mussar and European modernity, see ibid., 132, 134, 135, 138, 139, 140, 142. See also Shlomo Wolbe, *Quntres ha-Adam bi-Yeqar* (Jerusalem, 1999), 16, on Leibovitz and politics. Compare to the critiques of Haredi politics found in the collected works of R. Avraham Eliyahu Kaplan, a fascinating and understudied figure (*Be-'Iqvot ha-Yir'a* [Jerusalem: Mossad Harav Kook, 1988], 92–110).

51. Shmu'el Stern, *'Olam Hesed Yibane*, reprinted in *Shi'urei Da'at* (Collected Talks of Rabbi A. I. Bloch), 2nd ed. (Jerusalem: Feldheim, 2010), 289–91; Jonathan Garb, "Mussar as a Modern Movement," Paper delivered at the Third International Conference on Modern Religions and Religious Movements in Judaism, Christianity, Islam, and the Babi, Bahai Faith, Hebrew University of Jerusalem, March 2011 (http://www.academia.edu/1684906 /Mussar_as_a_Modern_Movement).

52. *Sifsei Hakhamim Committee* (eds.), *Memorial Volume for the Author of Mikhtav mi-Eliyahu*, vol. 2 (Bnei Brak, 2004) [Hebrew], 103–4, 105–6, 109–10.

53. See, e.g., Yitzhaq Hutner, *Pahad Yitzhaq: Purim* (New York, 1996), 'Inyan 29, 79–81. On soul-making, see Beruriah David (published anonymously), *Memorial Volume for Our Teacher, the Author of Pahad Yitzhaq* (New York and Jerusalem, 1997) [Hebrew], 85.

54. Yeruham Leibovitz, *Da'at Torah* (Jerusalem, 2001), vol. 2, 94–95.

55. Ibid., 95.

56. For the original text in its context, see Jacob Emden, *Birat Migdal 'Oz* (Zhitomir, 1873), fol. 42b–47b.

57. Leibovitz, *Da'at Torah*, vol. 2, 98–99.

58. Ibid., 99–100. Cf. also ibid., 222, where Leibovitz explains that the heart includes everything just as the Torah is "one point" that includes everything. Cf. the profound discussion of the depth of the heart in ibid., vol. 4, 96–98, where Leibovitz expands on a somewhat radical passage from ibn Ezra on the heart, not the external commandments, being the greater part of the Torah. See also the anonymously edited Yeruham Leibovitz, *Ma'amarei ha-Mashgiah Rabenu Yeruham ha-Levi: Elul ve-Tishrei* (Jerusalem, 2008), 4, on the depth of the heart as the essence of speech (and see also 65).

59. Yehezkel Levenstein, *Or Yekhezqel*, vol. 7 (*Darkhei 'Avoda*) (Bnei Brak, 2001), 279–82, and compare to 20. Cf. idem, vol. 6 (*Yir'a ve-Mussar* [Bnei Brak, 1996], 22–23), on the sense of the centrality of the soul as the basis of self-work in the Mussar fashion. One should also mention R. Eliyahu Lopian, of the school of Kelm, who came to Israel through London and devoted his *Lev Eliyahu* to talks on the heart. On his studies with the famous Lithuanian Kabbalist R. Shlomo Elyashiv, see the biographical introduction to *Lev Eliyahu* (Jerusalem, 2005), 12, and compare to 35.

60. On the current revival of Wolbe's teachings, see Jonathan Garb, "Towards the Study of the Spiritual-Mystical Renaissance in the Contemporary Ashkenazi Haredi World in Israel," in *Kabbalah and Contemporary Spiritual Revival*, ed. B. Huss (Beer Sheva: Ben Gurion University of the Negev Press, 2011), 129–34. For a preliminary discussion of Wolbe's early writing, see Tamar Ross, "The Musar Movement and the Issue of Hermeneutics in the Study of Torah," *Tarbiz* 59 (1990): 191–92 [Hebrew].

61. See Garb, *The Chosen*, 82–83 (and 16, 59).

62. Shlomo Wolbe, *Da'at Shlomo: Ma'amarei Zeman Matan Torateinu* (Jerusalem, 2006), 281.

63. Ibid., 407–8. See also idem, *Pirqei Qinyan Da'at* (Jerusalem, 2001), 19. On the various stages in the place of the Kabbalah in his world, see idem, *Igrot u-Khtavim (Letters and Writings)*, vol. 1 (Jerusalem, 2006), 169. For an explicit critique of psychoanalysis, see vol. 2 (2013), 290–92.

64. An oral tradition that I heard has it that a student once asked Leibovitz if he might go to study in Telz. The reply was: "Of course, but first forget everything that you have learned with us" (see however, Wolbe, *Igrot u-Khtavim (Letters and Writings)*, vol. 1, 105, where Bloch's works are mentioned as optional study material). The intense rivalry between (different) Mussar schools is apparent in the literary memoirs of Chaim Grade, as well as the diary of a Yeshiva student, Benjamin Ya'aqov Barkai, who immigrated to Palestine in the 1920s, printed in the memorial volume *Nahalat Binyamin* (Jerusalem, 2005) [edited by his son Shmu'el Barkai] also containing valuable material as to contacts with Kook and the inner life of the students. For the critique of Zionism by R. Yosef Leib Bloch, who was a founding member of the Agudat Israel party, see, e.g., his *Shi'urei Da'at* (Tel Aviv, 1953) [Hebrew], vol. 3, 47, 65.

65. Bloch, *Shi'urei Da'at*, vol. 1, 52–53. See Ernest L. Rossi, *The Psychobiology of*

NOTES TO PAGES 75–78

Mind-Body Healing: New Concepts of Therapeutic Hypnosis (New York: W. W. Norton & Co., 1993), 47–68.

66. Bloch, *Shi'urei Da'at*, 54.

67. Ibid., 55–56, and compare to vol. 3, 67–78, which was delivered as a sharp and rare explicit response to the students expressing envy of Yeshivas with more effective public relations and advertising in the press. On soul-making, see also the text by R. Yitzhaq Hutner in *Memorial Volume for R. Hayyim Shmuelevitz*, ed. Ya'aqov Boksboim (Jerusalem, 2000), 139.

68. Here, too, there is a contemporary context—most likely the critique of Kabbalah in the circles of the Haskalah. Lest one conclude that Leibovitz's rival discourse is devoid of Kabbalistic tones, see, e.g., his *Da'at Torah*, vol. 2, 241–42, on the "secret of the heart," which reaches to the "abyss of the heart," which is one with the divine heart (commenting on a text by R. Elijah de Vidas).

69. Bloch, *Shi'urei Da'at*, 58–61. This approach, found in Bloch's own Talmudic writings but especially in those of R. Shimeon Shkop (who taught at Telz with a slight overlap with the former's tenure as Rosh Yeshiva), seeks to uncover the rationale of the Halakha, while the rival approach of R. Hayyim of Brisk (made famous in the English-speaking world by his grandson, R. Joseph Baer Soloveitchik), regarded this attempt as futile and instead strove to describe the internal logic of the Halakhic structure. For R. Shimeon Shkop, see Shay Wozner, *Legal Thinking in the Lithuanian Yeshivot* (Jerusalem: Magnes Press, forthcoming) [Hebrew].

70. The Mussar teachings of Friedlander and Kotler (*Siftei Hayyim* and *Mishnat Rabbi Aharon* respectively) have been printed in recent years. One must note here that the former contains Kabbalistic elements (and see also chapter 5). For Wolbe's sharp critiques of *hasqafa* (and of academic "Jewish thought"), see Shlomo Wolbe, *'Alei Shur* (Jerusalem, 1986), vol. 2, 144–47; idem, *Da'at Shlomo*, 198. Besides internal textual evidence and oral accounts, this description relies on authoritative biographical accounts of Leibovitz and Bloch found in Shlomo Wolbe, *Quntres ha-'Adam bi-Yeqar* and the essay by R. Aharon Sorsky (reprinted as a preface to *Shi'urei Da'at*, vol. 1, 3–32).

71. See the numerous texts devoted to subtlety (as of the heart) in Eliyahu E. Dessler, *Mikhtav mi-Eliyahu: Elul and Rosh ha-Shana* (Bnei Brak, 2009), 124–25; idem, *Mikhtav mi-Eliyahu* (Bnei Brak, 2009), vol. 5, 120–43.

CHAPTER FOUR

1. Sorotzkin, *Orthodoxy and Modern Disciplination*, 55–60, 131–32. For the state in later periods, see the important collection by Pierre Birnbaum and Ira Katznelson (eds.), *Paths of Emancipation: Jews, States, and Citizenship* (Princeton: Princeton University Press, 1995).

2. On the modern reception of *Sefer ha-Kuzari*, see Adam Shear, *The Kuzari and the Shaping of Jewish Identity, 1167–1900* (Cambridge: Cambridge University Press, 2008).
3. See Robert S. Wistrich, *A Lethal Obsession: Anti-Semitism from Antiquity to the Global Jihad* (New York: Random House, 2010), 517; Ruth HaCohen, *The Music Libel Against the Jews* (New Haven: Yale University Press, 2011), 245–51 (and compare to 164). See also Sorotzkin, *Orthodoxy*, 49–55.
4. Jantzen, *Power, Gender, and Christian Mysticism*, 345. For the general theme of Jews and gentiles in Kabbalah, see at length in Wolfson, *Venturing Beyond*, as noted in chapter 1 (as well as the comment of Idel, *Enchanted Chains*, 226). For national mysticism in Prague, see Garb, "The Kabbalists of Prague," as well as idem, "Rabbi Kook and His Sources: From Kabbalistic Historiosophy to National Mysticism," 77–96.
5. For Machiavelli and Kabbalah, see Garb, *Manifestations of Power*. For Vico, see Jonathan Garb, "The Political Model in Modern Kabbalah: A Study of Ramhal and his Intellectual Surroundings," 13–45. See there and in Garb, "Modernization of Kabbalah," for politics in the thought of Luzzatto's circle.
6. See the crescendo-like ending of the work of Kook's most mystical disciple, R. David Kohen, *Qol ha-Nevu'a* (Jerusalem, 2002), 315–18. This includes a discussion of the indebtedness of modern Jewish movements to Luzzatto. See Garb, *Kabbalist in the Heart of the Storm*, 336–39.
7. For history and regional identity, see also Garb, *Kabbalist in the Heart of the Storm*, 173–74, 201–2, 89–90, and the earlier studies cited there. For psychology in earlier Italian Kabbalah, see Yosha, *Myth and Metaphor: Abraham Cohen Herrera's Philosophic Interpretation of Lurianic Kabbalah*, 307, 318, 350; Gershom Scholem, *Sabbatai Sevi: The Mystical Messiah, 1626–1676* (Princeton: Princeton University Press, 1973), 31. The national model can be found in late sixteenth-century Italian Kabbalah; see Yoram Jacobson, *Along the Paths of Exile and Redemption: The Doctrine of Redemption of Rabbi Mordecai Dato* (Jerusalem: Bialik Institute, 1996), 84–85, 78.
8. On Luzzatto and the Baroque, see Israel Bartal, "On Periodization, Mysticism, and Enlightenment: The Case of Moses Hayyim Luzzatto," *Simon Dubnow Institute Yearbook* 6 (2007): 201–14. On rhetoric and the soul, see Hillman, *Re-Visioning Psychology*, 213–21 (for his indebtedness to Italian psychology, see idem, *Loose Ends: Primary Papers in Archetypal Psychology* [Zurich: Spring Publications, 1975], 146–69). For Luzzatto's experience of communication with exalted souls and techniques related to soul rectification, see Garb, *Kabbalist in the Heart of the Storm*, 117–26, and see there, 98, 229–45, on Luzzatto's rhetoric and his theoretical organization. For other earlier research on Luzzatto's psychology, see Isaiah Tishby, *Messianic Mysticism: Moses Hayim Luzzatto and the Padua School*, trans. M. Hoffman (Oxford: Littman Library of Jewish Civilization, 2008), 229–34, 241–43

(focusing on messianism, as was his wont); Mopsik, *Sex of the Soul*, 69–71, as well as Joelle Hansel, *Moïse Hayyim Luzzatto (1707–1746): Kabbale et Philosophie* (Paris: Editions du Cerf, 2004), 235.

9. Moshe Hayyim Luzzatto, *Adir ba-Marom*, ed. J. Spinner (Jerusalem, 1995), 88 (and see also 111, 408), 460.

10. For the manuscript and printing history of *Da'at Tevunot*, its Kabbalistic parallels, and the question of Luzzatto's Kabbalistic writings, see Garb, "The Authentic Kabbalistic Writings," 175–77. For Gordon's *Mar'eh ha-Mussar*, see Garb, *Kabbalist in the Heart of the Storm*, 317. For an interesting discussion of the soul in a work attributed to Luzzatto, see H. Friedlander (ed.), *Ginzei Ramhal* (Bnei Brak, 1984), 259–61, and especially the "four basic forms of knowledge on Kabbalah," one of which is that of the secrets of the soul, printed in a convenient form in the highly valuable annotated edition of *Da'at Tevunot*, ed. J. Spinner (Jerusalem, 2012), 400–404.

11. Moshe Hayyim Luzzatto, *Daat Tevunot: The Knowing Heart*, trans. A. Kaplan (Jerusalem: Feldheim Publishers, 1982), 168–71, 272–73.

12. Moshe Hayyim Luzzatto, *Mesillat Yesharim*, trans. M. M. Kaplan (Philadelphia: Jewish Publication Society of America, 1948), 16; idem, *Derekh ha-Shem*, trans. A. Kaplan (Jerusalem: Feldheim, 1988), part 1, chap. 4, 60–62; idem, *Da'at Tevunot*, 20–21. See my extensive discussion of psychology and the trajectories of *Mesilat Yesharim* in Garb, *Kabbalist in the Heart of the Storm*, 290–316. For this-worldly messianic fulfillment, see the theoretical and comparative observations of Idel, *Messianic Mystics*, 283–85, 289–93 (critiquing the earlier theories of Scholem while evaluating the interrelationship of individual and national messianism), and see also chapter 3.

13. See Garb, "Circle of R. Moshe Hayyim Luzzatto." For Valle's importance, see Jonathan Garb, "A Renewed study of the Self-Image of R. Moshe David Valle, as Reflected in his Biblical Exegesis," *Tarbiz* 79/2 (2010–11): 263–303 [Hebrew]. For a possible adaptation of this study by the contemporary Kabbalist R. Yitzhaq Me'ir Morgenstern (to be discussed in chapter 5), see the record of his weekly talks in *Nishmatin ha-Datin: Ki Tisa* (e-mail distribution, 2011), 27.

14. Moshe David Valle, *Teshu'at 'Olamim*, ed. J. Spinner (Jerusalem, 1999), 366; idem, *Bi'ur Hamesh Megilot*, ed. J. Spinner (Jerusalem, 1988), part 1, 151. The Besht substituted "divinity" for "lights." On Valle and Hasidism, see Garb, "A Renewed Study," 265–66, 291n109, and the discussions by Tishby cited there.

15. See, e.g., Moshe David Valle, *Bi'ur Sefer Tehillim*, ed. J. Spinner, vol. 2, 102 (Jerusalem, 2008). On the rectification of the *Shekhina* in Luzzatto's circle, see Elliot Wolfson, "Tiqqun ha-Shekhinah: Redemption and the Overcoming of Gender Dimorphism in the Messianic Kabbalah of Moses Hayyim Luzatto," *History of Religions* 36 (1997): 289–332, where issues of distinction between nations, highly relevant for the present discussion, are also addressed.

16. Moshe David Valle, *Sefer ha-Liqqutim*, ed. J. Spinner (Jerusalem, 1997), vol. 1, 239 . On the king and the heart (a theme found in far earlier sources such as *Sefer Yetzira*) see idem, *Brit 'Olam: Bi'ur Sefer Shemot*, ed. J. Spinner (Jerusalem, 1995), vol. 1, 120–21; idem, *Bi'ur Shir ha-Shirim, Ruth, Kohelet, Esther: Mahadura Qama*, ed. J. Spinner (Jerusalem, 2010), 248. Cf. *Bi'ur Trei 'Asar 'al Derekh ha-Pardes*, ed. J. Spinner (Jerusalem, 2009), 197, on the king as the head. For a broader historical perspective, see Jacques Le Goff, "'Head or Heart?' The Political Use of Body Metaphors in the Middle Ages," in *Fragments for a History of the Human Body: Part Three*, ed. M. Feher, R. Naddaff, and N. Tazi (New York: Zone, 1989), 12–26. On the heart of the nation, see also Valle, *Brit 'Olam*, vol. 1, 207. (Valle often quotes R. Judah Halevi's well-known description of Israel as the heart of the nations. Compare to his psychic theory of the Land of Israel, as in ibid., 86–87, on the *Shekhina*, as the soul of the Holy Land, as well as Valle, *Bi'ur Sefer Tehillim*, vol. 2, 185).

17. Valle, *Sefer ha-Liqqutim*, 229; idem, *Mamlekhet Kohanim: Bi'ur Sefer Yehezkel*, ed. J. Spinner (Jerusalem, 2008), 29 (on the rectifying *tzaddiq* as a powerful warrior, see 31). Although Valle's focus is on the Jews, he writes that all kings, "even" Gentiles, have a divine spark, which hovers over them as the source of their authority. Valle, *Bi'ur Sefer Tehillim*, 47, and see also idem, *Moshia' Hosim: Bi'ur Sefer Shmu'el*, ed. J. Spinner (Jerusalem, 1998), 288. On Valle and Christology (discussed in a two-volume work of his in Italian whose translation, by Vadim Putzu, I am currently supervising), see Garb, "A Renewed Study," 293n116.

18. Valle, *Bi'ur Trei 'Asar 'al Derekh ha-Pardes*, ed. J. Spinner (Jerusalem, 2009), 359; idem, *Sefer ha-Liqqutim*, vol. 1, 250 (Garb, *Shamanic Trance*, 72–73 and cf. Tishby, *Messianic Mysticism*, 198–206, 306, 310). Valle's construction of this image also reflects the medical training that he shared with other members of Luzzatto's circle (see, e.g., *Sefer ha-Liqqutim*, vol. 2, 608, on the importance of pulse taking, which enables observation of the power of the heart, as source of the vital spirit of the body). On Luzzatto's circle, medicine, and the academic world in general, see Jonathan Garb, "Mussar, Curriculum and Exegesis in the Circle of Ramḥal," Tikvah Center Working Paper No. 01/12 (http://www.nyutikvah.org/pubs/1112/documents/WP 1Garb.pdf). Compare to the discussion of the health of the heart as king of the body in Valle, *Bi'ur Shir ha-Shirim, Ruth, Kohelet, Esther: Mahadura Qama*, 180.

19. Valle, *Brit 'Olam*, vol. 1, 281 (and compare to idem, *Bi'ur Hamesh Megilot*, vol. 2, 181). Actually, according to Valle (*Bi'ur Shir ha-Shirim, Ruth, Kohelet, Esther: Mahadura Qama*, 208), the Messiah is already "ready" in the world of *atzilut* ("emanation"), and will be disclosed in the world of *'assiyah* ("action") at the proper time. See also Valle, *Teshu'at 'Olamim*, 61.

20. See Valle, *Bi'ur Sefer Tehillim*, vol. 1, 50, and vol. 2, 164; idem, *Bi'ur Shir ha-Shirim, Ruth, Kohelet, Esther: Mahadura Qama*, 243, 260, 267, 277, 297,

303, and 355 respectively (and see also 372). On the soul of David and the world of emanation, see idem, *Moshia' Hosim*, 130.

21. Valle, *Sefer ha-Liqqutim*, vol. 1, 239; idem, *Bi'ur Shir ha-Shirim, Ruth, Kohelet, Esther: Mahadura Qama*, 224, 308. On power depending on one's soul root, see Valle, *Moshia' Hosim*, 122.

22. Valle, *Sefer ha-Liqqutim*, vol. 1, 26–27; idem, *Bi'ur Hamesh Megilot*, part 2, 163. Compare to idem, *Teshu'at 'Olamim*, 449, on the kindnesses of David as the source of prophecy, and see also idem, *Bi'ur Sefer Tehillim*, vol. 1, 80, on David describing himself in Psalms as *hasid*, as his intention in all his deeds is to draw down *Hesed* to the attribute of kingdom (*Malkhut*). On drawing down *Hesed* through roots of the soul, see Moshe David Valle, *Bi'ur Dani'el, 'Ezra u-Nehemia*, ed. J. Spinner (Jerusalem, 2010), 187.

23. See, e.g., Valle, *Bi'ur Shir ha-Shirim, Ruth, Kohelet, Esther: Mahadura Qama*, 216; idem, *Bi'ur Hamesh Megilot*, vol. 2, 205; idem, *Or 'Olam*, ed. J. Spinner (Jerusalem, 1993–94), vol. 2, 596. On the lack of new souls during the exile, see idem, *Bi'ur Sefer Tehillim*, vol. 2, 79. On the transformation of the king, see there, 97 (on David) (and see also idem, *Moshia' Hosim*, 118, on the new soul of David).

24. See Aryeh Ne'eman, " 'Iyunim ba-Hibur 'Kaf ha-Qtoret': Zmano, Meqomo, Ra'ayonotav ve-Tod'ato ha-Meshihit" (M.A. thesis, Hebrew University of Jerusalem, 2009) [Hebrew].

25. Valle, *Bi'ur Sefer Tehillim*, vol. 2, 269. The theory of psychic protection, which is also a constant theme in Habad discourse, cannot be discussed here.

26. Moshe David Valle, *Marp'e Lashon*, ed. J. Spinner (Jerusalem, 2003), 135. On David as a "general soul," see idem, *Moshia' Hosim*, 222. Compare to the proto-Hasidic discussion of the soul as the imperceptible and invisible "nothingness" in idem, *Bi'ur Shir ha-Shirim, Ruth, Kohelet, Esther: Mahadura Qama*, 212. See also there, 241, for a national distinction between the Jews, whose heart obtains the hidden truth, and the Gentiles, who follow the visible and external.

27. Valle, *Bi'ur Shir ha-Shirim, Ruth, Kohelet, Esther: Mahadura Qama*, 191–92. On the soul as the source of power in the struggle against evil, see idem, *Teshu'at 'Olamim*, 43.

28. Valle, *Bi'ur Shir ha-Shirim, Ruth, Kohelet, Esther: Mahadura Qama*, 205; idem, *Or 'Olam*, vol. 1, 186 (and compare to idem, *Teshu'at 'Olamim*, 47; idem, *Bi'ur Shir ha-Shirim, Ruth, Kohelet, Esther: Mahadura Qama*, 379; idem, *Moshia' Hosim*, 241–42); idem, *Teshu'at 'Olamim*, 364; idem, *Sefer ha-Liqqutim*, vol. 2, 516; idem, *Bi'ur Shir ha-Shirim, Ruth, Kohelet, Esther: Mahadura Qama*, 299. On the heart and the root, see also idem, *Brit 'Olam*, vol. 1, 37; idem, *Mamlekhet Kohanim*, 79. On the intimate connection between the soul of the "pious king" and the *Shekhina*, see idem, *Bi'ur Sefer Tehillim*, vol. 2, 268, 279; compare to idem, *Bi'ur Hamesh Megilot*, vol. 2, 176, on the intimate connection between the soul of the "sifting" *tzaddiq* and the *Shekhina*. For

the darkening of the soul in the period of "smallness," see idem, *Bi'ur Sefer Tehillim*, vol. 2, 74.

29. See Garb, "Rabbi Kook and His Sources" and the studies cited there, as well as Eliyahu Stern, *The Genius: Elijah of Vilna and the Making of Modern Judaism* (New Haven: Yale University Press, 2013), and cf. Eliyahu Krakowsky, "Between the Genius and the Gaon: Lost in Translation" (review essay), *Hakirah: The Flatbush Journal of Jewish Law and Thought* 16 (2013): 153–76.

30. On the question of Zionism, see the critical assessment of Israel Bartal, "Messianic Expectations in the Context of Historical Reality," *Cathedra* 31 (1984): 159–71. R. Menahem Mendel of Shklov's thought has been discussed in Hebrew-language studies by Moshe Idel, Yehuda Liebes, and most recently, by Eliezer Baumgarten, "Kabbalah within the Circle of the Vilna Gaon's Disciples: Torah in the Thought of R. Menachem Mendel of Shklov and R. Isaac Eisik Heber Wildmann" (Ph.D. diss., Ben Gurion University, 2010) (on the soul see 75, 79, 175, and see also 196). Baumgarten's reading seeks to uncover certain antinomian tendencies in the writing of R. Menahem Mendel.

31. Reuven Leuchter (ed.), *Nefesh ha-Hayyim* with *Meshivat Nefesh* (Jerusalem, 2013), gate 1, chapter 15, 108–12 (and compare to gate 1, chapter 5, 30–37), gate 1, chapter 16, 116–18, and see also the discussion that Iczkovitz himself links to (found in ibid., gate 2, chapter 17, 333–36, and see the incisive comments of Leuchter, 336n19, 340) for both the intellectual nature of the soul and the current inaccessibility of the soul-root. The source is probably in the commentary by Iczkovitz's teacher Kremer on the *Heikhalot* section of the *Zohar* (Jerusalem, 2006), 10, 15. Such qualifications reinforce Shaul Magid, "Deconstructing the Mystical: The Anti-mystical Kabbalism in Rabbi Hayyim of Volozhin's Nefesh ha-Hayyim," *Journal of Jewish Thought and Philosophy* 9/1(2000): 21–67, in describing the work as antimystical, an overall assessment challenged by other texts that I shall cite now (and see also Garb, *Shamanic Trance*, 106).

32. See respectively, Leuchter, *Nefesh ha-Hayyim*, gate 2, chapters 11–12, 281–97, gate 4, chapters 2–3, 557–65, gate 2, chapters 15–16, 317–32 (as well as Elijah Kremer, *Heikhalot ha-Zohar im-Bi'ur* [Jerusalem, 2006], printed with a commentary by R. Itzhak Haver [Hebrew], 69–71), unnumbered section between gates 3 and 4, chapter 5, 531–36, and see esp. the comment of Leuchter, 532–33n7, who relates this emphasis to the inaccessibility of the soul.

33. Leuchter, *Nefesh ha-Hayyim*, gate 1, chapter 4, 19. Compare to a similar internalizing visualization in ibid., gate 4, chapter 33, 725–26.

34. Ibid. See 20 for the heart as axis mundi (and compare to Leuchter's comments, 27–29).

35. Ibid., 21.

36. Ibid., gloss in unnumbered section, chapter 4, 526 (it is quite clear that this particular text is a response to a model of the heart similar to that found

in Rashaz's *Tanya*). For these themes in Lithuanian Mussar, see Yakir Englander, *Images of the Male Body in Lithuanian Ultra Orthodox Judaism as Reflected in Musar Movement Sources and "HaGedolim" Hagiographies (1945–2010)* (Jerusalem: Magnes Press, forthcoming) [Hebrew]. Englander's work focuses on the body and on sexuality; however, it contains insights on construction of the self within a broad context of European modernity.

37. Leora F. Batnitzky, *How Judaism Became a Religion: An Introduction to Modern Jewish Thought* (Princeton: Princeton University Press, 2011), 112, 122–27 and cf. Zeev Gries, "From Myth to Ethos—Outlines for the History of Rabbi Abraham of Kalisk," in *Uma ve-Toldoteiha (Nation and History)*, ed. S. Etinger, vol. 2, 117–46 (Jerusalem: Zalman Shazar Center, 1984) [Hebrew].

38. See respectively in Yitzhaq Haver, *Or ha-Torah* (Jerusalem, 1881, reprint edition), fol. 51a–b, 4b, 17b, 31a.

39. Ibid., fol. 21a, 31a, as well as 71b.

40. Yitzhaq Haver, *Afiqei Yam* (Jerusalem, 1994), vol. 2, 348–49 (and see also idem, *Or ha-Torah*, fol. 9b, 17a, as well as the discussion of the former text in Nir Stern, *Adam Hai*); idem, *Siah Yitzhaq* (Jerusalem, 2000), 440. Haver's writing on the soul, and especially the theme of creation of souls through Torah study, is discussed in the context of a discussion of his influence on Kook in Elchanan Shilo, "Rabbi Yizhak Isaac Haver's Influence on Rabbi Kook's Interpretation of the *Kabbalah*," *Daat* 79 (2015): 108–10 [Hebrew].

41. On Elyashiv, see Garb, "Kabbalist in the Heart of the Storm," 328–30, where I cite the few Hebrew-language studies; idem, *The Chosen*, 15, 40, 118–19; idem, "Shamanism and the Hidden History," 184–85. For Sephardic support for his positions, see Ya'aqov Moshe Hillel, *Shorshei ha-Yam* (Jerusalem, 1999), vol. 1, 62–66.

42. Shlomo Elyashiv, *Leshem Shvo ve-Ahlama: Drushei 'Olam ha-Tohu* (Jerusalem, 1976) [reprint], part 1, fol. 52a–b (and see also part 2, fol. 105b, 107b); idem, *Leshem Shvo ve-Ahlama: Haqdamot u-Shorashim* (Petrakov, Russia, 1909), fol. 45b. See also idem, *Leshem Shvo ve-Ahlama: Sefer ha-Kelalim* (Jerusalem, 1924), part 1, fol. 61a.

43. Elyashiv's letters were published in the first volume of the commentaries on *Mishnat Hasidim* (New York: Makhon ha-Gr"a, 2006). See esp. ibid., 50 (as well as 47 on the soul, 57and 59 on psychoid forces, and the sharp critique of Hasidism on 53). This letter is dated in 1884, some two decades after James Clerk Maxwell's classic work on electromagnetism. One must stress that the letters were published with some censorship (as discussed in my above-mentioned monograph on Luzzatto).

44. Shlomo Wolbe, *Igrot u-Khtavim*, vol. 1 (Jerusalem, 2006), 170. For the profoundly modern Lithuanian thinker R. Pinchas Horowitz and his psychology, see the studies cited in chapter 1 note 30.

45. See Uwe Wolfradt, *Ethnologie und Psychologie: Die Leipziger Schule der Völkerpsychologie* (Berlin: Dietrich Reimer Verlag, 2010); Dov Schwartz, *Challenge and Crisis in Rabbi Kook's Circle* (Tel Aviv: 'Am 'Oved, 2001) [Hebrew],

254–56; Garb, "Alien Culture," 255–57. On the soul of the city, compared to post-Jungian discussions, see Garb, "The Modernization of Kabbalah," 10–15 (to which one should add Valle, *Bi'ur Hamesh Megilot,* 150). See also James Hillman, *City and Soul* (Dallas: Spring Publications, 2006); Jonathan Lear, *Open Minded: Working Out the Logic of the Soul* (Cambridge, Mass.: Harvard University Press, 1998), 219–39. On *Völkerpsychologie* and the contemporary Israeli Im Tirtzu movement, see the discussion by Tomer Persico at: http://www.scribd.com/doc/81356629/Tazhir-Tomer-Persico. It is troubling that Persico refrained from publishing his findings on his website in order to avoid litigation. See Jeffrey J. Kripal, *The Serpent's Gift: Gnostic Reflections on the Study of Religion* (Chicago: University of Chicago Press, 2007), 156: "Academic freedom . . . is a very real human rights problem, and the the harassment of intellectuals . . . is inevitably an accurate marker of important thought and real challenge to oppressive social practices."

46. On Zionism and Kabbalah scholarship, see Moshe Idel, "Messianic Scholars: On Early Israeli Scholarship, Politics, and Messianism," *Modern Judaism* 32/1 (2012): 22–53. On Kook and the soul, see Shilo, *Kabbalah in the Works of S. Y. Agnon,* 339–45. It is interesting that one branch of Kook's school is currently publishing and widely distributing booklets containing interpretations of his psychology with a contemporary orientation. See, e.g., Yuval Freund, *Psychology of Above: R. Kook's Doctrine of the Soul* (Jerusalem, 2009) [Hebrew]. The first chapter is accessible online at http://www.hebpsy.net /files/4YqSSOjeXg5Y2zX7wBtU.pdf.

47. Garb, *The Chosen,* 23–29, 37–44, 62–64, 77–78, 88–93, 118–19; Schwartz, *Challenge and Crisis.* Uriel Barak, "New Perspectives on Rabbi Kook and his Circle: Rabbi Avraham Yitzhak ha-Kohen Kook and His Principal Disciples through the Prism of an Integrated Methodology" (Ph.D. diss., Bar-Ilan University, 2009) [Hebrew], responds at length to critiques of the notion of the Kook circle. In my view Barak's approach is borne out if one but takes a panoramic view of Kabbalistic modernity, in which circles played a foundational role. See also the numerous soul-related texts discussed in Uriel Barak, "Can Amalek Be Redeemed: A Comparative Study of the Views of Rabbi Kook and Rabbi Ya'akov Moshe Harlap," *Da'at* 73 (2012): xxix–lxix. One should note here the descriptions of Kook's soul penned by his students: M. Z. Neria, *Sihot ha-Re'iah* (Tel Aviv: Moreshet: 1979), 264; Tzevi Kaplan, *Be-Shiphulei Glimato: Something on Our Master, the Ra'ayah Kook and His Surroundings* (Jerusalem, 2009) [Hebrew], 36. See also Smadar Sherlo, *The Tzadiq is the Foundation of the World* (Ramat Gan: Bar Ilan University Press, 2012) [Hebrew], esp. 82–83, 317–23, 383–85, who recently collected her earlier articles on the Kook circle without referring to the scholarship of the last decade.

48. Shlomo Fischer, "Self-Expression and Democracy in Radical Religious Zionist Ideology" (Ph.D. diss., Hebrew University of Jerusalem, 2007), 76, 84–85, 91 (as well as, more generally, ibid., 95–96, 98, 105, 119, 122).

49. Ibid., 100–101. Compare to the important discussion of the primacy of natural morality in Kook's ethics, ibid., 113–14. For more on Kook and expressivism, see Yehudah Mirsky, "An Intellectual and Spiritual Biography of Rabbi Avraham Yitzhaq ha-Cohen Kook from 1865–1904" (Ph.D. diss., Harvard University, 2007), 221–22, 281–83, 373–79, and compare to 272–73, as well as the more popular yet eloquent discussion in idem, *Rav Kook: Mystic in a Time of Revolution* (New Haven: Yale University Press, 2014), 114–18. See Avraham Yitzhaq ha-Kohen Kook, *Middot ha-Re'iah*, in idem, *Mussar Avikha* (Jerusalem: Mossad ha-Rav Kook, 1979), 139, on the foundation of tolerance on a perception of the heart and deep soul of the other.

50. See Mirsky, "Intellectual and Spiritual Biography," 151–52, as well as 154–56, 185 (compare to 255–59, for an important discussion of "strategies of containment"). For Maharal, see the panoramic discussion by Sorotzkin, *Orthodoxy and Modern Disciplination*, 187–200.

51. Avraham Yitzhaq ha-Cohen Kook, *Ma'amarei ha-Re'iah* (Jerusalem, 1988), 113–17.

52. Avraham Yitzhaq ha-Kohen Kook, *Orot* (Jerusalem: Mossad ha-Rav Kook, 1980), 151; Garb, "Alien Culture." On the rejection of outside influences on the individual and national soul, see Avraham Yitzhaq ha-Kohen Kook, *Orot ha-Qodesh* (Jerualem: Mossad ha-Rav Kook, 1984), vol. 1, 95–96. For Fischer's analysis, see Fischer, "Self-Expression," 102–3. For a detailed and valuable discussion of embodiment, see ibid., 106–8, 114, as well as Jonathan Garb, "Working Out as Divine Work," in *Sport and Physical Education in Jewish History*, edited by G. Eisen, H. Kaufman, and M. Lämmer (Netanya: Wingate Institute, 2003), 7–14. See also Fischer's discussion of the "inner soul," and the "root of the soul," as both individual and national, based on recently published texts, in Fischer, "Self-Expression," 116–19.

53. Avraham Yitzhaq ha-Kohen Kook, *'Olat Re'iah*, vol. 1 (Jerusalem: Mossad ha-Rav Kook, 1978), 11 (cf. 250, more reminiscent of *Nefesh ha-Hayyim*).

54. idem, *Orot ha-Teshuva* (Jerusalem: Mossad ha-Rav Kook, 1977), 40, 33 (as there is no standard edition, one should add: chapters 6 and 5). Kook's two-volume commentary on the prayerbook, as well as the additional texts recently printed in the latest edition of the collection *Orot ha-Tefila* (Jerusalem, 2003), alongside with other recently published autobiographical texts (e.g. Avraham Yitzhaq ha-Kohen Kook, *Shemona Qevatzim* [Jerusalem, 1999], notebook 3, par. 244) show that his experiential and theoretical understanding of prayer are both a closed book without appreciating the centrality of the soul.

55. Kook, *Orot ha-Teshuva*, chapter 7, 50; chapter 6, 39.

56. Ibid., chapter 15, 143–44.

57. Avraham Yitzhaq ha-Kohen Kook, *Letters* (Jerusalem: Mossad ha-Rav Kook, 1981) [Hebrew], vol. 1, letter 64, 70.

58. Idem, *Orot*, 144, 150–51 (and see also idem, *Ma'amarei ha-Re'iah*, 280). It is in this light that one should interpret the infamous description (idem,

Orot, 156), of the soul of the Jews being more superior to that of the Gentiles than that of Man vis-à-vis the animal soul.

59. Kook, *Letters*, vol. 3, letter 753, 19–21. Compare to the collection of diary entries by Ya'aqov Moshe Harlap, *Mei Marom: Razi Li* (Jerusalem, 2012).

60. Kook, *Orot*, 79 (and see also idem, *Ma'amarei ha-Re'iah*, 70). On the power of the national soul, see, e.g., idem, *'Olat Re'ia*, vol. 1, 75. It is interesting that even a nonreligious figure such as Albert Einstein described "revival of Palestine" as "the liberation and the revival of the soul of the Jewish people." See, e.g., David F. Rowe and Robert J. Schulmann, *Einstein on Politics: His Private Thoughts and Public Stands on Nationalism, Zionism, War, Peace, and the Bomb* (Princeton: Princeton University Press, 2007), 163. Cf. Yehezkel Kaufman, "The Ruin of the Soul," in *Zionism Reconsidered: The Rejection of Jewish Normalcy*, ed. M. Selzer (New York: Macmillan, 1970), 117–29.

61. Kook, *Orot ha-Qodesh*, vol. 1, 151. The illuminatory terms used here recall Hasidic discussions of the shining of the soul.

62. Kook, *Letters*, vol. 1, letter 325, 363. For the image of waves breaking in the soul, see, e.g., idem, *Orot ha-Teshuva*, chapter 6, 44; idem, *'Olat Re'ia*, vol. 2 (Jerusalem: Mossad ha-Rav Kook, 1983), 78. Cf. idem, *Orot*, 165, for an overlooked passage on the need for renewal of individual souls alongside national renewal and see also idem, *Orot ha-Qodesh*, vol. 1, 407, on soul growth, showing that Kook was not exclusively committed to the model of the soul's innate divinity.

63. Kook, *Pinqesei ha-Re'iah*, vol. 1 (Jerusalem: Mossad ha-Rav Kook, 2008), 463.

64. Compare to the repeated statements on breaking the fetters of the soul in this collection (ibid., 28, 436). An autobiographical example of such a desire of the soul that must never be repressed is the study of Kabbalah itself; see ibid., 408, and compare to 414, on understanding Kabbalah by means of the soul, and ibid., 416, on recognizing one's soul root through one's talents and aspirations. See, however, the warning in ibid., 411–12, on the dangers of such soul-revelations of mystical lore. For a text that characteristically synthesizes these seemingly opposing statements, see 421.

65. Kook, *Pinqesei ha-Re'iah*, vol. 1, 407, 431–32, 441. For important comments and summaries of existing research on the influence of Yehuda Halevi on Kook and his circle, see Barak, "Can Amalek Be Redeemed?," 64–66, 399nn109–10; idem, "New Perspectives," 110, 46.

66. Kook, *Pinqesei ha-Re'iah*, vol. 1, 453. Compare to the slightly antinomian formulation in idem, *Pinqesei ha-Re'iah* (Jerusalem, 2010), vol. 2, 200, where Kook writes that as all of Torah, prayers, and good deeds are intended to reveal the soul's inner truth, it hates any deviance from its path, even if enclothed in "garments of holiness." See also Avraham Yitzhaq ha-Kohen Kook, *Qevatzim mi-Ketav Yad Qodsho* (Jerusalem, 2008), vol. 2, 104, on the revelation of the soul through its subtle movements.

67. Compare to Leibovitz, *Da'at Torah*, vol. 2, 139–40.
68. Kook, *Pinqesei ha-Re'iah*, vol. 1, 456. On Kook and Nietzsche, see most recently Mirsky, "Intellectual and Spiritual Biography," 335, 365, 389–90, 394 (and esp. 198, 341, and 386, on the soul). For an explicit reference to modern psychology, see, e.g., Kook, *Shemona Qevatzim*, notebook 1, par. 408. On Freudian psychology in Palestine in this period, see Eran Rolnik, *Freud in Zion: Psychoanalysis and the Making of Modern Jewish Identity*, trans. H. Watzman (London: Karnac Books, 2012).
69. See the text translated and analyzed in Mirsky, "Intellectual and Spiritual Biography," 187, 195, the text on giving each power of the soul its due place discussed in 199, as well as the discussions in 53–58, 66, 74, 98, 164–65, 176, 179–80, 200–203, 219–20, 225, 234–35, 295 (on the soul in the writings from this period, see 145, 192, 205; see also 159, 188–89, 229–30, 239, 274), and see also idem, *Rav Kook*, 28–30; Kook, *Mussar Avikha*, 30, 31. Idem, *Qevatzim mi-Ketav Yad Qodsho*, vol. 1, 60, joins an explicit critique of Salanter's movement with his reservations vis-à-vis Lithuanian Talmudics. For a more explicit text on the unconscious, see Kook, *Pinqesei ha-Re'iah*, vol. 1, 409–10. Cf. Leibovitz, *Da'at Torah*, vol. 2, 244–47, 251–53, who subtly deconstructs the separation of study and prayer that Kook upholds.
70. See Mirsky, "Intellectual and Spiritual Biography," 198 (in n95, he does distinguish between the school of Finkel and other Mussar schools, while claiming, incorrectly in my view, that Finkel's stress on human dignity does not entail an expansive apotheosis of the self). See also the similar claims in 204, 235 (and n54) as well as 100–101, 109 on Hertz. For passages that somewhat support Mirsky's interpretation of Kook's view of Mussar, see Kook, *Shemona Qevatzim*, notebook 2, par. 73; idem, *Pinqesei ha-Re'iah*, vol. 1, 563–66 4.
71. Don Seeman, "Violence, Ethics, and Divine Honor in Jewish Thought," *Journal of the American Academy of Religion* 73/4 (2005): 1028–35; Kook, *Shemona Qevatzim*, notebook 1, par. 51. A vivid portrayal of Karelitz's critique may be found in the literary memoirs of his study partner, the Yiddish writer Chaim Grade. See also Benjamin Brown, *The Hazon Ish: Halakhist, Believer and Leader of the Haredi Revolution* (Jerusalem: Magnes Press, 2011) [Hebrew], 135–36, 139–40, 153.
72. Kook, *Pinqesei ha-Re'iah*, vol. 1, 506–7, and compare to 373. On the Land of Israel and the greatness and freedom of the soul, see, e.g., 408–9.
73. For national psychology in Sephardic Kabbalah around the period of the second generation, see Garb, "Kabbalah Outside the Walls: The Response of Rabbi Haddayah to the State of Israel," 13–27.
74. Similar ideas may be found among other members of Tau's circle. See R. Moshe Bleicher's commentary on Maimonides' psychological treatise *Shemona Peraqim* (subtitled "Understanding the Soul from a Torah Perspective" [Kiryat Arba', 2009]) [Hebrew], aimed at explicating the powers of the soul from nationalist perspective.

75. See, respectively, Tzevi Yisra'el Tau, *Le-'Emunat 'Itenu* (Jerusalem, 1994), vol. 1, 115–18, 173, 188 (compare to vol. 7 [Jerusalem, 2006], 47, 49), on the "noise" of the media as an attempt on the part of the empty soul to distract itself from the suffering caused by the unrealized yearning to express its connection to the divine. See also the similar interpretation of sexual permissiveness in 135, 163, 171, 176; idem, *Tzaddiq be-'Emunato Yehiye* (Beit Shemesh, 2004), 279–81, 83–85 respectively (compare to 125–28, where the idea of the unity of the Torah and the national soul is utilized to reject a comparativist approach to Judaism), and Ishay Rosen-Zvi, "The Creation of Metaphysics: The Debate in the 'Mercaz Harav Yeshiva'—A Critical Study," in *A Hundred Years of Religious Zionism*, vol. 3, ed. A. Sagi and D. Schwartz (Ramat Gan: Bar-Ilan University Press, 2003) [Hebrew], 421–45.

76. See Tau, *Le-'Emunat 'Itenu*, vol. 9 (Jerusalem, 2009), 166; for psychic pain, see chapter 5.

77. Tau, *Le-'Emunat 'Itenu*, vol. 1, 172, 174–75, vol. 9, 177 (and compare to vol. 2 [Jerusalem, 1995], 69–74).

78. See Garb, "The Political Model"; idem, *Manifestations of Power*, esp. 253–55, 269–74; Zygmunt Bauman, *Liquid Modernity* (Cambridge, UK: Polity Press, 2000). See also the sweeping yet creative arguments of Yuri Slezkine, *The Jewish Century* (Princeton: Princeton University Press, 2004). One could argue, contra Scholem, that the expulsion from Spain marked a transition between the premodern pattern of expulsions and far more profound forms of instability in the modern period, culminating with the Holocaust.

79. Yaron Ezrahi, *Imagined Democracies: Necessary Political Fictions* (Cambridge, UK: Cambridge University Press, 2012), 234–35 (and compare to 187) 183–85 respectively. Compare to Garb, *The Chosen Will Become Herds*, 73–74.

CHAPTER FIVE

1. See Jonathan Garb, "Contemporary Kabbalah and Classical Kabbalah: Breaks and Continuities," in *After Spirituality: Studies in Mystical Traditions*, vol. 1, edited by Ph. Wexler and J. Garb (New York: Peter Lang, 2012), 19–46 (also for a precise definition of classical Kabbalah), as well as Jonathan Garb and Phillip Wexler, "After Spirituality: Introducing the Volume and the Series," in *After Spirituality: Studies in Mystical Traditions*, vol. 1, edited by Ph. Wexler and J. Garb (New York: Peter Lang, 2012). 1–15. I cannot address here the place of the soul and heart in non-Kabbalistic twentieth-century Jewish writing, e.g. that of Franz Rosenzweig or even in the more mystical works of A. D. Gordon.

2. See Homans, *The Ability to Mourn*, 142 (and see also 79, as well as 272–73 on the soul); William Parsons, "Psychologia Perennis and the Academic Study of Mysticism," in *Mourning Religion*, edited by W. B. Parsons, D. Jonte-Pace, and S. E. Henking (Charlottesville: University of Virginia Press, 2008),

97–123. The latter argument reflects the general conception of this collection, as phrased in W. B. Parsons, D. Jonte-Pace, and S. E. Henking, "Mourning Religion: An Introduction", in ibid., 5: "This volume proceeds from the notion that the study of religion in the academy . . . represents a socially legitimated, institutionalized forum for the mourning of religion . . . in contemporary culture."

3. Homans, *The Ability to Mourn*, 229.

4. Peale's oft-published book is available at http://www.guideposts.org /free-ebooks/positive-thinking-2012-rediscover-power-positive-thinking -norman-vincent-peale.

5. Sorotzkin, *Orthodoxy and Modern Disciplination*, 281–420. Returning to the present, it must be noted that even on the textual level, and certainly on other levels that are highly important in terms of sociology of knowledge, one cannot begin to encompass current Haredi mysticism without fieldwork; see Jonathan Garb, "Mystical and Spiritual Discourse in the Contemporary Ashkenazi Haredi Worlds," *Journal of Modern Jewish Studies* 9/1 (2010): 29–48; idem, "Towards the Study." Given the continued focus on esotericism and the complex sociopolitics of this world, it will be understandable if in several places I will not be able to provide written references, or even explicitly name my sources.

6. Garb, *The Chosen*, 52–57. See, however, Ashlag's own reservations regarding Schopenhauer in Yehuda Leib Ashlag, *The Future Generation*, ed. M. Laitman (Thornhill, ON: Laitman Kabbalah Publishers, 2006), 343–44. A picture of the interpersonal dynamics in the early Ashlagian school may be derived from the record of his classes found in the multivolume collection edited by his students, *Ha-Shem Shima'kha Sham'ati*, esp. vol. 3 and 4. Ashlagian psychology has also influenced some of the followers of Yemima Avital, perhaps the first female Kabbalist in history (see Garb, *The Chosen*, 114). For an introductory discussion of Ashlag's psychology see Tony Lavi, *The Secret of Cosmogony: The Law of Divinity and the Essence of Mankind in the Studies of R. Yehuda Halevi Ashlag* (Jerusalem: Bialik Institute, 2007) [Hebrew], 50–90, 375–98.

7. Elliot R. Wolfson, *Giving Beyond the Gift: Apophasis and Overcoming Theomania* (New York: Fordham University Press, 2014), esp. 259–60.

8. Yehuda Leib Ashlag, *Pri Hakham* (Bnei Brak, 1985), vol. 1, 174–80; see also idem, *Or ha-Bahir* (Jerusalem, 1991), 13; idem, *Talmud 'Eser ha-Sefirot* (Brooklyn, 1943), vol. 1, 26–27. For a general exposition of five-worlds theory in terms of the gradual acquisition of the five parts of the soul (clearly in the "soul-making" model) through refinement of the "will to receive," see his introduction to the *Zohar* in Yehuda Leib Ashlag, *Sefer ha-Haqdamot* (Or ha-Ganuz, Israel, 2005), 26–32. I cannot enter here the relationship between Ashlag's understanding of lights and vessels and those of Cordovero and Luria respectively. The term *hitpa'alut* is used in a different sense from the Hasidic one of emotional response, yet is not devoid of influence

by it. These texts reinforce my earlier insistence on the salience of the term "power" in Ashlag's writings. On soul and spirit, see here in chapters 2 and 6, as well as Garb, *Shamanic Trance*, 38–45. On Ashlag and socialism, see Garb, *The Chosen*, 56, 150–51n34 (in dialogue with Boaz Huss).

9. Ashlag, *Pri Hakham*, 1, 180–84 (and see also idem, *Or ha-Bahir*, 346). I wrote this in the thirtieth year of my studies of Kabbalah.

10. Yehuda Leib Ashlag, *Sefer Beit Sha'ar ha-Kavvanot me-ha-Ari z"l 'im Bi'ur Poqeah 'Enayyim Or Pashut* (Jerusalem, 1996), 133–39; see also idem, *Igrot ha-Sulam* (Bnei Brak, 2014), 264–67. Meir, *Rehovot ha-Nahar*, 50, in his thoroughly historical description of this clash, overlooks this central text that explains the Sephardic Kabbalists' unaccepting attitude towards Ashlag to this day. For my earlier discussion of the relationship between Ashlag and his predecessors, see Garb, *The Chosen*, 29–30. For brief discussions of Shar'abi's contemporary influence, see Giller, *Shalom Shar'abi*, 56–57, 62, 103–4, 121–24, as well as Shaul Magid, "'The King Is Dead [And Has Been for Three Decades], Long Live the King': Contemporary Kabbalah and Scholem's Shadow," *Jewish Quarterly Review* 102/1 (2012): 131–53, esp. 150–52, who relates my book on the twentieth century and Giller's book on this school in an interesting manner.

11. See Boaz Huss, "All You Need Is Lav: Madonna and Postmodern Kabbalah," *Jewish Quarterly Review* 95/4 (2005): 611–24; idem, "The New Age of Kabbalah," *Journal of Modern Jewish Studies* 6/2 (2007): 107–25; Shmuel N. Eisenstadt, "The Civilizational Dimension of Modernity," *International Sociology* 16/3 (2001): 334–38; idem, "The Reconstruction of Religious Arenas in the Framework of 'Multiple Modernities,'" *Millenium: Journal of International Studies* 29/3 (2000): 591–611.

12. For the comparison with Kook, see Michael Laitman, *Shnei ha-Me'orot ha-Gedolim* (Petah Tikva: Ashlag Research Institute, 2006). I myself was consulted during the preparation of this volume, though most of my suggestions were not incorporated in the final version. Laitman's close readings of Ashlag's exegetical works, containing some interesting psychological insights, are available at http://www.kab.co.il/heb/content/view/frame/2373?/heb /content/view/full/2373&main. For closer, though less creative readings, see R. Adam Sinai's site http://hasulam.co.il/.

13. For the Zoharic myth, see *Zohar* I, fol. 4a–4b, and see Michael Fishbane, *Biblical Myth and Rabbinic Mythmaking*, 7n29, 96–98, 162–67, 286–99. Y. Ashlag's commentary is in idem, *Zohar 'im ha-Sulam*, vol. 1, 69. On the Ashlagian concept of the barrier, see Garb, *The Chosen*, 54; Lavi, *The Secret of Cosmogony*, 145–53, 221–37, 276–85. For Betty Joseph's theory, see her *Psychic Equilibrium and Psychic Change: Selected Papers of Betty Joseph*, edited by M. Feldman and E. Bott Spillius (London: Tavistock/Routledge, 1991), esp. 88–97. For the history of Y. Ashlag's commentary on the Zohar (*perush ha-Sulam*), see Jonatan Meir, "The Revealed and the Revealed within the Concealed: On the Opposition to the 'Followers' of Rabbi Yehudah Ashlag

and the Dissemination of Esoteric Literature," *Kabbalah* 16 (2007): 151–258 [Hebrew]; idem, "Wrestling with the Esoteric: Hillel Zeitlin, Yehuda Ashlag and Kabbalah in the Land of Israel," in *Judaism, Topics, Tragments, Faces, Identities: Jubilee Volume in Honor of Rivka Horwitz*, ed. by H. Pedaya and E. Meir (Beer Sheva: Ben Gurion University of the Negev Press, 2007) [Hebrew], 585–647. For the perception of the importance of the Zohar commentary in the Ashlagian school, see Avraham M. Gottlieb, *Ha-Sulam: The Lives and Teachings of Our Holy Rebbes of the Ashlagian Dynasty and Their Disciples* (Jerusalem, 1997) [Hebrew], 162–68. For a popular-apologetic English treatment of this commentary, see S. Schneider, *Kabbalistic Writings on the Nature of Masculine & Feminine* (Northvale, NJ: Jason Aronson, 2001), 99–134. See Garb, "Contemporary Kabbalah," 21; idem, "The Psychological Turn," for some of the reasons why I do not consider the *Zohar* (which actually received its present form only in the modern period) a true classic for modern Kabbalah.

14. See respectively Yehuda Leib Ashlag, *The Future Generation*, 364 (and 373), 301–2, 384, 348–49 (and 353). These texts betray the influence of Gustave Le Bon's theories of mass psychology. I was also assisted here by an unpublished lecture by Avishai Bar-Asher entitled "Messianism, Language, and Society in Ashlag's Redemptive Doctrine and the Proliferation of Kabbalah in the Twentieth Century." On rationality, the hallmark of twentieth-century socioeconomic planning (as proclaimed by Weber very early in the century), as egotistical in essence, see the sources discussed in Garb, *The Chosen*, 54–55, as well as, e.g., Barukh Ashlag, *Birkat Shalom* (Bnei Brak, 2000), vol. 3, 223, 387.

15. See Garb, *The Chosen*, 30–31, 52–53 (and see also 58 on Leonora Leet); Ashlag, *Sefer ha-Haqdamot*, 36, and the statements by R. Barukh Ashlag in his *Dargot ha-Sulam*, vol. 1, 50, as well as 61 (yet cf. idem, *Birkat Shalom*, vol. 3, 363, 389, 411).

16. See, e.g., Daniel C. Matt, *The Essential Kabbalah: The Heart of Jewish Mysticism* (San Francisco: Harper, 1995), esp. 109–28, 147–58; Michael A. Fishbane, *Sacred Attunement: A Jewish Theology* (Chicago: University of Chicago Press, 2008), esp. 171 (and Homans, *Jung in Context*, xl). It is an indication of the successful marketing of Kabbalah that some of these books, though clearly intended for an audience without any access to Kabbalistic texts, are then translated into Hebrew! An example is Elie Wiesel's anthology of Hasidic tales, characteristically titled *Souls on Fire: Portraits and Legends of Hasidic Masters* (New York: Vintage Books, 1973).

17. See Marc Gafni, *Soul Prints: Your Path to Fulfillment*. For appropriations of Izbiche-Radzin teachings in Jewish Renewal circles in Israel, see Rachel Werczberger, "New Age of Judaism: Jewish Spiritual Renewal in Israel" (Ph.D. diss., Hebrew University of Jerusalem, 2011), 104–6 (forthcoming in book form through Peter Lang Publishing). For Schachter-Shalomi, see Shaul Magid, *American Post-Judaism: Identity and Renewal in a Postethnic So-*

ciety (Bloomington: Indiana University Press, 2013), 48–56, 64–73, 88–110, 178–84, 220–33, as well as Tomer Persico, ""Jewish Meditation": The Development of a Modern Form of Spiritual Practice in Contemporary Judaism" (Ph.D. diss., Tel Aviv University, 2013), 335–43, 391–423. For my call for a reassessment of Izbiche, see Garb, *Shamanic Trance*, 108, 110 (which joins certain voices in academic scholarship discussed in chapter 3). My thanks to Ido Harari for sharing with me his unpublished work on the New Age reception of Izbiche-Radzin.

18. See esp. Avivah Gottlieb Zornberg, *The Murmuring Deep: Reflections on the Biblical Unconscious* (New York: Schocken Books, 2009), as well as her exegetical works on the Pentateuch: idem, *Genesis: The Beginning of Desire* (Philadelphia: Jewish Publication Society, 1995); idem, *The Particulars of Rapture: Reflections on Exodus* (New York: Doubleday, 2001). See also the work of her student Ora Wiskind-Elper, *Wisdom of the Heart: The Teachings of Rabbi Ya'akov of Izbica-Radzyn*.

19. An interesting and at times radical work, responding to the New Age, is Odeya Zuriely, *Transitions* (Jerusalem: Rubin Mass, 2009) [Hebrew]. For psychology, including discussions of Freud, see esp. 55–82.

20. See Garb, *The Chosen*, 48–50, 55; 66–68. On the psychology of Ginsburgh, see the useful summary by Rafael Sagi, "The Mystery of Messianic Rectification in the Thought of R. Yitzchak Ginsburgh" (Ph.D. diss., Bar-Ilan University, Ramat Gan, 2010) [Hebrew], and the less textually meaningful (written as it was in media studies) Yehiel Harari, "Mysticism as a Messianic Rhetoric in the Works of Rabbi Yitzchak Ginsburgh" (Ph.D. diss., Tel Aviv University, 2005) [Hebrew], as well as Gedalyah Afterman, "Understanding the Theology of Israel's Extreme Religious Right: 'The Chosen People' and 'the Land of Israel' from Bible [*sic*] to the 'Expulsion from Gush Katif'" (Ph.D. diss., Melbourne University, 2007), 231–35. On psychological aspects of post-Schneerson Habad, see Michal Kravel-Tovi and Yoram Bilu, "The Work of the Present: Constructing Messianic Temporality in the Wake of Failed Prophecy among Chabad Hasidim," *American Ethnologist* 35/1 (2008): 64–80.

21. Schneerson's telling description of the role of the Jewish citizen as taking a good system and giving it a soul is quoted in Jan L. Feldman, *Lubavitchers as Citizens: A Paradox of Liberal Democracy* (Ithaca: Cornell University Press, 2003), 182. For the soul and heart in this rebbe's teachings, see Wolfson, *Open Secret*, 47–51, 141–44, 149–51, 154–58, as well as idem, "Revealing and Re/Veiling: Menahem Mendel Schneerson's Messianic Secret," *Kabbalah* 26 (2002): 63–73. For a study of the place of the soul in contemporary Haredi discourse, see Yoram Bilu and Yehuda C. Goodman, "'What Does the Soul Say?': Metaphysical Uses of Facilitated Communication in the Jewish Ultra-Orthodox Community," in *Perspectives on Israeli Anthropology*, ed. Esther Hertzog et al. (Detroit: Wayne State University Press, 2010), 529–53.

22. See, e.g., Yitzchak Ginsburgh, *Shekhina Beneyhem* (Jerusalem: Gal Einai, 1992), 93, 141–42.

23. For an explicit quote from R. Y. L. Ashlag, see Yitzchak Ginsburgh, *Yayin Mesameakh: The Mysteries of Wedding and Marriage*, vol. 1 (Jerusalem: Gal Einai, 2004) [Hebrew], 43.

24. See Huss, "The New Age of Kabbalah," 113, 115; Yitzchak Ginsburgh, *The Dynamic Corporation: Involvement, Quality and Flow: A Jewish Approach to Business Management Based on Kabbalah and Chassidut* (Jerusalem: Gal Einai, 1995). For his extreme positions, see esp. his unpaginated Kabbalistic introduction to the pseudo-Halakhic work by his students, Yitzhaq Shaper and Yosef Elitzur, *Torat ha-Melekh* (Yizhar: Od Yosef Chai Yeshiva, 2010), vol. 1, that, among other things, advocates indiscriminate attacks on enemy civilians in wartime (esp. 213–27). This being said, the picture is somewhat more complex. In his *Kabbalah and Meditation for the Nations* (Jerusalem: Gal Einai, 2007), Ginsburgh innovatively extends the Halakhic category of the Noahites, to embrace a legitimate form of Gentile spirituality affiliated with Judaism. However, one should recall that he denies such a status to the Palestinians (*Malkhut Israel*, vol. 1 [Rehovot: Gal Einai, 1999], 369–76).

25. Binyamin Efrati, *Torat ha-Nefesh be-Mishnat Ramhal* (Jerusalem: Feldheim, 2009); Avraham Ya'aqov Pritzky, *Adir bi-Melukha* (Jerusalem, 2009), esp. vol. 2, 59, 141–76; Garb, *Kabbalist in the Heart of the Storm*, 277–81.

26. Avraham Tzevi Kluger, *Nezer Yisra'el: Shi'urim, Sihot, u-Ma'amarim* (Beit Shemesh, 2007), 585; idem, *Qarva el Nafshi* (Beit Shemesh, 2012), esp. 343–48 (for a slightly more positive assessment by a member of Morgenstern's wider circle who passed away in 2003, see R. Avraham Yorovitz, *'Aravot Nahal* [Jerusalem, 2008], 197–98, 202); Nir Stern, "An Attempt to Describe the Teachings of R. Yeruham" (http://tshuvot.wordpress.com) (which also discusses phenomenology). On the Halakhic views of Nir'eh Likhora (Stern's alias), see Englander, "Images of the Male Body," 189–225. For Stern's influence, see the subversive website *Va-Yehi Or* (http://www.y-or .co.il).

27. See Garb, "Mystical and Spiritual Discourse," 26–28. It is worth citing the quote from Lichtenstein, quoted in Chaim Sabbato, *In Quest of Your Presence: Conversations with Rabbi Aharon Lichtenstein* (Tel Aviv: Yediot Ahronot, 2011) [Hebrew], 149: "I read things written by a Jew of my age. We had studied together at [R. Hutner's] Hayyim Berlin Yeshiva. He came to Israel and became a great Kabbalist. I read his words and my hair stood up! This is not the Judaism that I know." Based on the context, Lichtenstein is critiquing Weintraub's portrayal of an unbridgeable gap between Haredi scholars and other Jews. For the psychology of R. Joseph B. Soloveitchik, see Jonathan Garb, " 'The Joy of Torah' in the Thought of David Hartman: A Critical Examination of the Phenomenology of Halakhic Experience," in *Renewing Jewish Commitment: The Work and Thought of David Hartman*, edited by A. Sagi and Z. Zohar (Jerusalem: Shalom Hartman Institute; Tel

Aviv: Hakibbutz Hameuchad, 2001), 82–91, as well as Dov Schwartz, *Religion or Halakha: The Philosophy of Rabbi Joseph B. Soloveitchik* (Leiden: Brill, 2007), 222–45. For that of Teitelbaum, see Sorotzkin, *Orthodoxy and Modern Disciplination*, 378–420.

28. Israel Elijah Weintraub, *Be-Sod Yesharim: Ma'amarim 'al Seder ha-Parshiot u-Mo'adim* (Bnei Brak, 2008) 107–11 (and see also 146); Tzevi ha-Kohen Glick, *Bi-Hitoma shel Tequfa* (Jerusalem, 2011), 117; Israel Elijah Weintraub, *'Einei Yisra'el: Be-'Inyanei Mo'adim, Torah, va-'Avoda* (Bnei Brak, 2010), 344, 351 (and compare to the critique of Hasidism in 253–54). For the beginning of similar moves in the margins of the Kook circle following the 2005 disengagement, see Assaf Tamari, "Erev Rav," *Mafteach* 2 (2010): 43–74 [Hebrew]. There are obvious links between Weintraub's thought and that of the extreme Lithuanian critic of Zionism and Religious Zionism, R. Elhanan Wasserman, whom I shall not discuss here as the latter does not have a Kabbalistic layer.

29. As current Sephardic Kabablah, especially represented by R. Ya'aqov Moshe Hillel, is highly continuous with Shar'abi's teachings (see chapter 3) and I have little fieldwork to accompany textual research, I shall not address it here, beyond noting that at times Morgenstern appears to be critiquing the opinions of Hillel.

30. *Nishmatin Hadatin* are mostly extant in files dispatched via e-mail lists, although printed volumes of talks on Genesis and Exodus were published in limited editions in 2013 and 2015 respectively. For contemporary continuous Hasidism (including some figures discussed here), see Garb, "Mystical and Spiritual Discourse," 19–26; idem, "Towards the Study," 124–25; idem, "Contemporary Kabbalah," 27–30; the discussion of a psychological (and at times soul-related) treatise in Wolfson, *A Dream Interpreted*, 229–35; a poetic discussion of further texts in Aubrey Glazer, "Touching God: Vertigo, Exactitude, and Degrees of Devekut in the Contemporary Nondual Jewish Mysticism of R. Yitzhaq Maier Morgenstern," *Journal of Jewish Thought and Philosophy* 19 (2011): 147–92.

31. Yehiel Mikhel Hendler, *Barukh u-Mevurakh: Commentary on Intention of the Blessing in the Kabbalah of R. Shar'abi* (Jerusalem, 2011) [Hebrew], gate 1, 16–17.

32. Yitzhaq Me'ir Morgenstern, *Yam ha-Hokhma* (Jerusalem, 2011), 581–82, 585–96, 590, 596, and compare to the gendered discussion in idem, *Yam ha-Hokhma* (Jerusalem, 2007), 205–6.

33. Morgenstern, *Yam ha-Hokhma* (2011), 599, 602, 614, 618, 630–31, and cf. idem, *Yam ha-Hokhma* (2010), 206; Handler, *Barukh u-Mevurakh*, 189. Cf. Morgenstern, *Yam ha-Hokhma* (2009), 486.

34. Morgenstern, *Yam ha-Hokhma* (2011) 633–24, 638–41. For one sophisticated example of divinization in Bratzlav (responding to critiques from the Lithuanian world) see Gedalyahu Aharon Kening, *Hayyei Nefesh* (Jerusalem, 1968). Morgenstern's self-perception as an emanation of R. Nahman was

reflected in his recent move away from requiring pilgrimage on the New Year to the rebbe's gravesite in Ukraine towards occasionally celebrating R. Nahman's presence in his own Yeshiva in Jerusalem.

35. Morgenstern, *Yam ha-Hokhma* (2011), 647–49, 654; Garb, *Kabbalist in the Heart of the Storm,* 343–44.

36. Morgenstern, *Yam ha-Hokhma* (2011), 656, 661, and idem, *Yam ha-Hokhma* (2012), 269–70n21 (and see at greater length 281–87n26, and the numerous sources cited there, as well as the discussion devoted to adherence to the righteous in 622–60, which is clearly autobiographical).

37. Morgenstern, *Yam ha-Hokhma* (2012), 551–621.

38. Garb, "Mystical and Spiritual Discourse," 22–23; Meir, *Rehovot ha-Nahar,* 69–70, as well as 48–53, 65–73.

39. Tzevi Me'ir Zilberberg, *Le-Zekher 'Olam Yehiye Tzaddiq,* ed. Hanina H. Karfman (Jerusalem, 2009), 95–96, 99.

40. Yehuda Sheinfeld, *Sihot Mussar 'al Liqqutei Moharan* (Jerusalem, 2006), 56–57 (and see also 66 on the dependency of the imagination on the heart). One should mention that Sheinfeld openly inserts the more continuous of Ginsburgh's teachings into the Haredi discourse, as is especially apparent in this volume.

41. Yitzhaq Moshe Erlanger, *Quntres Akh be-Tzelem* (Jerusalem, 2011); idem, *Quntresei Hasidut: Mo'adim* (Jerusalem, 2007), 1, 311; idem, *Quntresei Hasidut: 'Inyanei Emunah* (Jerusalem, 2007), 202. For an exercise for imagining the world-soul, see idem, *Quntresei Hasidut: 'Inyanei Hasidut* (Jerusalem, 2007), 247. On psychology in contemporary Bratzlav, see esp. Zvi Mark, *Revelation and Rectification in the Revealed and Hidden Writings of R. Nahman of Breslav* (Jerusalem: Magnes Press, 2011) [Hebrew], 260–63, 268–74. On Shechter, see Garb, *The Chosen,* 58, as well as his *Ve-Nikhtav ba-Sefer* (Jerusalem, 1998), vol. 2, 287. For R. Moshe Weinberger, see his *Song of Teshuva: A Commentary on Rav Avraham Yitzchak HaKohen Kook's Oros HaTeshuvah* (Jerusalem, 2011), 22, as well as his discourse on the absence of the soul in contemporary Jewish life in http://klalperspectives.org/rabbi-moshe-weinberger (my thanks to Menachem Butler for calling this source to my attention).

42. For Milikovsky, see Garb, "Towards the Study," 124–25. As I wrote there, Morgenstern exhibits a more moderate form of Milikovsky's hypernomian approach to prayer. Apparently, due to lobbying by a prominent Haredi woman who heads a school for alternative medicine, neither the important Haredi rabbinical court (*badatz*) nor the late prominent "Lithuanian" Halakhist R. Shalom Elyashiv (grandson of the Kabbalist R. Shlomo Elyashiv) agreed to support the ban that Morgenstern and others campaigned for.

43. Schatz, *Ma'ayan Moshe,* 3, 24–25, 70–71, 78. See the more explicit discussion of modern science in idem, *Sparks of the Hidden Light: Seeing the Unified Nature of Kabbalah through Kabbalah* (Jerusalem: 'Ateret Tif'eret Institute,

1996), which aroused some interest in scientific circles. Goldstein's classes may be found at http://www.kesertorah.org/audio_shiurim.html.

44. Avraham Tzevi Kluger, *Divrei Hakhamim be-Nahat*, vol. 1 (Beit Shemesh, 2009), 331; idem, *Nezer Yisra'el: Makhon Shivtekha, Yasis 'Alayikh* (Beit Shemesh, 2010), 740. One should also add Morgenstern's closest student R. 'Aqiva Erlanger, a relative of R. Yitzhaq Moshe Erlanger and head of a Yeshiva in his own right, as well as R. Qaddish Waldman, a counselor who employs a range of techniques drawn from Western and Far Eastern psychology and has an academic background in Jewish studies.

45. On Itamar Schwartz, see Garb, "Mystical and Spiritual Discourse," 28–30; idem, "Contemporary Kabbalah," 29; Elliot Wolfson, "Building a Sanctuary of the Heart: The Kabbalistic-Pietistic Teachings of Itamar Schwartz," in *Kabbalah and Contemporary Spiritual Revival*, ed. Boaz Huss, 141–62 (Beer Sheva: Ben Gurion University of the Negev Press, 2011). Though this is but the tip of the iceberg, one can discern Morgenstern's criticism of his views of the Torah of the future in his appropriation to Schwartz's commentary on the beginning of Shar'abi's *Nahar Shalom* (Jerusalem, ca. 2007). For Schwartz's psychology, see his *Da' et 'Atzmekha: Le-Hakarat Kohot ha-Nefesh* (Israel, ca. 2008), 48–61, 70, 114, 201–3; idem, *Getting to Know Your Soul: Gateway to Understanding Your Personality* (Jerusalem: Bilvavi Books, 2010, published first in English!), 13. Internal Haredi critiques of the influence of Zionism have been partly discussed in the above-cited treatment of Erlanger. See also, e.g., Benzion Rabinovitch, *Le-Yeshu'atkha Qiviti ha-Shem* (Jerusalem, 2003), 230, and compare to my citation of R. Avraham Eliyahu Kaplan in chapter 3. Due to the identity politics discussed below these have been ignored in academic writing on the Haredim. For R. Qalonymus Qalman Shapira and his intellectual environment, see Garb, *Shamanic Trance*, 115–18, the sources cited there, and the recent study of Daniel Reiser, *Vision as a Mirror: Imagery Techniques in Twentieth Century Jewish Mysticism* (Los Angeles: Cherub Press, 2014) [Hebrew], which also addresses earlier studies. Reiser's archival work has contributed greatly to our understanding of twentieth-century Hasidic psychology, especially in his research on techniques of guided imagination. See esp. 194–98, 324–26, on the soul.

46. See Mordekhai Putsh (ed.), *Rahmana Liba Ba'i* (Jerusalem, 2006), a compilation of sayings on the role of the heart in the worship of the Creator, and the collective and anonymous *Ohel Shikhen ba-'Adam* (Jerusalem, 2009), on internal connection with God in the human heart.

47. See Garb, *The Chosen*; idem, *Shamanic Trance*, 5–6, 135–39; idem, "Towards the Study," 137–39. For Mussar on the Internet, see, e.g., http://www.mussarinstitute.org, as well as http://www.mussarleadership.org/index.html.

48. See Jonathan Garb, "The Challenges of Teaching Mysticism [review of W. Parsons, *Teaching Mysticism*]," *Religious Studies Review* 38:4 (2012): 207–12. On collaboration with Haredi scholarship, see Abrams, *Kabbalistic*

Manuscripts, 49–53, 522–23. Wolfson's stress on the continuous is especially apparent in his approach to contemporary and classical Habad. See Wolfson, *Open Secret*, esp. 22–24.

49. Compare to the astute comments of Abrams, *Kabbalistic Manuscripts*, 65–66, 150–52, 283, 287, 308, 374–76, 403, 409, 411, 430, 437, 467–68, 515–19, 537–38, 574, 584, 587–88. The findings of savvy studies of the predicament of academia such as Frank Donoghue, *The Last Professors: The Corporate University and the Fate of the Humanities* (New York: Fordham University Press, 2008), are already being overtaken by the march of "educational reform."

CHAPTER SIX

1. Harold J. Berman, *Faith and Order: The Reconciliation of Law and Religion* (Grand Rapids: William B. Eerdmans Publishing Company, 2000), 25; April DeConick, "Mysticism before Mysticism," in *Teaching Mysticism*, ed. W. B. Parsons (Oxford: Oxford University Press, 2011), 27–29.

2. On demography and modern Kabbalah, see my talk online at http://huji .academia.edu/JonathanGarb/Talks/32897/Kabbalah_Mussar_and_Jewish _Modernity.

3. For an example of a strongly conservative reaction to the growing openness to Jewish ideas in the "emergent" circles discussed later in this chapter, see Kevin L. DeYoung and Ted Kluck, *Why We're Not Emergent (By Two Guys Who Should Be)* (Chicago: Moody Publishers, 2008), 201–4.

4. See Gerhard Oestreich, *Neostoicism and the Early Modern State* (Cambridge: Cambridge University Press, 2008).

5. See Nancy Caciola, "Breath, Heart, Guts: The Body and Spirits in the Middle Ages," in *Communicating with the Spirits*, ed. G. Klaniczay et al. (Budapest: Central European University Press, 2005), 30–31.

6. For a learned yet accessible account of Sufi psychology, see Sara Sviri, *A Taste of Hidden Things: Images of the Sufi Path* (Inverness, CA: Golden Sufi Center, 1997) (esp. 1–22 on the centrality of the heart for Sufism). See also idem, "The Self and Its Transformation in Sufism," in *Self and Self-Transformation in the History of Religions*, ed. by D. Shulman and G. G. Stroumsa (Oxford: Oxford University Press, 2002), 195–215, esp. 195. On the heart in Sufism and Kabbalah in the context of a discussion of imagination, see Wolfson, *Through a Speculum*, 279–80. One should note a striking account of admiration of a Sufi sheikh, perhaps the eighteenth-century 'Abd al-Ghani al-Nablusi, who also visited Jerusalem, discussed in Zvi Zohar, "The Rabbi and the Sheikh," *Jewish Studies Quarterly* 17 (2010): 114–45.

7. See Kenneth Gergen, *The Saturated Self: Dilemmas of Identity in Contemporary Life* (New York: Basic Books, 1992), esp. 172–76, on the displacement of the Romantic soul by this saturated self. These processes have also been discussed in an interesting manner by Margolin, *The Inner Religion*, 431, 443–44. However, while Margolin is correct in critiquing reduction of contem-

porary spiritual trends to consumerism, he does not consider the impact of wider geopolitical processes of globalization, which have been analyzed at great length by scholars such as Immanuel Wallerstein.

8. On the soul from Islamic perspectives (especially Iranian), see Christian Kanzian and Muhammad Legenhausen (eds.), *Soul: A Comparative Approach* (Heusenstamm, Germany: Ontos Verlag, 2010). See the rich article there by Mahmoud Khatami, "Becoming Transcendent: Remarks on the Human Soul in the Philosophy of Illumination," 97–121, on ascent of the soul in Iranian (although pre-Safavid) Sufism. Though Idel, "Ascensions, Gender," very briefly (99) mentions Sufism, as we have already seen that the entire thrust of his argument is that Safedian Kabbalah responded to European developments. For a popular comparison of Sufi and Orthodox views of the heart, see James Cutsinger, *Paths to the Heart: Sufism and the Christian East* (Bloomington, IN: World Wisdom, 2003). For a discussion containing important comparisons between Kabbalah and the Babi-Bahai movement, see Moshe Sharon, "New Religions and Religious Movements: The Common Heritage" in *Studies in Modern Religions, Religious Movements and the Babi-Bahai Faiths,* ed. M. Sharon (Leiden: Brill, 2004), 3–37.

9. Weinstein, *Kabbalah and Jewish Modernity*, esp. 166, 253–55 (and compare to 408–21, as well as Sorotzkin, *Orthodoxy*, 270–72). For the soul in the counterreformation from a Foucauldian perspective, see Wietse de Boer, *The Conquest of the Soul: Confession, Discipline, and Public Order in Counter-Reformation Milan* (Leiden et al.: Brill, 2001). On Kabbalah in Protestant Europe, see, e.g., Allison Coudert, *The Impact of the Kabbalah in the Seventeenth Century: The Life and Thought of Francis Mercury van Helmont (1614–98)* (Leiden: Brill, 1999).

10. Gregory, *The Unintended Reformation*. For soul rescue and the reformation in a broad context, see Miller, *Hells and Holy Ghosts: A Theopoetics of Christian Belief*, 120. For Calvin, see, e.g., the texts on the visions of the soul once it is enlightened by faith and on faith sealed on the heart, quoted in Barbara Pitkin, *What Pure Eyes Could See: Calvin's Doctrine of Faith in its Exegetical Context* (Oxford: Oxford University Press, 1999), 3, 7; on the relationship of faith with the heart and soul, see Margolin, *The Inner Religion*, 342–45. For responses to the Reformation in sixteenth-century Kabbalah, see Idel, *Messianic Mystics*, 134. For the wider context, see Abraham David, "The Lutheran Reformation in Sixteenth-Century Jewish Historiography," *Jewish Studies Quarterly* 9 (2002): 124–39.

11. Victoria Nelson, *Gothicka: Vampire Heroes, Human Gods and the New Supernatural* (Cambridge: Harvard University Press, 2012), 48.

12. Christopher Rowland, *Radical Christianity: A Reading of Recovery* (New York: Orbis Books, 1988), 90–91, 97; compare to Hans Schneider, *German Radical Pietism*, trans. G. MacDonald (Plymouth: Scarecrow Press, 2007), 152–53. For earlier sources for personal internal religion in what later would become Protestant areas, see Oliver Davies, *God Within: The Mystical Tradition*

of Northern Europe (New York: Paulist Press, 1988), esp. 193–94 (and 47–59, 78–84, 131–45, 162, 180–83 for the heart and soul). I am not convinced at all by Davies' positing a mysticism focused on the personal relationship of the soul as bride to Christ versus a Northern European (and yet "purest and most timeless," 4) tradition focused on the return of the soul to God beyond the world. I thus prefer the organization of Northern European mysticism proposed by Amy Hollywood, *The Soul as Virgin Wife: Mechthild of Magdeburg, Marguerite Porete, and Meister Eckhart* (Notre Dame: University of Notre Dame Press, 1995).

13. Carter Lindberg, *The Pietist Theologians: An Introduction to Theology in the Seventeenth and Eighteenth Centuries* (Malden, MA: Blackwell Publishers, 2005), 13; Schneider, *German Radical Pietism*, esp. 131, 186. On Christian forms of Kabbalah in eighteenth-century Germany, see Elliot R. Wolfson, "Immanuel Frommann's Commentary on Luke and the Christianizing of Kabbalah: Some Sabbatean and Hasidic Affinities," in *Holy Dissent: Jewish and Christian Mystics in Eastern Europe*, ed. G. Dynner (Detroit: Wayne State University Press, 2011), 171–222.

14. Vassányi, *Anima Mundi*, 394, as well as 127–28, 143–46, 294–97, 304–5, 353–55 (and see chapter 2 for a critique of his view of the Kabbalistic tradition itself). On somewhat later German developments, see Corinna Treitel, *A Science for the Soul: Occultism and the Genesis of the German Modern* (Baltimore: Johns Hopkins University Press, 2004), esp. 35–37. The influence of modern (sixteenth-century) Kabbalah on Boehme was already noted by Scholem, *Major Trends in Jewish Mysticism*, 190, 237–38 (who also considers his impact on later Christian Kabbalah); idem, *Kabbalah*, 200. See also Shlomo Wolbe, *'Olam ha-Yedidut (with Or la-Shav)* (Jerusalem, 1994), 123–24 (who also discusses Hasidism and pietism); Elliot R. Wolfson, *Alef, Mem, Tau: Kabbalistic Musings on Time, Truth, and Death* (Berkeley: University of California Press, 2006), 34–38 (and see idem, *Language, Eros, Being*, 103); Shatil, "The Doctrine of Secrets of Emeq ha-Melech," 382 (and see 379). For a rich discussion of Eckhart and Kabbalah, see Elliot R. Wolfson, "Patriarchy and the Motherhood of God in Zoharic Kabbalah and Meister Eckhart," in *Envisioning Judaism: Studies in Honor of Peter Schäfer on the Occasion of His Seventieth Birthday*, ed. R. S. Boustan et al. (Tübingen: Mohr Siebeck, 2013), 1047–88. As Wolfson notes there (1063–64), Eckhart describes the source of his doctrines as the heart of God. One could conjecture that the receptivity of German romantics to Kabbalistic ideas was eased by the similarities between Eckhartian thought and Kabbalistic ideas. For the soul in Eckhart, see Amy Hollywood, *The Soul as Virgin Wife*, 143–79 (also discussing the influence of Marguerite Porete's *The Mirror of Simple Souls*, to which I shall return in chapter 7). One should also note Vassányi's important comments (*Anima Mundi*, 356) on the place of the world soul in the writing of Salomon Maimon in the eighteenth century. The latter had direct exposure to the Hasidic world, where such theories were widespread.

On the question of Boehme and radical pietism, see Schneider, *German Radical Pietism*, 6, 178–79.

15. See Jacob Boehme, *The Aurora*, trans. J. Sparrow (London: John M. Watkins, 1915), 485; Evelyn Underhill, *Mysticism* (Stilwell: Digireads, 2005), 45; Kathryn Wood Madden, *Dark Light of the Soul* (Great Barrington: Lindisfarne Books, 2008), 55, 64–66, 118, and the sources cited there (for the soul, see 119–26); Norman O. Brown, *Life against Death: The Psychoanalytical Meaning of History* (Middletown: Wesleyan University Press, 1959), esp. 33–34; idem, *Love's Body* (New York: Random House, 1966), esp. 214; Hamutal Bar-Yosef, *Mysticism in Modern Hebrew Poetry* (Tel Aviv: Miskal, 2008) [Hebrew]. Madden's title is of course an allusion to *The Dark Night of the Soul*, by the sixteenth-century Spanish mystic San Juan de la Cruz, one of the few modern Christian mystics to have been discussed in Israeli religious studies; see R. J. Zwi Werblowsky, "On the Mystical Rejection of Mystical Illuminations: A Note on St. John of the Cross," *Religious Studies* 1 (1965): 177–84. Following the rich suggestions by Weinstein, *Kabbalah and Jewish Modernity*, 517–19, 541–63, I hope to reflect elsewhere on the possible shared sources of the "Golden Age" of mysticism in Safed and Spain. For now see Garb, "Mystics' Critique," 307–10, and, on the role of the soul in Teresa of Avila's *The Interior Castle*, see Michel de Certeau, *The Mystic Fable: The Sixteenth and Seventeenth Centuries*, trans. Michael B. Smith (Chicago: University of Chicago Press, 1992), 188–200. The neglect of Boehme in Israel is surprising, as this was the topic of Martin Buber's doctoral thesis, "Beiträge zur Geschichte des Individuationsproblems" (on Jacob Böhme and Nikolaus Cusanus) (Ph.D. diss., University of Vienna, 1904).

16. Jacob Boehme, *Forty Questions of the Soul*, trans. J. Sparrow (London: John M. Watkins, 1911), 158 (image 104 in http://eebo.chadwyck.com). The theme of the soul's power is concentrated in the sixth and thirteenth questions. Although Cyril O'Regan, *Gnostic Apocalypse: Jacob's Boehme's Haunted Narrative* (Albany: State University of New York Press, 2002), is a strong reading (part of a wider thesis of a Gnostic return in modernity), it covers many of the interpretative and historical issues discussed here (see esp. 69–82 on Eckhart, offering a different narrative from that adopted here, 87–101; 157–58 on the Reformation; 112–13, 144–45, 193– 207 on Kabbalah: and 90–91, 161–75 on apocalyptic themes) as well as raising the issue of the modern impact of Gnosticism. However, the soul is rather absent in his discussion. On fire and Shamanic empowerment, see Garb, *Shamanic Trance*, 36–45, 82–88 (and 120 on the soul). Kahana, "An Esoteric Path to Modernity: Rabbi Jacob Emden's Alchemical Quest," concentrates on earlier discussions, most notably Gershom Scholem, *Alchemy and Kabbalah*, trans. K. Ottmann (Putnam, CT: Spring Publications, 2006).

17. On the question of esotericism in modernity, see Idel, *Kabbalah: New Perspectives*, 253–56; and cf. Garb, "Shamanism and the Hidden History," as well as the wider discussions of Elliot Wolfson, "Circumcision and the

Divine Name: A Study in the Transmission of Esoteric Doctrine," *Jewish Quarterly Review* 78 (1987): 77–112; idem, "Murmuring Secrets: Eroticism and Esotericism in Medieval Kabbalah," in *Hidden Intercourse: Eros and Sexuality in the History of Western Esotericism*, ed. J. Kripal and W. Hanegraff (Leiden: Brill, 2008), 65–109; idem, *Open Secret*, 171–79. The theme of modernity and messianism has been much discussed, and for now I shall but note the foundational study of Jacob L. Talmon, *Political Messianism: The Romantic Phase* (London: Secker & Waburg, 1960), esp. 506–7, representing the previous generation of Israeli scholarship. For a recent discussion of Boehme's sociopolitical views, see Michael L. Birkel and J. Bach, *Genius of the Transcendent: Mystical Writings of Jakob Boehme* (Boston: Shambhala Publications, 2011), 31–32, 61, 96, and the texts cited there.

18. The impact of Boehme on later Romanticism is a very large topic in and of itself. Here I should but note his influence on William Blake, whose debt to Kabbalah has also been the subject of several studies. See, e.g., Kevin Fischer, *Converse in the Spirit: William Blake, Jacob Boehme, and the Creative Spirit* (Teaneck: Fairleigh Dickinson University Press, 2004), esp. 32–34; Sheila A. Spector, *Wonders Divine: The Development of Blake's Kabbalistic Myth* (Lewisburg: Bucknell University Press, 2001) (the soul, and tellingly "the secret soul," being central in this innovative reading; see, e.g., 20, 84, 86–99, 107–10, 113–35, 141–64). Compare to Eric Jager, *The Book of the Heart* (Chicago: University of Chicago Press, 2000), 23–24, on the "secrets of the heart" in antiquity, and to my discussions of secrecy elsewhere in this chapter. On Romanticism and modern Kabbalah, see Boaz Huss, "Admiration and Disgust: The Ambivalent Re-Canonization of the *Zohar* in the Modern Period," in *Study and Knowledge in Jewish Thought*, ed. H. Kreisel (Beer Sheva: Ben Gurion University of the Negev Press, 2006), 210–19.

19. Porter, *Flesh*, 435, 448 (and compare to 374–75), 458, and see also chapter 3 for my comparative suggestion based on this study. For the Industrial Revolution and the study of modern Judaism, see Garb, "The Circle of Moshe Hayyim Luzzatto," 195–96.

20. Sorotzkin, *Orthodoxy*, 55–60, 131–32. Birnbaum and Katznelson, *Paths of Emancipation: Jews, States, and Citizenship*, though focused on later periods, remains a highly useful resource for the study of the role of the state in the construction of modern Judaism. For a refreshing view of the centrality of Catholic Spain for understanding modern culture, see Ivan Illich and Barry Sanders, *ABC: The Alphabetization of the Popular Mind* (San Fransisco: North Point, 1988), 65–70 (for Kabbalah, see, e.g., 119–21).

21. Raymond Jonas, *France and the Cult of the Sacred Heart: An Epic Tale for Modern Times* (Berkeley: University of California Press, 2000), esp. 17–18. On the soul and demonology in the early modern French mystical tradition, see Moshe Sluhovsky, *Believe Not Every Spirit: Possession, Mysticism, and Discernment in Early Modern Catholicism* (Chicago: University of Chicago Press, 2007), esp. 197–205.

22. For an important study that traces the roots of psychoanalysis in the care of souls in spiritual direction, see Benjamin Nelson, "Self-Images and Systems of Spiritual Direction in the History of European Civilization," in *The Quest for Self-Control: Classical Philosophies and Scientific Research*, ed. S. Z. Klausner (New York: Free Press; London: Collier-Macmillan, 1965), 49–103. Rivka Schatz-Uffenheimer, *Hasidism as Mysticism: Quietistic Elements in Eighteenth Century Hasidic Thought* (Princeton: Princeton University Press; Jerusalem: Magnes Press, 1993), represents a preliminary attempt to relate Hasidism to a modern Christian movement (Quietism). See also the analysis of mysticism and the inward turn during the sixteenth and seventeenth centuries in Certeau, *The Mystic Fable: The Sixteenth and Seventeenth Centuries*.

23. See Ted A. Campbell, *The Religion of the Heart: A Study of European Religious Life in the Seventeenth and Eighteenth Centuries* (Eugene: Wipf and Stock, 2000), 30–41, 47–53, 67 (and 150–51 on Hasidism). The role of the soul in this movement, as well as in Protestant parallels, has been discussed in an almost canonical volume by Jaroslav Pelikan, *Christian Doctrine and Modern Culture (Since 1700)* (Chicago: University of Chicago Press, 1989), see esp. 167, 171, 122. Pelikan adduced important texts on the "believing soul" as direct confirmation of religious truths and on the Holy Spirit as the natural feelings of the heart. For Idel's study, see for now his "R. Israel Ba'al Shem Tov 'In the State of Walachia,'" 85–88.

24. Alphonsus de Liguori, *Selected Writings*, ed. F. Jones (New York: Paulist Press, 1999), 222–23, 275, 284 (for the heart and soul connection that is very pronounced in his writing, see, e.g., 60); Garb, *Kabbalist in the Heart of the Storm*, 156, 194, 216. On theories of the soul in the period and locale of the Luzzatto circle, see Vincenzo Ferrone, *The Intellectual Roots of the Italian Enlightenment: Newtonian Science, Religion, and Politics in the Early Eighteenth Century* (Amherst: Prometheus Books, 1995), 115 (and see 100 for earlier debates on theories of the world soul influenced by Christian Kabbalah). The connection between Harvey's theories and the cult of the sacred heart has been noted in a general manner by Porter, *Flesh in the Age of Reason*, xiii–xiv.

25. William B. Parsons, "Psychoanalytic Spirituality," in *Spirituality and Religion: Psychoanalytic Perspectives, Mental Health Perspectives*, ed. J. Winer and J. Anderson (New York: Catskill, 2007), 83–97. For a strong opposition between soul and spirit and the upward tendency of the latter, see Hillman, "Peaks and Vales" (for a less dichotomous presentation, see idem, *Anima*, 177–82). On shamanism and the soul and for critiques of the universalization and popularization of the term, see Garb, *Shamanic Trance*, 24–25, 27–35. On shamanic themes such as soul rescue and soul possession and psychoanalysis see, e.g., C. Michael Smith, *Jung and Shamanism in Dialogue: Retrieving the Soul, Retrieving the Sacred* (Bloomington, IN: Trafford Publishing, 2007); Donald F. Sandner and Stephen H. Wong (eds.), *The Sacred Heritage: The Influence of Shamanism in Analytical Psychology* (New York: Routledge, 1997).

26. For worldly religion, see Kirschner, *The Religious and Romantic Origins*, 113, 133, 165; Taylor, *Sources of the Self*, 14. One must note the influence of Eckhart on this "mysticism of everyday life" (see Hollywood, *The Soul as Virgin Wife*, 10). For the Jewish context (only) see Tsippi Kauffman, *In All Your Ways Know Him: The Concept of God and Avodah be-Gashmiyut in the Early Stages of Hasidism* (Ramat Gan: Bar-Ilan University Press, 2009) [Hebrew].

27. See Harold Bloom, *The American Religion: The Emergence of the Post-Christian Nation* (New York: Simon & Schuster, 1992), 36–41, where Bloom also distances his writing from history of religion.

28. For the soul in early modern America, see Rivett, *The Science of the Soul in Colonial New England*. On the Shakers and Kabbalah, see Garb, *Shamanic Trance*, 15, 61, 156n54, where I cited additional studies on early modern religion relevant for the present discussion (and see also Fischer, *Converse in the Spirit*, 37–40 on Boehme's influence on the European sources of such groups and their views of the soul), as well as Carole D. Spencer, *Holiness—The Soul of Quakerism: A Historical Analysis of the Theology of Holiness in the Quaker Tradition* (Milton Keynes: Paternoster, 2007), 265–66, for a fruitful suggestion as to the influence of the sacred heart movement on the Quakers. On American Buddhism, see Jonathan Garb, "Returning the Chairs to Their Place: Buddhist Mussar Literature in Face of the Takeover of Mysticism by Psychology," in *From India Till Here: Israeli Thinkers Write about their Conception of Judaism and India*, ed. E. Nir, 127–42 (Jerusalem: Reuven Mass, 2006) [Hebrew], as well as chapter 1. For a fascinating textual and auditory collection of Tibetan materials on transmission from heart to heart, see Anne Klein, *The Heart Essence of the Vast Expanse: A Story of Transmission* (Ithaca, NY: Snow Lion Publications, 2009) esp. 45.

29. Tanya M. Luhrmann, *When God Talks Back: Understanding the American Evangelical Relationship with God* (New York: Alfred A. Knopf, 2012), 107; Wayne Jacobsen and Dave Coleman, *So You Don't Want to Go to Church Anymore: An Unexpected Journey* (Los Angeles: Windblown Media, 2006). See John Eldredge, *Waking the Dead: The Glory of a Heart Fully Alive* (Nashville: Thomas Nelson, 2003), esp. 218 (one should note that Eldredge also has a book on the female soul). For a critique of emergents' views of the soul, see R. Scott Smith, "Are Emergents Rejecting the Soul's Existence?" *Knowing & Doing* (Winter 2009): 1–6.

30. See Richard Rohr, *The Enneagram: A Christian Perspective* (New York: Crossroad Publishing. 2006). One can also detect influences of A. H. Almaas' "diamond heart" approach on Rohr's writing. For contemplative prayer, see, e.g., Thomas Keating, *Open Mind, Open Heart: The Contemplative Dimension of the Gospel* (New York: Continuum, 2012), esp. 11, 15–16, 169.

31. See Henri J. M. Nouwen, Michael J. Christensen, and Rebecca Laird, *Spiritual Formation: Following the Movements of the Spirit* (New York: Harper One, 2010); Wil Hernandez, *Henri Nouwen: A Spirituality of Imperfection* (New York: Paulist Press, 2006), who correctly places Nouwen's work within the

context of the current rediscovery of the soul (17–25). Though I have stated my reservations regarding psychobiography, I found Kenneth Bragan's Winnicotian *The Making of a Saint: A Psychological Study of Thomas Merton* (Durham: Strategic Book Group, 2011) a useful discussion of Merton's self-experience of soul. For a Jungian analysis focusing on Merton's relationship with his *anima*, see Robert Waldron, *The Wounded Heart of Thomas Merton* (New York: Paulist Press, 2011). For my view of the importance of Hasidic hagiography, see Garb, *Shamanic Trance in Modern Kabbalah*, 77–78.

32. Eric L. Johnson, *Foundations of Soul Care: A Christian Psychology Proposal* (Downers Grove, IL: IVP Academic, 2007), 17, 69–73, 190 (this work includes a very comprehensive review of literature on Christianity and psychology).

33. John S. Dunne, *The Homing Spirit: A Pilgrimage of the Mind, of the Heart, of the Soul* (New York: Crossroad Publishing Co,, 1987).

34. Idem, *The House of Wisdom: A Pilgrimage of the Heart* (Horktown Heights, NY: Meyer Stone Books, 1988), e.g. 6–8; idem, *A Journey with God in Time: A Spiritual Quest*, 77. For a fine discussion of the heart and soul and pilgrimage to Palestine, see Brouria Bitton-Ashkelony, *Encountering the Sacred: The Debate on Christian Pilgrimage in Late Antiquity* (Berkeley: University of California Press, 2005), 109–22, 161, 167, 177–78.

35. Wolfgang Giegerich, *What Is Soul?* (New Orleans: Spring Journal Books, 2012), 204, 208–10 (and see also, especially, 174–82, 286–92).

36. Rose, *Governing the Soul*, 214 (and see chapter 1); Jeremy R. Carrette and Richard King, *Selling Spirituality: The Silent Takeover of Religion* (New York: Routledge, 2005), 124 (and see my discussion in Garb, *The Chosen*, 106–15).

37. Leigh E. Schmidt, *Restless Souls: The Making of American Spirituality* (San Francisco: HarperCollins, 2005), 43 (for the soul, see 33, 48, 52, 60, 64, 85–87, 90, 110, 112–13, 131–32, 172; for "modern souls," see 45, and for the "liberal soul," see 246; for the soul in the thought of the Reform Jewish thinker Felix Adler, see 144); Courtney Bender, *The New Metaphysicals: Spirituality and the American Religious Imagination* (Chicago: University of Chicago Press, 2010). For the soul, see 39, 123, 132–52, 163–70.

38. See Schmidt, *Restless Souls*, esp. 82–83 (on Rumi). Patrick Laude, *Pathways to an Inner Islam: Massignon, Corbin, Guénon, and Schuon* (Albany: State University of New York Press, 2010), esp. 43, 46, 66, 72, 142, on the soul. Margolin's treatment of Sufism (*The Inner Religion*, 73–75, 90–91, 194–95), like his comments on German mysticism (73, 194, 233), focuses on the medieval period. For Corbin and Heschel, see Paul Fenton, "Abraham Heschel and Henry Corbin," *Daat* 68–9 (2010): 225–35. For popular Sufi psychology, see, e.g., the Ibn 'Arabi–focused Robert Frager, *Heart, Self and Soul: The Sufi Psychology of Growth, Balance, and Harmony* (Wheaton, IL: Quest Books, 1999). On the contemporary psychologization of Rumi, see Franklin D. Lewis, *Rumi: Past and Present, East and West: The Life, Teaching and Poetry of Jalâl al-Din Rumi* (Oxford: OneWorld Publications, 2001), 511–13.

39. See Irina Tweedie, "Spiritual Sufi Training Is a Process of Individuation Leading into the Infinite," VIII International Conference of the International Transpersonal Association, paper presented September 1, 1983, accessed September 1, 2014, http://www.goldensufi.org/a_sufi_training.html. Sara Sviri, "Daughter of Fire by Irina Tweedie: Documentation and Experiences of a Modern Naqshbandi Sufi," in *Women as Teachers and Disciples in Traditional and New Religions*, ed. E. Puttick and P. B. Clarke (Lewiston: Edwin Mellen Press, 1993), 84.

40. Llewellyn Vaughan-Lee, *Catching the Thread: Sufism, Dreamwork and Jungian Psychology* (Inverness, CA: Golden Sufi Center, 2003), xiv, ix, 43, 51, 68–69. See also idem, *Sufism: The Transformation of the Heart* (Point Reyes, CA: Golden Sufi Center, 1995), as well as J. Marvin Spiegelman, Pir Vilayat Inayat Khan, and Tasnim Fernandez (eds.), *Sufism, Islam and Jungian Psychology* (Las Vegas: New Falcon Publications, 1991); Adams, *For Love of the Imagination*, 84–95.

41. Muhammad al-Jamal Rifa'i, *Music of the Soul: Sufi Teachings* (Petaluma: Sidi Muhammad Press, 1997), 28, 85, 264 (for the litany), http://www.sufiheart.com/aboutus/musicofrahmatullah.htm; Garb, *The Chosen*, 98. For the theme of the transformations of the heart and soul in classical Sufism, see, e.g., Michael Chodkiewicz (ed.), *The Meccan Revelations*, vol. 1 (New York: Pir Press, 2002), 328n62, 65. The Wilaya discourse almost certainly influenced Safedian Kabbalists, as is apparent in R. El'azar Azikri's poem "Yedid Nefesh" (see chapter 2).

42. James Winston Morris, *The Reflective Heart: Discovering Spiritual intelligence in Ibn 'Arabi's Meccan Illuminations* (Louisville: Fons Vitae, 2005), 1, 130, 60, respectively. For a strongly universalistic interpretation of Ibn 'Arabi 's doctrine of purification of the heart, see 85–88. Morris notes that Ibn 'Arabi's "allusions to the purification of the heart frequently occur in connection to more concrete, practical aspects of Islamic worship" (51), yet like writers on Kabbalah discussed in chapter 7, he does not overly dwell on the implications of this observation (see however 76–79). For an interesting comparison with the *Zohar*'s hermeneutics, see 328n4.

43. Brian Daizen Victoria, *Zen At War* (Lanham, Maryland: Rowman and Littlefield, 2006, 2nd ed.); idem, *Zen War Stories* (London: RoutledgeCurzon, 2003). The Kook circle is the main instance of twentieth-century Jewish national mysticism, but not the only one (see Garb, *The Chosen*, 44–51; Baruch Falach, "The 'Sulam' Journal: Between Poetry and Politics," Ph.D diss., Bar Ilan University, 2010, [Hebrew]).

44. Robert H. Sharf, "The Zen of Japanese Nationalism," *History of Religions* 33/1 (1993): 2; see also idem, "Whose Zen: Zen Nationalism Revisited," in *Rude Awakenings: Zen, the Kyoto School, and the Question of Nationalism* (Nanzan Studies in Religion and Culture), ed. by J. W. Heisig and J. Maraldo (Honolulu: University of Hawai'i Press, 1995), 41–44.

45. Sharf, "The Zen of Japanese Nationalism," 6; Kook, *Igrot*, vol. 2, 279 (letter 669).

46. Suzuki's *Outlines of Mahayana Buddhism* is quoted in Sharf, "The Zen of Japanese Nationalism," 19. His *Japanese Spirituality* is analyzed in 26–28, and see also idem, "Whose Zen?," 48. Sōen's *Sermons of a Buddhist Abbot* is quoted on 9 (see also 12, 24).

47. Sharf, "The Zen of Japanese Nationalism," 41.

48. Sharf, "Whose Zen?," 47. See idem, "The Zen of Japanese Nationalism," 39, on the attraction of Westernized Zen, denuded of its national context, for the Catholic contemplative movement discussed in this chapter, and also on "therapeutized" Zen.

49. Sharf, "Whose Zen?," 44–46; and idem, "The Zen of Japanese Nationalism," 20–23; idem, "Buddhist Modernism and the Rhetoric of Meditative Experience," *Numen* 42 (1995): 228–83.

50. See Garb, *The Chosen*, 100–101, 106–15, on the social psychology of New Age globalization and commodification.

51. See James Hillman and Michael Ventura, *We've Had a Hundred Years of Psychotherapy—And the World's Getting Worse* (San Francisco: Harper One, 1993) (as well as Kirschner, *Religious and Romantic Origins*, 177).

52. For Freud, see the balanced comments of Kripal, *The Serpent's Gift*, 165–68. For Herbert Marcuse, see idem, *Eros and Civilization: Philosophical Inquiry Into Freud* (Boston: Beacon Press, 1955), 159–71. The above-mentioned writings of Norman O. Brown are obviously relevant to this discussion, as is José Brunner, *Freud and the Politics of Psychoanalysis* (New Brunswick: Transaction, 2001). See also Bettelheim, *Freud and Man's Soul*, 40, 107, for an important opposition between Freud's concern for the soul and the concern for adjustment in American psychoanalysis.

53. Bernard Brandchaft, Shelley Doctors, and Dorienne Sorter, *Toward an Emancipatory Psychoanalysis: Brandchaft's Intersubjective Vision* (New York: Routledge, 2010), 10

54. Michael Vannoy Adams, *For Love of the Imagination: Interdisicplinary Applications of Jungian Psychoanalysis* (London: Routledge, 2014). For applications, see xi–xii. For his complex attitude to resacralization, see 74.

55. Andrew Samuels, *Politics on the Couch: Citizenship and the Internal Life* (New York: Other Press, 2001), 30 (and see also 32 on his clinical work with mystically oriented right-wing Israelis); idem, *The Political Psyche* (London: Routledge, 1993), esp. 12 (and see 204–5 for interesting comments on Maimonides). For his courageous critique of the men's movement and its "male soul," see 181–95 (though I do not agree with every single point there). On mysticism, politics, and social psychology, see also Philip Wexler, "Society and Mysticism," in *After Spirituality*, ed. P. Wexler and J. Garb, 107–25 (New York: Peter Lang Publishing, 2012). One theoretician who is intensely resistant to compliance is William Pinar, whose *What Is Curriculum Theory*,

updated 2nd ed. (New York: Routledge, 2012), has inspired my thoughts on recovering the progressive potential of historical study through "reactivating the past" in the "complex conversations" of learning—"inspired by those who have gone before us, committed to those who are yet to come" (212, 218).

CHAPTER SEVEN

1. See Daniel Abrams, "'Text' in a Zoharic Parable: A Chapter in the History of Kabbalistic Textuality," *Kabbalah* 25 (2011): 7 (in my quote, I skipped Abrams' characterization of Kabbalah as "a late form of Rabbinic culture," which also guides his focus on a medieval text in this important article, as obviously I have a different view of these matters); Garb, *The Chosen*, 75–99; idem, *Shamanic Trance*, 119–41; de Vidas, *Reshit Hokhma*, vol. 1, 5–6, 12–13, 22. For an early modern view on the perfection of the soul in action, see Tirosh-Samuelson, "Jewish Philosophy on the Eve of Modernity," 499–573.

2. A major inspiration for this chapter is Moshe Halbertal, *People of the Book: Canon, Meaning, and Authority* (Cambridge, MA: Harvard University Press, 1997), and see esp. 119–24 on the modern period. For a critique of the place of law and the normative in Jewish studies and a sample of an integrative approach, see Garb, "Mussar, Curriculum and Exegesis."

3. Frederick E. Greenspahn, *Jewish Mysticism and Kabbalah: New Insights and Scholarship* (New York: New York University Press, 2011); Wolfson, *Abraham Abulafia*; Hugh B. Urban, *The Power of Tantra: Religion, Sexuality and the Politics of South Asian Studies* (Berkeley: University of California Press, 2003). On the dialectic of the inner and outer forms of religion as opposed to their binary opposition, see Patrick Laude, *Pathways to an Inner Islam*, 4.

4. For Luzzatto and his times, see the critical discussion in Garb, *Kabbalist in the Heart of the Storm*, 94–95, 167–70. See, however, my discussions of antinomianism, whose occasional presence in modern Kabbalah is undeniable, in chapters 3 and 4 here. See also Leuchter (ed.), *Nefesh ha-Hayyim*, gate 1, chapters 21–22, 165–75, for a critique of Hasidic views that at least in his interpretation subordinate the commandments to mystical perceptions of the requirements of the soul root (and see the editor's comment, 175, on the inaccessibility of the soul root according to this treatise). On the significance of *nigunim*, see Garb, *Shamanic Trance*, 132–33.

5. Margolin, *Inner Religion*, 323–27.

6. See *Zohar* III, fol. 152a; Wolfson, *Luminal Darkness*, 72–74 (and see also 67); idem, *Through a Speculum*, 379; Idel, *Absorbing Perfections*, 152–53; Pinchas Giller, *Reading the Zohar: The Sacred Text of the Kabbalah* (Oxford: Oxford University Press, 2001), 39, 41–42, 46–48, 52–53, 55–56, 61, 63–68; Boaz Huss, *Like the Radiance of the Sky: Chapters in the Reception History of the Zohar and the Construction of its Symbolic Value* (Jerusalem: Bialik Press and

Yad Ben-Zvi, 2008), [Hebrew], 252–53; 264. On the Torah as subsidiary to the soul, see Reuven Margolies (ed.), *Zohar Chadash (Tikunim me-Zohar Chadash)* (Jerusalem, 1994), 242.

7. Hayyim Vital, *Sha'ar Ma'amarei Raza"l* (Jerusalem, 1978), fol. 8b and see a different angle in Wolfson, *Luminal Darkness*, 95–96. On *penimiyut* in Safed, see Margolin, *Inner Religion*, 45–48, 317.

8. Shar'abi, *Nahar Shalom*, fol. 10b–11a, and compare to fol. 24b.

9. Ya'aqov Abuhatzeira, *Abir Ya'aqov* (Nahariya, Israel, 2001), vol. 4, 88–90; vol. 1, 156–57, 277; vol. 5, 335–77 respectively. The most sophisticated study on this writer is that of Avishai Bar-Asher, "'The White Appearance'— Mahsof ha-Lavan': Interpretation and Performance Commentary and Activity in the Kabbalah of Rabbi Ya'akov AbiHasira" (M.A. thesis, Hebrew University of Jerusalem, 2010) [Hebrew], who describes the rather disappointing current state of research.

10. Patton, *Religion of the Gods*, 171 (and see 173 on ritual as intensely reflexive); Hollywood, *The Soul as Virgin Wife: Mechthild of Magdeburg, Marguerite Porete, and Meister Eckhart*, 89–97, 113–19. For the triangular saying, see Tishby, *Messianic Mysticism*, 454–85 as well as Idel, *Absorbing Perfections*, 20.

11. Alter, *Sefat Emet*, vol. 2, 178 (this being one of many important statements in this work on the interrelationship of the Torah with the heart and soul); Zadoq ha-Kohen, *Resisei Laila*, 37; idem, *Liqqutei Ma'amarim*, vol. 1, 15 (and see also 35), as well as many more texts discussed in the exemplary study of Amira Liwer, "Oral Torah in the Writings of R. Zadok ha-Kohen of Lublin" (Ph.D. diss., Hebrew University of Jerualem, 2006), esp. 12, 42, 45–46, 74–77, 103–8, 193–96, 239–42, 290–92 (on written Torah and soul-making, see 363). On Mishna study, see Lawrence Fine, "Recitation of Mishnah as a Vehicle for Mystical Inspiration: A Contemplative Technique Taught by Hayyim Vital," *Revue des études juives* 141 (1982): 183–99 (on Torah study including Mishna study as soul-making, see the above-cited text from Vital's *Sha'ar ha-Mitzvot*). The mystical view of Mishna study may have contributed to a certain revival of study of this corpus in the early modern period in both Jewish and Christian circles.

12. Baumgarten, "Kabbalah within the Circle of the Vilna Gaon's Disciples," 70–71, 77, 99, 109, and esp. 148 (and see also 36–37, 113, 199, 213–14, 274–75 and the strikingly individualistic discussions of the soul in Torah study by Haver cited in 213, 275–76); Y. Safrin, *Heikhal ha-Brakha*, vol. 2, fol. 189a–b (and see also the *Otzar ha-Hayyim* commentary in vol. 5, fol. 187a–b). See also Liwer, "Oral Torah in the Writings of R. Zadok ha-Kohen of Lublin," 205, on the reception of R. Zadoq ha-Kohen's thought in Lithuanian Mussar.

13. Cf. my less nuanced comments in Garb, *Shamanic Trance*, 129–30, where I also adduced soul-related texts, as well as Idel, *Absorbing Perfections*, 473–81.

14. Garb, *Shamanic Trance*, 40–42.

15. See Shilo, *Kabbalah in the Works of Agnon*, 73, 262–66, 251–56. On Luzzatto

and Hebrew literature, see the sources and studies discussed in Garb, *Kabbalist in the Heart of the Storm*, esp. 26–27, 261–70. See also Harold Bloom, *Kabbalah and Criticism* (New York: Continuum, 1983), and my discussion of Bloom's approach in chapter 6.

16. See respectively Nahman of Bratzlav, *Liqqutei Moharan*, vol. 1, siman 20, pars. 1–4, siman 60, par. 6 (as well as vol. 1, siman 38, par. 5, siman 156, as well as siman 59, pars.1–2 on spirit, heart, and fire); Idel, *Kabbalah: New Perspectives*, 242–43 (and cf. idem, *Absorbing Perfections*, 191–97); Garb, *Shamanic Trance*, 43–44 (adducing further scholarly interpretations and Hasidic parallels); Arnold J. Band (trans.), *Nahman of Bratslav: The Tales* (New York: Paulist Press, 1978), 268–69; Dunne, *The Homing Spirit: A Pilgrimage of the Mind, of the Heart, of the Soul*, 45 (and cf. Margolin, *Inner Religion*, 273–74, 357–61). Compare to Dunne's analysis of William Morris' tale *The Well at the World's End* as describing the recovery of the modern soul in idem, *The Reasons of the Heart: A Journey into Solitude and Back Again into the Human Circle* (New York: Macmillan, 1978), 109–11. See also Marianne Schleicher, *Intertextuality in the Tales of Rabbi Nahman of Bratslav: A Close Reading of Sippurey Ma'asiyot* (Leiden: Brill, 2007), 60–76; Ora Wiskind-Elper, *Tradition and Fantasy in the Tales of Reb Nahman of Bratslav* (Albany: State University of New York Press, 1998), 209–15.

17. Nahman of Bratzlav, *Liqqutei Moharan*, vol. 1, siman 10, par. 7, siman 13, par. 2 (and pars. 1, 5). My interpretation is also based on siman 14, pars. 12–13. On the heart as the source of Law, see Valle, *Sefer Liqqutim*, vol. 1, 222. Yehuda Liebes, "The Novelty of Rabbi Nahman of Bretslav," *Daat* 45 (2000): 91–104 [Hebrew], reads R. Nahman's teachings and spiritual biography as a complex response to the Haskala.

18. Vital, *Sha'ar ha-Mitzvot* (Jerusalem, 1872, reprint) 33a–34a; Yo'el Sirkis, *Beit Hadash* on *Tur Orah Hayyim* (Vilna, 1900) [Hebrew], siman 47.

19. See, however, the important comment on the rooting of the hypernomian in a halakhic principle in Wolfson, *Open Secret*, 238, which obviously focuses on the last rebbe, rather than on Rashaz.

20. Loewental, *Communicating the Infinite*, 87, 159.

21. Shneur Zalman of Lyady, *Tanya: Liqqutei Amarim*, part 1, chapter 5, 9a–10a, and cf. ibid., chapter 46, 65a–66a. On this text, see the pioneering comments of Idel, *Kabbalah: New Perspectives*, 246 (as well as his later comments in *Enchanted Chains*, 157–59).

22. See Leuchter (ed.), *Nefesh ha-Hayyim*, gate 4, chapter 2, 559.

23. The triune structure of deed, speech, and thought in the soul is also important in *Nefesh ha-Hayyim*, though an attempt to see this as the very structure of the book is rather forced. One such attempt is that of Esther Eisenman, "The Structure and Content of R. Hayyim Volozhin's *Nefesh ha-Hayyim*," in *The Vilna Gaon and His Disciples*, ed. M. Hallamish, J. Rivlin, and R. Shuchat (Ramat Gan: Bar-Ilan University Press, 2003) [Hebrew], 185–94, esp. 187–94, for the heart and soul.

24. Shneur Zalman of Lyady, *Tanya*, part 1, chapter 23, 29a. See also Wolfson, *Open Secret*, 58–63.
25. Cf. Leuchter (ed.), *Nefesh ha-Hayyim*, gate 4, chapters 4–10, 566–96. See, however, Shneur Zalman of Lyady, *Tanya*, part 1, chapter 41, 56a–57a, which slightly weakens the distinction drawn here.
26. Shneur Zalman of Lyady, *Liqqutei Torah* (New York: Kehot Publication Society, 1984), part 5, fol. 16b.
27. See *Seder Eliahu Rabba (Tana de-Bey Eliyahu)*, ed. M. Friedmann (Jerusalem, 1969), 71.
28. See Wolfson, *Open Secret*, 64–65, 233–34. Heraclitus is quoted in Hillman, *Re-Visioning Psychology*, xvii.
29. Garb, *Shamanic Trance*, 145–47, as well as Maya Balakirsky Katz, "An Occupational Neurosis: A Psychoanalytic Case History of a Rabbi," *AJS Review* 34/1 (2010): 28, on Rashab's experience and theory of the head-heart and soul-body relationship from this historical perspective.
30. Shalom Dov Baer Schneerson, *Be-Sha'a she-Heqdimu* (New York: Kehot Publication Society, 2011), vol. 1, 356–57 (see also the important discussion at vol. 2, 902–3, on God knowing the Torah and the souls through his own self-knowledge); Roland Barthes, *The Pleasure of the Text*, trans. R. Miller (New York: Hill and Wang, 1975).
31. Shalom Dov Baer Schneerson, *Be-Sha'a she-Heqdimu*, vol. 1, 249–51, 253.
32. Ibid., vol. 1, 364. See also vol. 2, 912.
33. On the paradoxical advantage of the revealed (*nigle*) part of the Torah, see ibid., vol. 2, 745.
34. Ibid., vol. 1, 393–94.
35. Ibid., vol. 3, 1252. Elsewhere (vol. 3, 1404), Rashab discusses the conflict between the *Tana de-Bey Eliyahu* text on the superiority of Israel to the Torah and Zoharic formulations, where the Torah appears to be the superior element in the three-way link with the soul and God. Comparison to his 1906 text (Shalom Dov Baer Schneerson, *Yom Tov shel Rosh ha-Shana* [New York: Kehot Publications, 1984], 389, 507) discloses the gradual development of Rashab's thought in the direction of the superiority of the soul.
36. Shalom Dov Baer Schneerson, *Be-Sha'a she-Heqdimu*, vol. 3, 1403.
37. Ibid., 1407–8; vol. 2, 900.
38. See Leuchter (ed.), *Nefesh ha-Hayyim*, gate 4, chapter 12, 606–12 (and see 611 for the editor's important comment, lending itself to psychoanalytic interpretation, on *hiddush* as birth). An interesting statement on one's connection to the Torah rendering the soul a bucket drawing innovations directly from the *Sefirot* is found in the work of Yitzhaq Moshe Erlanger, *Shiv'a 'Enayim: Peqah 'Eneikha ve-Re'eh* (Jerusalem, 1990), 93. For concepts of Torah study in the nineteenth and early twentieth centuries, see the survey in Chana Kehat, "Changes in the Concept of Torah Study in the Modern Age" (Ph.D. diss, Hebrew University of Jerusalem, 2005) [Hebrew] (see 116, 168–70, 176–205, 209–11, 217–48, 256–61, 323–24, for numerous

texts on the soul that are discussed without any reference to the field of psychology, even when resorting to terms such as "individuation"). For an illuminating discussion of the relationship of ritual and innovation in a very different form of psychology (also critiquing the premodern/modern distinction through the Chinese case), see Michael Puett, "Innovation as Ritualization: The Fractured Cosmology of Early China," *Cardozo Law Review* 28/1 (2006): 23–36.

39. Elyashiv, *Leshem Shvo ve-Ahlama: Sefer ha-Kelalim*, fol. 61a; Shime'on Shkop, *Sha'arei Yosher* (Jerusalem, 1959), vol. 1, nonpaginated introduction, where one can possibly discern a resonance with the thought of Ashlag. Nonetheless, one can also find the notion of personal rectification based on the root of the soul that is a world of its own, devoid of any reference to Torah study, in other branches of this school; see, e.g., Yitzhaq Haver, *Beit 'Olamim* (Warsaw, 1889) (reprint), fol. 156b.

40. Here I shall just select, out of very many texts, discussions of reading the Scroll of Esther on Purim as effecting the shining of the soul of Mordechai (Levi Yitzhaq of Berditchev, *Qedushat Levi* [Jerusalem, n.a.], vol. 2, 448), diagnosing the movement of the soul in the body through the Havdala ceremony (Hayyim Vital, *Pri 'Etz Hayyim* [Jerusalem, n.d., reprint of Dubrovna, 1804], fol. 105a), the *miqve* as transition from the soulless state of impurity, thus a form of soul-making (see the text by R. Isaiah Horowitz adduced in Hallamish, *Kabbalah: In Liturgy, Halakhah and Customs*, 112) and compare to Garb, *Shamanic Trance*, 125–28. The theme of soul and prayer, though addressed throughout the book, deserves a comparative study. Here one should but mention the extensive Hasidic discussions of the fact that the morning prayers open with repeated mentions of the soul.

41. Elliot Ginsburg, *The Sabbath in the Classical Kabbalah* (Oxford,: Littman Library of Jewish Civilization, 2008), esp. 121–36 (and Scholem, *On the Kabbalah and Its Symbolism*, 139–40); Moshe Idel, "Sabbath: On Concepts of Time in Jewish Mysticism," in *Sabbath: Idea, History, Reality*, ed. G. J. Blidstein (Beer Sheva: Ben Gurion University Press, 2004),57–93; Vital, *Sha'ar ha-Kavvanot*, fol. 68a, as well as the parallel in idem, *'Olat Tamid*, fol. 55a (pointed out in Arenfeld, *Tevu'ot Shemesh*, 53). See also the texts and discussion in Wolfson, *Luminal Darkness*, 155–56. For a restriction of the extra soul to the righteous, see Aharon of Kremnitz, *Nishmat Adam*, fol. 7b. For a recent compilation of sources on the extra soul, see Ya'aqov Fisch, *Nishmat Ya'aqov* (Jerusalem, 1997), and see also Hallamish, *Kabbalah*, 323n232.

42. Tzevi Hirsch ben Yehoshua Moshe Horowitz, *Aspaklaria ha-Me'irah* (Jerusalem, 1983) [Hebrew], 46a–b; Menahem 'Azaria da Fano, *Ma'amar ha-Nefesh*, 55.

43. Zadoq ha-Kohen, *Pri Tzaddiq* (Jerusalem. 2005), vol. 1, 376–77; Yehuda Alter of Ger, *Sefat Emet*, vol. 4, 75 (and cf. the somewhat anomian formulation in Gershon Henokh Leiner, *Sod Yesharim* on the Torah, 191). For a

contemporary book on the Sabbath focusing on its identification with the soul, see Itamar Schwartz, *Shabbat Qodesh* (Jerusalem[?], ca. 2011). See also Jonathan Garb, "Soul Time in Modern Kabbalah" (forthcoming). For illuminatory discourse on the soul and the law, see, e.g., Nahman of Bratzlav, *Liqqutei Moharan*, vol. 1, siman 2, par. 6. For a comparative study of mystical illumination, see Matthew T. Kapstein (ed.), *The Presence of Light: Divine Radiance and Religious Experience* (Chicago: University of Chicago Press, 2004).

44. Yitzhaq Haver, *Pithei She'arim* (Tel Aviv, 1995), part 1, fol. 90a; vol. 2, fol. 97b and 133a.

45. Eliyahu E. Dessler, *Mikhtav mi-Eliyahu* (Bnei Brak, 2009), vol. 1, 72. Rivka Schatz-Uffenheimer's comparison of Hasidism to quietism should be recalled here; see idem, *Hasidism as Mysticism*, as well as chapter 6 and Garb, *Shamanic Trance*, 105–8.

46. See respectively, Ya'aqov Tzemah, *Nagid u-Metzave* (Jerusalem, 1880), 35, 6–7. For existing scholarship on *tefillin*, see, e.g., Elliot R. Wolfson, *Along the Path: Studies in Kabbalistic Myth, Symbolism, and Hermeneutics* (Albany: State University of New York Press, 1995), 36–39; Idel, *Enchanted Chains*, 110, 170n21, 182; Fishbane, *Light before Dawn*, 143–45; Garb, *Shamanic Trance*, 120, 127, as well as the classic discussion of *tefillin* in the intermediate festival days in Jacob Katz, *Divine Law in Human Hands: Case Studies in Halakhic Flexibility* (Jerusalem: Magnes Press, 1998), 34, 36, 42–44. This issue should be studied in the terms of liminality still current in anthropology of religion.

47. *Hemdat Yamim* (Jerusalem, 2011), vol. 1, 87.

48. Haver, *Pithei She'arim*, part 2, fol. 101a, 104a (and 106a); part 1, fol. 101a (and compare to the discussion of the snake as the Messiah, couched in similar esoteric terms in vol. 2, fol. 111b) respectively. On the association of the head and heart as seats of the soul and the temple, see, e.g., Hayyim Vital, *'Etz ha-Da'at Tov* (Jerusalem, 2001), vol. 1, 144b.

49. See Kook, *Shemona Kevatsim*, 1, par. 751, 161.

50. Jager, *The Book of the Heart*, 105–7, 141–56, 49; idem, "Reading the Book of the Heart from the Middle Ages to the Twenty-First Century" (http://press .uchicago.edu/Misc/Chicago/391167.html).

51. Robin M. Bower, "Ca Fallesció El Libro: Ascetic Reading and Restorative Hermeneutics in *La Vida de Santo Domingo de Silos*," *Hispanic Review* 73/2 (2005): 185–209, esp. 196; Meredith Sabini, "The 'Book of Knowledge' in Shamanism and Mysticism: Universal Image of the Source," in *The Sacred Heritage: The Influence of Shamanism in Analytical Psychology*, ed. D. F. Sandner and S. H. Wong (New York: Routledge, 1997), 45–59. For the Book of the Heart in Kabbalah, see Gershom Scholem, "The Name of God and the Linguistic Theory of the Kabbalah," trans. S. Pleasance, *Diogenes* 79 (1972), part 2, 188.

52. See, e.g., de Liguori, *Selected Writings*, 62, 121, 227, as well as the very lengthy and detailed discussion of internal and external modes of worship

of the sacred heart in the seventeenth-century Joseph de Galliffet, *The Adorable Heart of Jesus* (Philadelphia, 1890), 189–294 (available online at http://archive.org/details/theadorableheart00galluoft).

53. R. Ya'akov ben Asher, *Arba' Turim, Hoshen Mishpat*, 1, 2; Ann Shearer, *From Ancient Myth to Modern Healing: Themis—Goddess of Heart-Soul, Justice and Reconciliation* (New York: Routledge, 2008), esp. 21–23, 90, 94–97 (on Eckhart's idea of transformation into the "son of justice" to whom the soul gives birth, see Hollywood, *Soul as Virgin Wife*, esp. 4, 140–41, 194–96, 205).

54. Jan Patočka, *Plato and Europe*, trans. P. Lom (Stanford: Stanford University Press, 2002), 91, 222, 116, 120–21. See however, 128, for a problematic statement on the Jewish religion as not entirely moral, so that the Jewish element becomes part of European life only through Greek formation (see also 149). On Torah as empowering the divine soul to overcome the animal soul, see also Shneur Zalman of Lyady, *Torah Or*, fol. 67a.

55. David LeRoy Miller, *The New Polytheism: Rebirth of the Gods and Goddesses* (New York: Harper & Row, 1974), 38 (and see also 5, 43, 75). Hillman's discussion was printed in the less easily available 1981 (Dallas: Spring) edition of this book, 109–42. See also Michael Davis, *The Soul of the Greeks: An Inquiry* (Chicago: University of Chicago Press, 2011), 173. On Shaul Tchernichovsky's poem in cultural context, see Glenda Abramson, "'The First of Those Who Return': Incarnations of the New Jew in Modern Hebrew Literature," *Journal of Israeli History* 30/1 (2011): 52–56, and the earlier studies cited there. The mythopoetic studies of Liebes, based as they are on close reading in Greek, are an exemplary instance of the return of Greece in Zionist scholarship.

56. Weber, *The Protestant Ethic*, 182.

1. R. Shmu'el Landau, *Binyan Shmu'el,* Przemyśl 1906, unpaginated introduction.

2. Ibid., fol. 3a–4b (and see also 6b). See the detailed discussion of the life course in fol. 27a–28b (and esp. 28a for midlife).

3. Ibid., fol. 9a–10a. Compare to the illuminating synthesis with the doctrine of the *tzelem* in fol. 15a. In terms of our discussion in chapter 7, the treatments of tefillin and the psychology of sensory perception on 16a, and of Sabbath and circumcision in 18a–b are significant, as are the extensive discussions of prayer throughout.

Bibliography

Abrams, Daniel. "Chapters from an Emotional and Sexual Biography of God: Reflections on God's Attributes in the Bible, Midrash and Kabbalah." *Kabbalah* 6 (2001): 263–86 [Hebrew].

Abrams, Daniel. *The Female Body of God in Kabbalistic Literature: Embodied Forms of Love and Sexuality in the Divine Feminine.* Jerusalem: Hebrew University Magnes Press, 2004 [Hebrew].

Abrams, Daniel. *Kabbalistic Manuscripts and Texual Theory: Methodologies of Textual Scholarship and Editorial Practice in the Study of Jewish Mysticism.* 2d rev. ed. Jerusalem: Magnes Press; Los Angeles: Cherub Press, 2013.

Abrams, Daniel. "Knowing the Maiden without Eyes: Reading the Sexual Reconstruction of the Jewish Mystic in a Zoharic Parable." *Daat* 50/51 (2003): LIX–LXXXIII.

Abrams, Daniel. *Ten Psychoanalytic Aphorisms on the Kabbalah* (lecture delivered at the ceremony for the Gershom Scholem Prize for Kabbalah Scholarship at the Israel Academy of Sciences and Humanities on the anniversary of Gershom Scholem's birth, December 5, 2010). Los Angeles: Cherub Press, 2011.

Abrams, Daniel. " 'Text' in a Zoharic Parable: A Chapter in the History of Kabbalistic Textuality." *Kabbalah* 25 (2011): 7–54.

Abramson, Glenda. " 'The First of Those Who Return': Incarnations of the New Jew in Modern Hebrew Literature." *Journal of Israeli History* 30/1 March 2011): 45–63.

Abuhatzeira, Yaʿaqov. *Abir Yaʿaqov (Collected Commentaries on the Pentateuch).* 5 vols. Nahariya, Israel, 2001.

Adams, Michael Vannoy. *For Love of the Imagination: Interdisciplinary Applications of Jungian Psychoanalysis.* London: Routledge, 2014.

Afterman, Adam. *Devequt: Mystical Intimacy in Medieval Jewish Thought.* Los Angeles: Cherub Press, 2011 [Hebrew].

Afterman, Gedalyah. "Understanding the Theology of Israel's Extreme Religious Right: 'The Chosen People' and 'the Land of Israel' from Bible [*sic*] to the 'Expulsion from Gush Katif.'" Ph.D. diss., Melbourne University, 2007.

Aharon of Kremnitz. *Nishmat Adam*. Hannover 1617.

Aharon Horowitz of Staroselye. *'Avodat ha-Levi*. Jerusalem, 2004.

Aharon Horowitz of Staroselye. *Sha'arei ha-Yihud ve-Emunah and Sha'arei 'Avodah*. Jerusalem, circ. 1987 (11th pocket ed. of reprint of Shklov 1820).

Aharon Shmu'el of Kremnitz. *Nishmat Adam*. Hannover, 1617.

Altein, Leibel Y., et al. (eds.). *Chassidus Mvueres: Tanya*, vol. 1. New York: Kehot Publication Society, 2009.

Alter, Yehuda Arieh Leib, of Ger. 5 vols. *Sefat Emet*. Jerusalem, 2006.

Altmann, Alexander. *Essays in Jewish Intellectual History*. Hanover, NH: published for Brandeis University Press by University Press of New England, 1981.

Altmann, Alexander. "Notes on the Development of Rabbi Menaham Azariah Fano's Kabbalistic Doctrine." *Jerusalem Studies in Jewish Thought* 3 (1983/4): 241–67 [Hebrew].

Altshuler, Mor. "Prophecy and Maggidism in the Life and Writings of R. Joseph Karo." *Frankfurter Judaistische Beiträge* 33 (2006): 81–110.

Altshuler, Mor. " 'Revealing the Secret of His Wives': R. Joseph Karo's Concept of Reincarnation and Mystical Conception." *Frankfurter Judaistische Beiträge* 31 (2004): 91–104.

Anonymous and collective authorship. *Ohel Shikhen ba-'Adam*. Jerusalem, 2009.

Arenfeld, Shmu'el. *Ke-Tze'et ha-Shemesh*, 2 vols. Jerusalem, 2014.

Arenfeld, Shmu'el. *Tevu'ot Shemesh*. Jerusalem, 2012.

Arenfeld, Shmu'el. *Yira'ukah 'im-Shamesh*. Jerusalem, 2012.

Ashlag, Barukh. *Birkat Shalom*, vol. 3. Bnei Brak, 2000.

Ashlag, Yehuda Leib. *The Future Generation,* edited by M. Laitman. Thornhill, ON: Laitman Kabbalah Publishers, 2006 [Hebrew].

Ashlag, Yehuda Leib. *Ha-Shem Shima'kha Sham'ati: Articles on the Worship of God According to the Path of Truth*, 4 vols. Bnei Brak, 2009 [Hebrew].

Ashlag, Yehuda Leib. *Igrot ha-Sulam*. Bnei Brak, 2014.

Ashlag, Yehuda Leib. *Or ha-Bahir*. Jerusalem, 1991.

Ashlag, Yehuda Leib. *Pri Hakham*, 2 vols. Bnei Brak, 1985.

Ashlag, Yehuda Leib. *Sefer Beit Sha'ar Hakavanot me-ha-Ari z"l im Bi'ur Poqeah 'Eynayyim Or Pashut*. Jerusalem, 1996.

Ashlag, Yehuda Leib. *Sefer ha-Zohar im Perush ha-Sulam*, 24 vols. London, 1971.

Ashlag, Yehuda Leib. *Pri Hakham*, 2 vols. Bnei Brak, 1985 [Hebrew].

Ashlag, Yehuda Leib. *Sefer Beit Sha'ar ha-Kavvanot me-ha-Ari z''l 'im Bi'ur Poqeah 'Enayyim Or Pashut*. Jerusalem, 1996.

Ashlag, Yehuda Leib. *Sefer ha-Haqdamot* (Or ha-Ganuz, Israel, 2005).

Ashlag, Yehuda Leib. *Talmud 'Eser ha-Sefirot*, vol. 1. Brooklyn, 1943.

Assaf, David. *Untold Tales of the Hasidim: Crisis and Discontent in the History of Hasidism*. Translated by D. Ordan. Waltham, MA: University Press of New England, 2010.

Asulin, Shifra. "Midrash HaNe'elam Bereshit: Between Hebrew and Aramaic," In *And This Is for Yehuda: Studies Presented to our Friend, Professor Yehuda Liebes on the Occasion of His Sixty-Fifth Birthday*, edited by M. R. Niehoff, R. Meroz, and J. Garb, 222–53. Jerusalem: Mandel Institute of Jewish Studies and the Bialik Institute, 2012 [Hebrew].

Avens, Roberts. *The New Gnosis: Heidegger, Hillman, and Angels*. Dallas: Spring Publications, 1984.

Avivi, Yosef. *Binyan Ariel*. Jerusalem: Misgav Yerushalayim, 1987.

Avivi, Yosef. *Kabbala Luriana*, 3 vols. Jerusalem: Ben-Zvi Institute, 2008 [Hebrew].

Avivi, Yosef. *Kabbalat ha-Gr"a*. Jerusalem: Machon Kerem Eliyahu, 1993.

Avivi, Yosef. "The Kabbalistic Writings of R. Menahem Azaria of Fano." *Sefunot* 4 (1989): 347–76 [Hebrew].

Azulai, Avraham. *Hesed le-Avraham*. Jerusalem, ca. 1991.

Bachelard, Gaston. *The Psychoanalysis of Fire*. Boston: Beacon Press, 1964.

Bakhrakh, Naftali. *Emeq ha-Melekh*. Jerusalem, 1994.

Bakan, David, Dan Merkur, and David S. Weiss. *Maimonides' Cure of Souls: Medieval Precursor of Psychoanalysis*. Albany: State University of New York Press, 2009.

Balakirsky Katz, Maya. "An Occupational Neurosis: A Psychoanalytic Case History of a Rabbi." *AJS Review* 34/1 (2010): 1–31.

Band, Arnold J. (trans.). *Nahman of Bratslav: The Tales*. New York: Paulist Press, 1978.

Barak, Uriel. "Can Amalek Be Redeemed: A Comparative Study of the Views of Rabbi Kook and Rabbi Ya'akov Moshe Harlap." *Daat* 73 (2012): xxix–lxix.

Barak, Uriel. "The Development of the Doctrine of Redemption of Rabbi Ya'akov Moshe Charlap." M.A. thesis, Hebrew University of Jerusalem, 1997 [Hebrew].

Barak, Uriel. "New Perspectives on Rabbi Kook and His Circle: Rabbi Avraham Yitzhak ha-Kohen Kook and His Principal Disciples through the Prism of an Integrated Methodology." Ph.D. diss., Bar-Ilan University, 2009 [Hebrew].

Bar-Asher, Avishai. " 'The White Appearance'—Mahsof ha-Lavan': Interpretation and Performance Commentary and Activity in the Kabbalah of Rabbi Ya'akov AbiHasira." M.A. thesis, Hebrew University of Jerusalem, 2010 [Hebrew].

Bar-Yosef, Hamutal. *Mysticism in Modern Hebrew Poetry*. Tel Aviv: Miskal, 2008 [Hebrew].

Barnai, Jacob. "Nationalism and Jewish Historiography." In *Zionism and Empires*, edited by Y. Shenhav. Tel-Aviv and Jerusalem: Van Leer Institute and Hakibbutz Hameuchad, forthcoming [Hebrew].

Bartal, Israel, "Messianic Expectations on the Context of Historical Reality." *Cathedra* 31 (1984): 159–71.

Bartal, Israel. "On Periodization, Mysticism and Enlightenment: The Case of Moses Hayyim Luzzatto." *Simon Dubnow Institute Yearbook* 6 (2007): 201–14.

Barthes, Roland. *The Pleasure of the Text*. Translated by R. Miller. New York: Hill and Wang, 1975.

Bashir, Shahzad. *Messianic Hopes and Mystical Visions: The Nurbakhshiya between Medieval and Modern Islam.* Columbia: University of South Carolina Press, 2003.

Batnitzky, Leora F. *How Judaism Became a Religion: An Introduction to Modern Jewish Thought.* Princeton: Princeton University Press, 2011.

Bauman, Zygmunt. *Liquid Modernity.* Cambridge, UK: Polity Press, 2000.

Baumgarten, Eliezer. "The Gra and His Disciples' Attitude towards the Authority of the Ari," *Daat* 72 (2011): 53–74 [Hebrew].

Baumgarten, Eliezer, "Kabbalah within the Circle of the Vilna Gaon's Disciples: Torah in the Thought of R. Menachem Mendel of Shklov and R. Isaac Eisik Heber Wildmann." Ph.D. diss., Ben Gurion University, 2010.

Ben-Amos, Dan, and Jerome R. Mintz. *In Praise of the Baal Shem Tov: The Earliest Collection of Legends About the Founder of Hasidism (Shivḥei ha-Besht).* Bloomington: Indiana University Press, 1970.

Benarroch, Jonatan. "Sabba and Yanuqa, 'Two That Are One': Allegory, Symbol and Myth in Zoharic Literature." Ph.D. diss., Hebrew University of Jerusalem, 2011 [Hebrew].

Ben-David, Joseph, and Randall Collins. "Social Factors in the Origins of a New Science: The Case of Psychology." *American Sociological Review* 31/4 (1966): 451–65.

Bender, Courtney. *The New Metaphysicals: Spirituality and the American Religious Imagination.* Chicago: University of Chicago Press, 2010.

Ben-Dor, Yehuda. "A Study in R. Mordekhai Yosef of Izbicha's Mei ha-Shiloah." Ph.D. diss., Hebrew University of Jerusalem, 2008 [Hebrew].

Ben Israel, Menashe. *Nishmat Hayyim.* Jerusalem, 1998 (reprint of Leipzig 1862).

Berger, Peter. *A Rumor of Angels: Modern Society and the Rediscovery of the Supernatural.* Harmondsworth: Penguin, 1971

Berman, Harold J. *Faith and Order: The Reconciliation of Law and Religion.* Grand Rapids, MI: William B. Eerdmans Publishing Company, 2000.

Berman, Harold J. *Law and Revolution: The Formation of the Western Legal Tradition.* Cambridge, MA: Harvard University Press, 1983.

Berry, Patricia. "The Dogma of Gender." In idem., *Echo's Subtle Body: Contributions to an Archetypal Psychology,* 35–51. Dallas: Spring Publications, 2008.

Bettelheim, Bruno. *Freud and Man's Soul.* New York: Random House, 1984.

Bilu, Yoram. *Without Bounds: The Life and Death of Rabbi Ya'akov Wazana.* Detroit: Wayne State University Press, 2000.

Bilu, Yoram, and Yehuda C. Goodman. " 'What Does the Soul Say?': Metaphysical Uses of Facilitated Communication in the Jewish Ultra-Orthodox Community." In *Perspectives on Israeli Anthropology,* edited by E. Hertzog, O. Abuhav, H. E. Goldberg, et al., 529–53. Detroit: Wayne State University Press, 2010.

Bing, Yehezq'el. *Nequdot ha-Kesef,* vol. 1. Bnei Brak, 2008.

Birkel, Michael L., and J. Bach (eds.). *Genius of the Transcendent: Mystical Writings of Jakob Boehme.* Boston: Shambhala Publications, 2011.

Birnbaum, Pierre, and Ira Katznelson (eds.). *Paths of Emancipation: Jews, States, and Citizenship*. Princeton: Princeton University Press, 1995.

Bitton-Ashkelony, Brouria. *Encountering the Sacred: The Debate on Christian Pilgrimage in Late Antiquity*. Berkeley: University of California Press, 2005.

Bleicher, Moshe. *Maimonides' Shemona Peraqim—Understanding the Soul from a Torah Perspective*. Kiryat Arba', 2009 [Hebrew].

Bloch, Yosef Leib. *Shi'urei Da'at (Lectures on Mussar)*. Tel Aviv, 1953 [Hebrew].

Bloom, Harold. *The American Religion: The Emergence of the Post-Christian Nation*. New York: Simon and Schuster, 1992.

Bloom, Harold. *Kabbalah and Criticism*. New York: Continuum, 1983.

Boehme, Jacob. *The Aurora*. Translated by J. Sparrow. London: John M. Watkins, 1915.

Boehme, Jacob. *Forty Questions of the Soul*. Translated by J. Sparrow. London: John M. Watkins, 1911 (online version: http://meuser.awardspace.com /Boehme/JacobBoehmeFortyQuestions-electronictext.pdf).

Boksboim, Ya'aqov (ed.). *Memorial Volume for R. Hayyim Shmuelevitz*. Jerusalem: 2000 [Hebrew].

Bower, Robin M. "Ca Fallesció El Libro: Ascetic Reading and Restorative Hermeneutics in *La vida de Santo Domingo de Silos*." *Hispanic Review* 73 (2005): 185–209

Bragan, Kenneth. *The Making of a Saint: A Psychological Study of Thomas Merton*. Durham, CT: Strategic Book Group, 2011.

Brandchaft, Bernard, Shelley Doctors, and Dorienne Sorter. *Toward an Emancipatory Psychoanalysis: Brandchaft's Intersubjective Vision*. New York: Routledge, 2010.

Brown, Benjamin. *The Hazon Ish: Halakhist, Believer and Leader of the Haredi Revolution*. Jerusalem: Magnes Press, 2011 [Hebrew].

Brown, Benjamin. " 'It Does Not Relate to Me': Rabbi Israel Salanter and the Kabbalah." In *And This Is for Yehuda: Studies Presented to Our Friend, Professor Yehuda Liebes, on the Occasion of His Sixty-Fifth Birthday*, edited by M. R. Niehoff, R. Meroz, and J. Garb, 420–39. Jerusalem: Mandel Institute of Jewish Studies and Bialik Institute, 2012) [Hebrew].

Brown, Norman O. *Life against Death: The Psychoanalytical Meaning of History*. Middletown, CT: Wesleyan University Press; Scranton, PA: Harper & Row, 1959.

Brown, Norman O. *Love's Body*. New York: Random House, 1966.

Brunner, José. *Freud and the Politics of Psychoanalysis*. New Brunswick, NJ: Transaction, 2001.

Buber, Martin. "Beiträge zur Geschichte des Individuationsproblems." Ph.D. diss., University of Vienna, 1904.

Caciola, Nancy. "Breath, Heart, Guts: The Body and Spirits in the Middle Ages." In *Communicating with the Spirits*, edited by G. Klaniczay, É. Pócs, and E. Csonka-Takác, 21–39. Budapest: Central European University Press, 2005.

Campbell, Ted A. *The Religion of the Heart: A Study of European Religious Life in the Seventeenth and Eighteenth Centuries*. Eugene, OR: Wipf and Stock, 2000.

Cantor, Norman F. *Inventing the Middle Ages*. New York: Morrow, 1991.

Carrette, Jeremy R. *Foucault and Religion: Spiritual Corporality and Politial Spirituality*. London: Routledge, 2000.

Carrette, Jeremy R., and Richard King. *Selling Spirituality: The Silent Takeover of Religion*. New York: Routledge, 2005.

Certeau, Michel de. *The Mystic Fable: The Sixteenth and Seventeenth Centuries*. Translated by M. B. Smith. Chicago: University of Chicago Press, 1992.

Chajes, Joseph H. *Between Worlds: Dybbuks, Exorcists and Early Modern Judaism*, Philadelphia: University of Pennsylvania Press, 2003.

Cheetam, Tom. *The World Turned Inside Out: Henry Corbin and Islamic Mysticism*. Woodstock: Spring Journal, 2003.

Chodkiewicz, Michael. *The Meccan Revelations*, vol. 1. Translated by W. Chittick and J. W. Morris. New York: Pir Press, 2002.

Cohen, Aviezer. "Self-Consciousness in the Book Mei Hashiloach as the Nexus between God and Man." Ph.D. diss., Ben Gurion University of the Negev, 2006 [Hebrew].

Collins, Randall. *The Sociology of Philosophies: A Global Theory of Intellectual Change*. Cambridge, MA; Belknap Press of Harvard University Press, 1998.

Cooper, Paul C. *The Zen Impulse and the Psychoanalytic Encounter*. London: Routledge, 2010.

Cordovero, Moshe. *Or Ne'erav*. Jerusalem, 1990.

Cordovero, Moshe. *Or Yaqar*, 23 vols. Jerusalem, 1962–95.

Cordovero, Moshe. *Pardes Rimonim*. Jerusalem, 1962.

Cordovero, Moshe. *Sefer Eilima*. Jerusalem, 2013.

Cordovero, Moshe. *Tefila le-Moshe*. Ashdod, 2004.

Corrigan, John. *Business of the Heart: Religion and Emotion in the Nineteenth Century*. Berkeley: University of California Press, 2002.

Coudert, Allison. *The Impact of the Kabbalah in the Seventeenth Century: The Life and Thought of Francis Mercury van Helmont (1614–98)*. Leiden: Brill, 1999.

Cutsinger, James, *Paths to the Heart: Sufism and the Christian East*. Bloomington, IN: World Wisdom, 2003.

Dauber, Jonathan. *Knowledge of God and the Development of Early Kabbalah*. Leiden: Brill, 2012.

David, Abraham. "The Lutheran Reformation in Sixteenth-Century Jewish Historiography." *Jewish Studies Quartely* 9 (2002): 124–39.

David, Beruriah (published anonymously). *Memorial Volume for Our Teacher, the Author of Pahad Yitzhaq*. New York and Jerusalem, 1997.

Davidson, Eyal. "Safed's Sages between 1540–1615: Their Religious and Social Status." Ph.D. diss., Hebrew University of Jerusalem, 2009.

Davies, Oliver. *God Within: The Mystical Tradition of Northern Europe*. New York: Paulist Press, 1988.

Davis, Michael. *The Soul of the Greeks: An Inquiry*. Chicago: University of Chicago Press, 2011.

de Boer, Wietse. *The Conquest of the Soul. Confession, Discipline, and Public Order in Counter-Reformation Milan*. Leiden, Boston and Köln: Brill, 2001.

DeConick, April. "Mysticism before Mysticism: Teaching Christian Mysticism as a Historian of Religion." In *Teaching Mysticism*, edited by W. B. Parsons, 26–45. Oxford: Oxford University Press, 2011.

DeConick, April D. *Recovering the Original Gospel of Thomas: A History of the Gospel and Its Growth*. New York: T&T Clark International, 2005.

de Galliffet, Joseph. *The Adorable Heart of Jesus*. Philadelphia, 1890 (available online at http://archive.org/details/theadorableheart00galluoft).

De la Rossa, Hayyim. *Torat Hakham*. Jerusalem, 1999.

de Liguori, Alphonsus. *Selected Writings*, edited by F. Jones. New York: Paulist Press, 1999.

Dessler, Eliyahu E. *Mikhtav mi-Eliyahu*, 5 vols. Bnei Brak, 2009.

Dessler, Eliyahu E. *Mikhtav mi-Eliyahu: Elul and Rosh ha-Shana*. Bnei Brak, 2009.

De Swaan, Abram. "On the Sociogenesis of the Psychoanalytic Setting." In *Human Figurations: Essays for Nobert Elias*, edited by P. Gleichmann, J. Goudsblom, and H. Korte, 381–413. Amsterdam: Stichting Amsterdams Sociologisch Tijidschrift, 1977.

de Vidas, Elijah. *Reshit Hokhmah ha-Shalem*, 3 vols., edited by H. Y. Waldmann. Jerusalem, 1984.

DeYoung, Kevin L., and Ted Kluck. *Why We're Not Emergent (By Two Guys Who Should Be)*. Chicago: Moody Publishers, 2008.

Donoghue, Frank. *The Last Professors: The Corporate University and the Fate of the Humanities*. New York: Fordham University Press, 2008.

Drob, Sanford L. *Kabbalistic Visions: C. G. Jung and Jewish Mysticism*, New Orleans: Spring Journal Books, 2010.

Dunn, James D. (ed.), and Nathan Snyder (trans.). *Window of the Soul: The Kabbalah of R. Isaac Luria*. San Francisco: Weiserbooks, 2008.

Dunne, John S. *The Homing Spirit: A Pilgrimage of the Mind, of the Heart, of the Soul*. New York: Crossroad Publishing, 1987.

Dunne, John S. *The House of Wisdom: A Pilgrimage of the Heart*. Horktown Heights, NY: Meyer Stone Books, 1988.

Dunne, John S. *A Journey with God in Time: A Spiritual Quest*. Notre Dame, IN: University of Notre Dame Press, 2003.

Dunne, John S. *The Reasons of the Heart: A Journey into Solitude and Back Again into the Human Circle*. New York: Macmillan, 1978.

Dweck, Yaacob. *The Scandal of Kabbalah: Leon Modena, Jewish Mysticism, Early Modern Venice*. Princeton: Princeton University Press, 2011.

Dynner, Glenn. *Men of Silk: The Hasidic Conquest of Polish Jewish Society*. New York: Oxford University Press, 2006.

Efrati, Binyamin. *Torat ha-Nefesh be-Mishnat Ramhal*. Jerusalem: Feldheim, 2009.

Ehrenreich, Barbara. *Bright Sided: How the Relentless Promotion of Positive Thinking Has Undermined America*. New York: Metropolitan Books, 2009.

Eigen, Michael. *Ecstasy*. Middletown, Connecticut: Wesleyan University Press, 2001.

Eigen, Michael, *Kabbalah and Psychoanalysis*, London: Karnac Books, 2012.

Eigen, Michael. *The Psychoanalytic Mystic*, Binghamton, New York: ESF Publishers, 1998.

Eigen, Michael. *The Sensitive Self*. Middletown, Connecticut: Wesleyan University Press, 2004.

Eisenman, Esther. "The Structure and Content of R. Hayyim Volozhin's *Nefesh ha-Hayyim*." In *The Vilna Gaon and His Disciples*, edited by M. Hallamish, J. Rivlin, and R. Shuchat, 185–94. Ramat Gan: Bar-Ilan University Press, 2003 [Hebrew].

Eisenstadt, Shmuel N. "The Civilizational Dimension of Modernity." *International Sociology* 16/3 (2001): 320–40.

Eisenstadt, Shmuel N. *Comparative Civilizations and Multiple Modernities*. Leiden: Brill, 2003.

Eisenstadt, Shmuel N. "The Reconstruction of Religious Arenas in the Framework of 'Multiple Modernities', *Millenium: Journal of International Studies* 29/3 (2000): 591–611.

Eldredge, John. *Waking the Dead: The Glory of a Heart Fully Alive*. Nashville, Tennesee: Thomas Nelson, 2003.

Eleff, Zev. "Psychohistory and the Imaginary Couch: Diagnosing Historical and Biblical Figures." *Journal of the American Academy of Religion* 80/1 s(2012): 94–136.

Elior, Rachel. "The Doctrine of Transmigration in *Galya Raza*." In *Essential Papers on Kabbalah*, edited by L. Fine, 243–69. New York: New York University Press, 1995.

Elior, Rachel. "The Innovation of Polish Hasidism." *Tarbiz* 62 (1993): 381–432 [Hebrew].

Elior, Rachel. "Messianic Expectations and Spiritualization of Religious Life in the 16th Century." *Revue des études juives* 145 (1986): 35–49.

Elior, Rachel. *The Paradoxical Ascent to God: The Kabbalistic Theosophy of Habad Hasidism*. Translated by J. M. Green. Albany: State University of New York Press, 1993.

Elior, Rachel. "Soul—Nefesh: The Jewish Doctrine of the Soul." In *Contemporary Jewish Thought*, edited by A. Cohen and P. Mendes-Flohr, 887–96. New York: Scribner 1987.

Elior, Rachel. *The Theory of Divinity of Hasidut Habad*. Jerusalem: Magnes Press, 1982 [Hebrew].

Elqayam, Avraham. "Azamer bi-Svahin: On Ars Poetica of the God-Intoxicated R. Itzhak Luria." In *The Piyyut as a Cultural Prism: New Approaches*, edited by H. Pedaya, 68–150. Tel Aviv: Van Leer Jerusalem Institute and Hakibbutz Hameuchad Publishing House, 2012.

Elqayam, Avraham. "The Horizon of Reason: The Divine Madness of Sabbatai Sevi." *Kabbalah* 9 (2003): 7–61.

Elqayam, Avraham. "Nudity in Safed in the Sixteenth Century: Between Hasidism and Deviance." *Kabbalah* 30 (2013): 303–20. [Hebrew].

Elqayam, Avraham, "To Know the Messiah: The Dialectic of Sexual Discourse in the Messianic Thought of Nathan of Gaza." *Tarbiz* 65/4 (1996): 637–70 [Hebrew]

Elyashiv, Shlomo. *Leshem Shvo ve-Ahlama: Drushei 'Olam ha-Tohu*. Jerusalem, 1976.

Elyashiv, Shlomo. *Leshem Shvo ve-Ahlama: Haqdamot u-Shorashim*. Petrakov, Russia, 1909.

Elyashiv, Shlomo. *Leshem Shvo ve-Ahlama: Sefer ha-Kelalim*. Jerusalem. 1924.

Emden, Jacob. *Birat Migdal Oz*. Zhitomir, 1873.

Englander, Yakir. *Images of the Male Body in Lithuanian Ultra Orthodox Judaism as Reflected in Musar Movement Sources and 'HaGedolim' Hagiographies (1945–2010)*. Jerusalem: Magnes Press, forthcoming [Hebrew].

Epstein, Qalonymus Qalman. *Ma'or va-Shemesh*. Jerusalem, 1992.

Erlanger, Yitzhaq Moshe. *Quntres Akh be-Tzelem*. Jerusalem, 2011.

Erlanger, Yitzhaq Moshe. *Quntresei Hasidut: 'Inyanei Emunah*. Jerusalem, 2007.

Erlanger, Yitzhaq Moshe. *Quntresei Hasidut: Mo'adim*, 2 vols. Jerusalem, 2007.

Erlanger, Yitzhaq Moshe. *Shiv'a 'Enayim: Peqah 'Eneikha Ve-Re'eh*. Jerusalem, 1990.

Ernst, Waltraud (ed.). *Plural Medicine, Tradition and Modernity, 1800–2000*. London: Routledge, 2002.

Etkes, Immanuel. *Ba'al ha-Tanya: Rabbi Shneur Zalman of Liady and the Origins of Habad Hasidism*. Jerusalem: The Zalman Shazar Center for Jewish History, 2011 [Hebrew].

Etkes, Immanuel. *Rabbi Israel Salanter and the Mussar Movement: Seeking the Torah of Truth*. Translated by J. Chipman. Philadelphia and Jerusalem: The Jewish Publication Society, 1993.

Ezrahi, Yaron. *Imagined Democracies: Necessary Political Fictions*. Cambridge, UK: Cambridge University Press, 2012.

Faierstein, Morris M. (trans. and ed.). *Hayyim ben Joseph Vital and Isaac Judah Jehiel Safrin: Jewish Mystical Autobiographies: Book of Visions and Book of Secrets*. New York: Paulist Press, 1999.

Faierstein, Morris M. "Personal Redemption in Hasidism." In *Hasidism Reappraised*, edited by A. Rapoport-Albert, 214–24. London: Valentine, Mitchell, 1996.

Falach, Baruch. "The 'Sulam' Journal: Between Poetry and Politics." Ph.D diss., Bar Ilan University, 2010 [Hebrew].

Feldman, Jan L. *Lubavitchers as Citizens: A Paradox of Liberal Democracy*. Ithaca: Cornell University Press, 2003.

Fenton, Paul. "Abraham Heschel and Henry Corbin." *Daat* 68–69 (2010): 225–35.

Fenton, Paul. "Judaism and Sufism." In *The Cambridge Companion to Medieval Jewish Philosophy*, edited by D. H. Frank and O. Leaman, 201–17. Cambridge: Cambridge University Press, 2003.

Ferrone, Vincenzo. *The Intellectual Roots of the Italian Enlightenment: Newtonian Science, Religion, and Politics in the Early Eighteenth Century*. Amherst, NY: Prometheus Books, 1995.

Fine, Lawrence. *Physician of the Soul, Healer of the Cosmos: Isaac Luria and His Kabbalistic Fellowship*. Stanford: Stanford University Press, 2003.

Fine, Lawrence. "Recitation of Mishnah as a Vehicle for Mystical Inspiration: A Contemplative Technique Taught by Hayyim Vital." *Revue des études juives* 141 (1982): 183–99.

Fisch, Ya'aqov, *Nishmat Ya'aqov: Collections and Commentaries on the Extra Soul*. Jerusalem, 1997 [Hebrew].

Fischer, Kevin. *Converse in the Spirit: William Blake, Jacob Boehme, and the Creative Spirit*. Madison and Teaneck: Fairleigh Dickinson University Press, 2004.

Fischer, Shlomo. "Self-Expression and Democracy in Radical Religious Zionist Ideology." Ph.D. diss., Hebrew University of Jerusalem, 2007.

Fishbane, Eitan P. *As Light before Dawn: The Inner World of a Medieval Kabbalist*. Stanford, California: Stanford University Press, 2009.

Fishbane, Eitan P. "A Chariot for the Shekhinah: Identity and the Ideal Life in Sixteenth-Century Safed Kabbalah." *Journal of Religious Ethics* 37/3 (2009): 385–418.

Fishbane, Michael. *Biblical Myth and Rabbinic Mythmaking*. Oxford: Oxford University Press, 2003.

Fishbane, Michael. *The Kiss of God: Spiritual and Mystical Death in Judaism*. Seattle: University of Washington Press, 1994.

Fishbane, Michael A. *Sacred Attunement: A Jewish Theology*. Chicago: University of Chicago Press, 2008.

Fishbane, Michael. "Transcendental Consciousness and Stillness in the Mystical Theology of R. Yehudah Arieh Leib of Gur." In *Sabbath: Idea, History, Reality*, edited by G. Blidstein et al., 119–29. Beer Sheva: Ben Gurion University Press, 2004.

Flatto, Sharon. *The Kabbalistic Culture of Eighteenth-Century Prague: Ezekiel Landau and His Contemporaries*. Oxford: Littman Library of Jewish Civilization, 2010.

Fleischer, Cornell. "The Lawgiver as Messiah: The Making of the Imperial Image in the Reign of Süleymân." In *Soliman le magnifique et son temps*, edited by G. Veinstein, 159–77. Paris: La Documentation Française, 1992.

Fontaine, Resianne. "The Immortality of the Soul in Pinchas Hurwitz's 'Sefer ha-Berit': Philosophers versus Kabbalists." *Jewish Studies Quarterly* 13 (2006): 223–33.

Foucault, Michel. *Discipline and Punish: The Birth of the Prison*. Translated by A. Sheridan. New York: Vintage Books, 1995.

Frager, Robert. *Heart, Self and Soul: The Sufi Psychology of Growth, Balance, and Harmony*. Wheaton, Illinois: Quest Books, 1999.

Freud, Sigmund. *The Interpretation of Dreams*. Translated and edited by J. Stratchey. New York: Basic Books, 2010.

Freund, Yuval. *Psychology of Above: R. Kook's Doctrine of the Soul*. Jerusalem, 2009 [Hebrew].

Friedlander, H. (ed.). *Ginzei Ramhal*. Bnei Brak, 1984.

Fromm, Erich. *Psychoanalysis and Religion*. New Haven: Yale University Press, 1950.

Frosh, Stephen. *Hate and the Jewish Science: Anti-Semitism, Nazism, and Psycho-analysis*. New York, Palgrave Macmillan, 2005.

Fuchs, Thomas. *The Mechanization of the Heart: Harvey & Descartes*. Translated by M. Grene. Rochester, New York: University of Rochester Press, 2001.

Fuller, Andrew R. *Psychology and Religion: Classical Theorists and Contemporary Approaches*. Lanham, MD: Rowman and Littlefield Publishers, 2008.

Gafni, Marc. *Soul Prints: Your Path to Fulfillment*. New York: Pocket Books, 2001.

Gam-Hacohen, Moran. "Trends in Kabbalah Research in Israel, 1929–2010," Ph.D. diss., Ben Gurion University of the Negev, 2010 [Hebrew].

Gamlieli, Dvorah Bat-David. *Psychoanalysis and Kabbalah: The Masculine and Feminine in Lurianic Kabbalah*. Los Angeles: Cherub Press, 2006 [Hebrew].

Garb, Jonathan. "'Alien Culture' in the Thought of Rabbi Kook's Circle." In *Study and Knowledge in Jewish Thought*, edited by H. Kreisel, 253–64. Beer Sheva: Ben Gurion University of the Negev Press, 2006.

Garb, Jonathan. "The Authentic Kabbalistic Writings of Moshe Hayyim Luzzatto." *Kabbalah* 25 (2011): 165–222 [Hebrew].

Garb, Jonathan. "The Challenges of Teaching Mysticism," Review of *Teaching Mysticism* by William B. Parsons. *Religious Studies Review* 38/4 (2012): 207–12.

Garb, Jonathan. *The Chosen Will Become Herds: Studies in Twentieth Century Kabbalah*, trans. Y. Berkovits-Murciano. New Haven: Yale University Press, 2009.

Garb, Jonathan. "The Circle of Moshe Hayyim Luzzatto in Its Eighteenth-Century Context." *Eighteenth Century Studies* 44/2 (2011): 189–202.

Garb, Jonathan. "Contemporary Kabbalah and Classical Kabbalah: Breaks and Continuities," in *After Spirituality: Studies in Mystical Traditions*, eds. Ph. Wexler and J. Garb, 19–46 (New York: Peter Lang, 2012).

Garb, Jonathan. "The Cult of the Saints in Lurianic Kabbalah." *Jewish Quarterly Review* 98/2 (2008): 203–29.

Garb, Jonathan. "'The Joy of Torah' in the Thought of David Hartman: A Critical Examination of the Phenomenology of Halakhic Experience." In *Renewing Jewish Commitment: The Work and Thought of David Hartman*, edited by A. Sagi and Z. Zohar, 73–105. Jerusalem: Shalom Hartman Institute; Tel Aviv: Hakibbutz Hameuchad, 2001 [Hebrew].

Garb, Jonathan. "Kabbalah Outside the Walls: The Response of Rabbi Haddayah to the State of Israel." In *Rabbi Uziel and His Peers: Studies in the Religious*

Thought of Oriental Rabbis in 20th Century Israel, edited by Z. Zohar, 13–27. Tel Aviv: Tel Aviv University Press, 2009 [Hebrew].

Garb, Jonathan. *Kabbalist in the Heart of the Storm: R. Moshe Hayyim Luzzatto*. Tel Aviv: Tel Aviv University Press, 2014 [Hebrew].

Garb, Jonathan. *Manifestations of Power in Jewish Mysticism: From Rabbinic Literature to Safedian Kabbalah*. Jerusalem: Magnes Press, 2005 [Hebrew].

Garb, Jonathan. "The Modernization of Kabbalah: A Case Study." *Modern Judaism: A Journal of Jewish Ideas and Experience* 30/1 (2010): 1–22.

Garb Jonathan. "Mussar as a Modern Movement." Paper delivered at the Third International Conference on Modern Religions and Religious Movements in Judaism, Christianity, Islam, and the Babi, Bahai Faith, Hebrew University of Jerusalem, March 2011. Accessed September 1, 2014. http://www.academia.edu/1684906/Mussar_as_a_Modern_Movement.

Garb, Jonathan. "Mussar, Curriculum and Exegesis in the Circle of Ramhal." Tikvah Center Working Paper No. 01/12. Accessed September 1, 2014. http://www.nyutikvah.org/pubs/1112/documents/WP1Garb.pdf.

Garb, Jonathan. "Mystical and Spiritual Discourse in the Contemporary Ashkenazi Haredi Worlds." *Journal of Modern Jewish Studies* 9/1 (2010): 29–48.

Garb, Jonathan. "Mystics' Critique of Mystical Experience." *Revue de l'Histoire des Religions* 21 (2004): 293–325.

Garb, Jonathan. "On the Kabbalists of Prague." *Kabbalah* 14 (2006): 347–83 [Hebrew].

Garb, Jonathan. "The Political Model in Modern Kabbalah: A Study of Ramhal and His Intellectual Surroundings." In *'Al Da'at ha-Kahal–Religion and Politics in Jewish Thought: Festschrift in Honor of Aviezer Ravitzky*, edited by B. Brown, M. Lorberbaum, Y. Stern, and A. Rosenak, 13–45. Jerusalem: Zalman Shazar Center and Israel Democracy Institute [Hebrew].

Garb, Jonathan. "The Psychological Turn in Sixteenth Century Kabablah." In *Les Mystiques, juives, chrétiennes et musulmanes dans L'Egypte médiévale (VIIe–XVIe siècle): Interculturalités et contextes historiques*, edited by G. Cecere, M. Loubet, and S. Pagani, 109–24. Cairo: Institut français d'archéologie orientale, 2013.

Garb, Jonathan. "Rabbi Kook and His Sources: From Kabbalistic Historiosophy to National Mysticism." In *Studies in Modern Religions, Religious Movements and the Babi-Bahai Faiths*, edited by M. Sharon, 77–96. Leiden: Brill, 2004.

Garb, Jonathan. "A Renewed study of the Self-Image of R. Moshe David Valle, as Reflected in His Biblical Exegesis." *Tarbiz* 79/2 (2010–11): 263–303 [Hebrew].

Garb, Jonathan. "Returning the Chairs to Their Place: Buddhist Mussar Literature in Face of the Takeover of Mysticism by Psychology." In *From India Till Here: Israeli Thinkers Write about Their Conception of Judaism and India*, edited by E. Nir, 127–42. Jerusalem: Reuven Mass, 2006 [Hebrew].

Garb, Jonathan. Review of *Kabbalah and Jewish Modernity*, by Roni Weinstein. *Zion* 80 (2015): 148–53.

Garb, Jonathan. *Shamanic Trance in Modern Kabbalah*. Chicago: University of Chicago Press, 2011.

Garb, Jonathan. "Shamanism and the Hidden History of Modern Kabbalah." In *Histories of the Hidden God*, edited by A. DeConick and G. Adamson, 175–92. Durham: Acumen Publishing, 2013.

Garb, Jonathan. "Sixteenth-Century Kabbalah." In *The Cambridge Companion to Kabbalah*, edited by E. R. Wolfson. Cambridge: Cambridge University Press, forthcoming.

Garb, Jonathan. "Towards the Study of the Spiritual-Mystical Renaissance in the Contemporary Ashkenazi Haredi World in Israel." In *Kabbalah and Contemporary Spiritual Revival*, edited by B. Huss, 117–40. Beer Sheva. Ben Gurion University of the Negev Press, 2011.

Garb, Jonathan. "Working Out as Divine Work." In *Sport and Physical Education in Jewish History*, edited by G. Eisen, H. Kaufman, and M. Lämmer, 7–14. Netanya: Wingate Institute, 2003.

Garb, Jonathan. "Yehuda Liebes's Way in the Study of the Jewish Religion." In *And This Is for Yehuda: Studies Presented to Our Friend, Professor Yehuda Liebes, on the Occasion of his Sixty-Fifth Birthday*, edited by M. R. Niehoff, R. Meroz, and J. Garb, 11–16. Jerusalem: Mandel Institute of Jewish Studies and Bialik Institute, 2012 [Hebrew].

Garb, Jonathan, and Philip Wexler. "After Spirituality: Introducing the Volume and the Series." In *After Spirituality: Studies in Mystical Traditions*, edited by J. Garb and Ph. Wexler, 1–15. New York: Peter Lang Publishing, 2012.

Geels, Anton, and Jacob A. Belzen. "A Vast Domain and Numerous Perspectives: Introduction to the Volume," In *Mysticism: A Variety of Psychological Perspectives*, edited by J. A. Belzen and A. Geels, 7–15. Amsterdam: Rodopi, 2003.

Gellman, Yehuda (Jerome). "Hasidic Existentialism?" In *Hazon Nahum: Studies in Jewish Law, Thought, and History Presented to Dr. Norman Lamm on the Occasion of His Seventieth Birthday*, edited by Y. Elman and J. Gurock, 393–417. New York: Michael Scharf Publication Trust of the Yeshiva University Press, 1997.

Gergen, Kenneth. *The Saturated Self: Dilemmas of Identity in Contemporary Life*. New York: Basic Books, 1992.

Gerhold, Christine. "The Hero's Journey through Adolescence: A Jungian Archetypal Analysis of 'Harry Potter.'" Ph.D. diss., University of Chicago, 2010.

Giegerich, Wolfgang. *The Soul's Logical Life: Towards a Rigorous Notion of Psychology*. Frankfurt am Main: Peter Lang, 1998.

Giegerich, Wolfgang. *What Is Soul?* New Orleans: Spring Journal Books, 2012.

Gikatila, Joseph. *Shaare Ora*, 2 vols., edited with an introduction and notes by J. Ben Shlomo Jerusalem, 1970 [Hebrew].

Giller, Pinchas. *Kabbalah: A Guide for the Perplexed*. London: Continuum International Publishing Group, 2011.

Giller, Pinchas. *Reading the Zohar: The Sacred Text of the Kabbalah*. Oxford: Oxford University Press, 2001.

Giller, Pinchas. *Shalom Shar'abi and the Kabbalists of Beit El*. Oxford: Oxford University Press, 2008.

Ginsburg, Elliot. *The Sabbath in the Classical Kabbalah*. Oxford: Littman Library of Jewish Civilization, 2008.

Ginsburgh, Yitzchak. *The Dynamic Corporation: Involvement, Quality and Flow: A Jewish Approach to Business Management Based on Kabbalah and Chassidut*. Jerusalem: Gal Einai, 1995.

Ginsburgh, Yitzchak. *Kabbalah and Meditation for the Nations*. Jerusalem: Gal Einai, 2007.

Ginsburgh, Yitzchak. *Malkhut Israel*, vol. 1. Rehovot, Israel: Gal Einai, 1999.

Ginsburgh, Yitzchak. *Shekhina Beneyhem*. Jerusalem: Gal Einai, 1992.

Ginsburgh, Yitzhak. *Yayin Mesameah: The Mysteries of Wedding and Marriage*, vol. 1. Jerusalem: Gal Einai, 2004 [Hebrew].

Glassman, Reut. "The Magical Meaning of the Commandments in the Philosophy of Rabbi Shneur Zalman of Liady." M.A. thesis, Bar Ilan University, 2009 [Hebrew].

Glazer, Aubrey. "Touching God: Vertigo, Exactitude, and Degrees of Devekut in the Contemporary Nondual Jewish Mysticism of R. Yitzhaq Maier Morgenstern." *Journal of Jewish Thought and Philosophy* 19 (2011): 147–92.

Glick, Zvi ha-Kohen. *Bi-Hitoma shel Tequfa*. Jerusalem, 2011.

Goetschel, Roland. *Meir Ibn Gabbay: Le Discours de la Kabbale Espagnole*. Leuven: Peeters, 1981.

Goetz, Stewart, and Charles Taliaferro. *A Brief History of the Soul*. Oxford: Wiley-Blackwell, 2011.

Goldberg, Hillel. *Israel Salanter: Text, Structure, Idea: The Ethics and Theology of an Early Psychologist of the Unconscious*. New York: Ktav Publishing House, 1982.

Goldberg, Sheli. *The Spiritual Voyage of the Soul: The Soul of the Zaddik and the Eternity of the Spirit in Habbad's Doctrine*. Jerusalem: Rubin Mass, 2009 [Hebrew].

Gottlieb, Avraham M. *Ha-Sulam: The Lives and Teachings of Our Holy Rebbes of the Ashlagian Dynasty and Their Disciples*. Jerusalem, 1997 [Hebrew].

Gottlieb-Zornberg, Avivah. *Genesis: The Beginning of Desire*. Philadelphia: Jewish Publication Society, 1995.

Gottlieb-Zornberg, Avivah. *The Murmuring Deep: Reflections on the Biblical Unconscious*. New York: Schocken Books, 2009.

Gottlieb-Zornberg, Avivah. *The Particulars of Rapture: Reflections on Exodus*. New York: Doubleday, 2001.

Grange, Joseph. *Soul: A Cosmology*. Albany: State University of New York Press, 2011.

Green, Arthur (trans.). *The Language of Truth: The Torah Commentary of the Sefat Emet, Rabbi Yehudah Leib Alter of Ger*. Philadelphia: Jewish Publication Society, 1998.

Green, Arthur. *Tormented Master: The Life and Spiritual Quest of Rabbi Nahman of Bratslav*. Tuscaloosa: University of Alabama Press, 1979.

Greenspahn, Fredrick E. (ed.). *Jewish Mysticism and Kabbalah: New Insights and Scholarship*. New York: New York University Press, 2011.

Gregory, Brad S. *The Unintended Reformation: How a Religious Revolution Secularized Society*. Cambridge, MA: Harvard University Press, 2012.

Gries, Zeev. "From Myth to Ethos—Outlines for the History of Rabbi Abraham of Kalisk," In *Uma ve-Toldoteiha (Nation and History)*, vol. 2, edited by S. Etinger, 117–46. Jerusalem: Zalman Shazar Center, 1984 [Hebrew].

Gries, Zeev. "The Hasidic Managing Editor as an Agent of Culture." In A. Rapoport-Albert, ed., *Hasidism Reappraised*. London: Valentine, Mitchell, 1996.

HaCohen, Ruth. *The Music Libel Against the Jews*. New Haven: Yale University Press, 2011.

Hai Ricci, Immanuel. *Mishnat Hasidim* [with commentaries]. New York: Makhon ha-Gr"a, 2006.

Halberstam, Hayyim of Tzanz. *Divrei Hayyim*. 2 vols. New York, 2003.

Halbertal, Moshe. *By Way of Truth: Nahmanides and the Creation of Tradition*. Jerusalem: Hartman Institute, 2006 [Hebrew].

Halbertal, Moshe. *People of the Book: Canon, Meaning, and Authority*. Cambridge, Massachussets: Harvard University Press, 1997.

Hallamish, Moshe. *Kabbalah: In Liturgy, Halakhah and Customs*. Ramat Gan: Bar-Ilan University Press, 2000 [Hebrew].

Hansel, Joelle, *Moïse Hayyim Luzzatto (1707–1746): Kabbale et Philosophie*. Paris: Editions du Cerf, 2004.

Harari, Yehiel. "Mysticism as a Messianic Rhetoric in the Works of Rabbi Yitzchak Ginsburgh," Ph.D. diss., Tel Aviv University, 2005) [Hebrew].

Harlap, Ya'aqov Moshe, *Mei Marom: Razi Li*. Jerusalem, 2012.

Haver, Yitzhaq. *Afiqei Yam*. Jerusalem, 1994.

Haver, Yitzhaq, *Beit 'Olamim*. Warsaw, 1889.

Haver, Yitzhaq. *Or ha-Torah (Commentary on Ma'alot ha-Torah)*. Jerusalem, 1881 [reprint].

Haver, Yitzhaq. *Pithei She'arim*. Tel Aviv, 1995.

Haver, Yitzhaq. *Siah Yitzhaq*. Jerusalem, 2000.

Hecker, Joel. *Mystical Bodies, Mystical Meals: Eating and Embodiment in Medieval Kabbalah*. Detroit: Wayne State University Press, 2005.

Hellner-Eshed, Melila. *A River Flows From Eden: The Language of Mystical Experience in the Zohar*. Translated by N. Wolski. Stanford, California: Stanford University Press, 2009.

Hemdat Yamim. Jerusalem, 2011.

Hendler, Yehiel Mikhel. *Barukh u-Mevurakh: Commentary on Intention of the Blessing in the Kabbalah of R. Shar'abi*. Jerusalem, 2011 [Hebrew].

Hernandez, Wil. *Henri Nouwen: A Spirituality of Imperfection*. New York and Mahwah: Paulist Press, 2006.

Hillel, Ya'aqov Moshe. *Ahavat Shalom*. Jerusalem: Ahavat Shalom, 2002.

Hillel, Ya'aqov Moshe. *Shorshei ha-Yam*. Jerusalem, 1999.

Hillman, James. *Anima: An Anatomy of a Personified Notion*. Dallas: Spring Publications, 1985.

Hillman, James. *City and Soul*. Dallas: Spring Publications, 2006.

Hillman, James. *The Dream and the Underworld*. New York: Harper & Row, 1979.

Hillman, James. *Insearch: Psychology and Religion*. New York: Scribner, 1967.

Hillman, James. *Loose Ends: Primary Papers in Archetypal Psychology*. Zürich: Spring Publications, 1975.

Hillman, James. *The Myth of Analysis: Three Essays in Archetypal Psychology*. Evanston: Northwestern University Press, 1972.

Hillman, James. "Peaks and Vales: The Soul/Spirit Distinction as Basis for the Differences between Psychotherapy and Spiritual Discipline." In *On the Way to Self-Knowledge*, edited by J. Needleman and D. Lewis, 114–47. New York: Knopf, 1976.

Hillman, James. *Re-Visioning Psychology*. New York: Harper and Row, 1975.

Hillman, James. *The Soul's Code: In Search of Character and Calling*. New York: Random House, 1996.

Hillman, James. *Suicide and the Soul*. New York: Harper & Row, 1972.

Hillman, James. *The Thought of the Heart and the Soul of the World*. New York: Spring Publications, 2007.

Hillman, James, and Michael Ventura. *We've had a Hundred Years of Psychotherapy—And the World's Getting Worse*. San Francisco: Harper One, 1993.

Hollywood, Amy. *The Soul as Virgin Wife: Mechthild of Magdeburg, Marguerite Porete, and Meister Eckhart*, Notre Dame and London: University of Notre Dame Press, 1995.

Homans, Peter. *The Ability to Mourn: Disillusionment and the Social Origins of Psychoanalysis*. Chicago: University of Chicago Press, 1989.

Homans, Peter. *Jung in Context: Modernity and the Making of a Psychology*. Chicago: University of Chicago Press, 1995.

Horowitz, Aharon. *See* Aharon Horowitz of Staroselye.

Horowitz, Isaiah. *Shnei Luhot ha-Brit ha-Shalem*. Haifa: Machon Yad Rama, 1997.

Horowitz, Shabbetai Sheftel. *Shef'a Tal*. Jerusalem, 1971 (reprint of Warsaw, 1874).

Horowitz, Tzevi Hirsch ben Yehoshua Moshe. *Aspaklaria ha-Me'irah*. Jerusalem, 1983 [Hebrew].

Hoshen, Dalia. "*Zimzum* and R. Akiva's School: Kabbala and Midrash." *Daat*, 34 (1995): 34–60 [Hebrew].

Huss, Boaz. "Admiration and Disgust: The Ambivalent Re-Canonization of the *Zohar* in the Modern Period." In *Study and Knowledge in Jewish Thought*, edited by H. Kreisel, 203–37. Beer Sheva: Ben Gurion University of the Negev Press, 2006.

Huss, Boaz. "All You Need is Lav: Madonna and Postmodern Kabbalah." *The Jewish Quarterly Review* 95/4 (2005): 611–24.

Huss, Boaz. *Like the Radiance of the Sky: Chapters in the Reception History of the Zohar and the Construction of its Symbolic Value*. Jerusalem: Bialik Press and Yad Ben-Zvi, 2008 [Hebrew].

Huss, Boaz. "The New Age of Kabbalah." *Journal of Modern Jewish Studies* 6/2 (2007): 107–25.

Hutner, Yitzhaq. *Pahad Yitzhaq: Purim*. New York, 1996.

Ibn Gabbai, Meir. *'Avodat ha-Qodesh*. Jerusalem, 2004.

Idel, Moshe. *Absorbing Perfections: Kabbalah and Interpretation*. New Haven: Yale University Press, 2002.

Idel, Moshe. "Ascensions, Gender, and Pillars in Safedian Kabbalah," *Kabbalah* 25 (2011): 55–108.

Idel, Moshe. *Ascensions on High in Jewish Mysticism: Pillars, Lines, Ladders*. Budapest: Central European University Press, 2005.

Idel, Moshe. "The Battle of the Urges: Psychomacia in the Prophetic Kabbalah of Abraham Abulafia." In *War and Peace in Jewish Culture*, edited by A. Bar-Levav, 99–143. Jerusalem: Zalman Shazar Center; Haifa: Center for Jewish Culture in Haifa University, 2006 [Hebrew].

Idel, Moshe. *Ben: Sonship and Jewish Mysticism*. London: Continuum, 2007.

Idel, Moshe. " 'The Besht Passed His Hand over His Face': On the Besht's Influence on His Followers: Some Remarks." In *After Spirituality: Studies In Mystical Traditions*, edited by Ph. Wexler and J. Garb, 79–106. New York: Peter Lang Publications, 2012.

Idel, Moshe. *Enchanted Chains: Techniques and Rituals in Jewish Mysticism*. Los Angeles: Cherub Press, 2005.

Idel, Moshe. *Hasidism: Between Ecstasy and Magic*. Albany: State University of New York Press, 1995.

Idel, Moshe. "Italy in Safed, Safed in Italy: Toward an Interactive History of Sixteenth-Century Kabbalah." In *Cultural Intermediaries: Jewish Intellectuals in Early Modern Italy*, edited by D. Ruderman and G. Veltri, 239–69. Philadelphia: University of Pennsylvania Press, 2004.

Idel, Moshe. *Kabbalah and Eros*. New Haven: Yale University Press, 2005.

Idel, Moshe. *Kabbalah in Italy, 1280–1510: A Survey*. New Haven: Yale University Press, 2011.

Idel, Moshe. *Kabbalah: New Perspectives*. New Haven: Yale University Press, 1988.

Idel, Moshe. *Messianic Mystics*. New Haven: Yale Unversity Press, 1998.

Idel, Moshe. "Messianic Scholars: On Early Israeli Scholarship, Politics and Messianism." *Modern Judaism* 32/1 (2012): 22–53.

Idel, Moshe. "Metamorphoses of a Platonic Theme in Jewish Mysticism." *Jewish Studies at the Central European University* 3 (2002–3): 67–86.

Idel, Moshe. *Mircea Eliade: From Magic to Myth*. New York: Peter Lang Publishing, 2014.

Idel, Moshe. " 'Nishmat Eloha': The Divinity of the Soul in Nahmanidies and His School." In *Life as Midrash: Perspectives in Jewish Psychology*, edited by B. Kahana et al., 338–82. Tel Aviv: Yediot Aharonot, 2004 [Hebrew].

Idel, Moshe. *Old Worlds, New Mirrors: On Jewish Mysticism and Twentieth-Century Thought*. Philadelphia: University of Pennsylvania, 2010.

Idel, Moshe. "On Mobility, Individuals and Groups: Prolegomenon for a Sociological Approach to Sixteenth-Century Kabbalah." *Kabbalah* 3 (1998): 145–73.

Idel, Moshe. "On Some Forms of Order in Kabbalah." *Daat* 50–52 (2003): xxxi–lviii.

Idel, Moshe. "On the Theologization of Kabbalah in Modern Scholarship." In *Religious Apologetics—Philosophical Argumentation*, edited by Y. Schwartz and V. Krech, 123–74. Tübingen: Mohr Siebeck, 2004.

Idel, Moshe. "R. Israel Ba'al Shem Tov 'In the State of Wallachia': Widening the Besh't's Cultural Panorama." In *Holy Dissent: Jewish and Christian Mystics in Eastern Europe*, edited by G. Dynner, 69–103. Detroit: Wayne State University Press, 2011.

Idel, Moshe. "Revelation and the 'Crisis of Tradition' in Kabbalah: 1475–1575." In *Constructing Tradition: Means and Myths of Transmission in Western Esotericism*, edited by A. B. Kilcher, 255–92. Leiden: Brill, 2010.

Idel, Moshe. "Sabbath: On Concepts of Time in Jewish Mysticism." In *Sabbath: Idea, History, Reality*, edited by G. J. Blidstein. Beer Sheva: Ben Gurion University Press, 2004.

Idel, Moshe. *Saturn's Jews: On the Witches' Sabbat and Sabbateanism*. New York: Continumm, 2011.

Idel, Moshe. "The Secret of Impregnation as Metempsychosis in Kabbalah." In *Verwandlungen: Archäologie der literarischen Kommunikation*, edited by A. and J. Assman, 341–79. Munich: Wilhelm Fink, 2006.

Idel, Moshe. *Studies in Ecstatic Kabbalah*. Albany: State University of New York Press, 1988.

Idel, Moshe. "The Tsadik and His Soul's Sparks: From Kabbalah to Hasidism." *JQR* 103/2 (2013): 196–240.

Illich, Ivan, and Barry Sanders. *ABC: The Alphabetization of the Popular Mind*. San Fransisco: North Point, 1988.

Jacobs, Louis (trans.). *Rabbi Moses Cordovero: The Palm Tree of Deborah: Translated from the Hebrew with an Introduction and Notes*. London: Vallentine Mitchell, 1960.

Jacobs, Louis. "The Uplifting of Sparks in Later Jewish Mysticism." In *Jewish Spirituality from the Sixteenth-Century Revival to the Present*, edited by A. Green, 99–126. New York: Crossroad, 1987.

Jacobsen, Wayne, and Dave Coleman. *So You Don't Want to Go to Church Anymore: An Unexpected Journey*. Los Angeles: Windblown Media, 2006.

Jacobson, Yoram, *Along the Paths of Exile and Redmeption: The Doctrine of Redemption of Rabbi Mordecai Dato*. Jerusalem: Bialik Institute, 1996 [Hebrew].

Jacobson, Yoram. "Exile and Redemption in Gur Hasidism." *Daat* 2–3 (1978–79): 175–212 [Hebrew].

Jacobson, Yoram. "The Rectification of the Heart: Studies in the Psychic Teachings of R. Shneur Zalman of Liadi." *Teudah* 10 (1996): 359–409 [Hebrew].

Jager, Eric. *The Book of the Heart*, Chicago: The University of Chicago Press, 2000.

Jager, Eric. "Reading the Book of the Heart from the Middle Ages to the Twenty-First Century." Accessed September 1, 2014. http://press.uchicago.edu/Misc/Chicago/391167.html.

James, William, *The Varieties of Religious Experience*. New York: Mentor and Plume, 1958.

Jantzen, Grace. *Power, Gender, and Christian Mysticism*. Cambridge: Cambridge University Press, 1995.

Jay, Martin. *Songs of Experience: Modern American and European Variations on a Universal Theme*. Berkeley: University of California Press, 2005.

Johnson, Eric L. *Foundations of Soul Care: A Christian Psychology Proposal*. Downers Grove, IL: IVP Academic, 2007.

Johnson, Jeffrey. "The Future of the Social Sciences and Humanities in the Science of Complex Systems." *European Journal of Social Science Research* 23/2 (2010): 115–34.

Jonas, Raymond. *France and the Cult of the Sacred Heart: An Epic Tale for Modern Times*. Berkeley: University of California Press, 2000.

Jonte-Pace, Diane, and William B. Parsons. *Religion and Psychology: Mapping the Terrain*. New York: Routledge, 2001.

Joseph, Betty. *Psychic Equilibrium and Psychic Change: Selected Papers of Betty Joseph*, edited by M. Feldman and E. Bott Spillius. London: Tavistock/Routledge, 1991.

Joseph, Steven M. "Jung and Kabbalah: Imaginal and Noetic Aspects." *Journal of Analytical Psychology* 52 (2007): 321–41.

Jullien, François. *The Silent Transformations*, trans. M. Richardson and K. Fijalkowski. London: Seagull Books, 2011.

Jung, Carl. *Psychological Types*. Vol. 6 of *The Collected Works of C. G. Jung*. Edited by H. Read et al., translated by H. G. Baynes. London: Routledge and Kegan Paul, 1971.

Jung, Carl. *Psychology and Religion*. New Haven: Yale University Press, 1966.

Kahana, Maoz. "An Esoteric Path to Modernity: Rabbi Jacob Emden's Alchemical Quest," *Journal of Modern Jewish Studies:* 12, 2 (2013): 253–75.

Kahane, Barukh. *Breaking and Mending: A Hasidic Model for Clinical Psychology*. Jerusalem: Rubin Mass Publishing, 2010. [Hebrew].

Kallus, Menachem. *Pillar of Prayer: Teachings of Contemplative Guidance in Prayer, Sacred Study, and the Spiritual Life from the Baal Shem Tov and His Circle*. Louisville: Fons Vitae Pub, 2011.

Kallus, Menachem. "Pneumatic Mystical Possession and the Eschatology of the Soul in Lurianic Kabbalah." In *Spirit Possession in Judaism: Cases and Contexts From the Middle Ages to the Present*, edited by M. Goldish, 159–85, 385–413. Detroit: Wayne State University Press, 2003.

Kallus, Menachem. "The Theurgy of Prayer in the Lurianic Kabbalah." Ph.D. diss., Hebrew University of Jerusalem, 2002

Kanzian, Christian, and Muhammad Legenhausen (eds.). *Soul: A Comparative Approach*. Heusenstamm, Germany: Ontos Verlag, 2010.

Kaplan, Avraham Eliyahu. *Be-'Iqvot ha-Yir'a*. Jerusalem: Mossad ha-Rav Kook, 1988.

Kaplan, Tzevi. *Be-Shipulei Glimato: Something on Our Master, the Ra'ayah Kook and his Surroundings*. Jerusalem, 2009 [Hebrew].

Kapstein, Matthew T. (ed.). *The Presence of Light: Divine Radiance and Religious Experience*. Chicago: University of Chicago Press, 2004.

Karfman, Hanina H. (ed.). *Le-Zekher 'Olam Yehiye Tzaddiq*. Jerusalem, 2009.

Katz, Dov. *The Musar Movement: Its History, Leading Personalities, and Doctrines*, 2 vols. Tel-Aviv: Orly Press, 1900 [Hebrew].

Katz, Jacob. *Divine Law in Human Hands: Case Studies in Halakhic Flexibility*. Jerusalem: Magnes Press, 1998.

Kauffman, Tsippi. *In All Your Ways Know Him: The Concept of God and Avodah be-Gashmiyut in the Early Stages of Hasidism*. Ramat Gan: Bar-Ilan University Press, 2009 [Hebrew].

Kaufman, Yehezkel. "The Ruin of the Soul." In *Zionism Reconsidered: The Rejection of Jewish Normalcy*, edited by M. Selzer, 117–29. New York: Macmillan, 1970.

Keating, Thomas. *Open Mind, Open Heart: The Contemplative Dimension of the Gospel*. New York: Continuum, 2012.

Kehat, Chana. "Changes in the Concept of Torah Study in the Modern Age." Ph.D. diss., Hebrew University of Jerusalem, 2005 [Hebrew].

Kening, Gedalyahu Aharon. *Hayyei Nefesh*. Jerusalem, 1968.

Kerr, John. *A Most Dangerous Method: The Story of Jung, Freud, and Sabina Spielrein*. New York: Alfred A. Knopf, 1993.

Khatami, Mahmoud. "Becoming Transcendent: Remarks on the Human Soul in the Philosophy of Illumination." In *Soul: A Comparative Approach*, edited by Ch. Kanzian and M. Legenhausen, 97–121. Heusenstamm, Germany: Ontos Verlag, 2010.

Kirschner, Suzanne. *The Religious and Romantic Origins of Psychoanalysis: Individuation and Integration in Post-Freudian Theory*. New York: Cambridge University Press, 1996.

Klein, Anne. The *Heart Essence of the Vast Expanse: A Story of Transmission*. Ithaca, New York: Snow Lion Publications, 2009.

Kluger, Abraham Tzevi. *Divrei Hakhamim be-Nahat*, vol. 1 (of 2 vols.). Beit Shemesh, 2009.

Kluger, Avraham Tzevi. *Nezer Yisra'el: Makhon Shivtekha, Yasis 'Alayikh*. Beit Shemesh, 2010.

Kluger, Avraham Tzevi. *Nezer Yisra'el: Shi'urim, Sihot, u-Ma'amarim*. Beit Shemesh, 2007.

Kluger, Avraham Tzevi. *Qarva el Nafshi*. Beit Shemesh, 2012.

Koch, Patrick. "Cultivating the Emotions: Asceticism in R. Elijah De Vidas' *Reshit Hokhmah*." M.A. thesis, Hebrew University of Jerusalem, 2007.

Koch, Patrick. *Human Self-Perfection: A Re-Assessment of Kabbalistic Musar-Literature of Sixteenth-Century Safed*. Los Angeles: Cherub Press, 2015.

Kohen, David. *Qol ha-Nevu'a*. Jerusalem, 2002.

Kook, Avraham Yitzhaq ha-Kohen. *Letters [Igrot]*, 4 vols. Jerusalem: Mossad ha-Rav Kook, 1981.

Kook, Avraham Yitzhaq ha-Kohen. *Ma'amarei ha-Re'iah.* Jerusalem, 1988.

Kook, Avraham Yitzhaq ha-Kohen. *Middot ha-Re'iah,* in idem., *Mussar Avikha.* Jerusalem: Mossad ha-Rav Kook, 1979.

Kook, Avraham Yitzhaq ha-Kohen. *Mussar Avikha.* Jerusalem: Mossad ha-Rav Kook, 1979.

Kook, Avraham Yitzhaq ha-Kohen. *'Olat Re'iah,* 2 vols. Jerusalem: Mossad ha-Rav Kook, 1978–83.

Kook, Avraham Yitzhaq ha-Kohen. *Orot.* Jerusalem: Mossad ha-Rav Kook, 1980.

Kook, Avraham Yitzhaq ha-Kohen. *Orot ha-Qodesh.* Jerualem: Mossad ha-Rav Kook, 1984.

Kook, Avraham Yitzhaq ha-Kohen. *Orot ha-Tefila.* Jerusalem, 2003.

Kook, Avraham Yitzhaq ha-Kohen. *Orot ha-Teshuva.* Jerusalem: Mossad ha-Rav Kook, 1977.

Kook, Avraham Yitzhaq ha-Kohen. *Pinqesei ha-Re'iah,* 2 vols. Jerusalem: Mossad ha-Rav Kook, 2008–10.

Kook, Avraham Yitzhaq ha-Kohen. *Qevatzim mi-Ketav Yad Qodsho,* 2 vols. Jerusalem, 2008.

Kook, Avraham Yitzhaq ha-Kohen. *Shmona Qevatzim,* 3 vols. Jerusalem, 1999.

Krakowsky, Eliyahu. "Between the Genius and the Gaon: Lost in Translation" (review essay). *Hakirah: The Flatbush Journal of Jewish Law and Thought* 16 (2013): 153–76.

Kravel-Tovi, Michal, and Yoram Bilu. "The Work of the Present: Constructing Messianic Temporality in the Wake of Failed Prophecy among Chabad Hasidim." *American Ethnologist* 35/1 (2008): 64–80.

Kremer, Elijah. *Heikhalot ha-Zohar im-Bi'ur.* Jerusalem, 2006 (printed with a commentary by R. Itzhak Haver) [Hebrew].

Kripal, Jeffrey J. *Mutants and Mystics: Science Fiction, Superhero Comics, and the Paranormal.* Chicago: University of Chicago Press, 2011.

Kripal, Jeffrey J. *The Serpent's Gift: Gnostic Reflections on the Study of Religion.* Chicago: University of Chicago Press, 2007.

Krisspel, Dalia. "The Concept of Man in 'Shenei Luhot ha-Berit' ('The Two Tablets of the Covenant') by Rabbi Isaiah Horowitz." Ph.D. diss., Ben Gurion University of the Negev, 2004 [Hebrew].

Kristeva, Julia. *New Maladies of the Soul.* Translated by R. M. Guberman. New York: Columbia University Press, 1995.

Lachman, Gary. *Jung the Mystic: The Esoteric Dimensions of Carl Jung's Life and Teachings.* New York: Tarcher & Penguin, 2010.

Laitman, Michael. *Shnei ha-Me'orot ha-Gedolim.* Petah Tikva: Ashlag Research Institute, 2006.

Landau, Shmu'el. *Binyan Shmu'el.* Przemyśl, 1906.

Laude, Patrick. *Pathways to an Inner Islam: Massignon, Corbin, Guénon, and Schuon.* Albany: State University of New York Press, 2010.

Lavi, Tony. *The Secret of Cosmogony: The Law of Divinity and the Essence of Mankind in the Studies of R. Yehuda Halevi Ashlag*. Jerusalem: Bialik Institute, 2007 [Hebrew]

Lear, Jonathan. *Open Minded: Working Out the Logic of the Soul*. Cambridge, MA: Harvard University Press, 1998.

Lederberg, Netanel. *The Gateway to Infinity: Rabbi Dov Bear [sic], the Maggid Mesharim of Mezhirich*. Jerusalem: Rubin Mass, 2011 [Hebrew].

Le Goff, Jacques. " 'Head or Heart?' The Political Use of Body Metaphors in the Middle Ages." In *Fragments for a History of the Human Body, Part Three*, edited by M. Feher, R. Naddaff, and N. Tazi, 12–26. New York: Zone, 1989.

Leibovitz, Yeruham. *Da'at Torah: Limudei Mussarei ha-Torah*. 5 vols. Jerusalem, 2001.

Leibovitz, Yeruham. *Ma'amarei ha-Mashgiah Rabenu Yeruham ha-Levi: Elul ve-Tishrei*. Jerusalem, 2008.

Leiner, Gershon Hanokh (Henikh). *Sod Yesharim*. Jerusalem, 2002.

Leiner, Hayyim Simha. *Dor le-Yesharim*. Jerusalem, 1999.

Leiner, Mordekhai Yosef. *Mei ha-Shiloah*. Bnei Brak, 1995.

Leuchter, Reuven (ed.). *Nefesh ha-Hayyim 'im Perush Meshivat Nefesh*. Jerusalem, 2013.

Levanoni, Tsiri. "The Concept of Repentance in R. Dov Ber's Thought and Its Sources in R. Shneur Zalman of Liady's Thought." Ph.D. diss., Bar Ilan University, 2009 [Hebrew]

Levenstein, Yehezkel. "Nothing Is More Effective than Judgment." *Yeshurun* 27 (2012): 566–71.

Levenstein, Yehezkel. *Or Yekhezqel*, vol. 7 (*Darkhei 'Avoda*). Bnei Brak, 2001

Levi Yitzhaq of Berditchev. *Qedushat Levi*, 2 vols. Jerusalem, n.a.

Lewis, Franklin D. *Rumi: Past and Present, East and West: The Life, Teaching and Poetry of Jalâl al-Din Rumi*. Oxford: OneWorld Publications, 2001.

Liebes, Esther. "A New Examination of the Myth of the Kings of Edom: Cordovero and Luria." In *Ma'yan 'Ein Ya'acov*, edited by B. Sack, 32–60. Beer Sheva: Ben Gurion University of the Negev Press, 2009 [Hebrew].

Liebes, Esther. "The Novelty in Hasidism According to R. Barukh of Kossow." *Daat* 45 (2000): 75–90 [Hebrew].

Liebes, Yehuda. "Mysticism and Reality: Towards a Portrait of the Martyr and Kabbalist R. Samson Ostropoler." In *Jewish Thought in the Seventeenth Century*, edited by I. Twersky and B. Septimus, 221–55. Cambridge, MA: Harvard University Press, 1987.

Liebes, Yehuda. "Myth vs. Symbol in the Zohar and in Lurianic Kabbalah." In *Essential Papers on Kabbalah*, edited by L. Fine, 212–42. New York: New York University Press, 1995.

Liebes, Yehuda. "The Novelty of Rabbi Nahman of Bretslav." *Daat* 45 (2000): 91–104 [Hebrew].

Liebes, Yehuda. " 'Two Young Roes of a Doe': The Secret Sermon of Isaac Luria before His Death." *Jerusalem Studies in Jewish Thought* 10 (1992): 113–69 [Hebrew].

Lindberg, Carter. *The Pietist Theologians: An Introduction to Theology in the Seventeenth and Eighteenth Centuries.* Malden, MA: Blackwell Publishers, 2005.

Liwer, Amira. "Oral Torah in the Writings of R. Zadok ha-Kohen of Lublin." Ph.D. diss., Hebrew University of Jerusalem, 2006 [Hebrew].

Loewenthal, Naftali. *Communicating the Infinite: The Emergence of the Habad School.* Chicago: University of Chicago Press, 1990.

Lorberbaum, Menachem. "'Attain the attribute of *'Ayin'*: The Mystical Religiosity of *Maggid Devarav le-Ya'aqov.*" *Kabbalah* 31 (2014): 169–235 [Hebrew].

Lorberbaum, Menachem. *Dazzled by Beauty: Theology as Poetics in Hispanic Jewish Culture.* Jerusalem: Ben Zvi Institute and Hebrew University of Jerusalem, 2011 [Hebrew].

Lorberbaum, Yair. "Nahmanides' Kabbalah on the Creation of Man in the Image of God." *Kabbalah* 5 (2000): 287–326 [Hebrew].

Luhrmann, Tanya M. *When God Talks Back: Understanding the American Evangelical Relationship with God.* New York: Alfred A. Knopf, 2012.

Luzzatto, Moshe Hayyim. *Adir ba-Marom*, edited by J. Spinner. Jerusalem, 1995.

Luzzatto, Moshe Hayyim. *Da'at Tevunot*, edited by J. Spinner. Jerusalem, 2012.

Luzzatto, Moshe Hayyim. *Daat Tevunot: The Knowing Heart.* Translated by A. Kaplan. Jerusalem: Feldheim Publishers, 1982.

Luzzatto, Moshe Hayyim. *Mesillat Yesharim.* Translated by M. M. Kaplan. Philadelphia: Jewish Publication Society of America, 1948.

Lynch, David (ed.). *Divine Passions: The Social Construction of Emotion in India.* Berkeley: University of California Press, 1990.

Maciejko, Pawel. *The Mixed Multitude: Jacob Frank and the Frankist Movement, 1755–1816.* Philadelphia: University of Pennsylvania Press, 2011.

Madden, Kathryn Wood. *Dark Light of the Soul.* Great Barrington, MA: Lindisfarne Books, 2008.

Magid, Shaul. *American Post-Judaism: Identity and Renewal in a Postethnic Society.* Bloomington: Indiana University Press, 2013.

Magid, Shaul. "Deconstructing the Mystical: The Anti-Mystical Kabbalism in Rabbi Hayyim of Volozhin's Nefesh ha-Hayyim." *Journal of Jewish Thought and Philosophy* 9/1 (2000): 21–67.

Magid, Shaul. *From Metaphysics to Midrash: Myth, History, and the Interpretation of Scripture in Lurianic Kabbala.* Bloomington: Indiana University Press, 2008.

Magid, Shaul. *Hasidism Incarnate: Hasidism, Christianity and the Construction of Modern Judaism.* Stanford: Stanford University Press, 2014.

Magid, Shaul. *Hasidism on the Margin: Reconciliation, Antinomianism, and Messianism in Izbica and Radzin Hasidism.* Madison: University of Wisconsin Press, 2003.

Magid, Shaul. "'The King Is Dead [And Has Been for Three Decades], Long Live the King': Contemporary Kabbalah and Scholem's Shadow." *Jewish Quarterly Review* 102/1 (2012): 131–53.

Maitland, Frederic William. *The Collected Papers of Frederic William Maitland, Downing Professor of the Laws of England*, edited by H. A. L. Fisher. Cambridge: Cambridge University Press, 1911.

Malisov, Hillel Halevi. *Pelah ha-Rimon: Exodus*. New York, 1956.

Marcuse, Herbert. *Eros and Civilization: Philosophical Inquiry into Freud*. Boston: Beacon Press, 1955.

Margolies, Reuven (ed.). *Zohar Chadash (Tikunim me-Zohar Chadash)*. Jerusalem, 1994.

Margolin, Ron. *The Human Temple: Religious Interiorization and the Structuring of Inner Life in Early Hasidism*. Jerusalem: Magnes Press, 2005 [Hebrew].

Margolin, Ron. *Inner Religion: The Phenomenology of Inner Religious Life and Its Manifestation in Jewish Sources (From the Bible to Hasidic Texts)*. Ramat Gan: Bar Ilan University and Shalom Hartman Institute, 2011 [Hebrew].

Margolin, Ron. Review of *The Chosen Will Become Herds*, by Jonathan Garb. *Journal of Modern Jewish Studies* 10/3 (2011): 441–44.

Mark, Zvi. *Mysticism and Madness: The Religious Thought of Rabbi Nachman of Bratslav*. London: Continuum, 2009.

Mark, Zvi. *Revelation and Rectification in the Revealed and Hidden Writings of R. Nahman of Breslav*. Jerusalem: Magnes Press, 2011 [Hebrew].

Marlan, Stanton. "Mystical Light: Dream Images and the Alchemy of Psychic Momentum." In *Archetypal Psychologies: Reflections in Honor of James Hillman*, edited by S. Marlan, 341–49. New Orleans: Spring Journal Books, 2008.

Martin, Raymond, and John Barresi. *Naturalization of the Soul: Self and Personal Identity in the Eighteenth Century*. London: Routledge, 2000.

Martin, Raymond, and John Barresi, *The Rise and Fall of Soul and Self: An Intellectual History of Personal Identity*. New York: Columbia University Press, 2008.

Mathers, Dale, Melvin E. Miller, and Osamu Ando (eds.). *Self and No-Self: Continuing the Dialogue between Buddhism and Psychotherapy*. London: Routledge, 2009.

Matt, Daniel. *The Essential Kabbalah: The Heart of Jewish Mysticism*. San Francisco: Harper, 1995.

Meghnagi, David. "From the Dreams of a Generation to the Theory of Dreams: Freud's Roman Dreams." *International Journal of Psychoanalysis* 92/3 (2011): 675–94.

Meir, Jonatan. *Rehovot ha-Nahar: Kabbalah and Exotericism in Jerusalem (1896–1948)*. Jerusalem: Yad Yitzhak Ben-Zvi and the Mandel Institute of Jewish Studies, 2011 [Hebrew].

Meir, Jonatan. "The Revealed and the Revealed within the Concealed: On the Opposition to the 'Followers' of Rabbi Yehudah Ashlag and the Dissemination of Esoteric Literature." *Kabbalah* 16 (2007): 151–258 [Hebrew].

Meir, Jonatan. Review of *Shalom Shar'abi and the Kabbalists of Beit El*, by Pinchas Giller. *Journal of Religion* 89 (2009): 448–50.

Meir, Jonatan, "Wrestling with the Esoteric: Hillel Zeitlin, Yehuda Ashlag and Kabbalah in the Land of Israel." In *Judaism, Topics, Tragments, Faces, Identities: Jubilee Volume in Honor of Rivka Horwitz*, edited by H. Pedaya and E. Meir, 585–647. Beer Sheva: Ben Gurion University of the Negev Press, 2007 [Hebrew].

Melamed, Yitzhak. Review of Yirmiyahu Yovel, *The Other Within: The Marranos: Split Identity and Emerging Modernity.*" *Journal of Religion* 83/1 (2011): 198–200.

Menahem 'Azaria da Fano, *Ma'amar ha-Nefesh*, edited by Hanina H. Karfman. Jerusalem, 2011.

Menahem 'Azaria da Fano. *Pelah ha-Rimon.* Jerusalem, 2000.

Merkur, Dan. *Explorations of the Psychoanalytic Mystics.* Amsterdam: Rodopi, 2010.

Meroz, Ronit. "Faithful Transmission versus Innovation: Luria and His Disciples." In *Gershom Scholem's Major Trends in Jewish Mysticism, 50 Years After: Proceedings of the 6th International Conference on the History of Jewish Mysticism*, edited by P. Schäfer and J. Dan, 257–74. Tübingen: Mohr Siebeck, 1993.

Meroz, Ronit. "Hebetim be-Torat ha-Nevu'a ha-Lurianit." M.A. thesis, Hebrew University of Jerusalem, 1980.

Meroz, Ronit. "The Teachings of Redemption in Lurianic Kabbalah." Ph.D. diss., Hebrew University of Jerusalem, 1988 [Hebrew].

Mezuman, Yaniv. "Rabbi Shalom Shar'abi's Kabbalistic Intentions of Prayer for the Morning Blessings." M.A. thesis, Bar-Ilan University, Ramat Gan, 2000 [Hebrew].

Miller, David L. *Christs: Meditations on Archetypal Images in Christian Theology.* New York: Seabury Press, 1981.

Miller, David L. *Hells and Holy Ghosts: A Theopoetics of Christian Belief.* New Orleans: Spring Journal Books, 2004.

Miller, David L. *The New Polytheism: Rebirth of the Gods and Goddesses.* New York: Harper & Row, 1974.

Miller, David L. *Three Faces of God: Traces of the Trinity in Literature and Life.* New Orleans: Spring Journal Books, 2005.

Mirsky, Yehudah. "An Intellectual and Spiritual Biography of Rabbi Avraham Yitzhaq ha-Cohen Kook from 1865–1904." Ph.D. diss., Harvard University, 2007.

Mirsky, Yehudah. *Rav Kook: Mystic in a Time of Revolution.* New Haven: Yale University Press, 2014.

Mopsik, Charles. *Sex of the Soul: The Vicissitudes of Sexual Difference in Kabbalah.* Los Angeles: Cherub Press, 2005.

Morris, James Winston. *The Reflective Heart: Discovering Spiritual Intelligence in Ibn 'Arabi's Meccan Illuminations.* Louisville: Fons Vitae, 2005.

Morgenstern, Yitzhaq Me'ir. *Yam ha-Hokhma.* Jerusalem, 2007, 2009, 2011, 2012, 2014.

Moshe of Prague, *Va-Yakhel Moshe.* Zalkov, 1741.

Nabarro, Assaf. *Tikkun: From Lurianic Kabbalah to Popular Culture*, Ph.D. diss., Ben-Gurion University of the Negev, 2006 [Hebrew].

Nadler, Allan. *The Faith of the Mithnagdim: Rabbinic Response to Hasidic Rapture.* Baltimore: Johns Hopkins University Press, 1999.

Ne'eman, Aryeh. " 'Iyunim ba-Hibur 'Kaf ha-Qtoret': Zmano, Meqomo, Ra'ayonotav ve-Tod'ato ha-Meshihit." M.A. thesis, Hebrew University of Jerusalem, 2009 [Hebrew].

Nelson, Benjamin. "Self-Images and Systems of Spiritual Direction in the History of European Civilization." In *The Quest for Self-Control: Classical Philosophies and Scientific Research*, edited by S. Z. Klausner, 49–103. New York : Free Press; London: Collier-Macmillan, 1965.

Nelson, James M. *Psychology, Religion and Spirituality*. New York: Springer, 2009.

Nelson, Victoria. *Gothicka: Vampire Heroes, Human Gods and the New Supernatural*. Cambridge, MA: Harvard University Press, 2012.

Nelson, Victoria. *The Secret Life of Puppets*. Cambridge, MA: Harvard University Press, 2001.

Neria, Moshe Z. *Sihot ha-Re'iah*. Tel Aviv: Moreshet, 1979.

Neumann, Erich. *Amor and Psyche*. Translated by R. Manheim. Princeton: Princeton University Press, 1971

Nouwen, Henri J. M., Michael J. Christensen, and Rebecca. Laird. *Spiritual Formation: Following the Movements of the Spirit*. New York: Harper One, 2010.

Nussbaum, Martha. *Not for Profit: Why Democracy Needs the Humanities*. Princeton: Princeton University Press, 2010.

Oestreich, Gerhard. *Neostoicism and the Early Modern State*. Cambridge: Cambridge University Press, 2008.

Ogren, Brian. *Renaissance and Rebirth: Reincarnation in Early Modern Italian Kabbalah*. Leiden: Brill, 2009.

O'Regan, Cyril. *Gnostic Apocalypse: Jacob's Boehme's Haunted Narrative*. Albany: State University of New York Press, 2002.

Ornet, Leah. *"Ratzo Va-shov, Running and Returning": Ethical and Mystical Perspectives in the Teaching of R. Shneur Zalman of Liadi: A Comparative Study*. Tel-Aviv: Hakibbutz Hameuchad, 2007 [Hebrew].

Oron, Michal. "The Doctrine of the Soul and Reincarnation in the 13th Century." *Studies in Jewish Thought*, edited by Sara O. Haller Willensky and Moshe Idel, 277–90. Jerusalem: Magnes Press, 1989 [Hebrew]

Oron, Michal. *Window to the Stories of the Zohar: Studies in the Exegetical and Narrative Methods of the Zohar*. Los Angeles: Cherub Press, 2013 [Hebrew].

Otto, Rudolph. *Mysticism East and West: A Comparative Analysis of the Nature of Mysticism*. Translated by B. L. Bracey and R. C. Payne. New York: Meridian Books, 1959.

Pachter, Mordechai. "The Musar Movement and the Kabbalah." In *Let the Old Make Way for the New*, edited by D. Assaf and A. Rapoport-Albert, vol. 1, 223–50. Jerusalem: Zalman Shazar Center for Jewish History, 2009 [Hebrew].

Pachter, Mordechai. *Roots of Faith and Devequt: Studies in the History of Kabbalistic Ideas*. Los Angeles: Cherub Press, 2004.

Parsons, William B. *Freud and Augustine in Dialogue: Psychoanalysis, Mysticism and the Culture of Modern Spirituality*. Charlottesville: University of Virginia Press, 2013.

Parsons, William B. "Freud's Last Theory of Mysticism: The Return of the (Phylo-genetic) Repressed." In *After Spirituality: Studies in Mystical Traditions*, edited by Ph. Wexler and J. Garb, 173–86. New York: Peter Lang Publishing, 2012.

Parsons, William B. "Psychoanalysis Meets Buddhism: The Development of a Dialogue." In *Changing the Scientific Study of Religion: Beyond Freud?*, edited by J. A. Belzen, 179–209. Dordrecht: Springer, 2009.

Parsons, William B. "Psychoanalytic Spirituality." In *Spirituality and Religion: Psychoanalytic Perspectives, Mental Health Perspectives*, edited by J. Winer and J. Anderson, 83–97. New York: Catskill, 2007.

Parsons, William B. "Psychologia Perennis and the Academic Study of Mysti-cism." In *Mourning Religion*, edited by W. B. Parsons, D. Jonte-Pace, and S. E. Henking, 97–123. Charlottesville: University of Virginia Press, 2008.

Parsons, William B., Diane Jonte-Pace, and Susan E. Henking. "Mourning Reli-gion: An Introduction", In *Mourning Religion*, edited by W. B. Parsons, D. Jonte-Pace, and S. E. Henking, 1–9. Charlottesville: University of Vir-ginia Press, 2008.

Patočka, Jan. *Plato and Europe*. Translated by P. Lom. Stanford: Stanford Univer-sity Press, 2002.

Patton, Kimberly. *Religion of the Gods: Ritual, Paradox, and Reflexivity*. Oxford: Oxford University Press, 2009.

Pedaya, Haviva. *Expanses: An Essay on the Theological and Political Unconscious*. Tel Aviv: Hakibbutz Hameuchad, 2011 [Hebrew].

Pedaya, Haviva. *Nahmanides: Cyclical Time and Holy Text*. Tel Aviv: 'Am 'Oved, 2003 [Hebrew].

Pedaya, Haviva. *Name and Sanctuary in the Teaching of R. Isaac the Blind: A Com-parative Study in the Writings of the Earliest Kabbalists*. Jerusalem: Magnes Press, 2001 [Hebrew].

Pedaya, Haviva. "Text and Its Performance in the Poetry of R. Israel Najjara: Ban-ishing Sleep as a Practice of Exile in the Nocturnal Space." In *The Piyyut as a Cultural Prism: New Approaches*, edited by H. Pedaya, 29–67. Jerusalem: : Van Leer Institute; Tel Aviv: Hakibbutz Hameuchad, 2012 [Hebrew].

Pedaya, Haviva. *Vision and Speech: Models of Prophecy in Jewish Mysticism*. Los Angeles: Cherub Press, 2002 [Hebrew].

Pedaya, Haviva. *Walking through Trauma: Rituals of Movement in Jewish Myth Mys-ticism and History*. Tel Aviv: Resling, 2011 [Hebrew].

Pelikan, Jaroslav. *Christian Doctrine and Modern Culture (Since 1700)*. Chicago: University of Chicago Press, 1989.

Persico, Tomer. " 'Jewish Meditation': The Development of a Modern Form of Spiritual Practice in Contemporary Judaism," Ph.D. diss., Tel Aviv University, 2013.

Pinar, William. *What Is Curriculum Theory?* New York: Routledge, 2012.

Pitkin, Barbara. *What Pure Eyes Could See: Calvin's Doctrine of Faith in Its Exegetical Context*. Oxford: Oxford University Press, 1999.

Porter, Roy. *Flesh in the Age of Reason*. New York: W. W. Norton & Co, 2004.

Potok, Chaim. *The Chosen*. London: Penguin, 1970.

Pritzky, Avraham Ya'aqov. *Adir bi-Melukha*. Jerusalem, 2009.

Puett, Michael. "Innovation as Ritualization: The Fractured Cosmology of Early China." *Cardozo Law Review* 28/1 (2006): 23–36.

Putsh, Mordekhai (ed.). *Rahmana Liba Ba'i*. Jerusalem, 2006.

Quintaes, Marcus. "Hillman Revisioning Hillman: Polemics and Paranoia." In *Archetypal Psychologies: Reflections in Honor of James Hillman*, edited by S. Marlan, 73–94. New Orleans: Spring Journal Books, 2008.

Rabinovitch, Benzion. *Le-Yeshu'atkha Qiviti ha-Shem*. Jerusalem, 2003.

Rank, Otto. *Psychology and the Soul: A Study of the Origin, Conceptual Evolution, and Nature of the Soul*. Translated by G. C. Richter and E. J. Lieberman. Baltimore: Johns Hopkins University Presss, 1998.

Rapoport-Albert, Ada. *Women and the Messianic Heresy of Sabbatai Zevi 1666–1816*. Oxford: Littman Library of Jewish Civilization, 2011.

Rapp, Jennifer. "From the Self to the Soul: Platonic Religious Thought." Ph.D. diss., Stanford University, 2006.

Raviv, Zohar. *Decoding the Dogma within the Enigma: The Life, Works, Mystical Piety and Systematic Thought of Rabbi Moses Cordoeiro (Aka Cordovero; Safed, Israel, 1522–1570)*. Saarbrücken: Verlag Dr. Müller, 2008.

Raz-Krakotzkin, Amnon. "The National Narration of Exile: Zionist Historiography and Medieval Jewry." Ph.D. diss., Tel Aviv University, 1996 [Hebrew].

Reed, Edward S. *From Soul to Mind: The Emergence of Psychology, from Erasmus Darwin to William James*. New Haven: Yale University Press, 1997.

Reiser, Daniel. *Vision as a Mirror: Imagery Techniques in Twentieth Century Jewish Mysticism*. Los Angeles: Cherub Press, 2014 [Hebrew].

Reiser, Daniel, and Ariel Evan Mayse. "The Last Sermon of R. Judah Leib Alter of Gur and the Role of Yiddish in the Study of Hasidic Sermons," *Kabbalah* 30 (2013): 127–60 [Hebrew].

Ribi, Alfred. *The Search for Roots: C. G. Jung and the Tradition of Gnosis*. Los Angeles: Gnosis Archive Books, 2013.

Richards, Graham. *Psychology, Religion and the Nature of the Soul: A Historical Entanglement*. New York: Springer, 2011.

Rieff, Philip. *The Triumph of the Therapeutic: Uses of Faith after Freud*. Chicago: University of Chicago Press, 1987.

Ar-Rifa'i as-Shadhili, Muhammad al-Jamal. *Music of the Soul: Sufi Teachings*. Petaluma, CA: Sidi Muhammad Press, 1997.

Rivett, Sarah. *The Science of the Soul in Colonial New England*. Chapel Hill: University of North Carolina Press, 2011.

Rivlin, Eliezer (ed.). *HaTzaddik Rabbi Yosef Zundel from Salant*. Jerusalem, 1983.

Rohr, Richard. *The Enneagram: A Christian Perspective*. New York: Crossroad Publishing. 2006.

Rolnik, Eran, *Freud in Zion: Psychoanalysis and the Making of Modern Jewish Identity*. Translated by H. Watzman. London: Karnac Books, 2012.

Romanyshyn, Robert D. *The Wounded Researcher: Research with Soul in Mind*. New Orleans: Spring Journal Books, 2007.

Rose, Nikolas. *Governing the Soul: The Shaping of the Private Self*. London: Routledge, 1989.

Rosen, Michael. *The Quest for Authenticity: The Thought of Reb Simhah Bunim*. Jerusalem: Urim Publications, 2008.

Rosen-Zvi, Ishay. *Body and Soul in Ancient Jewish Thought*. Ben Shemen: Modan, 2012 [Hebrew].

Rosen-Zvi, Ishay. "The Creation of Metaphysics: The Debate in the 'Mercaz Harav Yeshiva'—A Critical Study." In *A Hundred Years of Religious Zionism*, vol. 3, edited by A. Sagi and D. Schwartz, 421–45. Ramat Gan: Bar-Ilan University Press, 2003 [Hebrew].

Ross, Tamar. "The Musar Movement and the Issue of Hermeneutics in the Study of Torah." *Tarbiz* 59 (1990): 191–214 [Hebrew].

Rossi, Ernest L. *The Psychobiology of Mind-Body Healing: New Concepts of Therapeutic Hypnosis*. New York: W. W. Norton & Co., 1993.

Rotenberg, Mordechai. *Dialogue with Deviance: The Hasidic Ethic and the Theory of Social Contraction*. Philadelphia: Institute for the Study of Human Issues, 1983.

Roth, Ariel. "The Habad Literary Corpus, its Components and Distribution as the Basis for Reading Habad Text." Ph.D. diss., Bar Ilan University, 2012 [Hebrew].

Rowe, David E., and Robert J. Schulmann. *Einstein on Politics: His Private Thoughts and Public Stands on Nationalism, Zionism, War, Peace, and the Bomb*. Princeton: Princeton University Press, 2007.

Rowland, Christopher. *Radical Christianity: A Reading of Recovery*. New York: Orbis Books, 1988.

Rubin, Jeffrey B. *Psychotherapy and Buddhism: Toward an Integration (Issues in the Practice of Psychology)*. New York: Springer, 1996.

Ruderman, David B. *A Best-Selling Hebrew Book of the Modern Era: The Book of the Covenant of Pinhas Hurwitz and Its Remarkable Legacy*. Seattle: University of Washington Press, 2014.

Ruderman, David B. *Early Modern Jewry: A New Cultural History*. Princeton, NJ: Princeton University Press, 2010.

Sabbato, Chaim. *In Quest of Your Presence—Conversations with Rabbi Aharon Lichtenstein*. Tel Aviv: Yediot Ahronot, 2011 [Hebrew].

Sabini, Meredith. "The 'Book of Knowledge' in Shamanism and Mysticism: Universal Image of the Source." In *The Sacred Heritage: The Influence of Shamanism in Analytical Psychology*, edited by D. F. Sandner and S. H. Wong, 45–59. New York: Routledge, 1997.

Sack, Bracha. "*Ben Ga'agu'im*: The Righteous in Some Unpublished Chapters of R. Moshe Cordovero's *Elimah*." In *And This Is for Yehuda: Studies Presented to Our Friend, Professor Yehuda Liebes, on the Occasion of his Sixty-Fifth Birthday*, edited by M. R. Niehoff, R. Meroz, and J. Garb, 344–58. Jerusalem: Mandel Institute of Jewish Studies and Bialik Institute, 2012 [Hebrew].

Sack, Bracha. *The Kabbalah of R. Moshe Cordovero*. Beer Sheva: Ben Gurion University Press, 1995 [Hebrew].

Sack, Bracha. "Me-'Eyin 'Nusaḥ Rishon' Shel Tomer Devorah Le-Rabbi Moshe Cordovero."*Asufot* 9 (1995): 161–88 [Hebrew].

Sack, Bracha. *Shomer ha-Pardes: The Kabbalist Rabbi Shabbetai Sheftel Horowitz of Prague*. Beer Sheva: Ben Gurion University Press, 2002 [Hebrew].

Sack, Bracha. "Some Remarks on Siddur *Tefillah Le-Moshe*." *Daat* 44 (2000): 59–84 [Hebrew].

Safrin, Ya'aqov Yosef. *Zohar Hai*. Jerusalem, 2006.

Safrin, Yitzhaq Yehiel. *Heikhal ha-Brakha*. Lemberg, 1866.

Sagi, Rafael. "The Mystery of Messianic Rectification in the Thought of R. Yitzchak Ginsburgh." Ph.D. diss., Bar-Ilan University, Ramat Gan, 2010 [Hebrew].

Sagiv, Gadi. *Dynasty: The Chernobyl Hasidic Dynasty and Its Place in the History of Hasidism*. Jerusalem: Zalman Shazar Center, 2014 [Hebrew].

Samuels, Andrew. *Jung and the Post-Jungians*. London: Routledge & K. Paul, 1985.

Samuels, Andrew. *The Plural Psyche: Personality, Morality, and the Father*. London: Routledge, 1989.

Samuels, Andrew. *The Political Psyche*. London: Routledge, 1993.

Samuels, Andrew. *Politics on the Couch: Citizenship and the Internal Life*. New York: Other Press, 2001.

Sandner, Donald F., and Stephen H. Wong (ed.). *The Sacred Heritage: The Influence of Shamanism in Analytical Psychology*. New York: Routledge, 1997.

Sardello, Robert. *Love and the Soul: Creating a Future for Earth*. Berkeley: North Atlantic Books, 2008.

Schachter-Shalomi, Zalman, and Netanel Miles-Yepez. *A Hidden Light: Stories and Teachings of Early HaBaD and Bratzlav Hasidism*. Santa Fe: Gaon Books, 2011.

Schafer, Roy. *Aspects of Internalization*. Madison: International Universities Press, 1990.

Schatz, Moshe. *Ma'ayan Moshe*. Jerusalem, 2011.

Schatz, Moshe. *Sparks of the Hidden Light: Seeing the Unified Nature of Kabbalah through Kabbalah*. Jerusalem: 'Atret Tif'eret Institute, 1996.

Schatz Uffenheimer, Rivka. *Hasidism as Mysticism: Quietistic Elements in Eighteenth Century Hasidic Thought*. Princeton, NJ: Princeton University Press; Jerusalem: Magnes Press, 1993.

Shechter, Ya'aqov Me'ir. *Ve-Nikhtav ba-Sefer: A Collection of Discourses to Awaken One to the Worship of the Creator and the Rectification of One's Traits,* vol. 2 (of 2 vols.). Jerusalem, 1998 [Hebrew].

Schleicher, Marianne. *Intertextuality in the Tales of Rabbi Nahman of Bratslav: A Close Reading of Sippurey Ma'asiyot*. Leiden: Brill, 2007.

Schmidt, Leigh E. *Restless Souls: The Making of American Spirituality*. San Francisco: HarperCollins, 2005.

Schneersohn, Fischel. *Chaim Gravitzer*. Translated by A. Shlonsky. Tel Aviv: Miskal, 2013 [Hebrew].

Schneerson, Menahem Mendel. *Heikhal ha-Negina*. Edited by Z. Wolff. Jerusalem, 2007.

Schneerson, Shalom Dov Baer. *Be-Sha'a she-Heqdimu*, 3 vols. New York: Kehot Publication Society, 2011.

Schneerson, Shalom Dov Baer. *Yom Tov shel Rosh ha-Shana*, New York: Kehot Publications, 1984.

Schneider, Hans. *German Radical Pietism*. Translated by G. MacDonald. Plymouth: Scarecrow Press, 2007.

Schneider, Sarah. *Kabbalistic Writings on the Nature of Masculine & Feminine*. Northvale, NJ: Jason Aronson, 2001.

Scholem, Gershom. *Alchemy and Kabbalah*. Translated by K. Ottmann. Putnam, CT: Spring Publications 2006.

Scholem, Gershom. *Devils, Demons, Souls: Essays on Demonology*, edited by E. Liebes. Jerusalem: Yad Ben Tzvi, 2004 [Hebrew].

Scholem, Gershom. *Kabbalah*. Jerusalem: Keter Publishing House, 1974.

Scholem, Gershom. *Major Trends in Jewish Mysticism*. New York: Schocken Books, 1961.

Scholem, Gershom. "The Name of God and the Linguistic Theory of the Kabbalah." Translated by S. Pleasance, *Diogenes* 79 (1972): part 2, 164–94.

Scholem, Gershom. *On the Kabbalah and Its Symbolism*. New York: Schocken Books, 1965.

Scholem, Gershom. *On the Mystical Shape of the Godhead: Basic Concepts on the Kabbalah*. New York: Schocken Books, 1991.

Scholem, Gershom. *On the Possibility of Jewish Mysticism in Our Time & Other Essays*. Translated by J. Chipman. Philadelphia and Jerusalem: The Jewish Publication Society, 1997.

Scholem, Gershom. *Sabbatai Sevi: The Mystical Messiah, 1626–1676*. Princeton, NJ: Princeton University Press, 1973.

Schwartz, Dov. *Central Problems of Jewish Medieval Philosophy*. Leiden: Brill, 2005.

Schwartz, Dov. *Challenge and Crisis in Rabbi Kook's Circle*. Tel Aviv: 'Am 'Oved, 2001 [Hebrew].

Schwartz, Dov. *Habad's Thought from Beginning to End*. Ramat Gan: Bar-Ilan University Press, 2011 [Hebrew].

Schwartz, Dov. *Religion or Halakha: The Philosophy of Rabbi Joseph B. Soloveitchik*. Leiden: Brill, 2007.

Schwartz, Itamar. *Da' et 'Atzmekha: Le-Hakarat Kohot ha-Nefesh*. Israel, ca. 2008.

Schwartz, Itamar. *Getting to Know Your Soul: Gateway to Understanding Your Personality*. Jerusalem: Bilvavi Books, 2010.

Schwartz, Itamar. *Hakdamat Nahar Shalom*. Jerusalem (?), ca. 2007.

Schwartz, Itamar, *Shabbat Qodesh,* Jerusalem(?), ca. 2011.

Seder Eliahu Rabba (Tana de-Bey Eliahu), edited by M. Friedmann. Jerusalem, 1969.

Seeman, Don. "Martyrdom, Emotion and the Work of Ritual in R. Mordecai Josef Leiner's *Mei ha-Shiloah." AJS Rewiew* 27:2 (2003): 253–80.

Seeman, Don. "Violence, Ethics, and Divine Honor in Jewish Thought." *Journal of the American Academy of Religion* 73/4 (2005): 1015–48.

Segal, Avraham. *The Path of Worship: Topics in the Hasidic Kabbalah of Rabbi Tzvi Hirsch of Zydachov.* Jerusalem, 2011 [Hebrew].

Shamdasani, Somu. *Jung and the Making of Modern Psychology: The Dream of a Science.* Cambridge: Cambridge University Press, 2012 [online edition].

Shaper, Yitzhaq, and Yosef Elitzur. *Torat ha-Melekh.* Yizhar: Od Yosef Chai Yeshiva, 2010.

Shar'abi, Shalom. *Nahar Shalom.* In Hayyim Vital, *'Etz Hayyim.* Jerusalem, 1990 (reprint of Jerusalem, 1910).

Sharf, Robert H. "Buddhist Modernism and the Rhetoric of Meditative Experience." *Numen* 42 (1995): 228–83.

Sharf, Robert H. "Whose Zen: Zen Nationalism Revisited." In *Rude Awakenings: Zen, the Kyoto School, and the Question of Nationalism* (Nanzan Studies in Religion and Culture), edited by J. W. Heisig and J. Maraldo, 40–51. Honolulu: University of Hawai'i Press, 1995.

Sharf, Robert H. "The Zen of Japanese Nationalism." *History of Religions* 33/1 (1993): 1–43.

Sharon, Moshe. "New Religions and Religious Movements: The Common Heritage." In *Studies in Modern Religions, Religious Movements and the Babi-Bahai Faiths,* edited by M. Sharon, 3–37. Leiden: Brill, 2004.

Shatil, Sharron. "The Doctrine of Secrets of Emeq ha-Melech." *Jewish Studies Quarterly* 17 (2010): 358–95.

Shear, Adam. *The Kuzari and the Shaping of Jewish Identity, 1167–1900.* Cambridge: Cambridge University Press, 2008.

Shearer, Ann. *From Ancient Myth to Modern Healing: Themis: Goddess of Heart-Soul, Justice and Reconciliation.* New York: Routledge, 2008.

Sheehan, Jonathan, and Dror Wharman, *Invisible Hands: Self-Organization in the Eighteenth Century.* Chicago: University of Chicago Press, 2015.

Sheinfeld, Yehuda. *Sihot Mussar 'al Liqqutei Moharan.* Jerusalem, 2006.

Sherlo, Smadar. *The Tzadiq is the Foundation of the World.* Ramat Gan: Bar Ilan University Press, 2012 [Hebrew].

Shilo, Elchanan. *The Kabbalah in the Works of S. Y. Agnon.* Ramat Gan: Bar Ilan University Press, 2011 [Hebrew].

Shilo, Elchanan. "Rabbi Kook's Interpretation of Lurianic Kabbalah, the Appearance of New Souls and *Tikkun ha-Olam." Iyunim Bitkumat Israel* 18 (2008): 55–77 [Hebrew].

Shilo, Elchanan. "Rabbi Yizhak Isaac Haver's Influence on Rabbi Kook's Interpretation of the *Kabbalah," Daat* 79 (2015): 89–111 [Hebrew].

Shivhei ha-Ari ha-Shalem ve-ha-Mevo'ar. Jerusalem: Ahavat Shalom, 1991.

Shkop, Shime'on. *Sha'arei Yosher*. Jerusalem, 1959).

Shneur Zalman of Lyady. *Liqqutei Torah*. New York: Kehot Publication Society, 1984.

Shneur Zalman of Lyady. *Ma'amarei Admor Hazaqen: Parshiot ha-Torah ve-haMo'adim*, vol. 1. New York: Kehot Publishing, 1983.

Shneur Zalman of Lyady. *Tanya*. New York: Kehot Publication Society, 1985.

Shneur Zalman of Lyady. *Torah Or*. New York: Kehot Publication Society, 1987.

Shneuri, Dov Baer. *Derekh Hayyim*. New York: Kehot Publishing Society, 1986.

Shokek, Shimon. *Kabbalah and the Art of Being*. New York: Routledge, 2011.

Sifsei Hakhamim Committee (eds.). *Memorial Volume for the Author of Mikhtav mi-Eliyahu*, vol. 2. Bnei Brak, 2004 [Hebrew].

Silman, Yohanan. "Psychology in the Teachings of R. Israel Lipkin (Salanter)." *Bar-Ilan* 12 (1973): 288–304 [Hebrew].

Singer, June. *Seeing Through the Visible World: Jung, Gnosis, and Chaos*. San Francisco: Harper & Row, 1990.

Sirkis, Yo'el. *Beit Hadash (Commentary on Tur Orah Hayyim)*. Vilna, 1900.

Slezkine, Yuri. *The Jewish Century*. Princeton, NJ: Princeton University Press, 2004.

Sluhovsky, Moshe. *Believe Not Every Spirit: Possession, Mysticism and Discernment in Early Modern Catholicism*. Chicago: University of Chicago Press, 2007.

Smith, Andrew Philip (trans.). *Gnostic Writings on the Soul: Annotated and Explained*. Woodstock, VT: Skylight Paths, 2007.

Smith, C. Michael. *Jung and Shamanism in Dialogue: Retrieving the Soul, Retrieving the Sacred*. Bloomington, IN: Trafford Publishing, 2007.

Smith, R. Scott. "Are Emergents Rejecting the Souls Existence?" *Knowing & Doing* (Winter 2009): 1–6.

Sorotzkin, David. *Orthodoxy and Modern Disciplination: The Production of the Jewish Tradition in Europe in Modern Times*. Tel Aviv:Hakibbutz Hameuchad, 2011 [Hebrew].

Spector, Sheila A. *Wonders Divine: The Development of Blake's Kabbalistic Myth*. Lewisburg, PA: Bucknell University Press, 2001.

Spencer, Carole Dale. *Holiness: The Soul of Quakerism: A Historical Analysis of the Theology of Holiness in the Quaker Tradition*. Milton Keynes: Paternoster, 2007.

Spiegelman, J. Marvin, Pir Vilayat Inayat Khan, and Tasnim Fernandez (eds.). *Sufism, Islam and Jungian Psychology*. Las Vegas: New Falcon Publications, 1991.

Spielmann, Ya'aqov Me'ir. *Tal Orot*. Lemberg, 1876.

Stern, David. "*Vayikra Rabbah* and My Life in Midrash." *Prooftexts* 21/1 (2001): 23–38.

Stern, Eliyahu. *The Genius: Elijah of Vilna and the Making of Modern Judaism*. New Haven: Yale University Press, 2013.

Stern, Nir. *Adam Hai* (forthcoming).

Stern, Nir. "An Attempt to Describe the Teachings of R. Yeruham," Accessed September 1, 2014. http://tshuvot.wordpress.com ("Nir'eh lichora" blog).

Stroud, Jonathan. *The Golem's Eye*. New York: Disney-Hyperion, 2004.

Stroumsa, Guy G. *A New Science: The Discovery of Religion in the Age of Reason*. Cambridge, MA: Harvard University Press, 2010.

Stroumsa, Guy G., and Paula Fredriksen. "Two Souls and the Divided Will." In *Self, Soul and Body in Religious Experience*, edited by A. I. Baumgarten, J. Assman, and G. G. Stroumsa, 198–217. Leiden: Brill, 1998.

Stroumsa, Sarah. "Soul-Searching at the Dawn of Jewish Philosophy: A Hitherto Lost Fragment of al-Muqammas's 'Twenty Chapters'." *Ginzei Qedem* 3 (2007): 137–61.

Sviri, Sara. "Daughter of Fire by Irina Tweedie: Documentation and Experiences of a Modern Naqshbandi Sufi." In *Women as Teachers and Disciples in Traditional and New Religions*, edited by E. Puttick and P. B. Clarke, 77–89. Lewiston: Edwin Mellen Press, 1993.

Sviri, Sara. "The Self and Its Transformation in Ṣūfīsm: With Special Reference to Early Literature." In *Self and Self-Transformation in the History of Religions*, edited by D. Shulman and G. G. Stroumsa, 195–215. Oxford: Oxford University Press, 2002.

Sviri, Sara. "Spiritual Trends in Pre-Kabbalistic Judeo-Spanish Literature: The Cases of Bahya ibn Paquda and Judah Halevi." *Donaire* 6 (1996): 78–84.

Sviri, Sara. *A Taste of Hidden Things: Images of the Sufi Path*. Inverness, CA: Golden Sufi Center, 1997.

Tallis, Frank. *Darkness Rising*. New York: Random House, 2009.

Talmon, Jacob. L. *Political Messianism: The Romantic Phase*. London: Secker & Waburg, 1960.

Tamari, Assaf. "Erev Rav." *Mafteach* 2 (2010): 43–74 [Hebrew].

Tamari, Assaf. "Human Sparks: Readings in the Lurianic Theory of Transmigration and Its Concept of the Human Subject." M.A. thesis, Tel Aviv University, 2009 [Hebrew].

Tanenbaum, Adena. *The Contemplative Soul: Hebrew Poetry and Philosophical Theory in Medieval Spain*. Leiden: Brill, 2002.

Tau, Tzevi Yisra'el. *Le-'Emunat 'Itenu*, 11 vols. Jerusalem, 1994–2013.

Tau, Tzevi Yisra'el. *Tzaddiq be-'Emunato Yihye*. Beit Shemesh, 2004.

Taylor, Charles. *Sources of the Self: The Making of the Modern Identity*. Cambridge, MA: Harvard University Press, 1989.

Tikochinsky, Shlomo. "The 'Musar Yeshivot' from Lithuania to Israel: 'Slabodka Yeshiva,' Its Education, Emigration and Establishment in Mandate Palestine." Ph.D. thesis, Hebrew University of Jerusalem, 2009.

Tirosh-Samuelson, Hava. "Gender in Jewish Mysticism." In *Jewish Mysticism and Kabbalah: New Insights and Scholarship*, edited by F. E. Greenspahn, 191–230. New York: New York University Press, 2011.

Tirosh-Samuelson, Hava. "Jewish Philosophy on the Eve of Modernity." In *History of Jewish Philosophy*, edited by D. H. Frank and O. Leaman, 499–573. London: Routledge, 1997.

Tishby, Isaiah. "The Confrontation between Lurianic Kabbalah and Cordoverian Kabbalah in the Writings and Life of Rabbi Aaron Berechiah of Modena." *Zion* 39 (1974): 8–85 [Hebrew].

Tishby, Isaiah. *The Doctrine of Evil in Lurianic Kabbalah*. Translated by D. Solomon. London: Kegan Paul, 2002.

Tishby, Isaiah. *Messianic Mysticism: Moses Hayim Luzzatto and the Padua School*. Translated by M. Hoffman. Oxford: Littman Library of Jewish Civilization, 2008.

Tishby, Isaiah. *The Wisdom of the Zohar: An Anthology of Texts*. Translated by D. Goldstein. Oxford: Oxford University Press, 1989.

Treitel, Corinna. *A Science for the Soul: Occultism and the Genesis of the German Modern*. Baltimore: Johns Hopkins University Press, 2004.

Tweedie, Irina. "Spiritual Sufi Training Is a Process of Individuation Leading into the Infinite." The VIII International Conference of the International Transpersonal Association, paper presented September 1, 1983. Accessed September 1, 2014. http://www.goldensufi.org/a_sufi_training.html.

Twersky, Menahem Nahum. *Ma'or 'Enayyim*. Ashdod, 2008.

Tzemah, Ya'aqov, *Nagid u-Metzave*. Jerusalem, 1880.

Underhill, Evelyn. *Mysticism*. Stilwell, KS: Digireads, 2005.

Urban, Hugh B. *The Power of Tantra: Religion, Sexuality and the Politics of South Asian Studies*. Berkeley, California: University of California Press, 2003.

Valle, Moshe David. *Bi'ur Dani'el, 'Ezra u-Nehemia*, edited by J. Spinner. Jerusalem, 2010.

Valle, Moshe David. *Bi'ur Hamesh Megilot*, edited by J. Spinner. Jerusalem, 1988.

Valle, Moshe David. *Bi'ur Sefer Tehilim*, 2 vols., edited by J. Spinner. Jerusalem, 2008.

Valle, Moshe David. *Bi'ur Shir ha-Shirim, Ruth, Kohelet, Esther: Mahadura Qama*, edited by J. Spinner. Jerusalem, 2010.

Valle, Moshe David. *Bi'ur Trei 'Asar 'al Derekh ha-Pardes*, edited by J. Spinner. Jerusalem, 2009.

Valle, Moshe David. *Brit 'Olam: Bi'ur Sefer Shemot*, 2 vols., edited by J. Spinner. Jerusalem, 1995.

Valle, Moshe David. *Mamlekhet Kohanim: Bi'ur Sefer Yehezkel*, edited by J. Spinner. Jerusalem, 2008.

Valle, Moshe David. *Marp'e Lashon: Bi'ur Sefer Yirmiyahu*, edited by J. Spinner. Jerusalem, 2003.

Valle, Moshe David. *Moshia' Hosim: Bi'ur Sefer Shmu'el*, edited by J. Spinner. Jerusalem, 1998.

Valle, Moshe David. *Or 'Olam: Bi'ur Sefer Bereshit*, 2 vols., edited by J. Spinner. Jerusalem, 1993–94.

Valle, Moshe David. *Sefer ha-Liqqutim*, 2. vols., edited by J. Spinner. Jerusalem, 1997.

Valle, Moshe David. *Teshu'at 'Olamim: Bi'ur Sefer Yesha'iah*, edited by J. Spinner. Jerusalem, 1999.

Vassalli, Giovanni, "The Birth of Psychoanalysis from the Spirit of Technique." *International Journal of Psychoanalysis* 82/3 (2001): 3–25.

Vassányi, Miklós. *Anima Mundi: The Rise of the World Soul Theory in Modern German Philosophy.* Dordrecht: Springer, 2011.

Vaughan-Lee, Llewellyn. *Catching the Thread: Sufism, Dreamwork and Jungian Psychology* (Inverness, CA: Golden Sufi Center, 2003.

Vaughan-Lee, Llewellyn. *Sufism: The Transformation of the Heart.* Point Reyes Station, CA: Golden Sufi Center, 1995.

Vick, Amiel. "Through Which All of Israel Can Ascend: On R. Shneur Zalman of Lyady's Composition of Nusah ha-Ari." M.A. thesis, Hebrew University of Jerusalem, 2012.

Victoria, Brian Daizen. *Zen at War*, 2d ed, Lanham, MD: Rowman and Littlefield, 2006.

Victoria, Brian Daizen. *Zen War Stories.* London: RoutledgeCurzon, 2003.

Vital, Hayyim. *'Etz ha-Da'at Tov*, 2 vols. Jerusalem, 2001.

Vital, Hayyim. *'Etz Hayyim* with annotations by R. Shlomo Elyashiv. Jerusalem, 1990 (reprint of Jerusalem, 1910).

Vital, Hayyim. *'Olat Tamid.* Jerusalem, 1872 [reprint].

Vital, Hayyim. *Pri 'Etz Hayyim* with annotations by R. Shlomo Elyashiv. Jerusalem, n.d. (reprint of Dubrovna, 1804).

Vital, Hayyim. *Sefer ha-Liqqutim.* Jerusalem, 1913.

Vital, Hayyim. *Sha'ar ha-Kavvanot*, with annotations by R. Shlomo Elyashiv. Jerusalem, 1985.

Vital, Hayyim. *Sha'ar ha-Mitzvot.* Jerusalem, 1872.

Vital, Hayyim. *Sha'ar Ma'amarei Razal* (printed with *Sha'ar Ma'amarei Rashbi*). Jerusalem, 1978 (reprint of Jerusalem, 1898).

Vital, Hayyim. *Sha'ar Ruah ha-Qodesh*, 3 vols. Jerusalem, 1999.

Vital, Hayyim. *Sha'arei Qedusha.* Jerusalem, 1986.

von Heyking, John. "From a Wooded Summit: Learning to Love through Augustinian Meditation at Ascona." In *Pioniere, Poeten, Professoren: Eranos und der Monte Verità in der Zivilisationsgeschichte des 20. Jahrhunderts*, edited by B. Elisabetta, M. Riedl, and A. Tischel, 83–96. Würzburg: Königshausen & Neumann, 2004.

Waldron, Robert. *The Wounded Heart of Thomas Merton.* New York: Paulist Press, 2011.

Wasserman, Dana Beth. "Chasidic Antecedents to the Psychoanalytic Theory of Sigmund Freud: A Biographical and Textual Analysis." Ph.D. diss., Wright Institute Graduate School of Psychology, Berkeley, CA, 2004.

Wasserstrom, Steven M. *Religion After Religion: Gershom Scholem, Mircea Eliade, and Henry Corbin At Eranos.* Princeton, New Jersey: Princeton University Press, 1999.

Weber, Max. *The Protestant Ethic and the Spirit of Capitalism.* London: Allen and Unwin, 1976.

Weinberg, Yehiel Ya'aqov. *Seridei Esh.* Jerusalem, 1977.

Weinberger, Moshe. *Song of Teshuva: A Commentary on Rav Avraham Yitzchak HaKohen Kook's Oros HaTeshuvah*. Jerusalem, 2011.

Weinstein, Roni. *Juvenile Sexuality, Kabbalah, and Catholic Reformation in Italy: Tiferet Bahurim by Pinhas Barukh Ben Pelatiyah Monselice*. Leiden: Brill, 2009.

Weinstein, Roni. *Kabbalah and Jewish Modernity*. Tel Aviv: Tel Aviv University Press, 2011 [Hebrew].

Weintraub, Israel Elijah. *Be-Sod Yesharim: Ma'amarim 'Al Seder Ha-harshiot ve-Mo'adim*. Bnei Brak, 2008.

Weintraub, Israel Elijah. *'Einei Yisra'el: Be-'Inyanei Mo'adim, Torah, ve 'Avoda*. Bnei Brak, 2010.

Werblowsky, R. J. Zwi. *Joseph Karo: Lawyer and Mystic*. Oxford: Oxford University Press, 1962.

Werblowsky, R. J. Zwi. "On the Mystical Rejection of Mystical Illuminations: A Note on St. John of the Cross." *Religious Studies* 1 (1965): 177–84.

Werczberger, Rachel. "New Age of Judaism: Jewish Spiritual Renewal in Israel." Ph.D. diss., Hebrew University of Jerusalem, 2011.

Wexler, Philip. *Holy Sparks: Social Theory, Education and Religion*. New York: St. Martin's, 1996.

Wexler, Philip. "Mystical Education: Social Theory and Pedagogical Prospects." In *Teaching Mysticism*, edited by W. Parsons, 268–87. Oxford: Oxford University Press, 2011.

Wexler, Philip. *Mystical Interactions: Sociology, Jewish Mysticism and Education*. Los Angeles: Cherub Press, 2007.

Wexler, Philip. *Mystical Sociology: Toward Cosmic Social Theory*. New York: Peter Lang, 2013.

Wexler, Philip. "Society and Mysticism." In *After Spirituality*, edited by Ph. Wexler and J. Garb, 107–25. New York: Peter Lang Publishing, 2012.

Wexler, Philip, and Jonathan. Garb. "After Spirituality: Introducing the Volume and the Series." In *After Spirituality: Studies in Mystical Traditions*. New York: Peter Lang Publishing, 2012.

Wharman, Dror. *The Making of the Modern Self: Identity and Culture in Eighteenth-Century England*. New Haven: Yale University Press, 2004.

White, Victor. *Soul and Psyche*. New York: Harper and Brothers, 1960.

Whitebook, Joel. "Freud, Foucault and 'The Dialogue with Unreason.'" *Philosophy and Social Criticism* 25/6 (1999): 29–66.

Wiesel, Elie. *Souls on Fire: Portraits and Legends of Hasidic Masters*. New York: Vintage Books, 1973.

Wiskind-Elper, Ora. *Tradition and Fantasy in the Tales of Reb Nahman of Bratslav*. Albany: State University of New York Press, 1998.

Wiskind-Elper, Ora. *Wisdom of the Heart: The Teachings of Rabbi Ya'akov of Izbica-Radzyn*. Philadelphia: Jewish Publication Society, 2010.

Wistrich, Robert S. *A Lethal Obsession: Anti-Semitism from Antiquity to the Global Jihad*. New York: Random House, 2010.

Wolbe, Shlomo. *'Alei Shur*, 2 vols. Jerusalem, 1986.

Wolbe, Shlomo. *Da'at Shlomo: Ma'amarei Zeman Matan Torateinu.* Jerusalem, 2006.

Wolbe, Shlomo. *Igrot u-Khtavim (Letters and Writings),* 2 vols. Jerusalem, 2006, 2013.

Wolbe, Shlomo. *'Olam he-Yedidut (with Or la-Shav).* Jerusalem, 1994.

Wolbe, Shlomo. *Pirqei Qinyan Da'at.* Jerusalem, 2001.

Wolbe, Shlomo. *Quntres ha-Adam bi-Yeqar.* Jerusalem, 1999.

Wolfradt, Uwe. *Ethnologie und Psychologie: Die Leipziger Schule der Völkerpsychologie.* Berlin: Dietrich Reimer Verlag, 2010.

Wolfson, Elliot R. *Abraham Abulafia—Kabbalist and Prophet: Hermeneutics, Theosophy and Theurgy.* Los Angeles: Cherub Press, 2000.

Wolfson, Elliot R. *Alef, Mem, Tau: Kabbalistic Musings on Time, Truth, and Death.* Berkeley: University of California Press, 2006.

Wolfson, Elliot R. *Along the Path: Studies in Kabbalistic Myth, Symbolism, and Hermeneutics.* Albany: State University of New York Press, 1995.

Wolfson, Elliot R. "Building a Sanctuary of the Heart: The Kabbalistic-Pietistic Teachings of Itamar Schwartz." In *Kabbalah and Contemporary Spiritual Revival,* edited by B. Huss, 141–62. Beer Sheva: Ben Gurion University of the Negev Press, 2011.

Wolfson, Elliot R. "Circumcision and the Divine Name: A Study in the Transmission of Esoteric Doctrine." *Jewish Quarterly Review* 78 (1987): 77–112.

Wolfson, Elliot R. "Divine Suffering and the Hermeneutics of Reading: Philosophical Reflections on Lurianic Mythology." In *Suffering Religion,* edited by R. Gibbs and E. R. Wolfson, 101–62. New York: Routledge, 2002.

Wolfson, Elliot R. *A Dream Interpreted Within a Dream: Oneiropoiesis and the Prism of Imagination.* New York: Zone Books, 2011.

Wolfson, Elliot R. *Giving Beyond the Gift: Apophasis and Overcoming Theomania.* New York: Fordham University Press, 2014

Wolfson, Elliot R. "Immanuel Frommann's Commentary on Luke and the Christianizing of Kabbalah: Some Sabbatean and Hasidic Affinities." In *Holy Dissent: Jewish and Christian Mystics in Eastern Europe,* edited by G. Dynner, 171–222. Detroit: Wayne State University Press, 2011.

Wolfson, Elliot R. *Language, Eros, Being: Kabbalistic Hermeneutics and Poetic Imagination.* New York: Fordham University Press, 2005.

Wolfson, Elliot R. *Luminal Darkness: Imaginal Gleanings from Zoharic Literature.* Oxford: Oneworld, 2007.

Wolfson, Elliot R. "Murmuring Secrets: Eroticism and Esotericism in Medieval Kabbalah." In *Hidden Intercourse: Eros and Sexuality in the History of Western Esotericism,* edited by J. Kripal and W. Hanegraff, 65–109. Leiden: Brill, 2008.

Wolfson, Elliot R. *Open Secret: Postmessianic Messianism and the Mystical Revision of Menahem Mendel Schneerson.* New York: Columbia University Press, 2009.

Wolfson, Elliot R. "Patriarchy and the Motherhood of God in Zoharic Kabbalah and Meister Eckhart." In *Envisioning Judaism: Studies in Honor of Peter Schäfer on the Occasion of his Seventieth Birthday,* edited by R. S. Boustan,

K. Herrmann, R. Leicht, A. Y. Reed, and G. Veltri, 1047–88. Tübingen: Mohr Siebeck, 2013.

Wolfson, Elliot R. "Revealing and Re/Veiling: Menahem Mendel Schneerson's Messianic Secret." *Kabbalah* 26 (2012): 25–96.

Wolfson, Elliot R. "Suffering Eros and Textual Incarnation: A Kristevan Reading of Kabbalistic Poetics." In *Toward a Theology of Eros: Transfiguring Passion at the Limits of Discipline*, edited by V. Burrus and C. Keller, 341–65. New York: Fordham University Press, 2006.

Wolfson, Elliot R. *Through a Speculum That Shines: Vision and Imagination in Medieval Jewish Mysticism*. Princeton, NJ: Princeton University Press, 1994.

Wolfson, Elliot. "Tiqqun ha-Shekhinah: Redemption and the Overcoming of Gender Dimorphism in the Messianic Kabbalah of Moses Hayyim Luzatto." *History of Religions* 36 (1997): 289–332.

Wolfson, Elliot R. *Venturing Beyond: Law and Morality in Kabbalistic Mysticism*. Oxford: Oxford University Press, 2006.

Wolfson, Elliot R. "Weeping, Death, and Spiritual Ascent in Sixteenth-Century Jewish Mysticism." In *Death, Ecstasy, and Other Worldly Journeys*, edited by J. J. Collins and M. Fishbane, 209–47. Albany: State University of New York Press, 1995.

Wolfson, Elliot R. "Woman—the Feminine as Other in Theosophic Kabbalah: Some Philosophical Observations on the Divine Androgyne." In *The Other in Jewish Thought and History: Constructions of Jewish Culture and Identity*, edited by L. J. Silberstein and R. L. Cohn, 166–204. New York: New York University Press, 1994.

Wolosky, Shira. *The Riddles of Harry Potter: Secret Passages and Interpretive Quests*. New York: Palgrave Macmillan, 2010.

Wozner, Shay. *Legal Thinking in the Lithuanian Yeshivot*. Jerusalem: Magnes Press, forthcoming [Hebrew].

Wozner, Shay, Hanina Ben Menahem, and Neil Hecht. *Controversy and Dialogue in the Halakhic Sources—Sources and Commentary*. Jerusalem: Institute for Research in Jewish Law, Faculty of Law, 2002 [Hebrew].

Ya'aqov Yosef of Polony. *Toledot Ya'aqov Yosef*, vol. 1. Jerusalem, 2011.

Yifrach, Yehuda. "The Elevation of Foreign Thoughts in the Traditions of R. Israel Baal Shem Tov as Transmitted in the Works of His Students." M.A. thesis, Bar Ilan University, 2008 [Hebrew].

Yorovitz, Avraham. *'Aravot Nahal*. Jerusalem, 2008.

Yosha, Nissim. *Myth and Metaphor: Abraham Cohen Herrera's Philosophical Interpretation of Lurianic Kabbalah*. Jerusalem: Magnes Press, 1994 [Hebrew].

Young-Eisendrath, P., and S. Muramuto (eds.). *Awakening and Insight: Zen Buddhism and Psychotherapy*. New York: Brunner-Routledge, 2002.

Yovel, Yirmiyahu. *The Other Within: The Marranos; Split Identity and Emerging Modernity,*" *Journal of Religion* 83/1 (2011): 198–200.

Zadoq ha-Kohen of Lublin. *Liqqutei Ma'amarim*. Jerusalem, 2002.

Zadoq ha-Kohen of Lublin. *Pri Tzaddiq*, 5 vols. Jerusalem, 2005.

Zadoq ha-Kohen of Lublin. *Resisei Laila*. Jerusalem, 2002.

Zalmanov, S. (ed.). *Sefer ha-Niggunim*. New York: Ninah [Nigunei Hasidei Habad], 1985.

Zohar, Zvi. "The Rabbi and the Sheikh." *Jewish Studies Quarterly* 17 (2010): 114–45.

Zuriely, Odeya. *Transitions*. Jerusalem: Rubin Mass, 2009 [Hebrew].

Index